THE HINDU MANIFESTO

THE HINDU MANIFESTO

Swami Vigyananand

ink | OCCAM

ISBN: 978-93-6547-497-8

First published in India 2025
This edition published 2025

BluOne Ink Pvt. Ltd
A-76, 2nd Floor, Sector 136, Noida
Uttar Pradesh 201301
www.bluone.ink
publisher@bluone.ink

Printed and bound in India by Thomson Press (India) Ltd

Kali and Occam are imprints of BluOne Ink

ink | OCCAM

त्वदीयं वस्तु गोविन्द तुभ्यमेव समर्पये।
tvadīyaṃ vastu govinda tubhyameva samarpaye.
Whatever belongs to you, I offer back to you alone.

With profound reverence, I dedicate this work to:
Maharishi Valmiki
Maharishi Vedavyasa
Acharya Ushana
Acharya Chanakya

The Hindu Sutra

धर्मस्य मूलं अर्थः
Dharmasya mūlam arthaḥ
Prosperity for All

Śatrūn jaya prajā rakṣa
Defeating Enemy, Defending Citizens

नास्ति विद्यासमं चक्षुः
Nāsti Vidyāsamaṃ Cakṣuḥ
Quality Education for All

अविश्रमोऽयं लोकतंत्राधिकारः
Aviśramo'yaṃ lokataṃtrādhikāraḥ
Responsible Democracy

अग्र एति युवतिरह्रयाणा
Agra eti yuvatirahrayāṇā
Highest Respect for Women

एकवर्णस्तदा लोको
Ekavarṇastadā loko
Non-discriminatory Social System

सर्वं शान्तिः
Sarvam śāntiḥ
Care for Nature

माता भूमि :
(Mātā bhūmiḥ)
Respect for the Land

Contents

List of Abbreviations	vii
Acknowledgements	ix
Preface	xi
The Hindu Sutra	xiii
Introduction	xvii
Chapter 1: Prosperity for All	3
Appendix 1: World Economic History	42
Appendix 2: The British Exploitation and Plunder of Bharat's Economy	44
Chapter 2: Defeating Enemy, Defending Citizens	63
Appendix 1: The Military Structure of Ancient Bharat	82
Appendix 2: Hindu Resistance to Muslim Invaders	92
Chapter 3: Quality Education for All	101
Appendix 1: The Beautiful Tree of Indigenous Education in Bharat	115
Appendix 2: Ancient Universities of Bharat: Guardians of Knowledge and Culture	120
Chapter 4: Responsible Democracy	125
Appendix: Excerpts from Hindu Polity	210
Chapter 5: Highest Respect for Women	217
Appendix: Suktas and Mantras of the Brahmavadini Rishis in the Rigveda	249

Chapter 6: Non-discriminatory Social System 269

Appendix 1: Debating Caste: Western Constructs, Misconceptions and the Search for Clarity 294

Appendix 2: Comprehensive History of Caste in Colonial Bharat 297

Appendix 3: The Role and Growth of Scheduled Tribes and Castes in Medieval Bharat 301

Chapter 7: Care for Nature 307

Chapter 8: Respect for the Land 347

Appendix: Bhumi Sukta: Vedic Prayer for the Reverence of the Motherland 368

Notes 391

References 409

About the Author 411

Abbreviations

Adh.	Adhikaran
Prak.	Prakaran
C.	Canto
Ch.	Chapter
GND	Gautam's Nyaya Darshan
GPGKP	Gita Press Gorakhpur
KA	Kautilya Arthashastra
KS	Kautilya Sutra
SS	Sukranitisara
RV	*Rigveda*
YV	*Yajurveda*
AV	*Atharvaveda*
MS	Manu Smriti
	Mahabharata
MBAPAsP	Mahabharata Aadi Parva Astika Parva
MBAPSaP	Mahabharata Aadi Parva Sambhava Parva
MBAPBaP	Mahabharata Aadi Parva Bakavadha Parva
MBAPSwP	Mahabharata Aadi Parva Swayamvara Parva
MBAPArVP	Mahabharata Aadi Parva Arjun Vanvasa Parva
MBAPAnAP	Mahabharata Aadi Parva Anshavatarana Parva
MBAPPaSP	Mahabharata Aadi Parva Parva Sangraha Parva
MBSPLoSP	Mahabharata Sabha Parva Lokpal Sabhakhyana Parva
MBSPDiVP	Mahabharata Sabha Parva Dig Vijaya Parva
MBSPDyP	Mahabharata Sabha Parva Dyuta Parva
MBSPAnP	Mahabharata Sabha Parva Anudyuta Parva
MBVPArAP	Mahabharata Van Parva Arjun Abhigamana Parva

MBVPNaP	Mahabharata Van Parva Nalopakhyana Parva
MBVPTiP	Mahabharata Van Parva Tirthyatra Parva
MBVPMaSP	Mahabharata Van Parva Markandeya Samasya Parva
MBVPKuP	Mahabharata Van Parva Kundlaharana Parva
MBVPRaOP	Mahabharata Van Parva Ramopakhyana Parva
MBVPAaP	Mahabharata Van Parva Aajgara Parva
MBVPDrSSP	Mahabharata Van Parva Draupadi Satyabhama Samvad Parva
MBVPArnP	Mahabharata Van Parva Arneya Parva
MBViPPaPP	Mahabharata Virat Parva Pandav Pravesha Parva
MBUPBhYP	Mahabharata Udyog Parva Bhagvad Yana Parva
MBUPSeP	Mahabharata Udyog Parva Senodyoga Parva
MBUPPrP	Mahabharata Udyog Parva Prajagara Parva
MBBPJaVP	Mahabharata Bheeshma Parva Jambukhanda Vinirmana Parva
MBBPBhuP	Mahabharata Bheeshma Parva Bhumi Parva
MBDPAbVP	Mahabharata Drona Parva Abhimanyu Vadha Parva
MBShPRaDP	Mahabharata Shanti Parva Raj Dharmanushasana Parva
MBShPApDP	Mahabharata Shanti Parva Apad Dharma Parva
MBShPMoDP	Mahabharata Shanti Parva Moksha Dharma Parva
MBAnPDaDP	Mahabharata Anushasan Parva Dandharma Parva
MBAsPAshP	Mahabharata Ashwamedhik Parva Ashwamedha Parva
MBAsPAnGP	Mahabharata Ashwamedhik Parva Anu Geeta Parva
MBAsPVaDP	Mahabharata Ashwamedhik Parva Vaishnava Dharma Parva

Valmiki Ramayana

VRBK	Valmiki Ramayana Balkanda
VRAK	Valmiki Ramayana Ayodhyakanda
VRArK	Valmiki Ramayana Aranyakanda
VRKK	Valmiki Ramayana Kishkindhakanda
VRSK	Valmiki Ramayana Sundarkanda
VRYK	Valmiki Ramayana Yuddhakanda

Acknowledgements

My deepest gratitude goes to my two acharyas: Swami Vivekanand Saraswati Jee Maharaj and Acharya Vijaypal Vidyavaridhi. Their extraordinary scholarship in Panini's grammar, Vedangas and Upangas was instrumental in my learning. Without their teachings, this book would not have been possible.

I extend my sincere thanks to Shri Mukut Bihari Sekasaria. When I embarked on writing *The Hindu Manifesto*, I immersed myself in my studies. I began this journey at his farmhouse, located behind his factory, where I set study targets as diligently as I had during my college days. His hospitality created an environment that was ideal for focused study.

I also benefited greatly from the library facilities and accommodation at the RMP Knowledge Excellence Centre in Thane, Maharashtra, where I stayed multiple times during my research.

I am deeply grateful to my colleague and team member E. Narayanan, who undertook the initial typing of the manuscript before passing on the responsibility to Nilesh. Their assistance was invaluable in ensuring the smooth completion of the book.

My sincere appreciation to Dr Jagmohan of Hindu College, University of Delhi, for his unwavering support in verifying and locating references as well as for arranging the typing and proofreading of the Sanskrit text.

My heartfelt thanks to Dr J.K. Bajaj for his invaluable guidance and for graciously summarizing Dr Dharampal's book *The Beautiful Tree*. I also extend my gratitude to Dr Soniya of IGNOU for her assistance in locating references, and to Dr Charu Kalra of Deen Dayal Upadhyaya College, University of Delhi, for verifying and correcting the botanical references.

I sincerely appreciate the publisher, BluOne Ink, under the leadership of Shri Praveen Tiwari, along with the editorial team, including Shri Thanglenhao Haokip, senior editor, and Aditi Chopra, for their meticulous editing, proofreading and typesetting of this work, and for bringing this book into physical form. I also extend my special thanks to Manvendra Singh of Odd Monk for designing the cover page.

Preface

My journey into Hindu scholarship began at the Gurukul, where I immersed myself in the rigorous discipline of traditional learning, delving into the profound teachings of Hindu Shastras. My studies encompassed Pāṇini's grammar—the foundation of Sanskrit language and literature—along with the Vedangas and Upangas, essential disciplines that refine one's understanding of the Vedas and Hindu philosophy. As I explored the vast ocean of Hindu Shastras, I encountered intricate philosophy and profound knowledge, invaluable for both the past and the present.

The Vedas, with their eternal truths, knowledge and wisdom, captivated my intellect. The Ramayana and the Mahabharata, along with other Sanskrit literary masterpieces, imparted profound lessons on dharma, ethics, leadership, and human values, leaving an indelible mark on me.

As I immersed myself in these sacred texts, I recognized their enduring relevance in addressing the complexities of modern society. This realization inspired a vision: to distil their timeless principles into a contemporary framework. The concepts of dharma, justice, economics and governance found in these scriptures offer valuable solutions to present-day challenges.

During this transformative period, I made a firm resolution: upon completing my studies, I would write a book that brings ancient wisdom into the modern world. My goal is to present the timeless teachings of Hindu Shastras on dharma, ethics, justice, economics, politics, administration and governance in a way that resonates with contemporary society, ensuring that this invaluable heritage continues to enlighten and guide future generations.

Though the desire to write this book had been in my mind for years, it was in 2009 that the idea truly crystallized during a discussion with Prof. Satish Modh and Shri Sandeep Singh in Mumbai. That very day, we outlined key points and drafted an initial structure, marking the inception of *The Hindu Manifesto*.

The Hindu Sutra

When I began writing *The Hindu Manifesto*, a profound question arose in my mind: How can the entire thought process, content, and philosophy of this book be conveyed succinctly in limited words? The challenge was not merely to summarize ideas but to distil their essence in a way that is both easily comprehensible and deeply impactful.

In our ancient tradition, the great rishis mastered the art of encapsulating vast and profound wisdom into brief yet powerful statements known as sutras (aphorisms). These sutras—concise yet carrying immense depth—served as guiding principles. Inspired by this approach, I sought a way to express the essence of *The Hindu Manifesto* in a similarly compact yet profound manner.

During my research, I explored various Vedic mantras and Sanskrit shlokas, carefully identifying key phrases that capture the core principles and vision outlined in *The Hindu Manifesto*. After deep reflection, I have selected eight specific padas (sections) from the Vedic mantras and shastras (treatise). I termed these 'Hindu Sutras', a set of concise yet meaningful statements that encapsulate the book's ideological foundation.

These Hindu Sutras serve as the guiding framework of *The Hindu Manifesto*, reflecting its core message in a distilled and timeless form. They are not merely quotations from the shastra; they are living principles that can inspire and guide Hindus and humanity on their journey towards unity, progress and the betterment of human life.

In essence, the Hindu Sutras encapsulate the spirit of *The Hindu Manifesto*, making its core principles easily memorable, shareable and internalizable by those who wish to understand and contribute to the Hindu renaissance, as well as by individuals, societies and nations from communities beyond Hindu society.

1. धर्मस्य मूलं अर्थः
   (Dharmasya mūlam arthaḥ)
2. शत्रून् जय प्रजा रक्ष
   (Śatrūn jaya prajā rakṣa)
3. नास्ति विद्यासमं चक्षुः
   (Nāsti Vidyāsamaṃ Cakṣuḥ)
4. अविश्रमोऽयं लोकतंत्राधिकारः
   (Aviśramo'yaṃ lokataṃtrādhikāraḥ)
5. अग्र एति युवतिरह्रयाणा
   (Agra eti yuvatirahrayāṇā)
6. एकवर्णस्तदा लोको
   (Ekavarṇastadā loko)
7. सर्वं शान्तिः
   (Sarvam śāntiḥ)
8. माता भूमिः
   (Mātā bhūmiḥ)

The following English translations precisely capture the essence and meaning of the Hindu Sutras.

1. Prosperity for All
2. Defeating Enemy, Defending Citizens
3. Quality Education for All
4. Responsible Democracy
5. Highest Respect for Women
6. Non-discriminatory Social System
7. Care for Nature
8. Respect for the Land

This translation is not a literal word-for-word rendering, but it effectively conveys the purpose of the Hindu Sutras in a concise form.

A nation's strength and longevity depend on two fundamental aspects: a solid foundational framework that ensures stability and progress, and a civilizational framework that nurtures values, identity and sustainability. Together, these aspects form the core philosophy of this book, with each of the eight sutras representing a crucial pillar of a thriving society.

The First Four Sutras: Building a Strong and Resilient Nation

Any country wishing to safeguard the interests of its society and nation must prioritize its economy, defence and security, education, and democracy and politics. Therefore, the first four Hindu Sutras are foundational principles upon which any society, nation, or civilization firmly stands, sustains itself and progresses.

Prosperity for all: A robust economy is the backbone of any nation. Economic growth, wealth generation and fair distribution are essential. This sutra emphasizes respect for wealth creation, entrepreneurship, and economic policies that uplift all sections of society. A prosperous economy reduces disparities and fosters national confidence.

Defeating enemy, defending citizens: A nation's sovereignty and security are paramount. This sutra emphasizes the importance of a strong, well-equipped military, robust intelligence capabilities and strategic foresight to counter both external and internal threats. A powerful defence not only safeguards territorial integrity but also deters adversaries and ensures long-term stability.

Beyond military security, a nation must protect its citizens from social and political threats. This includes maintaining effective law enforcement and a fair justice system. Ensuring safety, justice and accountability fosters trust and stability in society.

Quality education for all: Education is the foundation of progress. This sutra emphasizes the need for accessible, high-quality, affordable education that nurtures creativity, critical thinking and moral responsibility in citizens.

Responsible democracy: Democracy must be rooted in responsibility and accountability. This sutra stresses the importance of ethical leadership, transparent governance and active citizen participation. A responsible democracy ensures that power serves the people rather than personal or partisan interests.

Together, these four pillars create a strong foundation for a nation, protecting it from instability and external threats while driving continuous progress.

The Last Four Sutras: Sustaining Cultural Values

Once the foundational principles are established, the primary concern for any society aiming to progress and earn respect is addressing issues related to the advancement of civilization.

Highest respect for women: A civilization's advancement is judged by how it treats its women. This sutra calls for ensuring the dignity and safety of women in all spheres of life. Equal opportunities in education, employment, and leadership are crucial for a just and prosperous society.

A non-discriminatory social system: A strong society does not discriminate based on jati, varna, race, religion, gender or social status. Social cohesion is essential for long-term stability and progress.

Care for nature: A civilization that exploits nature without care is bound to collapse. This sutra highlights the need for ecological balance and responsible consumption. Respecting nature is not just an environmental necessity but also a spiritual and ethical duty.

Respect for the land: A nation thrives when its citizens take pride in their land, heritage, and values. This sutra emphasizes patriotism as a deep-rooted sense of responsibility towards one's country and culture.

These four sutras form the civilizational values that sustain a society beyond material progress, ensuring that development is rooted in ethical and cultural consciousness.

The Eight Sutras as a Unified Philosophy

A society or nation cannot rely on just one of these aspects—both the foundational and civilizational frameworks must work in harmony.

Each of these sutras is explored in depth in this book, with every chapter dedicated to one of these principles, examining its significance and pathways to implementation.

For a nation to progress with confidence, dignity and respect, these eight sutras must be embraced in both thought and action.

Introduction

The Hindu Manifesto is a call to reclaim and apply the profound wisdom of Hindu Shastras (Treatises) as a guiding force for a just, prosperous, and harmonious world. It is not merely a theoretical discourse but a transformative blueprint for individuals, societies, and nations seeking to align with the timeless principles of dharma.

At its core, this manifesto draws from the vast repository of knowledge found in the Vedas, Ramayana,[1] Mahabharata,[2] Kautilya's Arthashastra,[3] Shukranitisara[4] and other classical Hindu texts.

धर्मशास्त्रमिदं पुण्यमर्थशास्त्रमिदं परम्।
मोक्षशास्त्रमिदं प्रोक्तं व्यासेनामितबुद्धिना ।।23।।

dharmaśāstramidaṃ puṇyamarthaśāstramidaṃ param |
mokṣaśāstramidaṃ proktaṃ vyāsenāmitabuddhinā ||23||[5]

The illustrious and erudite Maharishi Vedavyasa spoke about the Mahabharata, stating:
The Mahabharata is a Dharma Shastra; it is the highest authority on economics, politics and administration. Moreover, it is also a Shastra that guides one towards moksha (liberation).

श्रुतिं धर्मं वदन्त्यन्ये मानान्याहुः परे जनाः ।
न च तं स्वभ्यसूयामो न हि सर्वं विधीयते ।।13।।

śrutiṃ dharmaṃ vadantyanye mānānyāhuḥ pare janāḥ |
na ca taṃ svabhyasūyāmo na hi sarvaṃ vidhīyate ||13||[6]

It is important to note that not everything is mentioned or explained in the Vedas.

धर्मे चार्थे च कामे च मोक्षे च भरतर्षभ ।
यदिहास्ति तदन्यत्र यन्नेहास्ति न कुत्रचित् ।।53।।

Dharme cārthe ca kāme ca mokṣe ca bharatarṣabha |
Yadihāsti tadanyatra yannehāsti na kutracit ||53||[7]

Everything about dharma, artha, kama and moksha is mentioned in the Mahabharata. If something is found in the Mahabharata, it is also present in other Shastras. Conversely, if something is not mentioned in the Mahabharata, it is not found anywhere.

These shastras present an integrated vision of life, where dharma (righteousness), artha (wealth and prosperity) and kama (fulfilment of worldly desires) harmonize to create a thriving society. For millennia, these principles have shaped civilizations, fostering prosperity and stability. Yet, in modern discourse, their relevance is often overlooked or misrepresented. When understood and applied in their true essence, these eternal ideals have the power to uplift and revitalize societies across time and geography.

Impact on Hindu Society

The universal and enduring principles of *The Hindu Manifesto* are designed to:

Enhance the quality of Hindu society: By fostering ethical governance, social cohesion and individual responsibility, it ensures that Hindus live with self-respect, dignity and purpose.

Promote prosperity and security: Hindu Shastras emphasize economic well-being, self-sufficiency and social stability, ensuring the empowerment and safety of individuals and society.

Ensure justice and good governance: The concept of 'rajdharma' establishes a strong foundation for justice, ethical governance and social order, safeguarding rights while upholding responsibilities for all citizens.

Foster Hindu resurgence and civilizational renaissance: Applying these time-tested principles revitalizes Hindu society, strengthening its cultural and intellectual traditions while encouraging self-reliance and pride in Hindu identity.

A Universal Framework for Humanity

Though deeply rooted in Hindu traditions, the wisdom of *The Hindu Manifesto* transcends religious and geographical boundaries. History has shown that societies grounded in dharma (universal principles) flourish, while those that disregard it face decline. *The Hindu Manifesto* offers a time-tested framework for justice, governance and economic stability—not just for Hindus but for all of humanity. By embracing these principles, societies can achieve:

Justice and fair governance: The Hindu model of rajadharma and nyaya (justice) upholds fairness and the rule of law, preventing oppression and tyranny.

Dharma-centred governance: Its principles of governance, social responsibility, and economic ethics provide sustainable solutions that benefit all of humanity.

Cultural and economic resurgence: Societies that align with these ideals reclaim their cultural foundations while ensuring justice, security, and prosperity.

The Hindu Manifesto is more than a vision—it is a blueprint for the resurgence of dharma. It calls upon every individual committed to justice, prosperity, and harmony to take action in shaping a world that upholds these eternal principles. This is not just a declaration of values; it is a call to awaken, act, and restore balance in the world through the wisdom of Hindu thought.

Chapter 1

The first chapter, 'Prosperity for All', emphasizes that Hindu society and its thought process have always valued prosperity at both the individual and collective levels. Unlike the misconception that Hindu dharma solely focuses on Moksha (spiritual liberation) while neglecting material well-being, this chapter clarifies that Hindu philosophy acknowledges and promotes wealth creation as an essential pillar of a flourishing society.

It explores how the pursuit of prosperity aligns with dharma (righteousness), ensuring that economic activities remain ethical and beneficial for all. The chapter also examines the role of wealth in building a strong and successful state, highlighting the importance of supporting key contributors to the economy, such as farmers and entrepreneurs. It discusses the need for moderate taxation policies that enable economic growth without overburdening individuals and enterprises. Furthermore, it underscores Hindu thought's opposition to exploitative capitalism, advocating for a balanced approach in which wealth is both generated and distributed in a way that upholds collective well-being.

Given the profound Hindu philosophy of wealth creation and its emphasis on the importance of prudent financial management, why did Hindu civilization—renowned for centuries for its immense wealth and economic prowess—eventually fall into impoverishment?

For the answer to this question, please refer to Appendix 2 of this chapter.

Chapter 2

The second chapter, 'Defeating Enemy, Defending Citizens', holds immense significance as it underscores the fundamental principles of national security, military strength, and strategic warfare. It highlights the necessity of not only possessing military power but also maintaining resilience and preparedness to defend the nation effectively. The chapter emphasizes that the victory of the armed forces and the decisive defeat of adversaries are imperative for preserving sovereignty and protecting citizens.

A well-planned strategic approach is essential for overcoming the enemy, ensuring that military operations are executed with precision, foresight, and adaptability. The effectiveness of military leadership—encompassing commanders, the commander-in-chief and soldiers—is a crucial factor in achieving success on the battlefield. Their skills, discipline and morale directly influence the outcome of conflicts, making their training, well-being and overall care a national priority.

Moreover, the chapter explores the importance of advanced armaments and fortifications, stressing that a nation must invest in defence and infrastructure to withstand external threats. In addition to physical strength, the safeguarding of military intelligence and classified information is highlighted as a vital component of defence strategy. Ensuring that sensitive details do not fall into enemy hands is just as critical as battlefield tactics, as it prevents strategic vulnerabilities and strengthens national security.

Hindu ancestors had a well-thought-out understanding of defence, military strategy, armaments, intelligence and fortifications. So why did we lose to the Arabs, Turks and Mughals?

For the answer to this question, please refer to Appendix 2 of this chapter.

Chapter 3

The third chapter, 'Quality Education for All', explores the profound importance of Vidya (knowledge and wisdom) in shaping individuals and society. It emphasizes that acquiring various forms of Vidya is essential not only for personal growth but also for national progress. The chapter categorizes different types of Vidya, each playing a significant role in developing an individual's intellectual, moral and professional capabilities.

Furthermore, the chapter examines the state's responsibility in fostering education and ensuring access to quality learning for all. It discusses how a well-educated and well-trained population contributes to economic prosperity and social harmony. The state must actively promote education, provide quality learning opportunities, and create avenues for higher education. Additionally, the discussion extends to the government's role in generating employment opportunities and ensuring that educated individuals receive appropriate recognition, respect and rewards for their contributions to society.

The chapter also highlights how societies that honour scholars, educators, and skilled professionals thrive. By fostering an environment where learning is encouraged and rewarded, a nation can secure its long-term development and stability.

During the Arab and Turk invasions of Bharat, they primarily destroyed grand universities and burned libraries. The British colonial rule systematically dismantled Bharat's vast Hindu education system, including traditional institutions such as Gurukulas and Pathshalas, during the early phase of colonization.

To understand this issue in greater detail, please refer to Appendices 1 and 2 of this chapter.

Chapter 4

The fourth chapter, 'Responsible Democracy', explores the fundamental role of politics in shaping a just and prosperous society. It draws historical references from Bharat's democratic traditions, including the election of a king, highlighting ancient republican states that practised self-governance long before modern democratic frameworks emerged. The chapter underscores the core responsibilities of the state, emphasizing public safety, welfare and good governance.

Ram Rajya is presented as an ideal model of governance—a system based on dharma, justice and the well-being of all citizens. The discussion extends to the essential characteristics of a republican state, illustrating how democracy derives its strength from citizen participation, ethical leadership and institutional integrity.

The chapter also elaborates on the state's moral obligation to care for the underprivileged, ensure economic stability and create employment opportunities, reinforcing the idea that governance should serve the people rather than oppress them. It further explores the qualities of a head of state, emphasising virtues such as wisdom, integrity and a deep commitment to welfare and justice. Similarly, it outlines the essential qualifications for ministers, highlighting ethical conduct and a strong sense of duty towards public service.

Additionally, the rule of law is given prominence, with discussions on justice, fairness and the necessity of a corruption-free administration. The chapter strongly condemns state oppression, advocating for a governance model where power is exercised responsibly and transparently.

The welfare and well-being of citizens remain central themes, with an emphasis on fair salaries and appropriate rewards for government employees to ensure efficiency and integrity in administration. Finally, it identifies the characteristics of a failed state, warning against corruption, authoritarianism and negligence, which can lead to the collapse of democratic institutions.

Through these discussions, the chapter reinforces the vision of a responsible and accountable democracy, rooted in ethical leadership, justice and an unwavering commitment to public welfare.

In this chapter, I have translated 'King' as 'the Head of State'. To understand the process of electing a king and the ancient democratic institutions in society, please refer to the appendix of this chapter.

Chapter 5

The fifth chapter, 'Highest Respect for Women', highlights the profound reverence historically accorded to women in Hindu society, where they were honoured as Rishis (sages) and held in the highest regard. Sons and daughters are considered equal and must be valued and treated as such.

Women deserve the utmost respect, and their safety and security should always be a priority. Society must ensure their care and protection at all times. Hindu tradition exempts women from death penalty, emphasizing their dignity and sacred status. The sale of girls is strictly condemned and prohibited, reinforcing the principle that women are not commodities but individuals with inherent dignity, value and rights.

Education is essential for women, enabling them to become learned, qualified, and actively involved in decision-making processes. As the cornerstone of society, women—especially mothers—must be treated with the highest respect. Under no circumstances should women ever be insulted.

A fundamental truth must be acknowledged: in cases of misconduct, the blame lies with the man, not the woman. Women possess the strength and ability to be warriors, and their rights must always be protected. Crimes against women, such as rape, demand the strictest punishment to ensure justice and reinforce the principle that a society's progress is measured by how it treats its women.

All the suktas and mantras of the *Rigveda* associated with women rishis are provided in the appendix of this chapter.

Chapter 6

The sixth chapter, 'Non-discriminatory Social System', provides an in-depth analysis of the fundamental concepts of varna, jati, jatiya and jnati, shedding light on their true meanings and dispelling widespread misconceptions. It emphasizes the singular origin of all human beings, reinforcing the idea that Hindu society, at its core, does not support or justify discrimination based on varna or jati.

The chapter clarifies that varna and jati were traditionally linked to one's profession and occupation rather than being determined by birth. This fluidity allowed individuals to adopt different roles based on their skills and knowledge, making varna and jati interchangeable rather than rigid, hereditary divisions.

The focus here is on the respect and dignity accorded to the Shudra community within Hindu society. Contrary to misconceptions, Hindu philosophy upholds the principle that every individual deserves dignity and respect. The text underscores that human dignity is of utmost importance and that a truly just society must ensure the well-being of its weaker and underprivileged sections without any discrimination.

Ultimately, this chapter reaffirms Hindu dharma and society's inclusive and egalitarian ideals, advocating for a society where compassion, respect and justice guide human interactions rather than rigid social hierarchies.

How Christian ideologies and Western scholarship, backed by British colonialism, created the caste system and established it as a central narrative of Hindu society? To understand their strategies and dismantle their false narrative, refer to Appendices 1 and 2 of this chapter.

During the Islamic invasions and the Mughal and Turkish rule, a large number of our artisans and craftsmen, who were once prosperous, became impoverished. This led to the formation and expansion of what is now classified as backward castes, scheduled castes and scheduled tribes in medieval Bharat. This period also contributed to the growth of the Muslim population in Bharat. For a deeper understanding, please refer to Appendix 3 of this chapter.

Chapter 7

The seventh chapter, 'Care for Nature', highlights the deep-rooted environmental consciousness embedded in Hindu philosophy and traditions. It underscores the principle of restrained utilization of natural resources, advocating for a balanced and sustainable approach to consumption. The chapter stresses non-violence, particularly towards animals, and refutes the misconception that sacred Vedic rituals involved animal sacrifices. Instead, it asserts that Vedic traditions emphasize compassion and reverence for life.

A central theme of this chapter is the sacred relationship between humans and nature. In Hindu thought, the Earth is not merely a resource but a revered entity—often addressed as Bhūmi Mata (Mother Earth)—worthy of respect and protection. Similarly, rivers are considered divine mothers, with special reverence given to Maa Ganga as a purifier. This perception fosters a sense of responsibility among Hindus to preserve and protect these water bodies.

The chapter also elaborates on the sanctity of trees and forests, portraying them as integral to human life. Trees are viewed as living beings and are protected and nurtured like one's own children. Hindu scriptures emphasize the virtue of planting trees and creating forests, considering it a noble act that brings both spiritual merit and ecological benefits. The chapter calls upon individuals and society to take an active role in afforestation and environmental conservation.

Additionally, it highlights the state's responsibility in protecting forests and wildlife, emphasizing that governance should include policies to ensure the preservation of biodiversity. Governments and institutions are urged to implement conservation measures.

Finally, the chapter emphasizes the significance of water as a life-giving force. The purity and cleanliness of water sources are deemed invaluable, and maintaining them is considered a sacred duty. Rituals and traditions surrounding water bodies reinforce the idea that they should not be polluted or misused.

In essence, 'Care for Nature' presents a holistic perspective on environmental stewardship, urging individuals, communities and governments to adopt sustainable practices, protect biodiversity and uphold the spiritual and ecological harmony between humans and nature.

Chapter 8

The eighth chapter, 'Respect for the Land', explores Hindu history and its deep connection to the sacred geography of Bharat. It traces the lineage of present-day Hindus in this eon to Dravideshwar Rajarshi Satyavrat (Vaivasvat Manu), the revered king of Dravida, highlighting the profound historical and spiritual roots of Hindu civilization.

A significant portion of the chapter is dedicated to the sacred geography of Bharat Mata, portraying Bharat not merely as a physical territory but as a divine entity embodying the essence of Hindu heritage and spirituality. The narrative extends to the vast expanse once ruled by the great Hindu king Mandhata, describing its majestic mountains, sacred rivers and Janapadas (ancient states). This reinforces the idea that Bharat was historically a unified land under Hindu rule, enriched with cultural, spiritual, political, and economic prosperity.

The text also references the grandeur of Yudhishthira's rule, illustrating how he received gifts and tributes from rulers across the world, signifying the global influence and recognition of Hindu civilization.

In addition to historical accounts, the chapter addresses contemporary concerns by discussing the identification of anti-national elements and emphasizing the need for accountability and just punishment for those who act against Bharat's integrity. This section underscores the importance of vigilance and responsibility in preserving the nation's unity and cultural values.

The chapter concludes on a deeply spiritual note with select mantras from the Prithvi Sukta, a Vedic hymn from the *Atharvaveda*, which glorifies and expresses profound reverence for Mother Earth. This sacred prayer encapsulates the essence of Hindu philosophy, urging devotion, protection and respect for the motherland as a divine and nurturing force.

The Bhūmi Sukta is provided in the appendix of this chapter.

धर्मस्य मूलं अर्थः[1]
Dharmasya Mūlam Arthaḥ

CHAPTER 1

Prosperity for All

The economy serves as the foundation of a society and its resilience. Economic prosperity is essential for any nation to advance and properly care for its people. A nation's power and prominence in world affairs are directly proportional to its economic power.

Profound Hindu knowledge and thought encourage and inspire us to prioritize the welfare of both the people and the state. It advocates for creating widespread prosperity so that everyone has sufficient resources to meet their needs with dignity. Therefore, the first Hindu Sutra, 'धर्मस्य मूलं अर्थः' (Dharmasya mūlam arthaḥ)—'Prosperity for All'—emphasizes this principle.

धर्मार्थकामाः सममेव सेव्या ....
स उत्तमो योऽभिरतस्त्रिवर्गे॥40॥

Dharmārthakāmāḥ samameva sevyā ....
Sa uttamo yo'bhiratastrivarge ||40||[2]

धर्मं चार्थं च कामं च यथावद् वदतां वर।
विभज्य काले कालज्ञः सर्वान् सेवेत पण्डितः।।42।।

Dharmaṃ cāthermaṃ ca kāmaṃ ca yathāvad vadatāṃ vara.
Vibhajya kāle kālajñaḥ sarvān seveta paṇḍitaḥ ||42||[3]

समं वा त्रिवर्गमन्योन्यानुबन्धम्।

Samaṃ vā trivargamanyonyānubandham.[4]

Dharma, artha and *kama* are collectively known as *Trivarga* (grouping of three) or *param Trivarga* (Supreme grouping of three) and are inseparable from one another. These three should be pursued in harmony. A person who follows all three harmoniously is considered knowledgeable and a superior individual.

Dharma holds the highest position among dharma, artha and kama. One should pursue artha in accordance with dharma and fulfill kama within the boundaries of dharma. When a householder follows artha and kama in alignment with dharma, moksha is attained effortlessly. Moksha is the natural outcome of harmoniously adhering to dharma while pursuing artha and kama.

Dharma

Dharma is the greatest and most valuable contribution Hindus have made to humanity. Its ancient origins, profound utility and universal relevance inspire a deep sense of moral awareness in both individuals and society. To fully appreciate its significance, one must comprehend the true essence of dharma.

धारणाद्धर्ममित्याहु धर्मेण विधृता: प्रजाः।
यः स्याद्धारणसंयुक्तः स धर्म इति निश्चयः ॥11॥

Dhāraṇād dharma mityāhu dharmeṇa vidhṛtāḥ prajāḥ.
Yaḥ syād dhāraṇasaṃyuktaḥ sa dharma iti niścayaḥ ॥11॥[5]

धर्मो धारयति प्रजा: ॥67॥

Dharmo dhārayati prajāḥ ॥67॥[6]

धर्मो धारयति प्रजा: ॥9॥

Dharmo dhārayati prajāḥ ॥9॥[7]

धर्मेण धार्यते लोकः ॥234॥

Dharmeṇa dhāryate lokaḥ ॥234॥[8]

Dharma means 'that which sustains'. It is what eternally sustains everything, including individuals, families, communities, societies, nature and both animate and inanimate entities.

The quality of a material is also called its dharma, such as the dharma of fire being warmness and the dharma of water being coldness.

In simple terms, the dharma of the head of the family is to care for the family; it is his duty and responsibility. The dharma of a police officer is to maintain law and order. The dharma of the head of state is to protect the state and take care of its people. The dharma of a teacher is to impart proper knowledge to students. The dharma of a farmer is to produce food, and the dharma of the sun is to provide light.

There is no alternative to the term 'dharma' because it is a non-translatable word. No equivalent in English or any other language captures the true essence of dharma. Therefore, dharma should simply be referred to as dharma.

It would be futile to attempt to provide a single definition of the word, as it can only be understood through its numerous meanings. These meanings encompass a wide range, allowing us to grasp the complexity of the term. For instance, the word 'dharma' can refer to justice, moral and ethical values, righteous conduct in all areas of life, pious obligations, duties and responsibilities, universal moral principles assisting other living beings and the natural qualities or duties of living beings.

Some of the Universal Principles of Dharma

धृतिः क्षमा दमोऽस्तेयं शौचमिन्द्रियनिग्रहः।
धीर्विद्या सत्यमक्रोधो दशकं धर्मलक्षणम्॥92॥

Dhṛtiḥ kṣamā damo'steyaṃ śaucamindriyanigrahaḥ.
Dhīrvidyā satyamakrodho daśakaṃ dharmalakṣaṇam. ॥92॥[9]

धृति *(steadfastness)*, क्षमा *(forgiveness)*, दम *(continence)*, अस्तेय *(non-stealing)*, शौच *(purity)*, इन्द्रिय निग्रह *(control of senses)*, धी *(wisdom)*, विद्या *(true knowledge)*, सत्यम *(truth)*, और अक्रोध *(non-anger)*. *These are some of the universal principles that everybody should adopt.*

Artha refers to wealth, riches, prosperity and resources.

Kama means worldly desire.

The Creation and Generation of Wealth and Prosperity Are Important Dharma Activity

अर्थ एव प्रधान इति कौटिल्यः, अर्थमूलौ हि धर्मकामाविति।

Artha eva pradhāna iti kauṭilyaḥ, arthamūlau hi dharmakāmāviti.[10]

According to Acharya Kautilya, artha is foremost among dharma, artha and kama. Dharma and kama depend on artha.

Acharya Kautilya, a prominent ancient Hindu economist, political realist and philosopher, posited that the concept of 'artha' holds paramount significance among the trio of 'dharma', 'artha' and 'kama' in Hindu thought. In his seminal work, the *Arthashastra*, Kautilya elaborates on the multifaceted nature of artha, which encompasses wealth, prosperity and the economy.

Kautilya's pragmatic approach and profound emphasis on material well-being and the pursuit of wealth are integral aspects of Hindu society. His assertion demonstrates a pragmatic understanding of societal order and emphasizes the central role of artha in shaping societal dynamics.

Moreover, it signifies a nuanced interplay between these three concepts. Kautilya argues that both dharma and kama are contingent upon artha. In other words, he suggests that without the proper acquisition of wealth and resources (artha), the pursuit of dharma and the fulfilment of desires (kama) would be challenging, if not impossible, to achieve.

धनाद्धर्मं ततः सुखम् ।।6।।

Dhanāddharmaṃ tataḥ sukham ।।6।।[11]

Wealth results in dharma, and then dharma brings happiness.

When a person possesses wealth, they are in a position to fulfil their duties and responsibilities towards themselves, their families and society as a whole. Wealth provides the means to perform dharma, and fulfilling one's dharma leads to happiness and contentment.

धनात् स्रवति धर्मो हि धारणाद् वेति निश्चयः ।।18।।

Dhanāt sravati dharmo hi dhāraṇād veti niścayaḥ ।।18।।[12]

It is undeniable that dharma is sustained by wealth.

Acquiring wealth through dharmic (righteous) means is considered important, as it entails recognizing the significance of material resources in fulfilling one's duties and responsibilities within society.

धनेन जयते लोकावुभौ परमिमं तथा ।।43।।

Dhanena jayate lokāvubhau paramimaṃ tathā ।।43।।[13]

Both worlds can be conquered with the wealth in this one and the next.

It encompasses a profound understanding of the human condition and the pursuit of wealth. By acquiring wealth in this world through dharmic means and using it to serve people and society, one aligns with these principles.

धर्मश्चार्थेन महता शक्यो राजन् निषेवितुम् ।।48।।

Dharmaścārthena mahatā śakyo rājan niṣevitum ।।48।।[14]

Dharma can only be served through great wealth.

With a substantial abundance of financial resources, fulfilling one's moral duties and obligations in alignment with dharma can be effectively achieved or enhanced. Wealth can serve as a tool for carrying out one's duties and responsibilities, supporting righteous actions and contributing positively to the world.

धनाद् धर्मः प्रवर्धते ।।22।।

Dhanād dharmaḥ pravardhate ।।22।।[15]

Wealth fosters the advancement of dharma.

Fulfilling one's dharma is facilitated by having access to resources, which can serve as a means of upholding righteous conduct and promoting societal well-being. In other words, wealth enables individuals to fulfil their dharma more effectively.

योऽर्थो धर्मेण संयुक्तो धर्मो यश्चार्थसंयुतः ।।24।।

Yo'rtho dharmeṇa saṃyukto dharmo yaścārthasaṃyutaḥ ।।24।।[16]

Artha is united with dharma, and dharma is united with artha.

The interdependent relationship between the two fundamental concepts of 'dharma' and 'artha' suggests that they are inseparable and mutually supportive. This implies that dharma and artha (wealth) are closely connected and cannot be considered separately. In this context, the pursuit of wealth should align with the principles of dharma.

धनमाहुः परं धर्मं धने सर्वं प्रतिष्ठितम् ।।23।।

Dhanamāhuḥ paraṃ dharmaṃ dhane sarvaṃ pratiṣṭhitam ।।23।।[17]

Wealth is said to constitute the supreme dharma.
Everything is rooted in wealth.

Prosperity and material abundance are not only desirable but also integral to fulfilling one's dharma. This implies that accumulating wealth ethically and using it judiciously can help manifest one's dharma.

The Significance of Economic Prosperity in Societal Structure and Personal Well-being

Prosperity serves as the foundation upon which various facets of personal and societal life thrive. It enables individuals to access education, healthcare and other essential services, fostering overall development and societal progress.

A prosperous state looks after the welfare of its people by providing healthcare, education and other essential services. Economic stability offers a sense of security and freedom, empowering individuals to pursue their aspirations and contribute positively to society.

अर्थे सर्वे समारम्भाः समायत्ता न संशयः ।।48।।

Arthe sarve samārambhāḥ samāyattā na saṃśayaḥ ।।48।।[18]

There is no doubt that all undertakings depend on 'artha' (prosperity and material resources).

The pivotal role of 'artha' in all undertakings underscores the undeniable significance of financial and material resources in achieving objectives—whether personal, societal or organizational. 'Artha' serves as the cornerstone for various pursuits, facilitating progress and sustenance. Whether pursuing ambitions, implementing plans or fostering growth, the availability and effective utilization of 'artha' are fundamental. Essentially, without wealth and resources, undertakings or initiatives may struggle, highlighting the essential nature of wealth and resources (artha).

अर्थार्थी पुरुषो राजन् बृहन्तं धर्ममिच्छति ।।31।।

Arthārthī puruṣo rājan bṛhantaṃ dharmamicchati ।।31।।[19]

A man who pursues artha also strives for great dharma.

Someone who seeks material wealth or prosperity (artha) in life is inherently inclined towards upholding dharma. The pursuit of material prosperity is considered a dharmic activity; therefore, the pursuit of material gain should be guided by the principles of dharma. This emphasizes the interconnectedness of worldly success and moral integrity.

सर्वथा धर्ममूलोऽर्थो धर्मश्चार्थपरिग्रहः।
इतरेतरयोर्नीतौ विद्धि मेघोदधी यथा ।।29।।

Sarvathā dharmamūlo'rtho dharmaścārthaparigrahaḥ.
Itaretarayornītau viddhi meghodadhī yathā ||29||[20]

Dharma is the source of all artha (prosperity and material resources), and dharma is inseparable from artha. Understand that these two are interconnected, much like the ocean and the clouds.

The profound connection between dharma and artha suggests that dharma is fundamental to acquiring and maintaining wealth. Furthermore, it emphasizes the inseparable relationship between the two, likening it to the interdependence of the ocean and clouds. Just as clouds cannot form without the ocean and yet return after rain to enrich it, wealth is generated to uphold and sustain dharma. Similarly, dharma facilitates the generation of wealth.

अर्थस्यावयवावेतौ धर्मकामाविति श्रुतिः।
अर्थसिद्ध्या विनिर्वृत्तावुभावेतौ भविष्यतः॥14॥

Arthasyāvayavāvetau dharmakāmāviti śrutiḥ.
Arthasiddhyā vinirvṛttāvubhāvetau bhaviṣyataḥ ||14||[21]

The sacred text, the Vedas, states that dharma and kama are two aspects of artha, and both can be achieved through the successful pursuit of artha.

The Vedas emphasize the importance of artha in enabling undertakings, stating that without it, Dharma and Kama remain unfulfilled.

The Vedas posit dharma and kama as integral components of artha, suggesting that the successful pursuit of wealth leads to the realization of both. Artha is depicted as a cornerstone that not only sustains life but also enables the practice of dharma and the pursuit of kama.

अर्थेभ्यो हि विवृद्धेभ्यः सम्भृतेभ्यस्ततस्ततः।
क्रियाः सर्वा प्रवर्तन्ते पर्वतेभ्य इवापगाः॥16॥

Arthebhyo hi vivṛddhebhyaḥ sambhṛtebhyastatastataḥ.
Kriyāḥ sarvā pravartante parvatebhya ivāpagāḥ ||16||[22]

All kinds of meritorious acts (dharma) flow abundantly from great wealth, like a stream flowing down mountains.

धनाद्धि धर्मः स्रवति शैलादभि नदी यथा ।।23।।

Dhanāddhi dharmaḥ sravati śailādabhi nadī yathā ।।23।।[23]

Dharma flows from wealth like mountain streams flow from mountains.

The comparison of wealth to mountainous streams flowing down mountains to illustrate the flow of dharma is quite profound. Just as streams originate from mountains and continuously flow downwards, wealth can serve as the source from which acts of dharma naturally manifest.

Streams flow continuously down mountains, symbolizing the ongoing and consistent nature of dharma. Similarly, when acts of dharma stem from righteous wealth, they can have a positive impact on society by aiding communities and reducing suffering. Wealth empowers individuals to give to charity and serve others regularly, thus providing lasting benefits to society.

अर्थैरर्था निबध्यन्ते गजैरिव महागजाः ।।20।।

Arthairarthā nibadhyante gajairiva mahāgajāḥ ।।20।।[24]

Wealth follows wealth like elephants follow mighty elephants.

Wealth tends to attract more wealth, much like how elephants follow the paths of larger, more dominant elephants in their herds. Just as elephants are drawn to the power and leadership of the largest members of their group, financial success often begets further success.

In the realm of economics, this indicates that wealth attracts further wealth. Individuals with wealth tend to enjoy greater opportunities and resources for pursuing better investment prospects, which can result in higher returns on their investments.

अर्थाद् धर्मश्च कामश्च स्वर्गश्चैव नराधिप।
प्राणयात्रापि लोकस्य विना ह्यर्थं न सिद्ध्यति ।।17।।

Arthād dharmaśca kāmaśca svargaścaiva narādhipa.
Prāṇayātrāpi lokasya vinā hyartham na siddhyati ।।17।।[25]

Dharma, kama and heaven result from artha. Without artha, life in the world would be unsustainable.

धर्मः कामश्च स्वर्गश्च हर्षः क्रोधः श्रुतं दमः।
अर्थादेतानि सर्वाणि प्रवर्तन्ते नराधिप ।।21।।

Dharmaḥ kāmaśca svargaśca harṣaḥ krodhaḥ śrutaṃ damaḥ.
Arthādetāni sarvāṇi pravartante narādhipa ।।21।।[26]

The practice of dharma, the fulfilment of kama, the attainment of heaven, the increase of delight, success in anger, learning and self-control—all these result from artha.

अर्थ इत्येव सर्वेषां कर्मणामव्यतिक्रमः।
न ह्यृतेऽर्थेन वर्तेते धर्मकामाविति श्रुतिः।।12।।

Artha ityeva sarveṣāṃ karmaṇāmavyatikramaḥ.
Na hyṛte'rthena vartete dharmakāmāviti śrutiḥ ।।12।।[27]

The sacred text, the Veda, states that artha is essential for fulfilling all undertakings; without artha, dharma and kama cannot be fulfilled.

The concepts of dharma, kama and heaven are intricately intertwined with artha, which serves as a foundational pillar for sustaining life in the world. Artha encompasses material prosperity and the resources necessary for existence. Without it, life would be unsustainable, lacking the means to fulfil essential needs.

Artha facilitates the practice of dharma, the pursuit of kama and the attainment of heaven. It acts as a catalyst for various aspects of life, including the fulfilment of desires, the cultivation of virtues such as self-control, and the pursuit of knowledge.

आसीनश्च शयानश्च विचरन्नपि वा स्थितः।
अर्थयोगं दृढं कुर्याद् योगैरुच्चावचैरपि ।।22।।

Āsīnaśca śayānaśca vicarannapi vā sthitaḥ.
Arthayogaṃ dṛḍhaṃ kuryād yogairuccāvacairapi ।।22।।[28]

Regardless of whether someone is seated, lying down, roaming around or standing, they should strive for the successful pursuit of artha firmly through all ethical means.

Regardless of our physical state or activity, the pursuit of artha remains an ethical constant. Whether we are actively engaged in the world or at rest, this pursuit persists. This principle applies universally, transcending individuals' social status, occupation or background. Therefore, whether one is a labourer, an entrepreneur, a merchant, a farmer, a scholar or a ruler, the pursuit of material wealth should always be a motivating factor.

What Is the Purpose of Wealth Creation in Hindu Dharma?

शतहस्त समाहर सहस्रहस्त सं किर।
कृतस्य कार्यस्य चेह स्फातिं समावह॥5॥

śatahasta samāhara sahasrahasta saṃ kira|
kṛtasya kāryasya ceha sphātiṃ samāvaha॥5॥[29]

Create wealth with a hundred hands and share it with a thousand hands. By doing so, you will fulfil your bounden duty.

This means one should actively engage in creating wealth through hard work, innovation and entrepreneurship. However, true success is not only measured by the accumulation of wealth but also by generously sharing it with those in need. By broadly sharing one's wealth and helping others, an individual fulfils their ethical and moral responsibilities. This approach underscores that while creating wealth is important, its ultimate purpose is to benefit and uplift society as a whole. In doing so, one honours their duty to contribute positively to the community and make a meaningful impact on many lives.

Hindu thought on wealth creation and its purpose differs substantially from other economic philosophies around the world.

अहं लक्ष्मीरहं भूतिः श्रीश्चाहं बलसूदन।
अहं श्रद्धा च मेधा च संनतिर्विजितिः स्थितिः ।।22।।
अहं धृतिरहं सिद्धिरहं त्विड् भूतिरेव च।
अहं स्वाहा स्वधा चैव संस्तुतिनियतिः स्मृतिः ।।23।।

Ahaṃ lakṣmīrahaṃ bhūtiḥ śrīścāhaṃ balasūdana.
Ahaṃ śraddhā ca medhā ca saṃnatirvijitiḥ sthitiḥ ।।22।।
Ahaṃ dhṛtirahaṃ siddhirahaṃ tviḍ bhūtireva ca.
Ahaṃ svāhā svadhā caiva saṃstutiniyatiḥ smṛtiḥ ।।23।।[30]

Shri (Lakshmi, the embodiment of wealth) says, 'I bring prosperity to all beings. I am Lakshmi (wealth), I am Bhuti (prosperity), I am Shri (grace and dignity), I am Shradha (faithfulness) and Medha (intelligence). I am Sannati (affluence), Vijiti (victory), Stithi (immutability). I am Dhriti (steadfastness), I am Siddhi (success), I am Kanti (splendour). I am Svaha (sacrifice) and Svadha (self-confidence). I am Samstuti (praise), Niyati (destiny) and Smriti (memory).'

यत्राहं तत्र मत्कान्ता मद्विशिष्टा मदर्पणाः ।।82।।
सप्त देव्यो जयाष्टम्यो वासमेष्यन्ति तेऽष्टधा।
आशाश्रद्धा धृतिः शान्तिर्विजितिः संनतिः क्षमा ।।83।।
अष्टमी वृत्तिरेतासां पुरोगा पाकशासन।

Yatrāhaṃ tatra matkāntā madviśiṣṭā madarpaṇāḥ ।।82।।
Sapta devyo jayāṣṭamyo vāsameṣyanti te'ṣṭadhā.
Āśāśraddhā dhṛtiḥ śāntirvijitiḥ saṃnatiḥ kṣamā ।।83।।
Aṣṭamī vṛttiretāsāṃ purogā pākaśāsana.[31]

Seven other goddesses exist wherever I am. They are devoted to me, follow my instructions, and have given themselves to me. There is an eighth

(Jaya); these eight desire to dwell with me here. Aasha (hope), shradha (faithfulness), dhriti (steadfastness), shanti (peace), vijiti (victory), sannati (affluence), kshama (forgiveness) and viriti (jaya) are at the forefront.

In this profound proclamation, Shri (Lakshmi), the embodiment of wealth, prosperity and abundance, asserts her identity as the personification of prosperity, dignity, intelligence, and faithfulness. Each attribute symbolizes a facet of life's richness and depth, ranging from wealth and success to steadfastness and memory. Beyond personal qualities, Shri (Lakshmi) encompasses the very fabric of existence, from destiny and sacrifice to victory and peace. The presence of seven other goddesses reflects a collective devotion to Shri (Lakshmi), symbolizing harmonious unity in the pursuit of shared ideals. The mention of an eighth goddess signifies an ultimate aspiration towards completeness, where hope, faithfulness, forgiveness and victory converge at the pinnacle of fulfilment.

Enterprise and Efforts as Primary Factors in Wealth Creation

सत्त्वं हि मूलमर्थस्य वितथं यदतोऽन्यथा ।।64।।

Sattvaṃ hi mūlamarthasya vitathaṃ yadato'nyathā ।।64।।[32]

Self-confidence and courage serve as sources of artha (prosperity and material resources).

Self-confidence and courage are indispensable traits for entrepreneurs, as starting a business necessitates a profound belief in oneself and the fortitude to embrace risks. Entrepreneurs often confront uncertainty, financial hurdles and setbacks. Without self-confidence and courage, many aspiring entrepreneurs might never dare to embark on the journey of starting a business.

Furthermore, self-confidence plays a pivotal role for investors. The process of making investment decisions inherently involves risk, and having unwavering confidence in one's abilities and judgements can lead to more assertive investment choices. Courageous investors are those who are willing to take calculated risks, potentially yielding higher returns.

In the economic domain, self-confidence and courage hold significant value, as they empower individuals to take risks, seize opportunities, foster innovation and persist in the face of adversity. These attributes are fundamental ingredients for wealth creation, both at the individual and societal levels.

विद्या तपो वा विपुलं धनं वा
सर्वं ह्येतद् व्यवसायेन शक्यम्।
बुद्ध्यायत्तं तन्निवसेद् देहवत्सु
तस्माद् विद्याद् व्यवसायं प्रभूतम् ।।45।।

Vidyā tapo vā vipulaṃ dhanaṃ vā
Sarvaṃ hyetad vyavasāyena śakyam.
Buddhyāyattaṃ tannivased dehavatsu
Tasmād vidyād vyavasāyaṃ prabhūtam ।।45।।[33]

Learning, penance and a great deal of wealth—all of these can be obtained through hard work, undertaking and enterprise (Udyog or Purushartha). Therefore, one should recognize the importance of hard work, undertaking and enterprise.

The significance of hard work, undertaking and enterprise lies in their role as pathways to desirable outcomes like learning, penance and wealth. Engaging in these practices allows individuals to achieve material prosperity as well as spiritual growth and knowledge. Emphasizing their importance highlights their role as catalysts for personal development and success in both worldly and inner pursuits. Their multifaceted significance shapes one's life and helps in achieving various aspirations.

अर्थो वा मित्रावर्गो वा ऐश्वर्यं वा कुलान्वितम्।
श्रिश्चापि दुर्लभा भोक्तुं तथैवाकृतकर्मभिः ।।15।।

artho vā mitrāvargo vā aiśvaryaṃ vā kulānvitam|
śriścāpi durlabhā bhoktuṃ tathaivākṛtakarmabhiḥ||15||[34]

Achieving wealth, a supportive circle of friends and prosperity is extremely difficult without enterprise, effort and initiative.

Achieving wealth, building strong friendships and attaining prosperity require proactive engagement in undertaking and enterprise. This implies that merely desiring these outcomes is insufficient; one must actively pursue opportunities and take risks to realize them. Whether in business, personal relationships or any aspect of life, success often demands initiative and perseverance. The importance of effort and initiative in creating a fulfilling and prosperous life is emphasized, as passive wishing alone is unlikely to lead to significant achievements.

दक्षे नरे कर्मणि वर्तमाने ।।6।।

Dakṣe nare karmaṇi vartamāne ।।6।।[35]

Lakshmi, the embodiment of wealth, dwells in persons who are competent.

Wealth is attracted to individuals who possess competence, which encompasses not just skill or knowledge but also qualities like diligence, creativity and resourcefulness. This implies that those who demonstrate proficiency and capability in their endeavours tend to attract prosperity. Success and abundance are often earned through one's abilities and efforts, supporting the belief that competence is key to achieving and maintaining wealth and prosperity in life.

नाकर्मशीले पुरुषे वसामि ।।7।।

Nākarmaśīle puruṣe vasāmi ।।7।।[36]

Lakshmi, the embodiment of wealth, does not dwell in individuals who are idle.

The profound idea that there is interconnectedness between action and outcome, as well as diligence and prosperity, serves as a guiding principle for both spiritual and worldly success. It urges individuals to transcend idleness and embrace a proactive and purposeful approach to life in order to attract wealth and achieve fulfilment in all its forms.

Daily Struggles and Challenges of Those Living in Poverty

नान्यद् दुःखतरं किञ्चिल्लोकेषु प्रतिभाति मे।
अर्थैर्विहीनः पुरुषः परैः सम्परिभूयते ॥20॥

Nānyad duḥkhataraṃ kiñcillokeṣu pratibhāti me.
Arthairvihīnaḥ puruṣaḥ paraiḥ samparibhūyate ॥20॥[37]

There is no more pitiable sight in the world than that of people destitute of wealth, struggling to make ends meet.

The profound and often heartbreaking challenges faced by individuals who lack financial resources and are entrenched in poverty speak of the poignant struggle they endure, highlighting the difficulties of navigating life. For those living in poverty, every day is a battle for survival, marked by relentless obstacles and uncertainties. This struggle involves not just material deprivation but also the emotional and psychological toll it takes on individuals and families.

नातः पापीयसीं काञ्चिदवस्थां शम्बरोऽब्रवीत् ॥22॥

Nātaḥ pāpīyasīṃ kāñcidavasthāṃ śambaro'bravīt ॥22॥[38]

Sage Shambara has stated that nothing is worse for a person than poverty.

The profound impact poverty can have on an individual's life is significant. Poverty not only takes away material possessions but also diminishes dignity, opportunity and hope, which can perpetuate a cycle of disadvantage. Beyond material deprivation, poverty inflicts psychological and emotional distress, eroding self-worth and mental well-being.

मृता ये त्वधाना नराः ।।23।।

Mṛtā ye tvadhānā narāḥ ।।23।।[39]

दारिद्रयं खलु पुरुषस्य जीवितं मरणम् ।।257।।

Dāridrayaṃ khalu puruṣasya jīvitaṃ maraṇam ।।257।।[40]

People who do not possess wealth often struggle to thrive in society, feeling as if they are like the walking dead.

The harsh reality for individuals without financial means portrays their struggle to flourish in society. Lacking wealth, they often encounter barriers that hinder their progress, leading to feelings of alienation and invisibility. This imagery underscores the profound societal challenges faced by those who lack economic resources.

Wealth Loss Can Diminish and Destroy Intelligence

अर्थेन हि विहीनस्य पुरुषस्याल्पमेधसः।
विच्छिद्यन्ते क्रियाः सर्वा ग्रीष्मे कुसरितो यथा ।।18।।

Arthena hi vihīnasya puruṣasyālpamedhasaḥ.
Vicchidyante kriyāḥ sarvā grīṣme kusarito yathā ।।18।।[41]

In the absence of wealth, all of a person's undertakings and actions are hindered, and without wealth, their intelligence diminishes. This is akin to how small rivers dry up during summer due to insufficient rainfall.

The lack of wealth can severely hinder an individual's ability to pursue undertakings and take action. Financial resources are often essential for implementing plans and ideas. Furthermore, without wealth, one's intelligence may appear diminished. Essentially, this passage underscores the significant role of wealth in enabling proactive endeavours and realizing intellectual potential. It highlights the interconnectedness of financial stability and personal development.

The Characteristics of a Prosperous State

तुष्टाः कृषीवलाः ।।77।।

Tuṣṭāḥ kṛṣīvalāḥ ।।77।।[42]

Farmers should be content and satisfied in the state.

Farmers should feel content and satisfied with their agricultural endeavours within the state's policies, infrastructure and support systems.

सीताध्यक्षः कृषितन्त्रशुल्बवृक्षायुर्वेदज्ञस्तज्ज्ञसखो वा सर्वधान्यपुष्पफलशाककन्दमूलवाल्लिक्यक्षौमकार्पास-बीजानि यथा कालं गृह्णीयात्।

Sītādhyakṣaḥ kṛṣitantraśulbavṛkṣāyurvedajñastajjñasakho vā sarv adhānyapuṣpaphalaśākakandamūlavāllikyakṣaumakārpāsa-bījāni yathā kālaṃ gṛhṇīyāt.[43]

The head of the agriculture department should possess expertise in agricultural science and land surveying. They should also oversee a team of assistants who are experts in this field and ensure the regular collection and preservation of seeds for grains, fruits, tubers, vegetables, cotton, etc.

As the leader of the agriculture department, it's crucial for the individual to possess a deep understanding of agricultural science and land surveying. This expertise allows them to make informed decisions regarding farming practices, land management and resource allocation. Moreover, they must assemble a proficient team of assistants who specialize in various aspects of agriculture, ensuring a comprehensive approach. One of their key responsibilities involves overseeing the systematic collection and preservation of seeds essential for various crops such as grains, fruits, tubers, vegetables and cotton. This ensures the continuity of agricultural productivity and contributes to food security.

कच्चिन्न भक्तं बीजं च कर्षकस्यावसीदति।
प्रत्येकं च शतं वृद्ध्या ददास्यृणमनुग्रहम् ।।79।।

Kaccinna bhaktaṃ bījaṃ ca karṣakasyāvasīdati.
Pratyekaṃ ca śataṃ vṛddhyā dadāsyṛṇamanugraham ।।79।।[44]

The state should ensure that the seeds and food grains of the farmer are not destroyed. Additionally, the state should grant loans generously to farmers at an annual rate of one per cent.

For strong agricultural support from the state, it is essential to protect farmers' resources, particularly seeds and food grains, to sustain agricultural productivity. Additionally, offering loans to farmers at a minimal interest rate of one per cent is proposed as a means of providing financial stability and enabling investments in farming practices. This approach aims to alleviate financial burdens on farmers while fostering agricultural growth, ultimately contributing to the overall welfare of the agricultural sector and the nation.

कच्चिद् राष्ट्रे तडागानि पूर्णानि च बृहन्ति च।
भागशो विनिविष्टानि न कृषिर्देवमातृका ।।78।।

Kaccid rāṣṭre taḍāgāni pūrṇāni ca bṛhanti ca.
Bhāgaśo viniviṣṭāni na kṛṣirdevamātṛkā ।।78।।[45]

Big water reservoirs should be built in all regions of the state and filled with water to ensure that crops are not destroyed due to lack of rainfall.

The importance of water availability for agriculture cannot be overstated. If there's a shortage of rainfall, these reservoirs serve as a backup water source for irrigation, ensuring that crops have enough water to grow and thrive. This proactive approach helps safeguard against crop failure and economic losses that can result from drought conditions.

अकृषतामाच्छिद्यान्येभ्यः प्रयच्छेत्। ग्रामभृतकवैदेह वा कृषेयुः।
अकृषन्तोऽपहीनं दद्युः। धान्यपशुहिरण्यैश्चैनानुगृह्णीयात्। तान्यनु सुखेन दद्युः।

Akṛṣatāmācchidyānyebhyaḥ prayacchet.
grāmabhṛtakavaideha vā kṛṣeyuḥ.
Akṛṣanto'pahīnaṃ dadyuḥ. dhānyapaśuhiraṇyaiścainānugṛhṇīyāt.
tānyanu sukhena dadyuḥ.[46]

The barren land made fertile through the toil of the farmers should not be acquired by the state. The farmers should have full rights over such land. If any farmer does not use the fertile land for agriculture and keeps it unused, the land should be transferred to another needy farmer. If there is no needy farmer available to cultivate the land, the village head may use the same land. If any farmer takes the land for cultivation but fails to do so, revenue should be charged from them. The state should always assist farmers with seeds, grains, money and bulls. After the harvest, the farmer should gradually repay the loan or money to the state.

कच्चित् स्वनुष्ठिता तात वार्ता ते साधुभिर्जनैः।
वार्तायां संश्रितस्तात लोकोऽयं सुखमेधते ।।80।।

kaccit svanuṣṭhitā tāta vārtā te sādhubhirjanaiḥ.
vārtāyāṃ saṃśritastāta loko'yaṃ sukhamedhate ।।80।।[47]

Agriculture and commerce should be undertaken by the industrious and virtuous members of society. The prosperity and happiness of the state's people depend on these two pillars: agriculture and commerce.

The crucial role of hardworking and morally upright individuals in advancing the sectors of agriculture and commerce cannot be overstated. The success and well-being of a society hinge upon the dedication and integrity of its members within these sectors. Agriculture sustains the population with food and resources, while commerce fuels economic growth and stability. Together, these sectors form the foundation upon which a prosperous and content community can thrive, underscoring the interconnectedness of diligence, virtue and societal prosperity.

In Hindu society, farmers and businessmen are regarded as diligent and principled members of the communities. They play vital roles in sustaining society by sharing the responsibilities of providing food, managing commerce and fostering stability. Both groups should offer mutual care and be cared for, protected and supported by the state and society. Unfortunately, in the modern socialist ideological environment, these two groups are often set against each other as conflicting and opposing factions.

The Attributes of a Prosperous State

व्याधितो वा कृशो वापि तस्मिन् नाभृन्नरः क्वचित् ।।15।।

Vyādhito vā kṛśo vāpi tasmin nābhṛnnaraḥ kvacit ।।15।।[48]

The state's residents should not be weak or malnourished; instead, they should have good health and remain free from illness.

The importance of prioritizing the well-being of a state's residents cannot be overstated. A population's strength and vitality are crucial elements for the prosperity and stability of a society. By emphasizing the necessity of good health and the absence of illness, it suggests that adequate nutrition is essential for societal advancement. Essentially, a healthy and well-nourished population can contribute more effectively to the economy, maintain social cohesion, and pursue personal and collective goals. This fosters overall progress and development within the state.

रत्नैर्धनैश्च पशुभिः सस्यैश्चापि पृथग्विधैः ।।14।।
नगरं विषयश्चास्य प्रतिपूर्णस्तदाभवत्।

Ratnairdhanaiśca paśubhiḥ sasyaiścāpi pṛthagvidhaiḥ ।।14।।
Nagaraṃ viṣayaścāsya pratipūrṇastadābhavat.[49]

The state's cities, towns and villages should be filled with wealth, gems, jewellery, cattle, and various sorts of grains and provisions.

The prosperity and abundance that should permeate states are crucial for the flourishing economies of cities, towns and villages, envisioning them as bustling hubs of wealth and resources. The inclusion of wealth, gems, jewellery, cattle, grains and provisions highlights a diverse range of riches, suggesting a well-rounded and thriving economy. Such prosperity not only represents material wealth but also implies the overall welfare and stability of the communities within these areas, fostering a vision of abundance and fulfilment for all inhabitants.

Entrepreneurs and Farmers Should Be Cared for and Protected by the State

गोमिनो धनिनश्चैव परिपाल्या विशेषतः ।।17।।

Gomino dhaninaścaiva paripālyā viśeṣataḥ ।।17।।[50]

The state should care for and look after both farmers and businesspersons.

The state has a responsibility to provide support and assistance to both farmers and entrepreneurs. This support encompasses various forms of aid, including financial assistance, access to resources, regulatory support, and policies and measures that make farming attractive and profitable while promoting entrepreneurship and business growth, as well as infrastructure development. By prioritizing the well-being of these key economic contributors, the state aims to foster a conducive environment for agricultural, entrepreneurial and commercial activities to thrive. Ultimately, such measures are designed to ensure the sustainability and prosperity of these vital sectors, thereby benefiting the overall economy and society at large.

In Hindu society, the farming profession is highly esteemed and respectfully referred to as 'annadata', which means 'provider of food'.

Farming is regarded as a vital enterprise (vanijya), and both agriculture and entrepreneurship are seen as integral to the role of the cultivator.

Entrepreneurs are respected and addressed honourifically as 'Shreshthi' in Sanskrit, meaning 'fine people'. Consequently, in various regional languages of Bharat, Shreshthi has several variations: 'Shreshtha' in Hindi and Nepali, 'Sethi' in Punjabi, 'Sethji' in Rajasthani, 'Seth' in Gujarati, 'Shetty' in the South and Western regions (Maharashtra, Goa, Karnataka, Andhra Pradesh, and Telangana), and 'Chetty' or 'Chettiar' in Tamil.

नमो॑ म॒न्त्रिणे॑ वाणि॒जाय॒ ॥19॥

namo mantriṇe vāṇijāya ||19||[51]

Salutations to expert and capable entrepreneurs.

Respect and honour to cultivator, intelligent, capable entrepreneurs and business professionals.

Recognizing and respecting capable and intelligent entrepreneurs and business professionals means acknowledging the dedication, vision and resilience they demonstrate in their fields. Such individuals often possess a unique blend of creativity, strategic thinking, innovation and leadership qualities, enabling them to transform ideas into successful ventures. They navigate complex challenges, adapt to market changes and maintain a strong sense of ethical responsibility, all while fostering growth, building teams and creating value. By combining creativity with strategic thinking, they play a pivotal role in shaping industries and advancing society.

Their impact extends beyond mere business success; they contribute to society by driving economic progress, generating employment and inspiring others to pursue entrepreneurial aspirations.

In Hindu society, both farmers and entrepreneurs are respected, regarded and valued for their contributions to food grain production, wealth generation and employment creation, which make the country self-reliant and strong. A country that does not respect its farmers and entrepreneurs will never progress or become strong.

सत्याचारास्तु धनिका व्यवहारे हता यदि।
राजा समुद्धरेत्तांस्तु तथाऽन्यांश्च कृषिबलान् ॥83॥

Satyācārāstu dhanikā vyavahāre hatā yadi.
Rājā samuddharettāṃstu tathā'nyāṃśca kṛṣibalān ॥83॥[52]

Sometimes, honest entrepreneurs and farmers fall into distress. During those times, the state should help them overcome their difficulties.

In times of economic hardship, even the most diligent and honest individuals, such as entrepreneurs and farmers, may find themselves struggling. Whether due to unforeseen circumstances, market instability or natural disasters, these hardworking members of society can face significant challenges. It is during these moments of adversity that the state has a responsibility to provide support and assistance. By offering aid and resources to meet their needs, the state can help alleviate their burdens and enable them to overcome their difficulties, ensuring the resilience and stability of both the individuals and the broader economy.

The State Should Not Disrupt Day-to-Day Business Activities

नावो न सन्ति सेनाया बह्व्यस्तारयितुं तथा।
वणिजामुपधातं च कथमस्मद्विधश्चरेत् ॥28॥

Nāvo na santi senāyā bahvyastārayituṃ tathā.
Vaṇijāmupadhātaṃ ca kathamasmadvidhaścaret ॥28॥[53]

Shri Rama stated that our army is sizable; however, we lack a sufficient number of boats to facilitate crossing the sea. We prefer not to utilize merchant vessels, as doing so would disrupt their regular activities.

A compelling discussion unfolded as Shri Rama, leading his army, endeavoured to cross the sea towards the shores of Lanka. Expressing apprehension, Shri Rama remarked, 'Although our army is substantial, we face a shortage of boats to navigate this vast ocean'. Furthermore, he articulated his hesitation to impede the routine operations of merchants, stating, 'I am reluctant to disrupt the customary affairs of the business community'.

Shri Rama demonstrates his ethical principles and respect for the livelihoods of others by expressing reluctance to disrupt the routine operations of merchants. He acknowledges that interfering with merchants would disrupt their business activities, causing inconvenience and potentially harming their livelihoods. This reflects Shri Rama's sense of fairness and consideration for others, even in the midst of his military campaign.

A state should avoid interfering in the daily activities of entrepreneurs, reserving the use of their resources only for emergency situations, such as war or natural calamities, rather than for regular circumstances.

The Strength of the Military Is Contingent upon the Economy

राज्ञः कोशबलं मूलं कोशमूलं पुनर्बलम् ।।35।।

Rājñaḥ kośabalaṃ mūlaṃ kośamūlaṃ punarbalam ।।35।।[54]

अकोशस्य कुतो बलम् ।।4।।

Akośasya kuto balam ।।4।।[55]

The state's power is rooted in its treasury and military, with the treasury serving as a vital source of strength for the military.

बलमूलो भवेत्कोशः कोशमूलं बलं स्मृतम् ।।14।।

Balamūlo bhavetkośaḥ kośamūlaṃ balaṃ smṛtam ।।14।।[56]

The treasury is the source of strength of the military.

The essential relationship between the treasury and the military within a state's power structure suggests that a state's stability and might are deeply intertwined with its financial resources and military capabilities. The treasury, symbolizing economic stability and resources, serves as the backbone upon which the military relies for defence-related needs. A well-funded treasury not only supports military operations but also enhances their effectiveness, ensuring the state's ability to assert influence and protect its interests both domestically and internationally.

How Should a State Protect Its Prosperity?

दण्डेन रक्ष्यते धान्यं धनं दण्डेन रक्ष्यते ।।14।।

Daṇḍena rakṣyate dhānyaṃ dhanaṃ daṇḍena rakṣyate ।।14।।[57]

Law enforcement protects the wealth and prosperity of both individuals and the state.

Law enforcement plays a crucial role in safeguarding the wealth and prosperity of both individuals and the state through various means. First, it ensures public safety and security, creating an environment conducive to economic activities and investments. By combating crimes such as theft, fraud and organized crime, law enforcement safeguards individuals' assets and businesses, fostering economic stability and growth. Additionally, it upholds the rule of law, ensuring fair and equitable enforcement of regulations and contracts, which is essential for maintaining trust and confidence in the economic system. Overall, law enforcement serves as a cornerstone in safeguarding the socioeconomic fabric of society and protecting the interests of both individuals and the state.

How Should Taxation Be Charged and Collected

यथैव पूर्णादुदधेः स्यन्दन्त्यापो दिशो दश।
एवं राजकुलाद् वित्तं पृथिवीं प्रति तिष्ठति ।।32।।

Yathaiva pūrṇādudadheḥ syandantyāpo diśo daśa
Evaṃ rājakulād vittaṃ pṛthivīṃ prati tiṣṭhati ।।32।।[58]

Ocean water is drawn up by the sun, which then spreads clouds that bring rain in all directions. Similarly, wealth emanates from the state and spreads throughout it.

Taxation is akin to the moisture of the earth evaporated by the sun, only to be later returned as fertilizing rain. Taxation mirrors the natural cycle of moisture within the ecosystem. Just as the sun evaporates moisture from the earth's surface, taxes are gathered from individuals and businesses. Similarly, akin to rain replenishing the soil, these taxes are subsequently redistributed by the state to support public services such as healthcare, education, security and infrastructure, thereby benefiting society as a whole. These benefits might include improved public services, job creation, business opportunities and overall economic growth. This underscores the cyclical essence of taxation, wherein the resources extracted are eventually reinvested back into the community for its advancement and prosperity.

लोके चायव्ययौ दृष्ट्वा बृहद्वृक्षमिवास्रवत् ।।9।।

Loke cāyavyayau dṛṣṭvā bṛhadvṛkṣamivāsravat ।।9।।[59]

Taxation is akin to extracting juice from a Palmyra tree.

The analogy of taxation to extracting juice from a Palmyra tree conveys the idea that while taxation is necessary for the sustenance of a state; it should be done with care and consideration. Just as one wouldn't destroy a tree while collecting its juice, taxes should not harm people or cripple their livelihoods. Instead, taxation should be approached with a balanced perspective, examining both the resources available to people and the needs of the state. By understanding the income and expenditure of people, taxes can be levied in a manner that is fair and sustainable, akin to extracting juice from a Palmyra tree without causing harm to it.

विक्रयं क्रयध्वानं भक्तं च सपरिच्छदम् ।
योगक्षेमं च सम्प्रेक्ष्य वणिजां कारयेत् करान् ।।13।।

Vikrayaṃ krayadhvānaṃ bhaktaṃ ca saparicchadam
Yogakṣemaṃ ca samprekṣya vaṇijāṃ kārayet karān ।।13।।[60]

A state must thoroughly examine the sales and purchases of goods, transportation costs, staff salaries, profits and the survival of businesses. Only then should taxes be imposed to ensure the survival of entrepreneurs.

उत्पत्तिं दानवृत्तिं च शिल्पं सम्प्रेक्ष्य चासकृत्।
शिल्पं प्रति करानेवं शिल्पिनः प्रति कारयेत् ।।14।।

Utpattiṃ dānavṛttiṃ ca śilpaṃ samprekṣya cāsakṛt
Śilpaṃ prati karānevaṃ śilpinaḥ prati kārayet ।।14।।[61]

A state must thoroughly examine the costs of production, the quality of products, and the type of technology ensuring that taxes are commensurate. Taxes must also be structured to guarantee industrialists a decent standard of living, fostering the growth of both industry and industrialists.

The state must carefully consider various factors before imposing taxes on businesses and industrialists. A comprehensive analysis should encompass economic elements such as the cost of raw materials, sales and purchases of goods, transportation costs, employee salaries, production expenses, product quality and the application of technology. By evaluating these aspects, the state can assess the overall health of businesses and impose taxes that support their survival and growth.

Furthermore, it is important to structure taxes to support existing industries, stimulate the development of new ones and encourage the growth of individual entrepreneurs. This approach seeks to balance the state's revenue requirements with the need to create an environment conducive to economic prosperity and entrepreneurial activity.

उत्पन्नानकच्चिदाढ्यस्य दरिद्रस्य च भारत।
अर्थान्न मिथ्या पश्यन्ति तवामात्या हृता धनैः ।।107।।

utpannānakaccidāḍhyasya daridrasya ca bhārata|
arthānna mithyā paśyanti tavāmātyā hṛtā dhanaiḥ|| 107||[62]

Some entrepreneurs, both poor and wealthy, have become prosperous in a short period. Ministers and tax collectors should not be misled by others into believing that their success was achieved through improper means.

Some entrepreneurs, regardless of their initial financial status—whether poor or wealthy—have managed to achieve remarkable prosperity within a short span of time. Their success may be attributed to factors such as innovative business strategies, market opportunities, perseverance, or sheer hard work. However, it is crucial for ministers and tax collectors to exercise caution and not be swayed by hearsay, unfounded suspicions, or misleading accusations. They should avoid assuming that such rapid financial growth is necessarily the result of unethical practices, corruption, or tax evasion. Instead, a fair and objective assessment should be made, ensuring that legitimate success is recognized and not unfairly scrutinized.

कच्चिदभ्यागता दूराद्वणिजो लाभकारणात्।
यथोक्तमवहार्यन्ते शुल्कं शुल्कोपजीविभिः ।।115।।

kaccidabhyāgatā dūrādvaṇijo lābhakāraṇāt|
yathoktamavahāryante śulkaṃ śulkopajīvibhiḥ ||115||[63]

Entrepreneurs who have travelled from far away to conduct business and earn a profit should be treated fairly. State tax collectors should collect the appropriate amount of tax, not more than necessary.

कच्चित्ते पुरुषा राजन्पुरे राष्ट्रे च मानिताः।
उपानयन्ति पण्यानि उपाधाभिरवञ्चिताः ।।116।।

kaccitte puruṣā rājanpure rāṣṭre ca mānitāḥ|
upānayanti paṇyāni upādhābhiravañcitāḥ ||116||[64]

Entrepreneurs and traders who bring valuable goods into the state deserve respect and honour. Tax collectors should not deceive or cheat them.

Taxation in Underdeveloped Regions Hinders Economic Growth

कच्चित् ते वणिजो राष्ट्रे नोद्विजन्ति करार्दिताः।
क्रीणन्तो बहुनाल्पेन कान्तारकृतविश्रमाः ।।23।।

Kaccit te vaṇijo rāṣṭre nodvijanti karārditāḥ.
Krīṇanto bahunālpena kāntārakṛtaviśramāḥ ।।23।।[65]

Entrepreneurs and industrialists tirelessly making efforts in a challenging region within the state should not be burdened with heavy taxes.

The fair treatment of entrepreneurs and industrialists operating in challenging environments within a state is crucial. These individuals exert significant effort in regions that may lack infrastructure or face instability. Heavy taxation could further burden them, potentially stifling economic activity and inhibiting growth. Therefore, it is suggested that tax policies should be mindful of the context in which businesspeople and industrialists operate, aiming to support rather than hinder their endeavours in such areas to foster economic resilience and development.

Taxation and the Globalization of Trade and Commerce

परभूमिजं पण्यमनुग्रहेणावाहयेत्। नाविकसार्थवाहेभ्यश्च परिहारमायतिक्षमं दद्यात्।

Parabhūmijaṃ paṇyamanugraheṇāvāhayet.
nāvikasārthavāhebhyaśca parihāramāyatikṣamaṃ dadyāt.[66]

Goods that are not available in one's own country should be imported with tax discounts and waived customs duties.

महोपकारमुच्छुल्कं कुर्याद्वीजं तु दुर्लभम् ।।

Mahopakāramucchulkaṃ kuryādvījaṃ tu durlabham.[67]

There are goods that are not available within the state and are procured with difficulty from foreign countries; taxes should not be imposed on the import of such goods.

To foster economic growth and availability for consumers, it's imperative to import goods that aren't locally available, incentivizing this process through tax discounts and waived customs duties. This strategy promotes international trade, expands consumer choices and ensures access to a diverse range of products. By eliminating barriers to importation, such as high taxes and customs fees, countries can stimulate domestic demand, encourage competition and facilitate the flow of goods across borders, ultimately contributing to a more dynamic and prosperous marketplace.

Prohibiting Taxation of Farmers and the General Population Is Essential

कच्चित् कृषिकरा राष्ट्रं न जहत्यतिपीडिताः ।।24।।

Kaccit kṛṣikarā rāṣṭraṃ na jahatyatipīḍitāḥ ।।24।।[68]

Farmers should not be burdened and oppressed by excessive taxes.

Farmers, as stewards of the land, play a vital role in sustaining communities and ensuring food security. However, their livelihoods are often precarious, reliant on unpredictable weather patterns and uncertain markets. Excessive taxation exacerbates these challenges, placing undue strain on already limited resources. Such burdens hinder agricultural innovation and investment, stifling the potential for growth and sustainability in the sector. By alleviating the tax burden on farmers, states can foster an environment conducive to agricultural prosperity, empowering farmers to thrive and contribute meaningfully to society's well-being.

अर्थमूलोऽपि हिंसां च कुरुते स्वयमात्मनः।
करैरशास्त्रदृष्टैर्हि मोहात् सम्पीडयन् प्रजाः ।।5।।

Arthamūlo'pi hiṃsāṃ ca kurute svayamātmanaḥ.
Karairaśāstradṛṣṭairhi mohāt sampīḍayan prajāḥ ।।5।।[69]

The state should not oppress its people by extracting excessive taxes from them as this undermines the prescribed rules and ultimately leads to the destruction of the state.

Taxes are crucial for financing essential services such as infrastructure, healthcare, education, and defence by the state. However, when state authority is unjustly exercised through oppressive and unfair tax policies that place an undue burden on the populace, it contradicts established principles or norms within a society, including legal frameworks and constitutions for both the government and its people. Excessive taxation can lead to the erosion of public trust in the government, economic stagnation, social unrest, and ultimately the collapse or weakening of the state. When people feel excessively burdened by taxes without seeing commensurate benefits, or when taxes are perceived as unfair, it can undermine the stability and legitimacy of the government. While taxation is necessary for the functioning of a state, it must be fair and reasonable. Excessive taxation that oppresses the people violates established rules of governance and can have detrimental consequences for the state's stability and longevity.

The Maximum Limit of Taxation

आददीत बलिं चापि प्रजाभ्यः कुरुनन्दन।
स षड्भागमपि प्राज्ञस्तासामेवाभिगुप्तये ।।25।।

Ādadīta baliṃ cāpi prajābhyaḥ kurunandana.
Sa ṣaḍbhāgamapi prājñastāsāmevābhiguptaye ।।25।।[70]

The state should collect only one-sixth of its people's income as taxes to fulfil its duties and responsibilities for their welfare and protection.

यो हरेद् बलिषड्भागम् ।।11।।

Yo hared baliṣaḍbhāgam ।।11।।[71]

A state should take only one-sixth of people's income as taxes.

It is proposed that within a state, the government should collect approximately one-sixth of people's income as taxes, reflecting a comparatively lighter tax burden. The primary aim of taxation is to enable the government to fulfil essential responsibilities including public services such as education, healthcare, infrastructure, and defence, as well as ensuring the safety and welfare of its people. This approach advocates for a restrained tax burden to support critical government functions such as welfare and protection. By adhering to this principle, a state aims to strike a balance between financing its operations and safeguarding people's financial independence. Allowing people to retain a significant portion of their earnings promotes economic liberty while securing necessary funds for public services and infrastructure. Such a proportional taxation strategy seeks to prevent undue government intervention in people's finances, thereby fostering an environment conducive to economic growth and prosperity.

The State Should Support Foreign Industrialists, Entrepreneurs and Local Industries to Ensure Fairness

अनभियोगश्चार्थिष्वागन्तूनामन्यत्रसभ्योपकारिभ्यः।

Anabhiyogaścārthiṣvāgantūnāmanyatrasabhyopakāribhyaḥ.[72]

The state should assist foreign industrialists
and entrepreneurs impartially.

The government should foster a supportive environment for foreign industrialists and entrepreneurs seeking to establish businesses or operate within its jurisdiction. This includes ensuring transparent and fair laws that protect and guarantee equal treatment under the law. Incentives, such as tax breaks or subsidies, should be provided to attract foreign entrepreneurs and stimulate economic growth and job creation.

Political stability and a strong rule of law are necessary to create a secure environment for investments and to uphold contracts and agreements.

The state aims to drive economic growth, generate employment opportunities, transfer technology and expertise, and enhance integration into global markets. This approach not only contributes to overall economic development but also strengthens diplomatic and trade relations with other countries.

It is crucial for governments to safeguard national interests and support domestic industries against activities that undermine them. In economic policy, governments must ensure that enterprises and individuals contribute positively to the national economy and comply with established laws.

To achieve this, governments enact measures to shield domestic industries from unfair competition and practices that could impair their competitiveness. These measures target actions such as unfair trade practices and unethical business behaviour that could disadvantage domestic businesses.

Antinational Individuals Are a Threat to National Prosperity

ये च राष्ट्रोपरोधेन वृद्धिं कुर्वन्ति केचन।
तानेवानुम्रियेरंस्ते कुणपं कृमयो यथा ।।21।।

ye ca rāṣṭroparodhena vṛddhiṃ kurvanti kecana|
tānevānumriyeraṃste kuṇapaṃ kṛmayo yathā ||21||[73]

Those who seek to increase their fortune through unscrupulous means, harming and betraying their country, are like vermin feeding on a corpse.

Individuals who resort to unscrupulous methods to amass wealth not only compromise their integrity but also inflict harm upon their nation. This behaviour often involves deception, exploitation and betrayal, undermining the very fabric of society. By prioritizing their own interests, these anti-national individuals erode trust and foster an environment of greed and corruption.

Anti-national individuals are parasitic to society. Just as vermin thrive on decay, these unscrupulous people benefit from the suffering and decline of their country. Their actions contribute to a cycle of destruction, where the values of loyalty, duty and societal well-being are disregarded in favour of self-serving pursuits.

Ultimately, the pursuit of fortune through dishonest means not only jeopardizes national prosperity but also threatens the social cohesion and moral foundation of society. Such behaviour should be condemned, as it signifies a betrayal of the shared values and collective responsibility that bind individuals to their nation. These individuals should be punished harshly so that their actions become a deterrent for others.

Hindu Dharma and Philosophy Oppose Capitalist Exploitation

ये धनादपकर्षन्ति नरं स्वबलमास्थिताः।
ते धर्ममर्थं कामं च प्रमथ्नन्ति नरं च तम्।।24।।

Ye dhanādapakarṣanti naraṃ svabalamāsthitāḥ
Te dharmamarthaṃ kāmaṃ ca pramathnanti naraṃ ca tam ।।24।।[74]

If a powerful person resorts to using their power to exploit another for their wealth, they not only devastate the victim but also undermine their dharma, artha and kama.

It reflects the profound Hindu ethos, emphasizing harmony between individual well-being and societal welfare. In this context, capitalist exploitation contradicts the principles of dharma, artha and kama. Exploiting others for personal gain harms victims and disrupts societal balance. Therefore, the state and society are responsible for ensuring justice and preventing exploitation, in line with the broader Hindu concept of societal welfare.

It is essential to emphasize that this viewpoint, which challenges and protects against capitalist exploitation, is rooted in a tradition that is at least five thousand years old. This ancient perspective contradicts the commonly held belief that opposition to capitalist exploitation began exclusively with European socialist and communist movements.

आपदेवास्य मरणात् पुरुषस्य गरीयसी।
श्रियोविनाशस्तद्ध्यस्य निमित्तं धर्मकामयोः ।।27।।

Āpadevāsya maraṇāt puruṣasya garīyasī.
Śriyovināśastaddhyasya nimittaṃ dharmakāmayoḥ ।।27।।[75]

For a person, the destruction of prosperity is a worse calamity than death, as prosperity is the source of dharma and kama.

एतामवस्थां प्राप्यैके मरणं वव्रिरे जनाः।
ग्रामायैके वनायैके नाष्ठायैके प्रवव्रजुः ।।25।।

Etāmavasthāṃ prāpyaike maraṇaṃ vavrire janāḥ.
Grāmāyaike vanāyaike nāṣṭṭhāyaike pravavrajuḥ ।।25।।[76]

In the state of poverty, a poor person may prefer death; some escape to the forest, while others wander around, seeking to destroy themselves.

From an individual perspective, the collapse of prosperity is often perceived as a profound tragedy, sometimes even surpassing the fear of death itself. This is because prosperity is seen as the source of dharma and kama. When someone is plunged into poverty, they may find themselves viewing death as a preferable option. Some may retreat to the solitude of forests, while others wander aimlessly, perhaps seeking an end to their suffering.

This sentiment reflects the fundamental values of Hindu thought, which emphasize the interconnectedness of personal fulfilment and the well-being of the community. In this economic framework, the exploitative nature of capitalism directly contradicts the foundational Hindu principles of dharma, artha and kama. It suggests that when individuals exploit others solely for their own gain, they not only harm the victim but also disrupt the balance of society itself.

Therefore, it becomes imperative for the state to uphold justice and prevent such exploitation, aligning with the overarching Hindu principle of societal welfare. This underscores the idea that societal harmony is contingent upon the fair and equitable treatment of all individuals.

The discussion covered the importance of wealth creation, taxation and the protection of prosperity, as well as state policies related to these areas. Furthermore, the following is a description of Ayodhya, illustrating how a prosperous state is depicted in ancient Hindu historical texts.

Valmiki Described the Prosperity of the State of Kosala and the City of Ayodhya

कोशलो नाम मुदितः स्फीतो जनपदो महान्।
निविष्टः सरयूतीरे प्रभूतधनधान्यवान् ।।5।।

Kośalo nāma muditaḥ sphīto janapado mahān.
Niviṣṭaḥ sarayūtīre prabhūtadhanadhānyavān ।।5।।[77]

The large state of Kosala extends along the banks of the Saryu River. It is happy and prosperous, filled with abundant riches and plenty.

अयोध्या नाम नगरी तत्रासील्लोकविश्रुता ।।6।।

Ayodhyā nāma nagarī tatrāsīllokaviśrutā ।।6।।[78]

Its territory includes the world-renowned city by the name of Ayodhya.

आयता दश च द्वे च योजनानि महापुरी।
श्रीमती त्रीणि विस्तीर्णा सुविभक्तमहापथा ।।7।।

Āyatā daśa ca dve ca yojanāni mahāpurī.
Śrīmatī trīṇi vistīrṇā suvibhaktamahāpathā ।।7।।[79]

The great and glorious city of Ayodhya, with its well-aligned roads, is twelve yojanas (ninety-six miles) long and three yojanas (twenty-four miles) wide.

राजामार्गेण महता सुविभक्तेन शोभिता।
मुक्तपुष्पावकीर्णेन जलसिक्तेन नित्यशः ।।8।।

Rājāmārgeṇa mahatā suvibhaktena śobhitā.
Muktapuṣpāvakīrṇena jalasiktena nityaśaḥ ।।8।।[80]

Ayodhya is graced with a beautifully ramified extensive highway, which is daily sprinkled with water all along.

कपाटतोरणवर्तीं सुविभक्तान्तरापणाम्।
सर्वयन्त्रायुधवतीमुषिता सर्वशिल्पिभिः।।10।।

Kapāṭatoraṇavartīṃ suvibhaktāntarāpaṇām.
Sarvayantrāyudhavatīmuṣitā sarvaśilpibhiḥ ।।8।।[81]

Ayodhya features an arched gateway with beautiful doors, well-laid-out markets and a diverse population of craftsmen from all classes, all while being equipped with various types of weapons.

सूतमागधसम्बाधां श्रीमतीमतुलप्रभाम्।
उच्चाट्टालध्वजवतीं शतघ्नीशतसंकुलाम्।।11।।

Sūtamāgadhasambādhāṃ śrīmatīmatulaprabhām.
Uccāṭṭāladhvajavatīṃ śataghnīśatasaṃkulām ।।11।।[82]

Ayodhya, filled with panegyrists and bards, is prosperous and possesses matchless splendour, marked by towering buildings and flags, and equipped with a myriad of weapons and numerous cannons.

तस्मिन् पुरवरे हृष्टा धर्मात्मानो बहुश्रुताः।
नरास्तुष्टा धनैः स्वैः स्वैरलुब्धाः सत्यवादिनः ।।6।।

Tasmin puravare hṛṣṭā dharmātmāno bahuśrutāḥ.
Narāstuṣṭā dhanaiḥ svaiḥ svairalubdhāḥ satyavādinaḥ ||6||[83]

The people of Ayodhya are happy, virtuous, learned, free from greed, truthful and content with their own fortune.

The ancient text's description of Ayodhya paints a vivid picture of a thriving, well-organized city with a peaceful and harmonious atmosphere. The city boasts a grand design, with spacious areas and outstanding infrastructure, including well-planned streets, wide highways and a skilled, diverse population. Its residents are depicted as virtuous, knowledgeable and satisfied, contributing to the city's overall atmosphere of tranquillity and prosperity.

APPENDIX 1

World Economic History

Professor Angus Maddison's extraordinary study of world economic history presents the following statistics:

(Per Cent of World Total)

Year	**0**	**1000**	**1500**	**1600**	**1700**	**1820**	**1870**	**1913**	**1950**	**1973**	**1998**
Austria			0.6	0.6	0.7	0.6	0.8	0.9	0.5	0.5	0.5
Belgium			0.5	0.5	0.6	0.7	1.2	1.2	0.9	0.7	0.6
Denmark			0.2	0.2	0.2	0.2	0.3	0.4	0.6	0.4	0.3
Finland			0.1	0.1	0.1	0.1	0.2	0.2	0.3	0.3	0.3
France			4.4	4.7	5.7	5.5	6.5	5.3	4.1	4.3	3.4
Germany			3.3	3.8	3.6	3.8	6.5	8.8	5.0	5.9	4.3
Italy			4.7	4.4	3.9	3.2	3.8	3.5	3.1	3.6	3.0
Netherlands			0.3	0.6	1.1	0.6	0.9	0.9	1.1	1.1	0.9
Norway			0.1	0.1	0.1	0.2	0.2	0.2	0.3	0.3	0.3
Sweden			0.2	0.2	0.3	0.4	0.6	0.6	0.9	0.7	0.5
Switzerland			0.2	0.3	0.3	0.3	0.5	0.6	0.8	0.7	0.5
United Kingdom			1.1	1.8	2.9	5.2	9.1	8.3	6.5	4.2	3.3
12 Countries Total			15.5	17.2	19.5	20.9	30.7	31.1	24.1	22.8	17.9
Portugal			0.3	0.3	0.5	0.5	0.4	0.3	0.3	0.4	0.4
Spain			1.9	2.1	2.2	1.9	2.0	1.7	1.3	1.9	1.7
Other			0.2	0.3	0.3	0.3	0.4	0.5	0.6	0.7	0.7
Total Western Europe	**10.8**	**8.7**	**17.9**	**19.9**	**22.5**	**23.6**	**33.6**	**33.5**	**26.3**	**25.7**	**20.6**
Eastern Europe	**1.9**	**2.2**	**2.5**	**2.7**	**2.9**	**3.3**	**4.1**	**4.5**	**3.5**	**3.4**	**2.0**
Former USSR	**1.5**	**2.4**	**3.4**	**3.5**	**4.4**	**5.4**	**7.6**	**8.6**	**9.6**	**9.4**	**3.4**
United States			0.3	0.2	0.1	1.8	8.9	19.1	27.3	22.0	21.9
Other Western Offshoots			0.1	0.1	0.1	0.1	1.3	2.5	3.4	3.2	3.1
Total Western Offshoots	**0.5**	**0.7**	**0.5**	**0.3**	**0.2**	**1.9**	**10.2**	**21.7**	**30.6**	**25.3**	**25.1**
Mexico			1.3	0.3	0.7	0.7	0.6	1.0	1.3	1.7	1.9
Other Latin America			1.7	0.8	1.0	1.3	2.0	3.5	6.7	7.0	6.8

Year	0	1000	1500	1600	1700	1820	1870	1913	1950	1973	1998
Total Latin America	2.2	3.9	2.9	1.1	1.7	2.0	2.5	4.5	7.9	8.7	8.7
Japan	1.2	2.7	3.1	2.9	4.1	3.0	2.3	2.6	3.0	7.7	7.7
China	26.2	22.7	25.0	29.2	22.3	32.9	17.2	8.9	4.5	4.6	11.5
India	32.9	28.9	24.5	22.6	24.4	16.0	12.2	7.6	4.2	3.1	5.0
Other Asia	16.1	16.0	12.7	11.2	10.9	7.3	6.6	5.4	6.8	8.7	13.0
Total Asia (excluding Japan)	75.1	67.6	62.1	62.9	57.6	56.2	36.0	21.9	15.5	16.4	29.5
Africa	6.8	11.8	7.4	6.7	6.6	4.5	3.6	2.7	3.6	3.3	3.1
World	100.0	100.0	100.0	100.0	100.0	100.0	100.0	100.0	100.0	100.0	100.0

Table 1: Shares of World GDP, 20 Countries and Regional Totals, 0–1998 ad.[84]

'The prosperity of Bharat, as per statistics, was primarily created by Hindus. At the beginning of the century, Bharat alone accounted for 32.9% of the world GDP. By around 1000 CE, this figure had decreased to 28.9%. Between 1000 and 1500 CE, it further declined to 24.9%, and from 1500 to 1700 CE, it stood at 24.4%.'[85]

APPENDIX 2

The British Exploitation and Plunder of Bharat's Economy during the Colonial Period

The analysis is primarily based on two sources: *The Case for India* by Will Durant and *The Economic History of India* by Romesh Chunder Dutt, which explore why Hindu civilization became impoverished.

> The British nation had spent millions of their own money in acquiring dominions in other parts of the world; but in India an empire had been acquired, wars had been waged, and the administration had been carried on, at the cost of the Indian people; the British nation had not contributed a shilling.[86]

***

> Those who have seen the unspeakable poverty and physiological weakness of the Hindus today will hardly believe that it was the wealth of eighteenth-century India which attracted the commercial pirates of England and France.
>
> > This wealth was created by the Hindus' vast and varied industries. Nearly every kind of manufacture or product known to the civilized world-nearly every kind of creation of Man's brain and hand, existing anywhere, and prized either for its utility or beauty-had long, long been produced in India. India was a far greater industrial and manufacturing nation than any in Europe or than any other in Asia. Her textile goods- the fine product of her looms, in cotton, wool, linen and silk-were famous over the civilized world; so her exquisite jewellery and her precious stones cut in every lovely form; so were her pottery, porcelains, ceramics

> of every kind, quality, colour and beautiful shape; so were her fine works in metal-iron, steel, silver and gold. She had great architecture-equal in beauty to any in the world. She had great businessman, great bankers and financiers. Not only was she the greatest ship-building nation, but she had great commerce and trade by land and sea which extended to all known civilized countries.
>
> [*India in Bondage: Her Right to Freedom*, J.T. Sunderland]

It was this wealth that the East India Company proposed to appropriate. Already in 1686 its Directors declared their intention to 'establish ... a large, well-grounded, sure English dominion in India for all time to come'. The company rented from the Hindu authorities' trading posts at Madras, Calcutta and Bombay, and fortified them, without permission of the authorities, with troops and cannon. Robert Clive defeated the Bengal forces at Plassey ... and thereupon declared his Company the owner of the richest province in India. He added further territory by forging and violating treaties, by playing one native prince against another, and by generous bribes given and received. Four million dollars were sent down the river to Calcutta in one shipment. He accepted 'presents' amounting to $1,170,000 from Hindu rulers dependent upon his favour and his guns; pocketed from them, in addition, an annual tribute of $140,000; took to opium, was investigated and exonerated by Parliament and killed himself. 'When I think', he said, 'of the marvelous riches of that country, and the comparatively small part which I took away, I am astonished at my own moderation'. Such were the morals of the men who proposed to bring civilization to India.

His successors in the management of the Company now began a century of unmitigated rape on the resources of India. They profiteered without hindrance: goods which they sold in England for $10,000,000 they bought for $2,000,000 in India. They engaged, corporately and individually, in inland trade, and by refusing to pay the tolls exacted of Hindu traders, acquired a lucrative monopoly. The company paid such fabulous dividends that its stock rose to $32,000 a share. Its agents deposed and set up Hindu rulers according to bribes refused or received; in ten years they took in, through such presents, $30,000,000. They forged documents as circumstances required, and hanged Hindus for forging documents. Clive had set up Mir Jafar as ruler of Bengal for $6,192,875; Clive's successors deposed him and set up Mir Kasim on payment of $1,001,345; three years later they restored Mir Jafar for $2,500,825; two years later they replaced him with Najim-ud-Daula for $1,151,780. They taxed the provinces under the Company so exorbitantly that two-thirds of the population fled; defaulters were confined in cages and exposed to the burning sun; fathers sold their children to meet rising rates. It was usual to demand 50% of the net produce of the land. 'Every effort, lawful and unlawful,' says a Bombay Administration report, written by Englishmen, 'was made to get the utmost out of the wretched peasantry, who were subjected to torture, in some instances cruel and revolting beyond all description, if they would not or could not yield what was demanded.' Warren Hastings exacted contributions as high as a quarter of a million dollars from native princes to the treasury of the Company; he accepted bribes to exact no more, exacted more and annexed the states that could not pay; he allowed his agents to use torture in extorting contributions; he helped the Nawab of Oudh to rob his mother and grandmother in order to pay the Company $5,000,000; he occupied the province of Oudh with his army, captured it and then sold it to a prince for $2,500,000; he 'lent' a British army to a Hindu rajah for $2,000,000 and made no complaint when it was used to slaughter and be slaughtered for savage purpose. 'Everybody and everything', says the *Oxford History of India* 'was on sale'. And [T.B.] Macaulay writes:

> During the five years which followed the departure of Clive from Bengal, the misgovernment of the English was carried to such a point as seemed incompatible with the existence of society.... The servants of the Company ... forced the natives to buy dear and to sell cheap.... Enormous fortunes were thus rapidly accumulated at Calcutta, while thirty millions of human beings were reduced to the extremity of wretchedness. They had been accustomed to live under tyranny, but never under tyranny like this.... Under their old masters they had at least one resource: when the evil became insupportable, the people rose and pulled down the government. But the English Government was not to be so shaken off. That government, oppressive as the most oppressive form of barbarian despotism, was strong with all the strength of civilization.

By 1858 the crimes of the Company so smelled to heaven that the British Government took over the captured and plundered territories as a colony of the Crown; a little island took over half a continent. England paid the Company handsomely, and added the purchase price to the public debt of India, to be redeemed, principal and interest (originally at 10 and half per cent), out of the taxes put upon the Hindu people. All the debts on the Company's books, together with the obligations of India, to be redeemed out of the taxes put upon the Hindu people. Exploitation was dressed now in all the forms of Law, i.e the rules laid down by the victors for the vanquished. Hypocrisy was added to brutality, while the robbery went on.[87]

***

The expropriation of state after state from the native rulers by the war or bribery, or the simple decree of Lord Dalhousie that whenever a Hindu prince died without leaving a direct heir, his territory should pass to the British; in Dalhousie's administration alone, eight states were absorbed in this peaceful way. Province after province was taken over by offering its ruler a choice between a pension and war. In the seventh decade of the nineteenth century, England added 4,000 square miles to her Indian territory; in the eighth decade, 15,000 square miles; in the ninth, 90,000; in the tenth, 133,000. John Morley estimated that during the nineteenth century alone England carried on one hundred and eleven wars in India, using for the most part Indian troops; millions of Hindus shed their blood that India might be slave. The cost of these wars for the conquest of India was met to the last penny out of Indian taxes; the English congratulated themselves on conquering India without spending a cent. Certainly it was a remarkable, if not a magnanimous, achievement, to steal in forty years a quarter of a million square miles, and make the victims pay every penny of the expense. When at last in 1857 the exhausted Hindus resisted, they were suppressed with 'medieval ferocity'; a favourite way of dealing with captured rebels was to blow them to bits from the mouths of cannon. 'We took', said the London Spectator, 'at least 100,000 Indian lives in the mutiny'. This is what the English call the Sepoy Mutiny, and what the Hindus call the War of Independence. There is much in a name.

Let Englishmen describe the result. A report to the House of Commons by one of its investigating committees in 1804 stated: 'It must give pain to an Englishman to think that since the accession of the Company the condition of the people of India has been worse than before'. In 1826 the English Bishop Heber wrote: 'The peasantry in the Company's provinces are, on the whole, worse off, poorer, and more dispirited, than the subjects of the Native Princes... I met with very few men who will not, in confidence, own their belief that the people are overtaxed, and that the country is in a gradual state of impoverishment.' James Mill, historian of India, wrote: 'Under their dependence upon the British Government ... the people of Oudh and Karnatic, two of the noblest provinces of India, were, by misgovernment, plunged into a state of wretchedness with which ... hardly any part of the earth has anything to compare.' 'I conscientiously believe', said Lt Col. Briggs in 1830, 'that under no Government whatever, Hindu or Mohammedan, professing to be actuated by law, was any system so suppressive of the prosperity of the people at large as that which has marked our administration'. F.J. Shore, British administrator in Bengal, testified as follows to the follows to the House of Commons in 1857:

> The fundamental principle of the English has been to make the whole Indian nation subservient, in every possible way, to the interests and benefits of themselves. They have been taxed to the utmost limit; every successive province, as it has fallen into our possession, has been made a field for higher exaction; and it has always been our boast how greatly we have raised the revenue above that which the native rulers were able to extort. The Indians have been excluded from every honor, dignity or office which the lowest Englishman could be prevailed upon to accept.

Such was the method of the British acquisition of India; this is the origin of the British claim to rule India today.[88]

***

Economic Destruction

The economic condition of India is the inevitable corollary of its political exploitation.

Even the casual traveler perceives the decay of agriculture (which absorbs 85% of the people), and the destitution of the peasant. He sees the Hindu riot in the rich fields, wading almost naked in the mud of a foreign tyrant's land; his loin-cloth is all the finery that he has. In 1915, the Statistical Department of Bengal, the most prosperous of India's provinces, calculated the average wage of the able-bodied agricultural laborer to be $3.60 per month. His hut is roofed with straw; or it is a square of dried mud adorned with a cot of entire house and furnishings of a family of six, including all newspapers or books, entertainments, tobacco, or drink. Almost half his earnings go to the Government; and if he cannot pay the tax, his holdings, which may have been in his family for centuries, is confiscated by the state.

If he is fortunate he escapes from the overtaxed land and takes refuge in the cities. Provided there are not too many other applicants, he may get work in Delhi, the capital of India, carrying away the white master's excrement; sanitary facilities are unnecessary when slaves are cheap. Or he can go to the factory, and become, if he is very lucky, one of the 1,409,000 'hands' of India. He will find difficulty in getting a place, for 33% of the factory workers are women, and 8% are children. In the mines 34% of the employees are women, of whom one-half work underground; 16% of the miners are children. In the cotton mills of Bombay the heat is exhausting, and the lungs are soon destroyed by the fluff-laden air; men work there until they reach a subsistence wage, and then their health breaks down. More than half the factories use their employees fifty-four hours a week. The average wage of the factory workers is sixty to seventy cents a day; though allowance must be made for the inferior skill and strength of the Hindu as compared with the European or American labourer long trained in the ways of machines. In Bombay, in 1922, despite the factory acts of that year, the average wage of the cotton workers was 33 cents. In that same year the profit of the better years, the owners of those mills was 125%. This was an 'off-year'. The workman's home is like his wage; usually it consists of one room, shared by the family with various animals; Zimand found one room with thirty tenants. Such is the industrial revolution that a British government has allowed to develop under its control, despite the example of enlightened legislation in America and England.

The people flock to the factories because the land cannot support them; and the land cannot support them because it is overtaxed, because it is overpopulated, and because the domestic industries with which the peasants formerly eked out in winter their gleanings from the summer fields, have been destroyed by British control of Indian tariffs and trade. For of old the handicrafts of India were known throughout the world; it was manufactured, i.e., hand-made-goods which European merchants brought from India to sell to the West. In 1680, says the British historian Orme, the manufacture of cotton was almost universal in India, and the busy spinning wheels enabled the women to round out the earnings of their men. But the English in India objected to this competition of domestic industry with their mills at home; they resolved that India should be reduced to a purely agricultural country, and be forced in consequences to become a vast market for British machine-made goods. The Directors of the East India Company gave orders that the production of raw silk should be discouraged; that silk-winders should be compelled to work in the Company's factories, and be prohibited, under severe penalties, from working outside. Parliament discussed ways and means of replacing Hindu by British industries. A tariff of 70-80% was placed upon Hindu textiles imported into free trade England, while India was compelled, by foreign control of her government, to admit English textiles almost duty free. Lest Indian industries should nevertheless continue somehow to exist, an excise tax was placed on the manufacture of cotton goods in India. As a British historian puts it:

> It is a melancholy instance of the wrong done to India by the country on which she has become dependent. Had India been independent, she would have retaliated, would have imposed prohibitive duties upon British goods, and would thus have preserved her own productive industry form annihilation. This act of self-defence was not permitted her; she was at the mercy of the stranger. British goods were forced upon her without paying any duty, and the foreign manufacturer employed the arm of political injustice to keep down and ultimately strangle a competitor with whom he could not have contended on equal terms.

And another Englishman wrote:

> We have done everything possible to impoverish still further the miserable beings subject to the cruel selfishness of English commerce. Under the pretense of free trade, England has compelled the Hindus to receive the products of the steam-looms of Lancashire, Yorkshire, Glasgow, etc., at merely nominal duties; while the hand wrought manufactures of Bengal and Behar, beautiful in fabric and durable in wear, have heavy and almost prohibitive duties imposed on their importation into England.

The result was that Manchester and Paisley flourished, and Indian industries declined; a country well on the way to prosperity was forcibly arrested in its development, and compelled to be only a rural hinterland for industrial England. The mineral wealth abounding in India's soil was not explored, for no competition with England was to be allowed. The millions of skilled artisans whom Indian handicrafts had maintained were added to the hundreds of millions who sought support from the land. 'India', says Kohn, 'was transformed into a purely agricultural country, and her people lived perpetually on the verge of starvation.' The vast population which might have been comfortably supported by a combination of tillage and industry became too great for the arid soil; and India was reduced to such penury that to-day nothing is left of her men, her women and her children but empty stomachs and fleshless bones.

It might have been supposed that the building of 30,000 miles of railways would have brought a measure of prosperity to India. But these railways were built not for India but for England; not for the benefit of the Hindu, but for the purposes of the British army and British trade. If this seems doubtful, observe their operation. Their greatest revenue comes, not, as in America, from the transport of goods (for the British trader controls the rates), but from the third-class passengers-----the Hindus; but these passengers are herded into almost barren coaches like animals bound for the slaughter, twenty or more in one compartment. The railroads are entirely in European hands, and the Government has refused to appoint even one Hindu to the Railway Board. The railways lose money year after year, and are helped by the Government out of the revenues of the people; these loans to date total over $100,000,000.

The Government guarantees of a minimum rate to built the roads ran no risk whatever. No play or encouragement is given to initiative, completion or private enterprise; the worst evils of a state monopoly are in force. All the losses are borne by the people; all the gains are gathered by the trader. So much for the railways.

Commerce on the sea is monopolized by the British, even more than transport on land. The Hindus are not permitted to organize a merchant marine of their own; all Indian goods must be carried in British bottoms, as an additional strain on the starving nation's purse; and the buildings of ships, which once gave employment to thousands of Hindus, is prohibited.

To this running of the land with taxation, this ruining of industry with tariffs and this ruining of commerce with foreign control, add the drainage of millions upon millions of dollars from India year after year, and the attempt to explain India's poverty as the result of her superstitions becomes a dastardly deception practiced upon a world too busy to be well informed. This drain having been denied, it is only necessary to state the facts, and to introduce them with a quotation from a document privately addressed by the British government in India to the Parliament of England.

> Great Britain, in addition to the tribute which she makes India pay her through the customs, derives benefits from the savings of the service of the three presidencies (the provinces Calcutta, Madras and Bombay) being spent in England instead of in India; and in addition to these savings, which probably amount to $500,000,000, she derives benefit from the fortunes realized by the European mercantile community, which are all remitted to England.

This is a general statement, let us fill it in. Consider first the drain on India through trade. Not merely is this carried in British ships; far worse than that, there is an astounding surplus of exports over imports. In the happy years of the Company there were such balances as $30,000,000 exports and $30,000,000 imports; latterly the indecency has been reduced, and the excess of goods taken from India over goods brought into India is now a moderate one-third. In 1927, e.g., imports were $651,600,000, exports were $892,800,000; the excess of exports $241,200,000. Where goes the money that pays for this excess? We are asked to believe that it takes the form of silver or gold imported and hoarded by the Hindus; but no man that has seen their poverty can believe so shameless a myth. Doubtless there is some hoarding, above all by the native princes, for India cannot be expected to put full faith in a banking system controlled by foreign masters. But it is the officials, the merchants and the manufacturers (most of whom are British) who take the great bulk of this profit, and return it to their countries in one form or another. As an East Indian merchant said in a Parliamentary report in 1853, when this process of bleeding was on a comparatively modest scale: 'Generally up to 1847, the imports were about $30,000,000 and the exports about $47,500,000. The difference is the tribute which the Company received from the country.'

Consider, second, the drain through fortunes, dividends and profits made in India and spent abroad. The British come as officials or soldiers or traders; they make their money and return to Great Britain. Let an Englishman, Edmund Burke, proportion to the growth of British positions, manufactures and commerce in India.

> They have no more social habits with the people than if they still resided in England; nor indeed any species of intercourse but that which is necessary to make a sudden fortune. Animated with all the avarice of age, and all the impetuosity of youth, they roll in one after another; wave after wave, and there is nothing before the eyes of the natives but an endless, hopeless prospect of new flights of birds of prey and passage, with appetites continually renewing for a food that is continually wasting. Every rupee of profit made by an Englishman is lost forever to India.

Consider, third, the drain through salaries and pensions derived from India and spent abroad. In 1927 Lord Winterton showed, in the House of Commons, that there were then some 7,500 retired officials in Great Britain drawing annually $17,500,000 in pensions from the Indian revenue; Ramsay MacDonald put the figure at $20,000,000 a year. When England, which is almost as over-populated as Bengal, sends its sons to India, she requires of them twenty-four years of service, reduced by four years of furloughs; she then retires them for life on a generous pension, paid by the Hindu people. Even during their service these officials send their families or their children to live for the most part in England; and they support them there with funds derived from India. Almost everything bought by the British in India, except the more perishable foods, is purchased from abroad. A great proportion of the funds appropriated for supplies by the Government of India is spent in England.

As early as 1783, Edmund Burke predicted that the annual drain of Indian resources to England without equivalent return would eventually destroy India. From Plassey to Waterloo, fifty-seven years the drain of India's wealth to England is computed by Brooks Adams at two-and-a-half to five billion dollars. He adds, what Macaulay suggested long ago, that it was this stolen wealth from India which supplied England with free capital for the development of mechanical inventions, and so made possible the Industrial Revolution. In 1901 Dutt estimated that one half of the net revenues of India flowed annually out of the country, never to return. In 1906 Mr. Hyndman reckoned the drain at $40,000,000 a year. A.J. Wilson valued it at one-tenth of the total annual production of India. Montgomery Martin, estimating the drain at $15,000,000 year in 1838, calculated that these annual sums, retained and gathering interest in India, would amount in half a century to $40,000,000,000. Though it may seem merely spectacular to juggle such figures, it is highly probable that the total wealth drained from India since 1757, if it had all been left and invested in India, would now amount, at a low rate of interest, to $400,000,000,000. Allow for money reinvested in India, and a sum remains easily equivalent to the difference between the poorest and the richest nations in the world. The same high rate of taxation which has bled India to perhaps a mortal weakness, might have done her no permanent injury if the wealth so taken had all been returned into the economy and circulation of the country; but bodily withdrawn from her as so much of it was, it has acted like a long-continued transfusion of vital blood. 'So great an economic drain out of the resources of the land', says Dutt, 'would impoverish the most prosperous countries on earth; it has reduced India to a land of famines more frequent, more widespread and more fatal, than any known before in the history of India, or of the world.'[89]

***

Over-Taxation on the Hindu by the British Administration

In England, the Land Tax was between one shilling and four shillings in the pound, i.e., between 5 and 20 per cent of the rental, during a hundred years before 1798, when it was made perpetual and redeemable by William Pitt. In Bengal the Land Tax was fixed at over 90 per cent of the rental and in Northern India at over 80 per cent of the rental between 1793 and 1882. It is true that British Government only followed the precedent of the previous Mahomedan rulers, who also claimed an enormous Land Tax. But the difference was this that what the Mahomedan rulers claimed they could never fully realize; what the British rulers claimed they realized with rigour. The Mahomedan ruler of Bengal, in the last year of his administration (1764), realized a land revenue of Sterling Pound 817,553; within thirty years the British rulers realized a land revenue of Sterling Pound 2,680,000 in the same province. In 1802, the Nawab of Oudh ceded Allahabad and some other rich districts in Northern India to the British Government. The land revenue which had been claimed by the Nawab in these ceded districts was Sterling Pound 1,352,347; the land revenue which was claimed by the British rulers within three years of the cession was Sterling Pound 1,682,306. In Madras, the Land Tax first imposed by the East India Company was one-half the gross produce of the Land! In Bombay, the land revenue of the territory conquered from the Mahrattas in 1817 was Sterling Pound 800,000 in the year of the conquest; it was raised to Sterling Pound 1,500,000 within a few years of British rule; and it has been continuously raised since. 'No Native Prince demands the rent which we do', wrote Bishop Heber in 1826, after travelling all through India, and visiting British and Native States. 'A Land Tax like that which now exists in India,' wrote Colonel Briggs in 1830, 'professing to absorb the whole of the landlord's rent, was never known under any Government in Europe or Asia'.

In Madras and Bombay, things are worse. There the Land Tax is paid generally by the cultivators of the soil, there being, in most parts of those provinces, no intervening landlords. The British Government declared its intention in 1864 of realizing as Land Tax about one-half of the economic rent. But what the British Government does take as Land Tax at the present day sometimes approximates to the whole of the economic rent, leaving the cultivators little beyond the wages of their labour and the profits of their agricultural stock. The Land Tax is revised once every thirty years; the cultivator does not know on what grounds it is enhanced: he has to submit to each renewed assessment, or to leave his ancestral fields and perish. This uncertainty of the Land

Tax paralyses agriculture, prevents saving and keeps the tiller of the soil in a state of poverty and indebtedness.

Taxation raised by a king, says the Indian poet, is like the moisture of the earth sucked up by the sun, to be returned to the earth as fertilizing rain; but the moisture raised from the Indian soil now descends as fertilizing rain largely on other lands, not on India.

They bought their merchandise out of the revenues of India, and sold it in Europe for their own profit. They vigorously exacted from India a high interest on their stock-in-trade. In one shape or another all that could be raised in India by an excessive taxation flowed to Europe, after paying for a starved administration.

The East India Company's trade was abolished in 1833, and the Company was abolished in 1858, but their policy remains. Their capital was paid off by loans which were made into an Indian Debt, on which interest is paid from Indian taxes. The empire was transferred from the Company to the Crown, but the people of India paid the purchase money. The Indian Debt which was Sterling Pound 51,000,000 in 1857, rose to Sterling Pound 97,000,000 in 1862. Within the forty years of peace which have succeeded, the Indian Debt has increased continuously, and now (1901) amounts to Sterling Pound 200,000,000. The 'Home Charges' remitted annually out of the Indian revenues to Great Britain haveincreased to sixteen millions. The pay of European officers in India, virtually monopolizing all the higher services, comes to ten millions. One-half of the net revenues of India, which are now forty-four millions sterling, flows annually out of India. Verily the moisture of India blesses and fertilizes other lands.[90]

***

Sir Wilfred Seawen Blunt sums it up from the point of view of a true Englishman:

> India's famines have been severe and more frequent, its agricultural poverty has deepened, its rural population has become more hopelessly in debt, their despair more desperate. The system of constantly enhancing the land values (i.e. raising the valuation and assessment) has not been altered. The salt tax ... still robs the very poor. What was bad twenty-five years ago is worse now. At any rate there is the same drain of India's

food to alien mouths. Endemic famines and endemic plagues are facts no official statistics can explain away. Though myself a good Conservative… I own to being shocked at the bondage in which the Indian people are held; … and I have come to the conclusion that if we go on developing the country at the present rate, the inhabitants, sooner or later, will have to resort to cannibalism, for there will be nothing left for them to eat.[91]

***

By a moderate calculation, the famines of 1877 and 1878, of 1889 and 1892, of 1897 and 1900, have carried off fifteen millions of people. The population of a fair-sized European country has been swept away from India within twenty-five years. A population equal to half of that of England has perished in India within a period which men and women, still in middle age, can remember.[92]

***

The very year of the Queen's accession revealed the vast difficulties of Indian administration. Famines had followed the wars of Lord Wellesley in Bombay and northern India in 1803 and 1804; a fresh famine has occurred in 1813; and Madras, with her wretched and oppressive land settlements, had been afflicted by famines in 1807, 1823, 1833. And now in the first year of the Queen's reign, Northern India, suffering equally from oppressive land settlements, was desolated by a famine more intense and more widespread than any of the preceding famines of the century. The new settlement of Robert Merttins Bird had not yet been completed; the people were resourceless and in chronic indebtedness, and a failure of rains in 1837 brought on the disastrous famine.

'I have never in my life,' wrote John Lawrence, afterwards Lord Lawrence, 'seen such utter desolation as that which is now spread over the parganas of Hodal and Palwal.' Deaths were numerous and were never reckoned. In Cawnpur a special establishment patrolled the streets and the river to remove the corpses. In Fatehpur and Agra, similar measures were adopted. Hundreds of thousands died in obscure villages, unknown and unheeded. The dead lay on the road-side unburied and unburnt, till they were devoured by wild animals.[93]

Pandit Madan Mohan Malaviya's Notes in Indian Industrial Commission, 1916[94]

'The skill of the Indians', says Professor Weber, 'in the production of delicate woven fabrics, in the mixing of colours, the working of metals and precious stones, the preparation of essences and in all manner of technical arts, has from early times enjoyed a world-wide celebrity.' There is evidence that Babylon traded with India in 3000 BC. Mummies in Egyptian tombs, dating from 2000 BC, have been found wrapped in Indian muslin of the finest quality. 'There was a very large consumption of Indian manufactures in Rome. This is confirmed by the elder Pliny, who complained that vast sums of money were annually absorbed by commerce with India.' "The muslins of Dacca were known to the Greeks under the name of Gangetika.... Thus it may be safely concluded that in India the arts of cotton spinning and cotton weaving were in a high state of proficiency two thousand years ago ... cotton weaving was only introduced into England in the seventeenth century". [*Imperial Gazetteer of India*, Volume III, page 195] p. 6.

As regards iron manufactures, Prof. Wilson says: 'Casting iron is an art that is practiced this manufacturing country (England) only within a few years. The Hindus have the art of smelting iron, of welding it, and of making steel, and have had these arts from time immemorial.' p. 6.[95]

Mr. Ranade wrote in 1892:[96]

> The iron industry not only supplied all local wants but it also enabled India to export its finished products to foreign countries. The quality of the material turned out had also a world-wide fame. The famous Iron Pillar near Delhi, which is at least fifteen hundred years old, indicates an amount of skill in the manufacture of wrought iron, which has been the marvel of all who have endeavoured to account for it. Mr. Ball (late of the Geological Survey of India) admits that it is not many years since the production of such a pillar would have been impossibility in the largest factories in the world, and, even now, there are comparatively very few factories where such a mass of metal could be turned out. Cannons were manufactured in Assam of the largest caliber, Indian *wootz* or steel furnished the materials out of which Damascus blades with a world-wide reputation were

made; and it paid Persian merchants in those old times to travel all the way to India to obtain these materials and export them to Asia. The Indian steel found once considerable demand for cutlery even in England. This manufacture of steel and wrought iron had reached a high perfection at least two thousand years ago" [Ranade's *Essays on Indian Economics*, pp. 169-160] pp. 6-7.

शत्रून् जय प्रजा रक्ष[1]

Śatrūn jaya prajā rakṣa

CHAPTER 2

Defeating Enemy, Defending Citizens

Ensuring a thriving economy is crucial for any state as it directly impacts the well-being of its people. Equally critical is the responsibility to protect the state from foreign invasion and to ensure the safety and security of its citizens. Therefore, the second Hindu Sutra is 'शत्रून् जय प्रजा रक्ष' 'Śatrūn jaya prajā rakṣa' (Defeating enemy, defending citizens).

Protecting the state's territory and sovereignty from external threats is a fundamental duty. This includes maintaining a robust defence force, forging strategic alliances and possessing defensive capabilities to deter or repel potential attacks. By securing national borders and ensuring stability, the state safeguards the physical safety of its citizens and maintains conditions essential for societal well-being and economic advancement.

Providing safety and security to its people encompasses protecting them from internal threats such as crime, terrorism and civil unrest. People rely on the state to uphold their rights, defend their freedoms and ensure their safety, thereby fostering trust and confidence in governmental institutions.

The principle 'Defeating Enemy, Defending Citizens' encapsulates these responsibilities, emphasizing the dual roles of the state: defeating external adversaries threatening sovereignty and ensuring the well-being of its populace. This underscores the necessity of a strong defence and proactive measures to promote prosperity and stability.

The Paramount Importance of Power and Strength

बलं धर्मोऽनुवर्तते ।।19।।

balaṃ dharmo'nuvartate ||19||[2]

Dharma follows strength.

Dharma follows strength because it is sustained and protected through physical power. A weak person, society or state may struggle to uphold dharma in the face of challenges, while strength in all its dimensions fortifies the path of righteousness and ensures its continuity in a world often fraught with adversity. Without strength, dharma remains a noble idea, but with strength, it becomes a living, guiding force for individuals, communities and nations.

A Strong Military Is of Paramount Importance

The importance and significance of having a strong military cannot be overstated.

सैन्याद्विना नैव राज्यं न धनं न पराक्रमः ।।4।।

Sainyādvinā naiva rājyaṃ na dhanaṃ na parākramaḥ ।।4।।[3]

Without the military, the state, wealth and valour are all unstable, putting their existence at risk.

The power of a nation is intrinsically tied to the robustness of its military. A powerful and well-equipped military serves as a shield against external threats and a deterrent to potential adversaries. Without such a military, the very fabric of the state can be undermined. The security and sovereignty of a nation hinge on its ability to defend itself and its interests.

Furthermore, the lack of a strong military would make the state vulnerable to attacks, invasions and subjugation by hostile forces, which could erode its stability and jeopardize its very existence. The safety, peace, prosperity, and wealth of a nation depend on a secure environment where commerce can flourish and people can thrive. A weak military leaves the nation open to disruption and turmoil, impacting its economic growth and overall well-being.

Therefore, a strong military is not just a means of defence but a cornerstone for the survival, stability and success of the state. It upholds the integrity of the nation, supports its wealth and fosters an environment where the courage and resolve of the populace can manifest. The importance of a robust military cannot be overstated in safeguarding the future of the state and its people.

A Strong Military Is the Foundation of a State

राज्ञः कोशबलं मूलम् ।।35।।

Rājñaḥ kośabalaṃ mūlam ।।35।।[4]

The state's source of power is rooted in its military and treasury.

The state's source of power is rooted in its military and treasury, emphasizing the crucial roles of military capability and financial resources in ensuring the stability and security of the state.

The military serves as the primary means of defending a state against external threats such as invasions, attacks or conflicts with other nations. A strong military can also act as a deterrent, dissuading potential adversaries from considering an attack due to the perceived costs and risks involved, while also providing humanitarian assistance and upholding the state's sovereignty during emergencies such as natural disasters or internal disturbances.

A robust military and a healthy treasury are intertwined elements of state power. The military relies on the treasury for funding and logistical support, while the treasury benefits from the security and stability provided by the military. Together, they form a solid foundation upon which a state can project power, maintain sovereignty and pursue its interests both domestically and internationally.

The Importance of Wealth in Maintaining an Army

कोशमूलं पुनर्बलम् ।।35।।

Kośamūlaṃ punarbalam ।।35।।[5]

कोशमूलं बलं स्मृतम् ।।14।।

Kośamūlaṃ balaṃ smṛtam ।।14।।[6]

अकोशस्य कुतो बलम् ।।4।।

Akośasya kuto balam ।।14।।[7]

The treasury is the source of the military's power; without it, the military cannot maintain its power.

The state's stability and power are closely linked to its financial resources and military capabilities. The treasury, representing economic stability and resources, is depicted as the source of power on which the military, signifying defence, relies. In summary, a well-financed treasury not only supports the military's activities but also enhances its efficiency, thereby ensuring the state's ability to project influence and safeguard its interests both domestically and internationally.

The Bravery of Heroes Is Paramount as It Protects Both Society and the State

न हि शौर्यात् परं किञ्चित् त्रिषु लोकेषु विद्यते।
शूरः सर्वं पालयति सर्वं शूरे प्रतिष्ठितम् ।।18।।

Na hi śauryāt paraṃ kiñcit triṣu lokeṣu vidyate.
Śūraḥ sarvaṃ pālayati sarvaṃ śūre pratiṣṭhitam ।।18।।[8]

There is nothing in the world superior to bravery. The hero protects and upholds everything, and the whole world depends on the hero.

Courage is considered one of the most important qualities a person can possess. Bravery enables individuals to confront challenges and dangers directly, and to protect themselves, society and their nation.

The hero assumes the responsibility of safeguarding and plays a crucial role in maintaining balance and stability within society, the state and the world, standing up for what is right and striving to preserve justice, peace and harmony.

शूरबाहुषु लोकोऽयं लम्बते पुत्रवत् सदा।
तस्मात् सर्वास्ववस्थासु शूरः सम्मानमर्हति ।।17।।

Śūrabāhuṣu loko'yaṃ lambate putravat sadā.
Tasmāt sarvāsvavasthāsu śūraḥ sammānamarhati ।।17।।[9]

This world depends on the strength and bravery of heroes; therefore, they deserve to be honoured in all circumstances.

The essential role that heroes play in shaping and safeguarding the world emphasizes the importance of heroes as individuals who possess exceptional strength and courage, enabling them to confront and overcome challenges that may otherwise seem insurmountable. These heroes often step up in the face of adversity, protecting others and striving to uphold justice, peace and integrity.

Their bravery allows them to take risks and make sacrifices for the greater good; sometimes even putting their own lives on the line. This strength of character and willingness to act selflessly in the service of others make them stand out as beacons of hope and inspiration for many.

Given the profound impact heroes can have on society and the lives of individuals, it is fitting to honour them in all circumstances. Honouring heroes also serves to inspire others to embody similar virtues of courage, strength and selflessness, potentially creating a cycle of heroism that benefits society as a whole.

एवमेवात्मनस्त्यागान्नान्यं धर्मं विदुर्जनाः ।।29।।

Evamevātmanastyāgānnānyaṃ dharmaṃ vidurjanāḥ ।।29।।[10]

There is no higher dharma than sacrificing one's life fighting in a war to defend society and the nation.

The ultimate act of selflessness and bravery in combat is the value placed on protecting the sovereignty of the nation and the collective interests of society over one's own life. Such a sacrifice is often seen as the pinnacle of honour and loyalty because it entails putting the needs and defence of the nation above personal survival.

Victory Is Paramount in War

जयं जानीत धर्मस्य मूलं सर्वसुखस्य च ।।40।।

Jayaṃ jānīta dharmasya mūlaṃ sarvasukhasya ca ।।40।।[11]

Victory in war is dharma, and it is the source of all forms of happiness.

Victory in war is seen as a noble pursuit. It is not just about physical conquest but also a reflection of one's skill, valour and adherence to duty.

Happiness is not only a matter of personal satisfaction; it also includes a sense of fulfillment in effectively carrying out one's purpose and responsibilities. Victory in war, particularly when fighting for a just and noble cause, such as defending the nation, contributes to the security and stability of society and the nation. This larger sense of communal well-being can also be a source of happiness for everyone, knowing that their actions have brought about peace and safety.

The Defeat of the Enemy Army Is of Utmost Importance

कच्चिदष्टाङ्गसंयुक्ता चतुर्विधबला चमूः।
बलमुख्यैः सुनीता ते द्विषतां प्रतिवर्धिनी ।।64।।

kaccidaṣṭāṅgasaṃyuktā caturvidhabalā camūḥ |
balamukhyaiḥ sunītā te dviṣatāṃ prativardhinī ||64||[12]

A military force composed of infantry, cavalry, artillery, armored vehicles, engineers, medical personnel, supply and logistics units, and intelligence operatives is well-equipped to attack, destroy and defeat the enemy when commanded by a skilled leader.

Strategies for defeating enemies are important

एकाग्रः स्यादविवृतो नित्यं विवरदर्शकः ||18||

Ekāgraḥ syādavivṛto nityaṃ vivaradarśakaḥ ||18||[13]

The state should always monitor the weaknesses of its enemies and remain vigilant of them.

The state should carefully monitor its adversaries to identify any vulnerabilities or weaknesses they may have. By doing so, it can maintain awareness of potential threats and risks, allowing it to prepare defensive measures and strategies accordingly. The state should always stay attentive and alert to any changes in its enemies' conditions, such as shifts in strategy, internal conflicts or resource depletion. This ongoing monitoring can help the state maintain a strategic advantage, mitigate potential risks and protect its own interests and security. In essence, the state needs to stay proactive in assessing and responding to the weaknesses of its adversaries.

वधमेव प्रशंसन्ति शत्रूणामपकारिणाम्।
सुविदीर्णं सुविक्रान्तं सुयुद्धं सुपलायितम् ||10||
आपद्यापदि काले च कुर्वीत न विचारयेत्।
नावज्ञेयो रिपुस्तात दुर्बलोऽपि कथंचन ||11||

Vadhameva praśaṃsanti śatrūṇāmapakāriṇām.
Suvidīrṇaṃ suvikrāntaṃ suyuddhaṃ supalāyitam ||10||
Āpadyāpadi kāle ca kurvīta na vicārayet.
Nāvajñeyo ripustāta durbalo'pi kathaṃcana ||11||[14]

The vanquishing of an enemy is always praised by strategists. If the enemy is stronger, they should be destroyed mercilessly when they are vulnerable. Therefore, an enemy who fights well should be driven away when they suffer a setback. In times of crisis, one must certainly vanquish the foe. During such times, do not consider their relations or other ties. Even if the enemy is weak, they should still not be ignored.

Strategists celebrate the defeat of an enemy because it signifies a successful outcome in a conflict, solidifying one's position and achieving strategic objectives. It suggests taking advantage of any weaknesses an enemy may have, particularly if they are stronger. When a powerful adversary becomes vulnerable, it is crucial to strike decisively and mercilessly to maximize the advantage. When an enemy experiences a setback or loss, it is important to take the opportunity to push them further back or out of the situation entirely. By capitalizing on their moment of weakness, one can secure a strategic position and diminish the enemy's ability to retaliate.

In moments of crisis, it is crucial to decisively defeat the enemy without being swayed by relationships or other considerations. The focus should be on survival and achieving victory in a challenging situation. Regardless of whether the enemy is perceived as weak, it is important not to ignore them. Even a weak enemy can pose a threat if left unchecked, as they may regroup, gain strength or exploit a moment of inattention. Therefore, it is essential not to underestimate any enemy and to take decisive action when opportunities arise to secure one's position and achieve strategic goals.

दया न तस्मिन् कर्तव्या शरणागत इत्युत।
निरुद्विग्नो हि भवति न हताज्जायते भयम् ।।14।।

Dayā na tasmin kartavyā śaraṇāgata ityuta.
Nirudvigno hi bhavati na hatājjāyate bhayam ।।14।।[15]

The enemy has sought refuge with me, which should not evoke pity. Given the need for a fearless state, the enemy must be completely eradicated. If the enemy is not entirely defeated, danger will persist.

A strong stance is taken against an enemy who has sought refuge or protection. Despite this, it warns against feeling pity or sympathy for the enemy. The reasoning is that, to ensure a fearless and secure state, the enemy must be completely eradicated. It argues that if the enemy is not fully defeated, the danger they pose will persist and threaten the safety and stability of the state. This perspective emphasizes the need for decisive action to maintain security and protect against future threats.

In the past, Hindu states have granted refuge to enemies out of pity and sympathy. Many times, we have had to fight wars to protect those very enemies whom we had taken in. Hindu civilization has paid a heavy price for this misguided compassion towards its adversaries.

The use of stratagems for defeating the enemy is crucial for victory

निकृत्या निकृतिप्रज्ञा हन्तव्या इति निश्चयः।
न हि नैकृतिकं हत्वा निकृत्या पापमुच्यते ।।22।।

Nikṛtyā nikṛtiprajñā hantavyā iti niścayaḥ.
Na hi naikṛtikaṃ hatvā nikṛtyā pāpamucyate ।।22।।[16]

There is a principle that deceitful enemies should be destroyed through deceitful means; surely it is no sin to use fraud to destroy someone who commits fraud against others.

व्रजन्ति ते मूढधियः पराभवं भवन्ति मायाविषु ये न मायिनः ।
प्रविश्य हि घ्नन्ति शठास्तथाविधा नसंवृताङ्गान्निशिता इवेषवः॥30॥

vrajanti te mūḍhadhiyaḥ parābhavaṃ bhavanti māyāviṣu ye na māyinaḥ.
praviśya hi ghnanti śaṭṭhāstathāvidhā
nasaṃvṛtāṅgānniśitā iveṣavaḥ॥30॥[17]

Those who are foolish or naive and fail to use deceit when dealing with deceitful enemies are inevitably defeated. Crooked enemies infiltrate and destroy such people. Those who are honest but lack practical insight are destroyed just as sharp arrows pierce and destroy unprotected bodies without armour.

There is a principle that when dealing with deceitful enemies, it is permissible to use deceitful means in return. Employing fraud to counteract and ultimately neutralize someone who engages in fraudulent behaviour against others is not inherently unethical. Essentially, using the same tactics against those who commit deceitful acts is considered a justified response.

Those who are naive or overly honest, and who fail to recognize the necessity of employing deceit in such circumstances, are destined to face defeat. Individuals who cannot adapt to the deceitful nature of their adversaries are vulnerable to being overpowered. Just as sharp arrows can pierce and destroy unprotected bodies, individuals who lack practical insight and fail to use strategic deception are similarly vulnerable to being overwhelmed and destroyed by deceitful opponents.

This principle extends beyond individual interactions and applies to broader contexts, such as society and the state. In societal and state matters, when confronted with deceitful forces or entities, using strategic deception can be a necessary measure to ensure protection and survival. Ignoring this principle in larger contexts can lead to the downfall of entire systems of society and state, just as naive individuals can fall prey to deceitful adversaries.

Hindu society has lost many wars and battles against Islamic invaders and European colonialists due to its naivety. The Hindu society and state failed to employ deceitful tactics against these deceitful enemies, resulting in a heavy price paid by Hindu civilization, which continues to this day. Even in this challenging situation, the leadership of Hindu civilization has not learned from past lessons. Despite enduring over a thousand years of Islamic rule and more than two hundred years of colonial rule, there has been no significant change in approach.

जहि शत्रून् महाबाहो परां निकृतिमास्थितः ।।61।।

Jahi śatrūn mahābāho parāṃ nikṛtimāsthitaḥ ।।61।।[18]

The enemy must be vanquished through a clever stratagem.

If an opponent engages in dishonest or fraudulent behaviour, it is acceptable to use similar tactics against them. In other words, when facing an enemy who uses deceit and manipulation, it may be necessary to employ clever and cunning strategies to defeat them. This approach views using fraud to counteract fraud as justifiable, as it aims to neutralize the harm caused by the dishonest enemy. Essentially, it advocates for fighting fire with fire to overcome a deceptive adversary. Nonetheless, it emphasizes the importance of being strategic and resourceful in combating those who operate dishonestly.

The Qualities of a Commander

कच्चिद् धृष्टश्च शूरश्च धृतिमान् मतिमाञ्छुचिः।
कुलीनश्चानुरक्तश्च दक्षः सेनापतिः कृतः ।।30।।

Kaccid dhṛṣṭaśca śūraśca dhṛtimān matimāñchuciḥ.
Kulīnaścānuraktaśca dakṣaḥ senāpatiḥ kṛtaḥ ।।30।।[19]

The ideal military commander should be content, heroic, intelligent and possess high self-esteem while also being a seasoned fighter.

कच्चिद्धृष्टश्च शूरश्च मतिमान् धृतिमाञ्छुचिः।
कुलीनश्चानुरक्तश्च दक्षः सेनापतिस्तथा ।।47।।

Kacciddhṛṣṭaśca śūraśca matimān dhṛtimāñchuciḥ.
Kulīnaścānuraktaśca dakṣaḥ senāpatistathā ।।47।।[20]

The commander-in-chief should be full of joy and enthusiasm, brave, intelligent, patient, pure, devoted and skilled in his work.

कच्चिद् बलस्य ते मुख्याः सर्वयुद्धविशारदाः।
धृष्टा दाता विक्रान्तास्त्वया सत्कृत्य मानिताः ।।48।।

Kaccid balasya te mukhyāḥ sarvayuddhaviśāradāḥ.
Dhṛṣṭā dātā vikrāntāstvayā satkṛtya mānitāḥ ।।48।।[21]

The commander-in-chief should be suitably respected and esteemed, while the principal military commanders should be well-trained, skilled in all aspects of warfare, fearless, honest and endowed with immense prowess.

बलवन्तश्च कच्चित् ते मुख्या युद्धविशारदाः।
दृष्टापदाना विक्रान्तास्त्वया सत्कृत्य मानिताः ।।31।।

Balavantaśca kaccit te mukhyā yuddhaviśāradāḥ.
Dṛṣṭāpadānā vikrāntāstvayā satkṛtya mānitāḥ ।।31।।[22]

The principal commanders and warriors should possess great strength, be skilled in warfare and demonstrate immense prowess. Their courage should be tested, and they should be treated with the honour they deserve.

धर्मशास्त्रार्थतत्त्वज्ञः सांधिविग्रहिको भवेत्।
मतिमान् धृतिमान् ह्रीमान् रहस्यविनिगूहिता ।।30।।
कुलीनः सत्त्वसम्पन्नः शुक्लोऽमात्यः प्रशस्यते।
एतैरेव गुणैर्युक्तस्तथा सेनापतिर्भवेत् ।।31।।

Dharmaśāstrārthatattvajñaḥ sāṃdhivigrahiko bhavet.
Matimān dhṛtimān hrīmān rahasyavinigūhitā ।।30।।
Kulīnaḥ sattvasampannaḥ śuklo'mātyaḥ praśasyate.
Etaireva guṇairyuktastathā senāpatirbhavet ।।31।।[23]

The supreme commander-in-chief is one who discerns the opportune moments for war, peace, diplomacy and attack, possesses domain knowledge of military sciences and warfare, demonstrates intelligence, patience and decorum, maintains secrecy, and possesses a brave and pure heart.

The Qualities and Training of Commanders and the Commander-in-Chief Are Crucial for Effective Leadership

नीतिशस्त्रास्त्राव्यूहादिनीतिविद्याविशारदाः।
अबाला मध्यवयसः शूरा दान्ता दृढाङ्गकाः ।।135।।

स्वधर्मनिरता नित्यं स्वामिभक्ता रिपुद्विषः।
शूद्रा वा क्षत्रिया वैश्या म्लेच्छाः संकरसम्भवाः।
सेनाधिपाः सैनिकाश्च कार्या राज्ञा जयार्थिना ।।136।।

Nītiśastrāstrāvyūhādinītividyāviśāradāḥ.
Abālā madhyavayasaḥ śūrā dāntā dṛḍhāṅgakāḥ ।।135।।
Svadharmaniratā nityaṃ svāmibhaktā ripudviṣaḥ.
Śūdrā vā kṣatriyā vaiśyā mlecchāḥ saṃkarasambhavāḥ.
Senādhipāḥ sainikāśca kāryā rājñā jayārthinā ।।136।।[24]

States that desire victory should appoint individuals skilled in realpolitik, weaponry and armament, military formation, strategic planning and other relevant areas as commanders. These individuals should be young, brave, talented, and possess strong resolve, remaining focused on their duties, disciplined and determined to confront the enemy. They may come from any community and should be appointed without discrimination. Select brave, valiant and capable individuals from every community to serve as commanders, including the commander-in-chief.

The Qualities of Soldiers

The attributes of soldiers are essential for assessing their effectiveness and performance

सिंहशार्दूलवाङ्नेत्राः सिंहशार्दूलगामिनः।
पारावतकुलिङ्गाक्षाः सर्वे शूराः प्रमाथिनः ।।7।।

Siṃhaśārdūlavāṅnetrāḥ siṃhaśārdūlagāminaḥ.
Pārāvatakuliṅgākṣāḥ sarve śūrāḥ pramāthinaḥ ।।7।।[25]

Those with strong voices, eyes and the movements of lions or tigers, as well as those with eyes like pigeons or sparrows, are all heroes capable of challenging enemy forces.

मृगस्वरा द्वीपिनेत्रा ऋषभाक्षास्तरस्विनः।
प्रमादिनश्च मन्दाश्च क्रोधनाः किङ्किणीस्वनाः ।।8।।

Mṛgasvarā dvīpinetrā ṛṣabhākṣāstarasvinaḥ.
Pramādinaśca mandāśca krodhanāḥ kiṅkiṇīsvanāḥ ।।8।।[26]

Those individuals whose voices resemble those of deer and whose eyes are similar to those of a leopard or a bull are brave, bold and reckless. Additionally, those with naturally strong voices can become exceedingly wrathful.

मेघस्वनाः क्रोधमुखाः केचित् करभसंनिभाः।
जिह्मनासाग्रजिह्वाश्च दूरगा दूरपातिनः ।।9।।

Meghasvanāḥ krodhamukhāḥ kecit karabhasaṃnibhāḥ.
Jihmanāsāgrajihvāśca dūragā dūrapātinaḥ ।।9।।[27]

Those individuals who roar like thunderclouds, with faces marked by anger, bodies resembling camels and sporting crooked noses and tongues, can run great distances and strike targets from afar.

सुसंहताः सुतनवो व्यूढोरस्काः सुसंस्थिताः।
प्रवादितेषु कुप्यन्ति हृष्यन्ति कलहेषु च ।।12।।

Susaṃhatāḥ sutanavo vyūḍhoraskāḥ susaṃsthitāḥ.
Pravāditeṣu kupyanti hṛṣyanti kalaheṣu ca ।।12।।[28]

Those with muscular bodies and broad chests, or those who stand firm in battle—these brave men become furious upon hearing the battle cry. They find pleasure solely in grappling during conflict.

गम्भीराक्षा निःसृताक्षा पिङ्गाक्षा भ्रुकुटीमुखाः।
नकुलाक्षास्तथा चैव सर्वे शूरास्तनुत्यजः ।।13।।

Gambhīrākṣā niḥsṛtākṣā piṅgākṣā bhrukuṭīmukhāḥ.
Nakulākṣāstathā caiva sarve śūrāstanutyajaḥ ।।13।।[29]

Those who have large, protruding eyes or long, drawn eyebrows are very brave and can sacrifice their lives on the battlefield.

Characteristics of Soldiers from Different Regions of Bharat and Various Countries

गान्धाराः सिन्धुसौवीरा नखरप्रासयोधिनः।
अभीरवः सुबलिनस्तद्बलं सर्वपारगम्।।3।।

Gāndhārāḥ sindhusauvīrā nakharaprāsayodhinaḥ.
Abhīravaḥ subalinastadbalaṃ sarvapāragam ।।3।।[30]

The warriors from Gandhara, Sindhu and
Sauvira fight with tiger claws and lances.
They possess strong characteristics, and their armies are
capable of defeating any force.

सर्वशस्त्रेषु कुशलाः सत्त्ववन्तो ह्युशीनराः।
प्राच्या मातङ्गयुद्धेषु कुशलाः कूटयोधिनः ।।4।।

Sarvaśastreṣu kuśalāḥ sattvavanto hyuśīnarāḥ.
Prācyā mātaṅgayuddheṣu kuśalāḥ kūṭayodhinaḥ ।।4।।[31]

The brave soldiers of Ushinaras are skilled in using all types
of weapons. Additionally, the eastern warriors excel in
fighting from atop elephants and possess great strength.
They are also experts in deceitful warfare and are
exceptionally powerful.

तथा यवनकाम्बोजा मथुरामभितश्च ये
एते नियुद्धकुशला दाक्षिणात्यासिपाणयः ।।5।।

Tathā yavanakāmbojā mathurāmabhitaśca ye
Ete niyuddhakuśalā dākṣiṇātyāsipāṇayaḥ ।।5।।[32]

The Yavana, Kamboja and warriors living around
Mathura are skilled in martial arts. Those who reside
in the south are proficient
in wielding swords.

The Military's Salary, Care and Welfare

The importance of taking care of soldiers and ensuring their welfare

कच्चिद् बलस्य भक्तं च वेतनं च यथोचितम्।
सम्प्राप्तकालं दातव्यं ददासि न विलम्बसे ।।32।।

Kaccid balasya bhaktaṃ ca vetanaṃ ca yathocitam.
Samprāptakālaṃ dātavyaṃ dadāsi na vilambase ।।32।।[33]

Soldiers should receive their full salaries and adequate provisions on time; the state should not delay in providing what is owed to them.

कच्चिद् बलस्य भक्तं च वेतनं च यथोचितम्।
सम्प्राप्तकाले दातव्यं ददासि न विकर्षसि ।।49।।

Kaccid balasya bhaktaṃ ca vetanaṃ ca yathocitam.
Samprāptakāle dātavyaṃ dadāsi na vikarṣasi ।।49।।[34]

Soldiers should receive proper food and pay on time. Their payments and dues should not be delayed.

The importance of providing timely salary and proper food to the soldiers

तत्रादानेन भिद्यन्ते गणाः संघातवृत्तयः।
भिन्ना विमनसः सर्वे गच्छन्त्यरिवशं भयात् ।।13।।

Tatrādānena bhidyante gaṇāḥ saṃghātavṛttayaḥ.
Bhinnā vimanasaḥ sarve gacchantyarivaśaṃ bhayāt ।।13।।[35]

Even in a republic where people are united and live together, soldiers may disperse if they do not receive food and salary on time. Once scattered, they can turn against each other and be captured by enemies.

Fortifications and Their Preparedness

कच्चिद्दुर्गाणि सर्वाणि धनधान्यायुधोदकैः।
यन्त्रैश्च परिपूर्णानि तथा शिल्पिधनुर्धरैः ॥36॥

kacciddurgāṇi sarvāṇi dhanadhānyāyudhodakaiḥ|
yantraiśca paripūrṇāni tathā śilpidhanurdharaiḥ ॥36॥[36]

Defence fortifications should be equipped with weapons, combat vehicles, engineers, fighting forces and adequate supplies.

The Importance of Armaments for the Military

The proper storage, care and maintenance of weapons are essential

एतानि रक्ष्यमाणानि धनंजय यथागमम्।
बलवन्ति सुखार्हाणि भविष्यन्ति न संशयः ॥21॥

Etāni rakṣyamāṇāni dhanaṃjaya yathāgamam.
Balavanti sukhārhāṇi bhaviṣyanti na saṃśayaḥ ॥21॥[37]

Strategic weapons should be kept secure according to proper guidelines as they are powerful and can ensure victory in war.

अरक्ष्यमाणान्येतानि त्रैलोक्यस्यापि पाण्डव।
भवन्ति स्म विनाशाय मैवं भूयः कृथाः क्वचित् ॥22॥

Arakṣyamāṇānyetāni trailokyasyāpi pāṇḍava.
Bhavanti sma vināśāya maivaṃ bhūyaḥ kṛthāḥ kvacit ॥22॥[38]

If strategic weapons are not properly stored and maintained, they can cause destruction.

The responsible storage, maintenance and handling of large and powerful weapons, particularly strategic ones, are essential to avoid accidental harm and ensure their effectiveness when needed. Proper storage in secure facilities prevents unauthorized access and accidental discharge. Regular maintenance and inspection keep weapons in working order and safe to operate. Poorly maintained weapons pose a danger and are less effective in use. Access should be restricted to authorized personnel to maintain safety and security. By managing weapons responsibly, military organizations can minimize the risk of unintended destruction and maximize their effectiveness in achieving victory during war.

It is important to note that discussions about the secure storage and maintenance of strategic weapons are at least 5,000 years old.

Safeguarding the secrecy of the military is paramount

भाण्डागारायुधागारान् योधागारांश्च सर्वशः।
अश्वागारान् गजागारान् बलाधिकरणानि च ।।54।।
परिखाश्चैव कौरव्य प्रतोलीखर्निष्कुटानि च।
न जात्वन्यः प्रपश्येत गुह्यमेतद् युधिष्ठिर ।।55।।

Bhāṇḍāgārāyudhāgārān yodhāgārāṃśca sarvaśaḥ.
Aśvāgārān gajāgārān balādhikaraṇāni ca ।।54।।
Parikhāścaiva kauravya pratolīkharniṣkuṭāni ca.
Na jātvanyaḥ prapaśyeta guhyametad yudhiṣṭhira ।।55।।[39]

Arsenals, soldiers' camps, food grain storehouses, soldiers' quarters, encampments and trenches should be positioned discreetly so that the enemy and others cannot see or monitor them.

In military strategy and operations, it is vital to maintain the secrecy and security of various critical assets and positions to preserve a strategic advantage and protect personnel and resources. This entails meticulously planning the location and placement of different military installations and infrastructure to evade detection by enemy forces or other parties. By safeguarding these key aspects of military infrastructure and operations from enemy monitoring and observation, a military force can enhance its operational security and strengthen its strategic positioning during conflicts.

The Importance of Psychological Strategies in Securing Triumph

सम्प्रयुक्ते निकृष्टे वा सत्यं वा यदि वानृतम्।
प्रगृह्य बाहुन् क्रोशेत भग्नाः परे इति ॥48॥
आगतं मे मित्रबलं प्रहरध्वमभीतवत्।

Samprayukte nikṛṣṭe vā satyaṃ vā yadi vānṛtam.
Pragṛhya bāhūn krośeta bhagnāḥ pare iti ॥48॥
Āgataṃ me mitrabalaṃ praharadhvamabhītavat.[40]

Regardless of whether our army is combative or not and whether the issue is false or true, raising our hands and shouting out creates a furore: 'The enemy is routed! The enemy is routed!' They are fleeing the battlefield. Our ally's army is approaching to support us, raising a fearsome battle cry and preparing to attack the enemy.

In the heat of battle, psychological strategies can be just as crucial as physical combat in determining the outcome of an engagement. Leveraging tactics that manipulate the enemy's perception can lead to significant advantages. By using strategic declarations and support, an army can influence the enemy's psychological state, thereby increasing the chance of victory. This type of psychological warfare is an essential component of an effective battle strategy.

APPENDIX 1

The Military Structure of Ancient Bharat

एको रथो गजश्चैको नराः पञ्च पदातयः।
त्रयश्च तुरगास्तज्ज्ञैः पत्तिरित्यभिधीयतेः।।19।।

Eko ratho gajaścaiko narāḥ pañca padātayaḥ.
Trayaśca turagāstajjñaiḥ pattirityabhidhīyateḥ ।।19।।[41]

One chariot and one elephant, along with five foot-soldiers and three horsemen, form a 'Patti'.

पत्तिं तु त्रिगुणामेतामाहुः सेनामुखं बुधाः।
त्रीणि सेनामुखान्येको गुल्म इत्यभिधीयते ।।20।।

Pattiṃ tu triguṇāmetāmāhuḥ senāmukhaṃ budhāḥ.
Trīṇi senāmukhānyeko gulma ityabhidhīyate ।।20।।[42]

Three Pattis form a 'Senamukha', and three Senamukhas form a 'Gulma'.

त्रयो गुल्मा गणो नाम वाहिनी तु गणास्त्रयः।
स्मृतास्तिस्रस्तु वाहिन्यः पृतनेति विचक्षणैः।।21।।

Trayo gulmā gaṇo nāma vāhinī tu gaṇāstrayaḥ.
Smṛtāstisrastu vāhinyaḥ pṛtaneti vicakṣaṇaiḥ।।21।।[43]

Three Gulmas form a 'Gana', three Ganas form a 'Vahini' and three Vahinis together form a 'Pritana'.

चमूस्तु पृतनास्तिस्रस्तिस्रञ्चम्वस्त्वनीकिनी।
अनीकिनीं दशगुणां प्राहुरक्षौहिणीं बुधाः।।22।।

Camūstu pṛtanāstisrastisrañcamvastvanīkinī.
Anīkinīṃ daśaguṇāṃ prāhurakṣauhiṇīṃ budhāḥ ।।22।।[44]

Three Pritanas form a 'Chamu', three Chamus form an 'Anikini' and ten Anikinis together are called an 'Akshauhini'.

अक्षौहिण्याः प्रसंख्याता रथानां द्विजसत्तमाः।
संख्या गणिततत्त्वज्ञैः सहस्राण्येक¯वशतिः ।।23।।
शतान्युपरि चैवाष्टौ तथा भूयश्च सप्ततिः।
गजानां च परीमाणमेतदेव विनिर्दिशेत् ।।24।।

Akṣauhiṇyāḥ prasaṃkhyātā rathānāṃ dvijasattamāḥ.
Saṃkhyā gaṇitatattvajñaiḥ sahasrāṇyeka¯vaśatiḥ ।।23।।
Śatānyupari caivāṣṭau tathā bhūyaśca saptatiḥ.
Gajānāṃ ca parīmāṇametadeva vinirdiśet ।।24।।[45]

There are twenty-one thousand, eight hundred and seventy (21,870) chariots in an Akshauhini and the number of elephants (21,870) is the same.

ज्ञेयं शतसहस्रं तु सहस्राणि नवैव तु।
नराणमपि पञ्चाशच्छतानि त्रीणि चानघाः।।25।।

Jñeyaṃ śatasahasraṃ tu sahasrāṇi navaiva tu.
Narāṇamapi pañcāśacchatāni trīṇi cānaghāḥ ।।25।।[46]

An Akshauhini consists of one hundred and nine thousand, three hundred and fifty foot soldiers (109,350).

पञ्चषष्टिसहस्राणि तथाश्वानां शतानि च।
दशोत्तराणि षट् प्राहुर्यथावदिह संख्यया।।26।।

Pañcaṣaṣṭisahasrāṇi tathāśvānāṃ śatāni ca.
Daśottarāṇi ṣaṭ prāhuryathāvadiha saṃkhyayā ।।26।।[47]

The number of horses in one Akshauhini is said to be sixty-five thousand, six hundred and ten (65,610).

एतामक्षौहिणीं प्राहुः संख्यातत्त्वविदो जनाः।
यां वः कथितवानस्मि विस्तरेण तपोधनाः ॥27॥

Etāmakṣauhiṇīṃ prāhuḥ saṃkhyātattvavido janāḥ.
Yāṃ vaḥ kathitavānasmi vistareṇa tapodhanāḥ ॥27॥[48]

Those who understand the principles of numbers refer to this as an Akshauhini.

Table 1: The number of soldiers in each troop or formation in Army

Name	Number	Multiply	Total	Name
Soldier	10	1	10	Pati
Patti	10	3	30	Senamukh
Senamukh	30	3	90	Gulma
Gulma	90	3	270	Gana
Gana	270	3	810	Vahini
Vahini	810	3	2,430	Pritna
Pritna	2,430	3	7,290	Chamu
Chamu	7,290	3	21,870	Anikini
Anikini	21,870	10	218,700	Akshauhini

In one Akshauhini, the number of foot soldiers, chariots, elephants, horses are two hundred and eighteen thousand, and seven hundred (218,700).

Name	The number of soldiers and warriors in one Akshauhini
Foot Soldier	109,350
Chariot warriors	21,870
Elephant warriors	21,870
Horses warriors	65,610
Total	218,700

In the Mahabharata, a total of eighteen (18) Akshauhinis went to war, with eleven (11) Akshauhinis on the Kaurava side and seven (7) Akshauhinis on the Pandava side. Each Akshauhini consists of two hundred and eighteen thousand, and seven hundred (218,700) soldiers. Therefore, the total number of soldiers who went to war in the Mahabharata was three million, nine hundred and thirty-six thousand, and six hundred (3,936,600).

Additionally, each Akshauhini includes twenty-one thousand, eight hundred and seventy (21,870) charioteers and an equal number of chariot warriors, totaling three hundred and ninety-three thousand six hundred and sixty (393,660) when multiplied by eighteen (18) Akshauhinis. An equal number of mahouts also participated in the war, adding another seven hundred and eighty-seven thousand, three hundred and twenty (787,320).

In total, the number of warriors who participated in the Mahabharata war was three million, nine hundred and thirty-six thousand, and six hundred (3,936,600) soldiers, plus seven hundred and eighty-seven thousand, three hundred and twenty (787,320) charioteers and mahouts, amounting to a total of four million seven hundred and twenty-three thousand, nine hundred and twenty (4,723,920) individuals.

Name	Number in one Akshauhini	Akshauhini	Total
Foot Soldier	109,350	18	1,968,300
Chariot Warriors	21,870	18	393,660
Charioteers	21,870	18	393,660
Cavalry (Elephant)	21,870	18	393,660
Mahout	21,870	18	393,660
Cavalry (Horses)	65,610	18	1,180,980
Total	262,440	18	4,723,920

The total number of chariots used in the Mahabharata war was three hundred and ninety-three thousand, six hundred and sixty (393,660), and an equal number of elephants was used in the Mahabharata war, also totaling three hundred and ninety-three thousand, six hundred and sixty (393,660). The total number of horses used in the Mahabharata war was one million, one hundred and eighty thousand, nine hundred and eighty (1,180,980).

Name	Number	Number of Akshauhinis	Total Number
Chariot	21,870	18	393,660
Elephant	21,870	18	393,660
Horses	65,610	18	1,180,980

The number and strength of the Kaurava army during the Mahabharata War were significant, comprising eleven Akshauhinis of soldiers.

Further details are provided below.

भगदत्तो महीपालः सेनामक्षौहिणीं ददौ।
तस्य चीनैः किरातैश्च काञ्चनैरिव संवृतम् ।।15।।
बभौ बलमनाधृष्यं कर्णिकारवनं यथा।

Bhagadatto mahīpālaḥ senāmakṣauhiṇīṃ dadau.
Tasya cīnaiḥ kirātaiśca kāñcanairiva saṃvṛtam ।।15।।
Babhau balamanādhṛṣyaṃ karṇikāravanaṃ yathā.[49]

Bhagadatta gave Duryodhana an army consisting of one Akshauhini, which was composed of Chinese and Kirata soldiers.

तथा भूरिश्रवाः शूरः शल्यश्च कुरुनन्दन ।।16।।
दुर्योधनमुपायातावक्षौहिण्या पृथक् पृथक्।

Tathā bhūriśravāḥ śūraḥ śalyaśca kurunandana
Duryodhanamupāyātāvakṣauhiṇyā pṛthak pṛthak ।।16।।[50]

Bhurishravas and Shalya each went to Duryodhana with an army numbering one Akshauhini.

कृतवर्मा च हार्दिक्यो भोजान्धककुरैः सह।।17।।
अक्षौहिण्यैव सेनाया दुर्योधनमुपागमत्।

Kṛtavarmā ca hārdikyo bhojāndhakukuraiḥ saha ।।17।।
Akṣauhiṇyaiva senāyā duryodhanamupāgamat.[51]

Kritavarma, the son of Hridika, along with the Bhojas, the Andhakas and the Kukuras went to Duryodhana with an Akshauhini of troops.

सुदक्षिणश्च काम्बोजो यवनैश्च शकैस्तथा ।।21।।
उपाजगाम कौरव्यमक्षौहिण्या विशाम्पते।

Sudakṣiṇaśca kāmbojo yavanaiśca śakaistathā ।।21।।
Upājagāma kauravyamakṣauhiṇyā viśāmpate.[52]

Sudakshina, the ruler of Kamboja, along with the Yavanas and Shakas, joined Duryodhana with an Akshauhini of troops.

तथा माहिष्मतीवासी नीलो नीलायुधैः सह।।23।।
महीपालो महावीर्यैर्दक्षिणापथवासिभिः।

Tathā māhiṣmatīvāsī nīlo nīlāyudhaiḥ saha ।।23।।
Mahīpālo mahāvīryairdakṣiṇāpathavāsibhiḥ.[53]

Nila, the king of Mahishmati, along with the powerful soldiers from the southern region, joins Duryodhana's side.

आवन्त्यौ च महीपालौ महाबलसुसंवृतौ ।।24।।
अक्षौहिण्या च कौरव्यं दुर्योधनमुपागतौ ।

Āvantyau ca mahīpālau mahābalasusaṃvṛtau ।।24।।
Akṣauhiṇyā ca kauravyaṃ duryodhanamupāgatau.[54]

Vinda and Anuvinda, two kings of Avanti, each come to Duryodhana with an Akshauhini of troops.

केकयाश्च नरव्याघ्राः सोदर्याः पञ्च पार्थिवाः ।।25।।
संहर्षयन्तः कौरव्यमक्षौहिण्या समाद्रवन्।

Kekayāśca naravyāghrāḥ sodaryāḥ pañca pārthivāḥ ||25||
Saṃharṣayantaḥ kauravyamakṣauhiṇyā samādravan.[55]

The five rulers of Kaikay, who were brothers, came with an Akshauhini of troops to join Duryodhana's side.

ततस्ततस्तु सर्वेषां भूमिपानां महात्मनाम् ||26||
तिस्रोऽन्याः समवर्तन्त वाहिन्यो भरतर्षभ।

Tatastatastu sarveṣāṃ bhūmipānāṃ mahātmanām ||26||
Tisro'nyāḥ samavartanta vāhinyo bharatarṣabha.[56]

Three Akshauhini forces led by different kings from various regions joined Duryodhana's side.

एवमेकादशावृत्ताः सेना दुर्योधनस्य ताः ||27||

Evamekādaśāvṛttāḥ senā duryodhanasya tāḥ ||27||[57]

Duryodhana, on the Kaurava side, was surrounded by a strong army of eleven Akshauhinis.

The Pandava army's size and strength during the Mahabharata War were considerable, consisting of seven Akshauhinis of soldiers.

More details are provided below.

Army of Pandava during the Mahabharat War

युयुधानस्ततो वीरः सात्वतानां महारथः ।
महता चतुरङ्गेण बलेनागाद् युधिष्ठिरम् ||1||

Yuyudhānastato vīraḥ sātvatānāṃ mahārathaḥ.
Mahatā caturaṅgeṇa balenāgād yudhiṣṭhiram ||1||[58]

अक्षौहिणीं तु सा सेना तदा यौधिष्ठिरं बलम् ||6||

Akṣauhiṇīṃ tu sā senā tadā yaudhiṣṭhiraṃ balam ।।6।।[59]

Yuyudhana (Satyaki) of the Satvata dynasty came with the Chaturangini army of an Akshauhini to the side of Yudhishthira.

तथैवाक्षौहिणीं गृह्य चेदीनामृषभे बली।
धृष्टकेतुरुपागच्छत् पाण्डवानमितौजसः।।7।।

Tathaivākṣauhiṇīṃ gṛhya cedīnāmṛṣabhe balī.
Dhṛṣṭaketurupāgacchat pāṇḍavānamitaujasaḥ ।।7।।[60]

Chediraj Dhrishtaketu came with an army, an Akshauhini in size, to support Pandava Yudhishthira.

मागधश्च जयत्सेनो जारासन्धिर्महाबलः।
अक्षौहिण्यैव सैन्यस्य धर्मराजमुपागमत्।।8।।

Māgadhaśca jayatseno jārāsandhirmahābalaḥ.
Akṣauhiṇyaiva sainyasya dharmarājamupāgamat ।।8।।[61]

The mighty Magadh warrior Jayatsen and Sahdev, the son of Jarasandh, each brought an Akshauhini army to support Yudhishthira.

तथैव पाण्डयो राजेन्द्र सागरानूपवासिभिः।
वृतो बहुविधैर्योधैर्युधिष्ठिरमुपागमत्।।9।।

Tathaiva pāṇḍayo rājendra sāgarānūpavāsibhiḥ.
Vṛto bahuvidhairyodhairyudhiṣṭhiramupāgamat।।9।।[62]

Pandya, the king of the coastal area, brought his army in support of Yudhishthira.

द्रुपदस्याप्यभूत् सेना नानादेशसमागतैः ।।11।।

Drupadasyāpyabhūt senā nānādeśasamāgataiḥ।।11।।[63]

तथैव राजा मत्स्यानां विराटो वाहिनीपतिः ॥12॥

Tathaiva rājā matsyānāṃ virāṭo vāhinīpatiḥ॥12॥[64]

Drupada's and Virata's armies were ready on the side of the Pandavas.

इतश्चेतश्च पाण्डूनां समाजग्मुर्महात्मनाम्।
अक्षौहिण्यस्तु सप्तैता विविधध्वजसंकुलाः ॥13॥

Itaścetaśca pāṇḍūnāṃ samājagamurmahātmanām.
Akṣauhiṇyastu saptaitā vividhadhvajasaṃkulāḥ॥13॥[65]

Seven Akshauhini armies were gathered from various regions and came to support the Pandavas.

The Types of Weapons Described by Shukracharya

नालिकं द्विविधं ज्ञेयं बृहत्क्षुद्रविभेदतः ।
तिर्यगूर्ध्वच्छिद्रमूलं नालं पञ्चवितस्तिकम् ॥184॥
मूलाग्रयोर्लक्ष्यभेदितिलबिन्दुयुतं सदा ।
यन्त्राघाताग्निकृद् ग्रावचूर्णधृक्कर्णमूलकम् ॥185॥
सुकाष्ठोपाङ्गबुध्नञ्च मध्याङ्गुलविलान्तरम् ।
स्वान्तेऽग्निचूर्णसन्धातृ शलाकासंयुतं दृढम् ।
लघुनालिकमप्येतत् प्रधार्य्यं पत्तिसादिभिः ॥186॥

Nālikaṃ dvividhaṃ jñeyaṃ bṛhatkṣudravibhedataḥ.
Tiryagūrdhvacchidramūlaṃ nālaṃ pañcavitastikam ॥184॥
Mūlāgrayorlakṣyabheditilabinduyutaṃ sadā.
Yantrāghātāgnikṛd grāvacūrṇadhṛkkarṇamūlakam ॥185॥
Sukāṣṭhopāṅgabudhnañca madhyāṅgulavilāntaram.
Svānte'gnicūrṇasandhātṛ śalākāsaṃyutaṃ dṛḍham.
Laghunālikamapyetat pradhāryyaṃ pattisādibhiḥ ॥186॥[66]

The weapon named Nalik has two types: cannon and gun. The Laghunalika, or gun, features a slanted aperture in its barrel starting from the base, measuring five hands in length. A honing device for target detection is attached to the base and front of the gun. Gunpowder is used to fill the base's ear during assault operations. The gripping portion of the base should be crafted from high-quality wood. The aperture in the barrel should measure one finger in width, with an attached funnel for filling it with gunpowder. This robust weapon, known as Laghunalika, is carried by both foot soldiers and horsemen.

यथा यथा तु त्वक्सारं यथा स्थूलबिलान्तरम्।
यथा दीर्घं बृहद्गोलं दूरभेदि तथा यथा।।187।।
मूलकीलभ्रमाल्लक्ष्यसमसन्धानभाजि यत्।
बृहन्नालिकसंज्ञं तत्काष्ठबुध्नविवर्जितम्।
प्रवाह्यं शकटाद्यैस्तु सुयुक्तं विजयप्रदम्।।188।।

Yathā yathā tu tvaksāraṃ yathā sthūlabilāntaram.
Yathā dīrghaṃ bṛhadgolaṃ dūrabhedi tathā yathā ।।187।।
Mūlakīlabhramāllakṣyasamasandhānabhāji yat.
Bṛhannālikasaṃjñaṃ tatkāṣṭhabudhnavivarjitam.
Pravāhyaṃ śakaṭādyaistu suyuktaṃ vijayapradam ।।188।।[67]

When the gun barrel's covering thickens and the aperture widens, the barrel lengthens and the shape of the projectile changes. The cannon homes in on distant targets. By adjusting the screw at the base, the cannon can launch the projectile accurately towards the target. Unlike traditional guns, the base is not made of wood; instead, it can be attached to a cart for mobility. Properly utilizing this equipment can lead to victory in battle.

APPENDIX 2

Hindu Resistance to Muslim Invaders

A summary of Dr Ram Gopal Misra's PhD thesis, published in the form of a book titled *Indian Resistance to Early Muslim Invaders up to 1206 AD*, along with a detailed review of his book by Shri Sita Ram Goel, published as 'Heroic Hindu Resistance to Muslim Invaders (636 AD to 1206 AD)'

In the case of Bharat, where political and cultural contact with Islam began soon after the death of Prophet Muhammad, the story is quite different. Here, Islam encountered a thriving Hindu Dharma and a civilization as old as humanity itself, which had flourished for more than a thousand years before the advent of Islam. This challenges the dominant narrative of Bharat's history, which often portrays Hindus as passive victims of foreign conquest and emphasizes the heroic resistance of Hindus to successive waves of Muslim invaders.

These books meticulously detail the story of Hindu resistance to Muslim invaders, starting with the Arabs' attempts to conquer Sindh, Kabul and Zabul. Despite their rapid conquests across the Middle East and North Africa, the Arabs encountered significant resistance from Hindus, leading to notable failures.

The Arabs had long faced disastrous outcomes in their attempts to conquer any of the frontier states of Bharat, including Sindh, Kabul and Zabul.

The first Arab attack on Sindh occurred during a naval raid on Debal. According to the *Tarikh-i-Hind-wa-Sind* or *Chach Nama*, the raid ended in failure. 'Samah, son of Dewaiji, ruled the area on behalf of Chach Rai when the Arab army arrived at Debal. He emerged from the fort and engaged them in battle.'[68] The leader of the Arab army, Mughairah, was defeated and killed.

News of Mughairah's defeat, especially at a time when Arab armies were securing victories elsewhere, must have surprised Caliph Umar, prompting him to dispatch an army by land against Makran (modern-day Baluchistan), which was then part of the Kingdom of Sindh. However, the governor of Iraq, Abu Musa, advised Caliph Umar against a land assault on Sindh. Upon learning of Mughairah's defeat and death, and that a particularly headstrong and aggressive Hindu king ruled Sindh, Abu Musa urged the Caliph to abandon any further plans for the region.

Al-Ḥajjāj, the governor of Iraq under the Umayyad Caliphate, after receiving permission from the Caliph, dispatched Ubaidullah to raid Debal. However, Ubaidullah was killed. Al-Ḥajjāj then instructed Budail, who was in Oman, to proceed to Debal. Budail travelled by sea, landing on the Sindh coast. After receiving reinforcements—a 'large army'—from Muhammad Hanm at Nerun, he advanced towards Debal. The residents of Debal sent a messenger to King Dahir in Alor (the capital of Sindh) to inform him of Budail's arrival at Nerun. Dahir quickly dispatched his son, Jaisiah, with 4,000 soldiers on horseback and camels, who hurried to Debal. Jaisiah engaged the invading forces, and a pitched battle ensued, lasting from early morning until dusk.

In the end, the Muslim army was routed, and Budail was killed. This crushing defeat must have left the Caliph crestfallen, for when Al-Ḥajjāj requested permission for another expedition, the Caliph responded that it must be postponed. 'Every time the army undertakes such an expedition, vast numbers of Muslims are killed. Therefore, think no more of such a plan.'[69]

Another important incident is recorded in these books. With the rapid decline of Abbasid Caliphate power in the ninth and tenth centuries CE, and their inability to support distant viceroys with men and money, Arab control over Sindh weakened further. Accounts of Arab travellers in Bharat during the tenth century CE, such as Ibn Khurdadbih (912 CE), Al-Masudi (915 CE), Istakhri (951 CE), and Ibn Haukal (976 CE), mention only two independent Arab principalities, with Multan and Mansurah as their capitals. Al-Masudi describes

Multan as 'one of the strongest frontier places of the Muslims' and provides fascinating details about the famous Hindu idol (deity) of the city. Both Al-Masudi and Al-Istakhri write: 'When the Hindus march against Multan, and the Muslims do not feel strong enough to oppose them, they threaten to destroy the idol (deities), causing the enemies to immediately withdraw.'[70]

Had it not been for this temple in Multan, the Arab principality of Multan might have fallen to the mighty army of the Hindu king of Gurjara-Pratiharas. After three centuries of relentless efforts, Arab dominion in Bharat was reduced to two small states—Multan and Mansurah. Even here, their existence was possible only after abandoning their iconoclastic zeal and using idols (deities) for political purposes. It is ironic to see them seeking protection behind the very idols (deities) they originally came to destroy.

These books emphasize the early Arab campaigns, particularly highlighting their initial defeats and the steadfast Hindu resistance, especially in the kingdom of Sindh, where the Arabs suffered repeated setbacks. The authors argue that the Arab victory in Sindh was more a result of opportunism and treachery than military strength.

In conclusion, the Arab invasion of Bharat ultimately failed, as they could neither conquer nor assimilate the land and its people. The narrative challenges the popular belief that the Arabs easily subdued these regions, demonstrating that Hindu warriors fiercely resisted for several centuries. Arab successes, when they occurred, are attributed primarily to treachery and deceit rather than military superiority.

In 977 CE, when Subuktigin ascended the throne of Ghazni, he launched frequent raids against the territories of Jayapala, the Hindu Shahi ruler of Udabhanda. In response, Jayapala gathered all his princes, feudatories, nobles, and allies, and with a large army, marched towards Muslim territory. This marked the first of two campaigns led by Jayapala against the Ghazni region. He was perhaps the last Hindu ruler to exhibit such a spirit of aggression. They also examine the failed attempts of Muslim armies to conquer Kabul and Zabul, highlighting the determined resistance and eventual expulsion of the invaders.

The arrival of Mahmud Ghaznavi, notorious for his brutality and the destruction of Hindu temples, did not lead to the complete conquest of Bharat. The narrative of Mahmud's so-called victories is largely exaggerated; despite his military prowess, he failed to establish a lasting empire in Bharat. His campaigns were repeatedly thwarted by fierce Hindu resistance, forcing him to rely on plunder and raids rather than achieving sustained dominance.

Historians who claim that Hindu kings were always divided and never united against invaders are proven wrong. Anandpala, the successor of Jayapala, offers a clear example. In 1008 CE, when Mahmud attacked Anandpala, he sent emissaries to seek support from other Hindu rulers across Bharat. Recognizing the expulsion of the Muslims as a sacred duty, these rulers united. The kings of Ujjain, Gwalior, Kalinjar, Kanauj, Delhi, and Ajmer formed a confederation and brought their armies together, marching towards Punjab with the largest force ever assembled. For forty days, the Hindu and Muslim armies remained encamped at Waihind (near Peshawar) without engaging in battle, while the strength of the Hindu forces continued to grow. In a remarkable act of devotion, Hindu women sold their jewels and melted their gold ornaments to fund the war effort.

These works further explore the struggles of the Hindu kingdoms of Kabul and Zabul against the Arabs, showcasing the resilience and determination of Hindus in defending their homeland. They recount the numerous defeats suffered by the invading Arab armies and emphasize the refusal of Hindu rulers to submit to Islamic imperialism. When Ghaznavi raids on the Shahiya kingdom of Peshawar are examined, it reveals the bravery and tenacity of Hindu rulers in their battles against Mahmud Ghaznavi, whose military resistance often forced him to retreat and undermined his efforts to establish permanent rule in Bharat.

The determined defiance of the Chandellas of Kalanjar and Khajuraho against Mahmud's incursions is also emphasized. Vidyadhara, the Chandella king, refused to surrender to Mahmud's demands, ultimately forcing him to retreat. The formation of a confederacy with other Hindu rulers to resist Mahmud exemplifies the enduring spirit of Hindu resistance against Islamic imperialism.

Challenging the conventional narrative of Mahmud Ghaznavi's conquests, the book presents a nuanced interpretation of his campaigns. It argues that while Mahmud sought to conquer Bharat and establish an empire, his ambitions were continually thwarted by the staunch resistance of Hindu kingdoms. The meticulous analysis of Mahmud's campaigns against the Shahiyas of Punjab, the Chandellas of Kalanjar and Khajuraho and the Jats of Sindh reveals that many of his victories resulted from treachery and deception rather than military superiority. Ultimately, Mahmud's dream of conquering Bharat remained unfulfilled.

The Battle of Somnath saw Mahmud Ghaznavi plundering the temple and destroying the revered Shiva linga. However, it also underscores the significant Hindu resistance that ultimately forced him to retreat, shaken by their tenacity.

Hindu kings formed a confederacy under Mahipala, the Tomar king of Delhi, to oppose Mahmud Ghaznavi. The confederacy included Raja Bhoja of the Paramara dynasty, Kama of the Kalachuri dynasty and the Chahamana ruler of Anahilla. According to Muhammad Qasim Firishta, the Raja of Delhi, in alliance with other Hindu rulers, recaptured Hansi, Thaneshwar and their dependencies from governors appointed by Madood, the successor of Masud, who was Mahmud's heir. The Hindu forces then marched towards the fort of Nagarkot, laying siege for four months. With the garrison running low on provisions and receiving no reinforcements from Lahore, they were forced to capitulate. The Hindus, as per tradition, erected new idols (deities).

Ahmad Nialtigin's expedition to Banaras coincided with the death of Salar Masud, a legendary Islamic general, at Bahraich, Uttar Pradesh. Abdur Rahman Chishti, in his work *Mirat-i-Masudi*, describes Salar Masud's death in great detail. Salar Masud is said to have been the son of Salar Sahu and Mahmud's sister, Mamal. The Rais of Hindu Kot and the surrounding regions amassed innumerable forces, encamping on the banks of the Saryu River at Bahraich. The Hindu army, as numerous as the mountains on all sides, decimated the army of Islam like grass during the battle. Many of the greatest nobles lost their lives. From morning until evening prayer, two-thirds of the Islamic army was slain, leaving only a third to mourn their losses.

Meanwhile, Rai Sahar Deo (Suheldev) and Har Deo, along with several other chiefs who had kept their troops in reserve, saw that the army of Islam had been reduced to nothing. On 14 June 1033 CE, they launched a united attack on the bodyguard of Prince Salar Masud.

An enemy arrow pierced the main artery in Salar Masud's arm, causing his sun-like countenance to pale like the new moon, and he died.

After Salar Masud's death, Muzaffar Khan also perished. The Hindus drove his descendants from Ajmer and re-established their idols (deities), leading to a resurgence of idol (deity) worship throughout the land of Bharat.

This analysis delves into the key factors behind the success of Muslim invaders, particularly the roles of treachery and deceit in weakening Hindu kingdoms.

It examines the rise of Muhammad Ghuri (Muizzuddin Muhammad bin Sam) and his ambitious campaign to conquer Bharat. While Ghuri successfully subdued much of northern Bharat, he faced formidable challenges from valiant Hindu rulers in Gujarat and Ajmer. The fierce battles between Ghuri and Prithviraj III of Ajmer highlight the bravery and resilience of the Hindu forces against the encroaching Islamic empire.

The texts analyze Muhammad Ghuri's tactics, emphasizing his cunning approach and strategic use of deception to overcome Hindu resistance. They argue that Ghuri's success stemmed less from military prowess and more from his understanding of Hindu culture, particularly its values of chivalry and magnanimity, which he exploited to his advantage.

This narrative counters the prevailing view that Hindus were passive victims of Islamic aggression, instead highlighting the courage and determination of Hindu rulers who fought valiantly against the invaders. While Hindu tolerance is presented as admirable, it often became a vulnerability exploited by Muslim forces.

The account of the Battle of Tarain describes how Ghuri, having previously been defeated by Prithviraj Chauhan, employed treachery to secure victory through his tried stratagems. He wrote to Prithviraj, 'I have marched into Bharat at the command of my brother, whose general I am. Both honour and duty bind me to exert myself to the utmost… but I shall be glad to obtain a truce until he is informed of the situation and I have received his answer.'[71]

The Hindus fell into the trap. Firishta records, 'The Sultan made preparations for battle… and when the Hindus had left their camp to obey the call of nature and to perform ablutions, he entered the plain with his ranks marshaled. Although the unbelievers were amazed and confounded, they stood their ground as best as they could.'[72] The Hindus were defeated and suffered great losses.

The text criticizes Prithviraj for his misplaced magnanimity and failure to capitalize on Ghuri's weaknesses, as well as the inability of the Hindus to exploit opportunities, which ultimately contributed to their defeat.

These works also detail Ghuri's campaigns, including his setbacks in Gujarat at the hands of the Chaulukya king Mularaja.

The epic history of the Hindu resistance against early Muslim invaders, who sought to impose an alien faith, culture and rule over Hindu soil, began with the first Arab expedition against Thana, near Mumbai (Bombay), in 636 CE. Despite relentless efforts over 570 years, the Muslims succeeded in establishing the Delhi Sultanate only in 1206 CE. The magnitude of Hindu resistance becomes evident when considering that effective Muslim rule over northern Bharat lasted only 500 years, up until the death of Aurangzeb in 1707 CE, and even less over the whole of Bharat, if at all.

The narrative challenges the notion of Hindu passivity, emphasizing the crucial role of resistance in shaping history. Ultimately, the work stands as a powerful testament to the resilience and courage of Hindus, offering valuable insights into the ongoing struggle for Hindu identity and survival against Islamic imperialism. It is an essential read for understanding the complexities of Bharat's past and present, providing a roadmap for navigating future challenges.

नास्ति विद्यासमं चक्षुः[1]

Nāsti Vidyāsamaṃ Cakṣuḥ

CHAPTER 3

Quality Education for All

In a thriving society, education emerges as the vital thread binding progress, sustainability and societal well-being. It stands as the cornerstone upon which societal resilience rests, equipping individuals with knowledge, critical thinking abilities and the skills to adapt, innovate and contribute meaningfully to their societies and state. Education also cultivates values of empathy and social responsibility essential for cohesive, inclusive societies, nurturing an informed populace who actively engage in national progress, thereby promoting stable governance and effective policymaking crucial for sustained national advancement.

The transformative power of education extends beyond individual lives to shape the trajectory of entire nations, stimulating economic growth by fostering a skilled populace capable of driving innovation and competitiveness. It plays a pivotal role in breaking cycles of poverty and inequality, offering pathways to social mobility and reducing disparities that undermine social cohesion. Without a well-educated populace, societies struggle to innovate and effectively address complex challenges.

Nations that prioritize education tend to experience sustained economic growth and development. A society's long-term sustainability heavily depends on the education level of its population.

Ancient Hindu ancestors possessed a keen awareness of education's importance and its role in societal enlightenment. They developed a profound approach and philosophy towards fostering knowledge, establishing a robust foundation and system of educational institutions spanning from primary to tertiary levels. This dedication ensured quality education was accessible to all members of society, enabling Hindu civilization to persevere through challenging periods, including continuous attacks and invasions. Education is always of paramount importance for societies and will remain so indefinitely into the future. Therefore, the third Hindu Sutra is 'नास्ति विद्यासमं चक्षुः', '*Nāsti vidyāsamaṃ cakṣuḥ*'—Quality Education for All.

The Significance of Education

नास्ति विद्यासमं चक्षुर्नास्ति विद्यासमं फलम् ।।35।।

Nāsti vidyāsamaṃ cakṣurnāsti vidyāsamaṃ phalam ।।35।।[2]

There is no greater vision in the world than education (vidya), and there is no greater reward than education.

Education (vidya) is the most transformative force in the world and the key to unlocking potential and shaping a brighter future. It is not only a profound vision but also the most valuable gift one can receive. Through education, individuals achieve personal growth, intellectual development and the skills needed to succeed. Education is the foundation of progress, prosperity and empowerment, making it the most precious reward one can attain.

विद्याभ्यासैर्वृद्धयोगैरात्मानं विनयं नयेत् ।
विद्या धर्मार्थफलिनी तद्विदो वृद्धसंज्ञिताः ।।

Vidyābhyāsairvṛddhayogairātmānaṃ vinayaṃ nayet.
Vidyā dharmārthaphalinī tadvido vṛddhasaṃjñitāḥ.[3]

Through the pursuit of learning (vidya) and by gaining wisdom from the company of the wise, one should become humble. Vidya grants both dharma and artha. The learned are truly knowledgeable and respected.

The pursuit of vidya, or knowledge, is a foundational concept deeply rooted in Hindu dharma and its traditions. It involves the acquisition of various forms of knowledge, including intellectual and practical wisdom. Being in the company of wise and knowledgeable individuals provides opportunities for growth and learning. By listening to and observing the wise, one can gain valuable insights and wisdom.

True learning and wisdom should lead to humility. When one gains knowledge, it often reveals how much there is yet to learn. This realization fosters a sense of humility, as the individual acknowledges their limitations and the vastness of what is unknown. A humble attitude is also more receptive to further learning and growth.

Those who have acquired a deep understanding and wisdom through the pursuit of learning and association with the wise are considered truly knowledgeable. This knowledge is respected by society because it encompasses not only academic or technical expertise but also moral and ethical insights. Such individuals are often seen as guides or mentors who can help others navigate life's challenges.

विद्यायाश्च फलं ज्ञानम् ।।92।।

Vidyāyāśca phalaṃ jñānam ।।92।।[4]

The pursuit of vidya (Knowledge) ultimately results in the attainment of wisdom.

Vidya represents not just the acquisition of information or facts but also the cultivation of understanding, insight and wisdom.

Wisdom involves gaining a deeper understanding of the interconnectedness of things and developing the ability to apply knowledge judiciously in various contexts. It emerges from reflection, introspection and the integration of knowledge with experience.

विद्यैका परमा तृप्तिः ।।52।।

Vidyaikā paramā tṛptiḥ. ।।52।।[5]

Vidya brings the greatest sense of fulfilment.

Acquiring knowledge, education or wisdom provides a deep sense of satisfaction and completeness. It brings a profound sense of fulfilment because these experiences encompass personal growth, empowerment, meaning, connection, contribution, self-esteem and impact—all of which are deeply rewarding in life.

विद्या नाम नरस्य रूपमधिकं प्रच्छन्नगुप्तं धनं
विद्या भोगकरी यश:सुखकरी विद्या गुरुणां गुरुः ।
विद्या बंधुजनो विदेशगमने विद्या परा देवता
विद्या राजसु पूज्यते न तु धनं विद्याविहीन: पशु: ।।20।।

vidyā nāma narasya rūpamadhikaṃ pracchannaguptaṃ dhanaṃ
vidyā bhogakarī yaśa:sukhakarī vidyā guruṇāṃ guruḥ|
vidyā baṃdhujano videśagamane vidyā parā devatā
vidyā rājasu pūjyate na tu dhanaṃ vidyāvihīna: paśu: ||20||[6]

Knowledge and wisdom are forms of virtue. They represent a hidden treasure that brings recognition, fame, happiness, and comfort. Serving as the ultimate teachers, knowledge and wisdom become your most trusted companions when travelling abroad. They are revered as the highest deities and command more respect than material wealth, even in the presence of kings and wealthy individuals. Without knowledge and wisdom, a person is comparable to an animal.

Knowledge and wisdom are not merely attributes; they are forms of virtue that illuminate the essence of an individual's character. This beauty is not visible to the eye but is a hidden treasure that can transform a person's life in profound ways. It brings recognition and fame, but, more importantly, it imparts a deep sense of happiness and comfort.

When travelling abroad, knowledge and wisdom become invaluable companions. They help navigate unfamiliar territories with confidence, enrich interactions with diverse cultures and enable informed decisions. They act as a compass that guides an individual through the vast landscape of global experiences, ensuring that each journey is not just a physical voyage but also a personal enrichment.

Knowledge and wisdom are revered as the highest deities in the realm of personal growth. Unlike material wealth, which can be fleeting and superficial, they provide a deep, enduring respect that surpasses any worldly possession. Even in the presence of kings and the wealthiest individuals, the respect commanded by knowledge and wisdom remains unmatched.

Without these qualities, a person's existence may lack depth and purpose. Knowledge and wisdom are what differentiate humans from animals, imbuing them with the capacity for critical thinking, moral judgement and the pursuit of a meaningful life. They are the cornerstones of human dignity and excellence, elevating one's existence from mere survival to a life of true fulfilment and impact.

विद्या वार्ता च सेवा च कारुत्वं नाट्यता तथा।
इत्येते जीवनार्थाय मर्त्यानां विहिताः प्रिये।।

Vidyā vārtā ca sevā ca kārutvaṃ nāṭyatā tathā.
Ityete jīvanārthāya martyānāṃ vihitāḥ priye.[7]

Vidya (knowledge), business, service, art and craft and acting are five essential pursuits for human subsistence.

Education, business, service, art and craft and acting are five areas that people often choose to engage in for their livelihoods and sustenance. These fields offer different ways to make a living and contribute to society. Education and research empower individuals and advance society. Business involves the production and exchange of goods and services, driving economic growth. Service includes roles that benefit others, such as healthcare. Art and craft provide creative outlets and the chance to produce unique works for personal satisfaction or public appreciation. Acting, encompassing performance arts, enables storytelling and entertainment, enriching cultural life. Together, these areas reflect the diverse ways humans find purpose, fulfilment and means of subsistence.

विद्यायोगस्तु सर्वेषां पूर्वमेव विधीयते।
कार्याकार्ये विजानन्ति विद्यया देवि नान्यथा।।

Vidyāyogastu sarveṣāṃ pūrvameva vidhīyate.
Kāryākārye vijānanti vidyayā devi nānyathā.[8]

Through vidya (knowledge), individuals can determine their responsibilities and discern right from wrong. Without knowledge, they are unable to make these distinctions.

Knowledge enhances an individual's ability to think critically and analyse situations from multiple perspectives, enabling them to make more nuanced judgements. Knowledge is essential for guiding individuals in making ethical decisions, fulfilling their responsibilities, and distinguishing right from wrong. It provides a foundation for informed, thoughtful decision-making and moral growth.

अविद्याविनयः पुरुषव्यसनहेतुः। अविनीतो हि व्यसनदोषान्न पश्यति।

Avidyāvinayaḥ puruṣavyasanahetuḥ. avinīto hi
vyasanadoṣānna paśyati.[9]

Uneducated people may become addicted because they do not understand the profound harm of addiction.

People who lack education might be more vulnerable to addiction for several reasons. First, without a solid understanding of the potential consequences, they may not fully grasp the long-term risks and dangers involved. This can lead them to underestimate the seriousness of addiction and its potential impact on their health. As a result, uneducated individuals might also delay seeking treatment or support when needed.

क्षणशः कणशश्चैव विद्यामर्थं च साधयेत्।
न त्याज्यौ तु क्षणकणौ नित्यं विद्याधनार्थिना।।172।।

Kṣaṇaśaḥ kaṇaśaścaiva vidyāmarthaṃ ca sādhayet.
Na tyājyau tu kṣaṇakaṇau nityaṃ vidyādhanārthinā ।।172।।[10]

One who desires knowledge and wealth should not dismiss the importance of time and the accumulation of wealth. Instead, they should utilize every minute in the pursuit of knowledge and collect wealth in the same manner.

The importance of managing time wisely in the pursuit of knowledge and wealth cannot be overstated. Those who aim to advance in these areas should understand the value of time and use it efficiently and effectively. This involves dedicating time to learning through reading, studying or other forms of education, as well as actively engaging in activities that lead to financial growth.

Making the most of every minute requires a consistent and disciplined approach, involving deliberate choices about how to allocate time and energy. This includes prioritizing tasks that contribute to knowledge and wealth while minimizing distractions. It also means being mindful of how time is spent while striving for these goals. By maximizing the use of every minute, individuals can achieve their goals more efficiently and find success in both areas.

Diligence and Effort Are Crucial for Acquiring Vidya

विद्या तपो वा विपुलं धनं वा
सर्वे ह्येतद् व्यवसायेन शक्यम् ।।45।।

Vidyā tapo vā vipulaṃ dhanaṃ vā
Sarve hyetad vyavasāyena śakyam ।।45।।[11]

Learning, penance and a great deal of wealth—all of these can be obtained through diligent work. Therefore, one should recognize the importance of hard work.

The significance of diligent effort suggests that it provides a pathway to acquiring various desirable outcomes such as learning, discipline and wealth. By engaging in hard work and putting forth effort, individuals can gain knowledge as well as material prosperity. Recognizing the importance of diligent work and effort implies that they serve as catalysts for personal development and success in both worldly and inner pursuits. This highlights their multifaceted role in shaping one's life and achieving aspirations.

पञ्चविंशत्यब्दपूरं तदर्धं वा तदर्धकम्।।175।।

Pañcaviṃśatyabdapūraṃ tadardhaṃ vā tadardhakam ।।175।।[12]

A student should study for at least twenty-five years, or at least half that time, which is twelve and a half years, with a minimum of six and a quarter years.

The value of education and learning in a person's life is demonstrated by suggesting specific durations for study and highlighting their importance. Twenty-five years is a substantial period of study, representing a significant commitment to education and personal development over many years. Twelve and a half years, or half of the twenty-five-year duration, signifies a considerable investment in education. This time frame underscores the value of long-term learning, even if it is not as extensive as the full twenty-five years. Six and a quarter years, a quarter of the twenty-five-year duration, represents the minimum threshold for the length of education one should pursue. This shorter span is essential for acquiring foundational knowledge and skills crucial for life.

विद्याधनं श्रेष्ठतरं तन्मूलमितरद्धनम्।
दानेन वर्धते नित्यं न भाराय न नीयते।।176।।

Vidyādhanaṃ śreṣṭhataraṃ tanmūlamitaraddhanam.
Dānena vardhate nityaṃ na bhārāya na nīyate ।।176।।[13]

Knowledge and wisdom are immensely superior to other forms of wealth, which can also be acquired through education. Vidya cannot be stolen; it increases more through donation and distribution.

Vidya (knowledge and wisdom) stands as a superior quality due to its role in fostering personal growth, deep understanding and effective navigation through life's challenges. It is highly esteemed for profoundly enriching life, surpassing the achievements that material wealth alone can provide. This quality empowers individuals to innovate, tackle problems and lead fulfilling lives that transcend mere financial success. Achieving success in acquiring both material wealth and other types of wealth can be facilitated by a strong educational foundation.

Knowledge and education are the only forms of wealth that increase when donated and distributed. Vidya (knowledge) cannot be stolen by anyone.

Various Types of Vidya (Knowledge)

शिक्षा व्याकरणं कल्पो निरुक्तं ज्यौतिषं तथा।
छन्दः षडङ्गानीमानि वेदानां कीर्तितानि हि ।।26।।
मीमांसातर्कसांख्यानि वेदान्तो योग एव च।
इतिहासाः पुराणानि स्मृतयो नास्तिकं मतम् ।।27।।
अर्थशास्त्रं कामशास्त्रं तथा शिल्पमलङ्कृतिः।
काव्यानि देशभाषाऽवसरोक्तिर्यावनं मतम् ।।28।।
देशादिधर्मा द्वात्रिंशदेता विद्याभिसंज्ञिताः ।।29।।

Śikṣā vyākaraṇaṃ kalpo niruktaṃ jyautiṣaṃ tathā.
Chandaḥ ṣaḍaṅgānīmāni vedānāṃ kīrtitāni hi ।।26।।
Mīmāṃsātarkasāṃkhyāni vedānto yoga eva ca.
Itihāsāḥ purāṇāni smṛtayo nāstikaṃ matam ।।27।।
Arthaśāstraṃ kāmaśāstraṃ tathā śilpamalaṅkṛtiḥ.
Kāvyāni deśabhāṣā'vasaroktiryāvanaṃ matam ।।28।।
Deśādidharmā dvātriṃśadetā vidyābhisaṃjñitāḥ ।।29।।[14]

Shiksha, vyakaran (grammar), kalpa, nirukta (etymology), jyotish (mathematics and astronomy) and chhand (meter) are the six Vedangas. Together with the four Vedas and four Upavedas (Ayurveda, Dhanurveda, Gandharvaveda and Arthaveda), they form the fourteen vidyas. Mimansa, tarka (nyaya and vaisheshika), sankhya, Vedanta, Yoga, history, Puranas, Smriti, atheist philosophy, economics, kamashastra, science and technology, alankara shastra, poetry, language, ukti, yavan philosophy and popular practices of a country, along with the fourteen vidyas, together comprise the thirty-two (32) vidyas.

आन्वीक्षिक्यां तर्कशास्त्रं वेदान्ताद्यं प्रतिष्ठितम्।
त्रय्यां धर्मो ह्यधर्मश्च कामोऽकामः प्रतिष्ठितः।।153।।
अर्थानर्थौ तु वार्तायां दण्डनीत्यां नयानयौ।

Ānvīkṣikyāṃ tarkaśāstraṃ vedāntādyaṃ pratiṣṭhitam.
Trayyāṃ dharmo hyadharmaśca kāmo'kāmaḥ pratiṣṭhitaḥ।।153।।
Aarthānarthau tu vārtāyāṃ daṇḍanītyāṃ nayānayau.[15]

Logic and philosophy fall under the category of Anvikshiki. Dharma, artha, kama and moksha pertain to the study of Trayee Vidya. Agriculture and wealth creation come under the field of Varta. Law and enforcement belong to the realm of Dandaniti.

अर्थकरी च विद्या।।82।।

Arthakarī ca vidyā।।82।।[16]

Vidya (knowledge) should generate wealth and prosperity; individuals should seek to acquire such knowledge.

Effectively applied knowledge (vidya) fosters wealth and prosperity. Education and learning contribute not only to personal growth but also to economic and social progress. Recognizing the value of acquiring practical knowledge (vidya) capable of generating prosperity is crucial. Individuals should seek to acquire such knowledge. Knowledge (vidya) should transcend theory, actively improving economic well-being and overall prosperity. It promotes acquiring and applying relevant knowledge productively in society.

यदि चेद् विद्यया चैव वृत्तिं काङ्क्षेदथात्मनः।।
राजविद्यां तु वा देवि लोकविद्यामथापि वा।

yadi ced vidyayā caiva vṛttiṃ kāṅkṣedathātmanaḥ.
rājavidyāṃ tu vā devi lokavidyāmathāpi vā.[17]

Receiving education and training in statecraft and public administration can lead to a decent income and standard of living for an individual.

The State's Responsibility in Education and Employment

गुणसाधनसंदक्षः स्वप्रजायाः पिता यथा ।।78।।

Guṇasādhanasaṃdakṣaḥ svaprajāyāḥ pitā yat hā ।।78।।[18]

Just as a father strives to nurture his children and make them worthy, the state should succeed in educating and training its people and making them competent and capable.

Comparing the state to a father nurturing his children emphasizes the state's responsibility to provide education and training to its people, ensuring they are competent and capable. The state must actively nurture its people through quality education and training opportunities.

The state should ensure all people have access to quality education, from early childhood through higher education. This encompasses formal schooling as well as vocational and technical training programmes that cater to a diverse range of interests and career paths.

The state should create and maintain an educational infrastructure that supports lifelong learning. This includes adequate funding for schools, resources for teachers and students and access to technology and materials for effective learning.

The state should continually evaluate and update educational curricula to keep pace with the changing needs of society and the workforce. This involves integrating practical skills, critical thinking, creativity, and problem-solving abilities into educational programmes.

Teachers play a crucial role in shaping students' minds. The state must invest in teacher training and professional development to ensure educators have the skills and resources necessary to deliver quality instruction.

There should be systems in place to help students make informed decisions about their future careers and educational paths. This includes exposure to a variety of career options and industries.

By nurturing its people and providing them with the knowledge and skills they need to succeed in their personal and professional lives, the state contributes to the overall prosperity and progress of society.

समाप्तविद्यं सन्दृष्ट्वा तत्कार्ये तं नियोजयेत् ।।369।।
विद्याकलोत्तमान्दृष्ट्वा वत्सरे पूजयेच्च तान्।
विद्याकलानां वृद्धिः स्यात्तथा कुर्यान्नृपः सदा ।।370।।

Samāptavidyaṃ sandṛṣṭvā tatkārye taṃ niyojayet ।।369।।
Vidyākalottamāndṛṣṭvā vatsare pūjayecca tān.
Vidyākalānāṃ vṛddhiḥ syāttathā kuryānnṛpaḥ sadā ।।370।।[19]

After students complete their studies, the state should thoroughly test them and assign them suitable employment based on their knowledge and skills. Those who excel in academics, science, technology and the arts should be annually awarded to recognize their achievements. The state should continuously strive to promote progress in education, science and technology.

It outlines a vision for a comprehensive approach to education and career development that involves testing, employment and recognition of student achievements.

After students finish their studies, the state would assume the responsibility of evaluating their skills and knowledge through comprehensive testing and other assessments to measure their abilities in various areas such as academics, the arts, technical skills and other relevant fields.

Once the assessments are completed, the state would match students with suitable job opportunities based on their skills and test results. This system aims to align students with job opportunities that correspond to their qualifications and abilities, ensuring they can effectively contribute to the productive workforce and the economy.

It proposes annual awards for those who excel in academics, science, technology and the arts. This recognition serves multiple purposes: motivating individuals to strive for excellence, publicly acknowledging their achievements and inspiring others to pursue similar paths of achievement. By celebrating students' successes, the state encourages continuous improvement and sets high standards for future generations. Such awards can also contribute to the prestige associated with these fields, potentially attracting more talent and fostering innovation.

Promoting the arts could include funding for artistic programmes, cultural events and educational opportunities in music, theatre, dance, visual arts and more. By nurturing these fields, the state not only enriches the cultural landscape but also supports the development of well-rounded individuals.

The state is called upon to actively promote progress in these critical areas. This could involve initiatives such as increasing funding for education, supporting research and development in science and technology, fostering innovation through incentives and infrastructure, and promoting a culture that values continuous learning and advancement in knowledge.

The vision suggests a system where the state plays a significant role in guiding students from education to employment, recognizing their achievements and fostering a thriving environment for education and the advancement of science, technology and the arts.

Respect and Reward for the Educated and Qualified

कच्चिद् विद्याविनीतांश्च नराञ्ज्ञानविशारदान्।
यथार्हं गुणतश्चैव दानेनाभ्युपपद्यसे ।।54।।

Kaccid vidyāvinītāṃśca narāñjñānaviśāradān.
Yathārhaṃ guṇataścaiva dānenābhyupapadyase ।।54।।[20]

Those who are knowledgeable, humble and proficient
in their fields should be honoured and rewarded in accordance
with their abilities and should receive the wealth and
other rewards they deserve.

Recognizing and rewarding people who are knowledgeable, humble and skilled in their fields are essential for fostering excellence and innovation. These individuals possess deep expertise in their areas of work and stay current with developments and best practices. Their knowledge allows them to contribute effectively and innovate within their domain.

These individuals exhibit humility through their modesty and openness to learn from others, despite their proficiency. They respect differing perspectives and foster a collaborative work environment, which enhances teamwork and inclusivity.

Proficiency means these individuals excel in their work, consistently delivering high-quality results and efficiently solving complex problems. Their expertise is the product of dedicated practice and a commitment to excellence.

Recognizing these people involves acknowledging their contributions through awards or promotions. Fair compensation in the form of competitive salaries, bonuses or other financial rewards should align with their abilities and achievements.

Honouring and rewarding knowledgeable, humble and skilled individuals helps organizations and societies retain talent, motivate others and nurture a culture of respect and appreciation. This leads to greater success and innovation, benefiting the entire country or state.

APPENDIX 1

The Beautiful Tree of Indigenous Education in Bharat

Summary of *The Beautiful Tree: Indigenous Indian Education in the Eighteenth Century*

Dharampal (1922–2006) was a Gandhian historian of the eighteenth-century Bharat. He spent several years in the British archives on Bharat in England to painstakingly study what the British administrators and other European observers had written about different aspects of the society that they first encountered here in Bharat, before they destroyed it. *The Beautiful Tree* is one of the several books that Dharampal wrote on the basis of his exploration into the British archives of that period.[21] The book describes the wide spread of indigenous education that prevailed in Bharat before the British. His other books tell us about indigenous sciences and technologies, about indigenous social and political organizations and about many other aspects of society of Bharat in the eighteenth and the early nineteenth century.

The Beautiful Tree presents mainly the data of a survey of indigenous education that Thomas Munro, then Governor of Madras Presidency, had ordered in 1822. He asked the collectors of the twenty-one districts that comprised the Presidency to compile data on the number of native schools and colleges in their districts and the number of scholars studying in them in a specific format, with separate columns for Brahmins, Vaisyas, Shoodras, Other Classes and Muslims.

Besides this survey of Madras Presidency, which was published for the first time in *The Beautiful Tree*, the book also contains extracts from the voluminous reports of William Adam on the state of education in some districts of Bengal and Bihar, which were published between 1835 and 1838. The book also includes brief extracts from the *History of Education in the Punjab since Annexation and in 1882* by G.W. Leitner.

The data covered in *The Beautiful Tree* thus encompasses a large part of Bharat. The twenty-one districts of Madras Presidency comprised the whole of the current states of Tamil Nadu and Andhra Pradesh and included large parts of Kerala, Karnataka, Telangana and Odisha. Adam's reports covered selected districts of the Bengal Presidency. Leitner's book covered all of Punjab including western Punjab, which now forms part of Pakistan. The data presented in the book thus covers nearly all parts of Bharat. On the basis of this data, we can confidently assert the following about education in Bharat before the British:

Extent of Education

The main lesson that one learns from this book is that, before the coming of the British here, school education was widely prevalent in all parts of Bharat. Adam and Leitner suggest that elementary education was in fact universal. Adam's reports famously state that there were one lakh indigenous schools in the Bengal Presidency. 'This amounted to a school for every 400 persons or for every thirty-one or thirty-two boys of the relevant age. A school for every thirty or so boys does indeed imply universal education.'[22]

Leitner suggests that there were 330,000 pupils in Punjab at the time of annexation in 1849, which number had declined to 190,000 in 1867 after nineteen years of British rule. He also says that in the Punjab:

> There was not a mosque, a temple, a dharmasala that had not a school attached to it.... There were also thousands of secular schools, frequented alike by Muhammadans, Hindus and Sikhs.... There were hundreds of learned men who gratuitously taught their co-religionists, and sometimes all-comers.... In respectable Muhammadan families, husbands taught their wives, and these their children; nor did the Sikh prove in that respect to be unworthy of their appellation of 'learners and disciples'.[23]
>
> Munro of the Madras Presidency, on the basis of the data received from the Collectors, estimated that at least one-fourth of the male population of the Presidency in the relevant age group was receiving school education. He also suggested that there were a large number

> of boys who received education at home. For Madras District, the Collector reported that the number taught at home was five times greater than that taught in schools. If we take the proportion of home schooling to be the same for other districts of the Presidency, it implies that all boys of the school going age were receiving education either at home or in a school.[24]
>
> The number of girls recorded in the schools was not significant, except in Malabar. But all of the observers suggest that girls were largely taught at home and as Leitner says wives were taught by their husbands and they in turn taught their children.[25]

It should be remembered that these surveys in different parts of the country were undertaken several decades after the establishment of British rule in a particular area, by that time the indigenous system had largely degraded because of official neglect and obstruction.

Inclusiveness of Education

We have been taught to believe that if there was any education in the pre-British Bharat, it must have been confined to the Brahmins and other 'upper castes'. 'The surveys compiled in *The Beautiful Tree* indicate that it was the Shoodras and the castes below them that formed the overwhelming majority of the scholars in the indigenous schools.'[22] This was true for both the survey of the Madras Presidency and the survey of Bengal and Bihar in Adam's report.

Dharampal has compiled caste-wise tables of scholars and teachers in the schools of different districts on the basis of Adam's reports. The tables list scholars from as many as ninety-five Hindu castes and teachers from thirty-five, besides Christians and Muslims.

The tables look similar to the current lists of Other Backward Classes and of Scheduled Castes. This inclusiveness disappeared during the British period and it is doubtful whether the list of castes of students and teachers in our educational system would be as inclusive even today.

Efficiency of School Education

Adam in his reports describes the system of school education in detail. 'A very similar system is described by the Collector of Bellary in his relatively detailed report to the Governor of Madras.'[23] Both insist that the emphasis in elementary education was to impart literacy and numeracy that equipped the child to engage in the actual business of his native society. This practical tendency was so pronounced that children from different sections of the society were taught different kinds of books and different kinds of accounts.

> Adam's Reports give separate numbers for schools teaching commercial accounts, or agricultural accounts or both. The Collector of Bellary wrote that while Ramayana, Mahabharata and Bhagavata were studied by all, yet the manufacturing class of people had, in addition to these, books peculiar to their own tenets; such as Nagalingayana Katha, Vishvakarma Purana, etc., and those who wore the Lingum have their own books, and so on.[28]

After describing the content of education in the Bengali schools in some detail, Adam says:

> In the matter of instruction there are some grounds for commendation for the course I have described has a direct practical tendency; and, if it were taught in all parts, *is well adapted to qualify the scholar for engaging in the actual business of native society.* My recollection of the village schools of Scotland do not enable me to pronounce that the instruction given in them has a more direct bearing upon the daily interests of life than which I find given, or professed to be given, in the humbler village schools of Bengal.[29]

It seems that students in the indigenous schools, in about five years of schooling, achieved what we today term foundational literacy and numeracy. They could efficiently conduct the ordinary business of their native society. While granting this, many of the European observers keep regretting that the students hardly knew any morals, by which they meant knowledge of Christianity, or that the students did not know any of Euclid, by which they meant Western sciences and technologies. Unfortunately, these concerns of the Europeans continue to distort our early schooling even today, with the result that many of our students fail to achieve foundational literacy and numeracy even after passing the middle stage.

Respect for Education

From the documents collected in *The Beautiful Tree*, it is obvious that education was held in very high esteem in all parts of Bharat. Leitner in his report from Punjab expresses this universal respect for education and learning rather colourfully, when he says:

> Respect for learning has always been the redeeming feature of "the East". To this the Punjab has formed no exception. Torn by invasion and civil war, it ever preserved and added to educational endowments. The most unscrupulous chief, the avaricious money-lender, and even the free-booter, vied with the small landowner in making peace with his conscience by founding schools and rewarding the learned.[30]

Wilting of the Beautiful Tree

This extensive system of education that the reports from Madras, Bengal, Bihar and Punjab compiled in *The Beautiful Tree* describe was disrupted soon after the onset of the British rule, notwithstanding the solicitous concern of occasional officers like Thomas Munro. The near universality of education that the system had provided was soon replaced by widespread illiteracy. And soon the educated Bhartiya came to believe that this state of illiteracy had always been the reality of Bharat.

Mahatma Gandhi, during his visit to England for the Round Table Conference in 1931, gave a public speech at the Chatham House. In this speech, along with several other issues, he spoke about education in Bharat and its destruction by the British, thus:

> I say without fear of my figures being challenged successfully, that today Bharat is more illiterate than it was fifty or hundred years ago, and so is Burma, because the British administrators, when they came to Bharat, instead of taking hold of things as they were, began to look at the root, and left the root like that, and the beautiful tree perished.[31]

Dharampal took the name of his book from this reference of Mahatma Gandhi to the beautiful tree of indigenous education. That beautiful tree has still not been revived to its full glory and refulgence.

APPENDIX 2

Ancient Universities of Bharat: Guardians of Knowledge and Culture

Summary of Prof. Shailendra Raj Mehta's Lecture at the University of Oxford

When Alexander of Macedonia arrived in Bharat at Takshashila in the fourth century BCE, he encountered a university (Takshashila University) unlike any in Greece. The origins of Takshashila are lost in antiquity, first mentioned in ancient epics and referenced during the time of the Buddha. The Buddha himself sent disciples to Takshashila and appointed them as head monks at its renowned university. It continued to thrive when the Chinese pilgrim Fa-Hien visited around 400 CE, although its full historical significance remains inadequately explored.

Takshashila University, along with Nalanda, Valabhi, Vikramashila, Jagaddala, Odantapuri and Sompura, was among the most important centres of learning in ancient Bharat. Established around the sixth or seventh century BCE, Takshashila was renowned for its extensive curriculum, which included the three Vedas, grammar, mathematics, astronomy, medicine, surgery, politics, military science and music theory. Eighteen arts, including archery and elephant lore, were also taught. Many notable historical figures, such as Panini (the great grammarian), Charaka (the physician), Jivaka (the surgeon), Vishnu Sharma (author of the Panchatantra), Chanakya (author of the *Arthashastra*) and Chandragupta Maurya (founder of the Maurya dynasty), were students of Takshashila. Admission required the completion of basic education by the age of sixteen, with a strong emphasis on practical knowledge.

Nalanda, which flourished from the fifth to the twelfth century CE, was another great institution, famed for its international reputation and rigorous admissions process. It housed over 10,000 students and 2,000 teachers, attracting scholars from across Asia, including Korea, Japan, China, Tibet, Indonesia, Persia, Turkey and Greece. Nalanda exemplified a university that drew students from around the world, received significant support, and endured for centuries, possibly over a millennium.

Its impressive library system, consisting of three major libraries—Ratnasagara, Ratnadadhi and Ratnaranjaka—was so vast that, when invaders burned them, they reportedly burned for several months. The university was a hub of intellectual activity, not just a place of learning but also a centre for generating new knowledge, where scholars produced numerous original works and commentaries.

Valabhi University in Gujarat, founded by a princess from the Maitraka dynasty, thrived between the sixth and eighth centuries. It was financially supported by the ruling family and had a well-organized administration with chancellors and vice-chancellors. The curriculum included law, administration and commerce, and the campus housed an extensive library.

Vikramashila, founded in the eighth century by King Dharmapala, was renowned for its specialization in Buddhist studies and its well-organized administration. Like Nalanda, it was destroyed by invaders in the twelfth century. Odantapuri, Jagaddala and Somapura existed between the eighth and twelfth centuries.

These universities were not just places of learning but also hubs of cultural and intellectual exchange. Their vast curricula emphasized both theoretical and practical knowledge, attracting students from across Asia. However, invasions led to their decline, destroying both the universities and their libraries, resulting in the loss of vast amounts of knowledge.

Despite their decline, the legacy of these institutions lives on, with their knowledge spreading across Bharat, Central Asia, Southeast Asia, East Asia, the Arab world and even Europe. Their influence endures, continuing to inspire generations to this day.

In conclusion, these ancient universities were unique for their size, subject diversity, international appeal, and longevity. They left behind a legacy of cultural exchange and practical knowledge that continues to inspire today.

अविश्रमोऽयं लोकतंत्राधिकारः[1]

Aviśramo'yaṃ lokataṃtrādhikāraḥ

CHAPTER 4

Responsible Democracy

Political processes and institutions significantly influence the functioning and development of society. They establish the framework of rules, institutions and practices that govern individuals, organizations and society, shaping the processes through which decisions are made and executed.

Effective political leadership is crucial during times of crisis, such as invasions and threats to national security, as well as in achieving civilizational and national aspirations.

Politics is essential in crafting laws and policies that shape societal behaviour. Legislative processes allow political entities to transform societal needs and values into legal frameworks that regulate various aspects of life. Political decisions set economic policies, including taxation, government spending and resource allocation, which influence wealth distribution, economic growth and social welfare. Furthermore, these decisions affect national defence and security.

The provision and quality of social services, such as education, healthcare and safety, are also determined by political priorities. Institutions like the judiciary, police and regulatory bodies play crucial roles in maintaining social order and upholding justice.

In democratic societies, politics enables public participation in governance through elections and debates, allowing individuals to influence decision-making and hold leaders accountable. It also provides a platform for diverse interest groups to represent their concerns and shape societal structures.

Internationally, politics extends through diplomacy, with national decisions having global repercussions. Politics is a decisive force in shaping societal discourse and governance, impacting every aspect of life, from individual values to economic policies, defence and global relations. Understanding the role of politics is essential for comprehending how societies function and evolve.

In Hindu dharma and society, ancestors have placed significant emphasis on the importance of politics. Its relevance has always been paramount: it was in the past, it is in the present, and it will remain so in the future. Politics is always contemporary. Therefore, the fourth Hindu Sutra is 'अविश्रमोऽयं लोकतंत्राधिकारः', '*Aviśramo'yaṃ lokataṃtrādhikāraḥ*'—Responsible Democracy.

The Significance of Politics

सर्वस्य जीवलोकस्य राजधर्मः परायणम् ।।3।।

Sarvasya jīvalokasya rājadharmaḥ parāyaṇam ।।3।।[2]

Politics is a refuge, a place of safety, for all living beings.

The purpose of politics is to offer protection and security to all members of society, including humans and other living beings. Effective political systems establish laws and frameworks that govern society, providing structure and order, which lead to a stable and safe environment for everyone.

Politics often involves defining and defending the rights and duties of various groups within society. When rights are protected and people fulfil their duties, they feel safer and more secure in their environment.

Politics also plays a crucial role in organizing essential services such as healthcare, education, housing and public safety, which contribute to the well-being of individuals and communities, thereby creating a sense of safety and security.

Politics can act as a safeguard by establishing policies and practices aimed at protecting the environment and biodiversity. Such policies can preserve habitats and natural resources, thereby creating a safe place for non-human life.

Political systems can offer support through social programmes and economic assistance to those in need, ensuring a safety net for vulnerable populations.

Politics enables individuals and groups to advocate for their interests and work towards change that can improve their situation and the environment in which they live.

The concept of politics as a refuge aligns with the ideal that political systems should strive to create environments where all living beings can thrive safely and securely.

त्रिवर्गो हि समासक्तो राजधर्मेषु कौरव।
मोक्षधर्मश्च विस्पष्टः सकलोऽत्र समाहिताः॥4॥

Trivargo hi samāsakto rājadharmeṣu kaurava.
Mokṣadharmaśca vispaṣṭaḥ sakalo'tra samāhitāḥ ॥4॥[3]

In rajdharma (politics), dharma, artha and kama are all included, and it is clear that moksha (liberation from worldly bondage) is also inherent in Rajdharma.

Politics (rajdharma) encompasses a range of duties and principles that guide society, including justice, fairness and the welfare of the people. It balances and integrates the three main aspects of human life—dharma, artha and kama—in its practice.

The principles of politics guide the state in managing resources efficiently, promoting economic growth and meeting the needs of the people, thereby fostering an environment in which individuals can thrive.

Moksha, or liberation, can be achieved by those involved in managing the state and its governance through the proper execution of their duties. By acting selflessly for the benefit of the people, they may attain a state of liberation.

क्षात्रो धर्मो ह्यादिदेवात् प्रवृत्तः पश्चादन्ये शेषभूताश्च धर्माः॥64॥

Kṣātro dharmo hyādidevāt pravṛttaḥ paścādanye
śeṣabhūtāśca dharmāḥ ॥64॥[4]

Rajdharma (also known as kshatradharma) was the first to emerge from the primordial god. All other dharmas are part of it and appeared subsequently.

The concept of rajdharma (politics) is viewed as the foundational principle that creates the framework for other forms of dharma to develop and function within society. The emergence of rajdharma from the primordial emphasizes the vital role of politics as the starting point for social order and the subsequent practise of different dharmas. This viewpoint implies that other dharmas appeared later, suggesting that rajdharma acts as their foundation. Rajdharma establishes the essential conditions and structure needed for the effective practice and observance of other forms of dharma.

लोकेवेदोत्तराश्चैव क्षात्रधर्मे समाहिताः ।।1।।

Lokevedottarāścaiva kṣātradharme samāhitāḥ ।।1।।[5]

All aspects of societal dharma are vested in rajdharma.

Rajdharma is one of the key aspects of societal dharma in Hindu thought. The idea that all aspects of societal dharma are vested in rajdharma suggests that the responsibilities and principles of rajdharma play a central role in maintaining and guiding the order and harmony of society as a whole.

शेषाः सृष्टा ह्यन्तवन्तो ह्यनन्ताः सप्रस्थानाः क्षात्रधर्मा विशिष्टाः।
अस्मिन् धर्मे सर्वधर्माः प्रविष्टा स्तस्माद् धर्मं श्रेष्ठमिमं वदन्ति ।।22।।

Śeṣāḥ sṛṣṭā hyantavanto hyanantāḥ saprasthānāḥ
kṣātradharmā viśiṣṭāḥ.
Asmin dharme sarvadharmāḥ praviṣṭā stasmād dharmaṃ
śreṣṭhamimaṃ vadanti ।।22।।[6]

Rajdharma is paramount, while other dharmas are numerous and transient. All dharma is inherent in rajdharma.

Rajdharma (Politics) is considered the highest form of dharma because it involves the stewardship and welfare of the entire state and its people. Politics and governance play a central role in maintaining societal harmony and are crucial for upholding the overall balance and harmony within society.

While there are various forms of dharma beyond politics, these other forms can change and evolve depending on circumstances and shifting contexts. However, the essence of all forms of dharma is ultimately embedded within the framework of rajdharma.

The successful execution of rajdharma inherently supports and fulfils other dharmas, serving as the foundation upon which other forms of dharma rest. This ensures a just and fair society that can nurture all other aspects of life.

नष्टा धर्माः शतधा शाश्वतास्ते क्षात्रेण धर्मेण पुनः प्रवृद्धाः।
युगे युगे ह्यादिधर्माः प्रवृत्ता लोकज्येष्ठं क्षात्रधर्मे वदन्ति।।26।।

Naṣṭā dharmāḥ śatadhā śāśvatāste kṣātreṇa
dharmeṇa punaḥ pravṛddhāḥ.
Yuge yuge hyādidharmāḥ pravṛttā lokajyeṣṭhaṃ
kṣātradharme vadanti ।।26।।[7]

All forms of dharma have been repeatedly disrupted, yet they have been revived through the exercise of rajdharma (politics). In every era, the original principles of rajdharma have prevailed; therefore, rajdharma is considered the superior form of dharma in the world.

When a state or society loses political power, its social fabric is disrupted, its economy is ruined, and the safety of its people is destroyed. Conversely, when a society or state regains its political power, its economy is revived, and the safety of the society is restored.

Political power is crucial for the proper functioning and well-being of a society. Losing it can result in societal disarray, economic downturn and insecurity; while regaining it can lead to economic revitalization and the restoration of safety and stability.

बाह्वायत्तं क्षत्रियैर्मानवानां लोकश्रेष्ठं धर्ममासेवमानैः।
सर्वे धर्माः सोपधर्मास्त्रयाणां राज्ञो धर्मादिति वेदाच्छृणोमि।।24।।

Bāhvāyattaṃ kṣatriyairmānavānāṃ lokaśreṣṭhaṃ dharmamāsevamānaiḥ.
Sarve dharmāḥ sopadharmāsrayāṇāṃ rājño dharmāditi vedācchṛṇomi।।24।।[8]

Rajdharma depends on strength. Rajdharma is the world's paramount dharma; those who observe it protect humanity. All other dharma is safeguarded by rajdharma.

The concept of rajdharma suggests that a state must possess power to govern effectively and protect its people. This power can be interpreted in various ways, such as military and economic power.

Rajdharma is regarded as the highest and most crucial form of dharma in the world because it encompasses the governance and protection of society. It provides the framework for a well-functioning and just society.

A state adhering to rajdharma upholds the principles of justice, fairness and order. This protects the well-being of humanity by ensuring that people live in a society governed by just laws and ethical leadership. Good governance helps maintain peace, security and stability, thereby safeguarding humanity.

Rajdharma serves as the guiding principle for the state, ensuring it uses its strength and authority to maintain order, justice and welfare in society. By doing so, the state provides the foundation upon which other forms of dharma can be effectively carried out.

सर्वे धर्मा राजधर्मप्रधानाः सर्वे वर्णाः पाल्यमाना भवन्ति।
सर्वस्त्यागो राजधर्मेषु राजंस्त्यागं धर्मं चाहुरग्रयं पुराणम्।।27।।

Sarve dharmā rājadharmapradhānāḥ sarve varṇāḥ pālyamānā bhavanti.
Sarvastyāgo rājadharmeṣu rājaṃstyāgaṃ dharmaṃ cāhuragrayaṃ purāṇam ।।27।।[9]

Rajdharma is foremost among all dharmas. This is because everyone is sustained by rajdharma. Every form of renunciation is encompassed within rajdharma, which is said to be the paramount and oldest dharma.

Rajdharma also includes aspects of renunciation. A person practising Rajdharma must prioritize the needs and welfare of the state and its people over personal desires or interests. This selflessness aligns with the concept of renunciation.

One may need to relinquish power, control or delegate authority for the greater good of the people. This act of renunciation involves prioritizing the interests of the state above personal ambition.

To govern fairly and justly, one must renounce any form of bias, attachment or partiality. This includes avoiding favouritism, nepotism and prejudices of any kind.

Rajdharma also involves setting an example for the people by renouncing excessive luxury, indulgence or material pursuits and leading a life of moderation and simplicity.

सर्वे त्यागा राजधर्मेषु दृष्टाः सर्वा दीक्षा राजधर्मेषु चोक्ताः।
सर्वा विद्या राजधर्मेषु युक्ताः सर्वे लोका राजधर्मे प्रविष्टाः।।29।।

Sarve tyāgā rājadharmeṣu dṛṣṭāḥ sarvā dīkṣā rājadharmeṣu coktāḥ.
Sarvā vidyā rājadharmeṣu yuktāḥ sarve lokā rājadharme praviṣṭāḥ।।29।।[10]

All forms of renunciation are encompassed within rajdharma. Rajdharma conveys all types of teachings. Rajdharma intertwines with all forms of knowledge. Rajdharma encompasses all spheres.

Rajdharma provides insights into the political management of the state, covering concepts such as diplomacy, military strategy and statecraft. It emphasizes the importance of justice and the rule of law, requiring a deep understanding of legal systems and the ability to interpret and apply them appropriately. Rajdharma also encompasses knowledge of economics and finance to ensure the prosperity of the state, including an understanding of taxation, trade, agriculture and resource management to support the well-being of the people and the state's growth. Rajdharma encompasses all spheres of knowledge, teaching with wisdom, fairness and compassion. By intertwining various forms of knowledge, rajdharma aims to create a just and harmonious society, ensuring the well-being and prosperity of all its people.

Practicing and promoting rajdharma in its true spirit requires detachment from personal interests and wholehearted dedication to the welfare and common good of the people. This selfless devotion is regarded as a renunciation.

यथा राजन् हस्तिपदे पदानि संलीयन्ते सर्वसत्त्वोद्भवानि।
एवं धर्मान् राजधर्मेषु सर्वान् सर्वावस्थान् सम्प्रलीनान् निबोध॥25॥

Yathā rājan hastipade padāni saṃlīyante sarvasattvodbhavāni.
Evaṃ dharmān rājadharmeṣu sarvān sarvāvasthān sampralīnān nibodha ॥25॥[11]

Just as the footprints of all other animals fit within the footprints of an elephant, so too do all other forms of dharma fall within the scope of rajdharma.

All other forms of dharma fall within the scope of rajdharma, as rajdharma encompasses and upholds them. This perspective highlights the holistic and comprehensive nature of rajdharma in governance, viewing it as a foundational and overarching framework that includes and supports all other forms of dharma within its domain, much like the large footprint of an elephant contains all smaller footprints within it.

धर्मे स्थिता सत्त्ववीर्या धर्मसेतुवटारका।
त्यागवाताध्वगा शीघ्रा नौस्तं संतारयिष्यति ॥37॥

Dharme sthitā sattvavīryā dharmasetuvaṭārakā.
Tyāgavātādhvagā śīghrā naustaṃ saṃtārayiṣyati ॥37॥[12]

Rajdharma (politics) is like a boat that floats on the ocean of dharma. The attributes of satva (truth and purity) serve as the oars to steer the boat. Dharmashastra acts as the ropes that tie it. With the help of renunciation in the form of wind, the boat moves swiftly, allowing it to cross the worldly sea.

Satva represents truth and purity, serving as the oars that steer the boat. In rajdharma, adhering to the principles of truthfulness and maintaining purity of intention and conduct are essential for effective governance. Leaders guided by truth and integrity can navigate the complexities of politics with a clear sense of direction and purpose, making just and equitable decisions that benefit the society they govern.

Dharmashastra acts as the ropes that tie the boat. This represents the established constitution, laws, codes and moral principles that form the foundation of good governance. Dharmashastra provides the framework and guidelines for political leadership, ensuring that decisions align with moral and ethical standards.

Renunciation, depicted as the wind that propels the boat, plays a vital role in moving the boat across the ocean of dharma. In the context of politics, renunciation refers to leaders' willingness to detach themselves from personal gain, ambition and ego for the greater good. This selflessness fuels the progress of the boat (rajdharma) and keeps it aligned with the principles of dharma.

Together, these elements create a well-rounded and harmonious approach to governance. By adhering to truth and purity, grounding governance in Dharmashastra, and being propelled by renunciation, political leaders can navigate the ocean of dharma effectively, ensuring the welfare of society and the preservation of ethical governance. This approach upholds the moral fabric of society and ensures that leaders act as stewards of the common good.

उत्थानं हि नरेन्द्राणां बृहस्पतिरभाषत।
राजधर्मस्य तन्मूलं श्लोकांश्चात्र निबोध मे ।।13।।

Utthānaṃ hi narendrāṇāṃ bṛhaspatirabhāṣata.
Rājadharmasya tanmūlaṃ ślokāṃścātra nibodha me ।।13।।[13]

Perseverance and the right efforts are very important for rajdharma. They form the foundation of rajdharma.

Perseverance and the right efforts form the foundation of rajdharma by ensuring that leaders remain steadfast and committed to the welfare of their people, making thoughtful, ethical and compassionate decisions. This combination builds a stable and just society where both the governed and those who govern work towards common goals and mutual prosperity.

प्रवृत्तस्य हि धर्मस्य बुद्ध्या यः स्मरते गतिम्।
स मे मान्यश्च पूज्यश्च तत्र क्षत्रं प्रतिष्ठितम्।।31।।

Pravṛttasya hi dharmasya buddhyā yaḥ smarate gatim.
Sa me mānyaśca pūjyaśca tatra kṣatraṃ pratiṣṭhitam।।31।।[14]

A person whose intellect is centred on the path of dharma deserves respect and honour, as rajdharma holds high regard for such individuals.

Living according to dharma underscores the responsibility of those in power to govern justly, with integrity, and for the welfare of people. Individuals dedicated to dharma are inclined to uphold rajdharma if they hold positions of authority. They serve as exemplary figures, inspiring others to lead equally righteous lives and contribute positively to the common good.

पालनात् सर्वभूतानां स्वराष्ट्रपरिपालनात्।
दीक्षा बहुविधा राजन् सत्याश्रमपदं भवेत्।।13।।

Pālanāt sarvabhūtānāṃ svarāṣṭraparipālanāt.
Dīkṣā bahuvidhā rājan satyāśramapadaṃ bhavet ।।13।।[15]

By sustaining all living beings and protecting the nation and state, a head of state acquires the merit of various yajnas (sacred rituals). In doing so, they attain the merits of a renunciate (sannyasin).

By fulfilling their duties of sustaining all living beings and protecting the nation and state, the head of state gains immense spiritual merit equivalent to that acquired through the performance of various yajnas. The head of state attains spiritual benefits similar to those of individuals who have renounced worldly attachments in pursuit of spiritual liberation. The idea is that governance, when carried out with a sense of duty, selflessness and commitment to the welfare of all beings, can be a profoundly spiritual endeavour. Through their service-oriented leadership, the head of state can accumulate spiritual merit equivalent to that of renunciation.

Democratic State in Bharat: Election of King or Head of State

समानो मन्त्रः समितिः समानी समानं व्रतं सहचित्तमेषाम्॥2॥

Samāno mantraḥ samitiḥ samānī samānaṃ vrataṃ saha cittameṣām॥2॥[16]

समानो मन्त्र: समिति: समानी समानं मन: सहचित्तमेषाम्॥3॥

Samāno mantraḥ samitiḥ samānī samānaṃ manaḥ sahacittameṣām॥3॥[17]

सभा च मा समितिश्चावतां प्रजापतेर्दुहितरौ संविदाने ।।1।।

Sabhā ca mā samitiścāvatāṃ prajāpaterduhitarau saṃvidāne।।1।।[18]

ये ग्रामा यदरण्यं याः सभा अधि भूम्याम्॥56॥

Ye grāmā yadaraṇyaṃ yāḥ sabhā adhi bhūmyām॥56॥[19]

The most significant institution of its kind was the samiti or sabha of our ancestors. The term samiti or sabha denotes a gathering or assembly. The samiti or sabha functioned as the national assembly representing the entire populace. One of its crucial roles was the election and re-election of the king (head of state). The assembly was intended to include the entire populace and their representatives.

The primary function of the samiti or sabha was to elect the king or head of state, a task it could perform repeatedly. Consequently, it held sovereign authority from a constitutional perspective. In the *Atharvaveda*, there is a hymn praying for unity and harmony, and in the *Rigveda*, there is a prayer for a unified samiti and a common state policy, goal and mindset. This underscores that matters of governance were deliberated in the samiti or sabha, which the king or head of state was required to attend (see the appendix of this chapter).

The Core Responsibility of the State Is Public Safety and Welfare

स्त्रियश्चापुरुषा मार्गं सर्वालङ्कारभूषिताः।
निर्भयाः प्रतिपद्यन्ते यदि रक्षति भूमिपः॥32॥

Striyaścāpuruṣā mārgaṃ sarvālaṅkārabhūṣitāḥ.
Nirbhayāḥ pratipadyante yadi rakṣati bhūmipaḥ॥32॥[20]

When the head of state ensures the maintenance of the rule of law, oversees the implementation of justice and protects their people, women adorned with beautiful ornaments can move around fearlessly even when alone.

The head of state bears the responsibility of maintaining the rule of law, encompassing the enforcement of laws, prevention of crime and facilitation of smooth societal functioning devoid of chaos or unrest. Additionally, they oversee the justice system, ensuring its fair and impartial operation. One fundamental duty of a head of state is to protect the people of their country. When women in society feel safe and confident, moving around fearlessly alone, adorned with beautiful ornaments, it signifies a sense of freedom and security. This indicates the highest form of safety and security in the state. The fearless movement of a woman alone, adorned with beautiful ornaments, is the gold standard of safety and security in the state.

न मे राष्ट्रे विधवा ब्रह्मबन्धु-
र्न ब्राह्मणः कितवो नोत चोरः ॥26॥

Na me rāṣṭre vidhavā brahmabandhu-
Rna brāhmaṇaḥ kitavo nota coraḥ ॥26॥[21]

In the state of Kekai Raj, there are no widows, scoundrels, thieves or bad scholars. Consequently, there is absolutely no fear.

न मे स्तेनो जनपदे न कदर्यो न मद्यपः।।8।।

Na me steno janapade na kadaryo na madyapaḥ ।।8।।[22]

In my state, there are neither thieves, nor misers, nor drunkards.

In the state of Kekay, no individuals are engaging in morally or legally questionable behaviour. There are no thieves who steal, misers who hoard wealth or drunkards. This creates a relatively peaceful and orderly environment characterized by honesty, generosity and sobriety among its inhabitants.

न तस्य विषये चाभूत् कृपणो नापि दुर्गतः।।15।।
व्याधितो वा कृशो वापि तस्मिन् नाभृन्नरः क्वचित्।।26।।

Na tasya viṣaye cābhūt kṛpaṇo nāpi durgataḥ ।।15।।
Vyādhito vā kṛśo vāpi tasmin nābhṛnnaraḥ kvacit ।।26।।[23]

In the state, neither a miser nor any person afflicted with misfortune, disease or physical feebleness could be seen.

धर्ममेव प्रपद्यन्ते न हिंसन्ति परस्परम्।
अनुगृह्णन्ति चान्योन्यं यदा रक्षति भूमिपः।।33।।

Dharmameva prapadyante na hiṃsanti parasparam.
Anugṛhṇanti cānyonyaṃ yadā rakṣati bhūmipaḥ ।।33।।[24]

When the state protects everyone, people follow dharma by refraining from injuring others and by being gracious towards each other.

The state is responsible for maintaining law, order and justice within society, ensuring the safety, security and well-being of all individuals. This entails treating people with respect, empathy and understanding, irrespective of differences in status or background, fostering harmonious relationships and promoting mutual goodwill within the community. In such a society, people are encouraged to cultivate virtues such as compassion, honesty and integrity, thereby contributing to the overall welfare and harmony of the community.

In prosperous states characterized by well-maintained law, order and justice enforcement, the needs of the people are carefully attended to.

Ayodhya Is Characterized by Prosperity and Stability

तस्मिन् पुरवरे हृष्टा धर्मात्मानो बहुश्रुताः।
नरास्तुष्टा धनैः स्वैः स्वैरलुब्धाः सत्यवादिनः।।6।।

Tasmin puravare hṛṣṭā dharmātmāno bahuśrutāḥ.
Narāstuṣṭā dhanaiḥ svaiḥ svairalubdhāḥ satyavādinaḥ ।।6।।[25]

All residents of Ayodhya were happy, virtuous, learned and well-qualified. They were truthful, free from greed and content with their wealth.

The society of Ayodhya is characterized by happiness, moral integrity, knowledge and contentment. It is a society where individuals live harmoniously with each other and with their environment. It represents a vision of a community that serves as a model for ethical living and societal organization.

नाल्पसंनिचयः कश्चिदासीत् तस्मिन् पुरोत्तमे।
कुटुम्बी यो ह्यसिद्धार्थोऽगवाश्वधनधान्यवान्।।7।।

Nālpasaṃnicayaḥ kaścidāsīt tasmin purottame.
Kuṭumbī yo hyasiddhārtho'gavāśvadhanadhānyavān ।।7।।[26]

Every householder had plenty of essential items in his store and had acquired objects of human pursuit and material wealth.

In Ayodhya, there exists a community where each homeowner diligently prepares for their needs by storing a collection of items such as food, clothing, household supplies and other necessities for daily living. These provisions not only cater to practical requirements but also contribute to their overall sense of material prosperity.

कामी वा न कदर्यो वा नृशंसः पुरुषः क्वचित्।
द्रष्टुं शक्यमयोध्यायां नाविद्वान् न च नास्तिकः ।।8।।

Kāmī vā na kadaryo vā nṛśaṃsaḥ puruṣaḥ kvacit.
Draṣṭuṃ śakyamayodhyāyāṃ nāvidvān na ca nāstikaḥ।।8।।[27]

In Ayodhya, there was no one who was a sensualist, miserly, cruel or ignorant.

Ayodhya is characterized by virtue, compassion, generosity and wisdom, with negative traits such as sensuality, greed, cruelty and ignorance notably absent among its inhabitants.

सर्वे नराश्च नार्यश्च धर्मशीलाः सुसंयताः।
मुदिताः शीलवृत्ताभ्यां महर्षय इवामलाः।।9।।

Sarve narāśca nāryaśca dharmaśīlāḥ susaṃyatāḥ.
Muditāḥ śīlavṛttābhyāṃ maharṣaya ivāmalāḥ ।।9।।[28]

The men and women of Ayodhya were disciplined,
always cheerful and morally pure,
exhibiting kindness and compassion.

In Ayodhya, society is guided by principles of discipline, cheerfulness, moral purity, kindness and compassion. These qualities contribute to a harmonious and thriving community where people coexist peacefully and contribute positively to each other's well-being.

नाकुण्डली नामुकुटी नास्रग्वी नाल्पभोगवान्।
नामृष्टो न नलिप्ताङ्गो नासुगन्धश्च विद्यते ।।10।।

Nākuṇḍalī nāmukuṭī nāsragvī nālpabhogavān.
Nāmṛṣṭo na naliptāṅgo nāsugandhaśca vidyate ।।10।।[29]

Everyone possesses gold earrings, a diadem and a flower garland. No individual lacks objects of enjoyment. Each person maintains a smart appearance after bathing and applies sandal paste to their body.

दीर्घायुषो नराः सर्वे धर्मं सत्यं च संश्रिताः।
सहिताः पुत्रपौत्रैश्च नित्यं स्त्रीभिः पुरोत्तमे।।18।।

Dīrghāyuṣo narāḥ sarve dharmaṃ satyaṃ ca saṃśritāḥ.
Sahitāḥ putrapautraiśca nityaṃ srībhiḥ purottame।।18।।[30]

All the residents lived long lives, adhering to truth and dharma and finding refuge in them. They lived happily with their wives, children and grandchildren.

शुचीनामेकबुद्धीनां सर्वेषां सम्प्रजानताम्।
नासीत्पुरे वा राष्ट्रे वा मृषावादी नरः क्वचित्।।14।।
प्रशान्तं सर्वमेवासीद् राष्ट्रं पुरवरं च तत्।।15।।

Śucīnāmekabuddhīnāṃ sarveṣāṃ samprajānatām.
Nāsītpure vā rāṣṭre vā mṛṣāvādī naraḥ kvacit ।।14।।
Praśāntaṃ sarvamevāsīd rāṣṭraṃ puravaraṃ ca tat ।।15।।[31]

Everyone's thinking was pure and united,
and they knew of no liars or rogues.
There was peace throughout the entire state.

न तस्करा वा व्याधिर्वा विविधोपद्रवाः क्वचित्।
अनावृष्टिमयं चात्र दुर्भिक्षो व्याधयः क्वचित्।।
सर्वं प्रसन्नमेवासीदत्यन्तसुखसंयुतम्।
एवं लोकोऽभवत् सर्वो रामे राज्यं प्रशासति ।।19।।

Na taskarā vā vyādhirvā vividhopadravāḥ kvacit.
Anāvṛṣṭimayaṃ cātra durbhikṣo vyādhayaḥ kvacit.
Sarvaṃ prasannamevāsīdatyantasukhasaṃyutam.
Evaṃ loko'bhavat sarvo rāme rājyaṃ praśāsati ।।19।।[32]

Rama Rajya (Rama's Reign)

प्रहष्टमुदितो लोकस्तुष्टः पुष्टः सुधार्मिकः।
निरामयो ह्यरोगश्च दुर्भिक्षभयवर्जितः।।10।।

Prahaṣṭamudito lokastuṣṭaḥ puṣṭaḥ sudhārmikaḥ.
Nirāmayo hyarogaśca durbhikṣabhayavarjitaḥ ।।10।।[33]

In the state of Sri Rama, there were no thieves, various ailments or different kinds of turmoil. There was no fear arising from lack of rain, drought or disease. People were happy, healthy and satisfied. The entire world appeared to be fully joyful and content. Consequently, all the people were exceedingly happy.

न पुत्रमरणं केचिद् द्रक्ष्यन्ति पुरुषाः क्वचित्।
नार्यश्चाविधवा।।91।।

Na putramaraṇaṃ kecid drakṣyanti puruṣāḥ kvacit.
Nāryaścāvidhavā।।91।[34]

Parents do not witness the death of their children anywhere, and wives do not become widows.

In Ayodhya, child mortality was nonexistent, reflecting the desire for spouses to live long and healthy lives together without experiencing the loss of their partner. This desire reflects the preservation of family bonds and the avoidance of the profound grief that accompanies losing loved ones. It expresses a wish for lives to unfold in the expected order, with parents passing before their children and spouses growing old together.

न चाग्निजं भयं किंचिन्नाप्सु मज्जन्ति जन्तवः।
न वातजं भयं किंचिन्नापि ज्वरकृतं तथा।।92।।

Na cāgnijaṃ bhayaṃ kiṃcinnāpsu majjanti jantavaḥ.
Na vātajaṃ bhayaṃ kiṃcinnāpi jvarakṛtaṃ tathā ।।92।।[35]

There is no fear from fire, nor does anyone drown in water. There is no fear from wind or any fear of fever.

न चापि क्षुद्भयं तत्र न तस्करभयं तथा।
नगराणि च राष्ट्राणि धनधान्ययुतानि च।।93।।
नित्यं प्रमुदिताः सर्वे यथा कृतयुगे तथा।

Na cāpi kṣudbhayaṃ tatra na taskarabhayaṃ tathā.
Nagarāṇi ca rāṣṭrāṇi dhanadhānyayutāni ca ।।93।।
Nityaṃ pramuditāḥ sarve yathā kṛtayuge tathā.[36]

Neither fear of starvation nor threat of thieves exists; the urban and rural areas are filled with riches and abundant food grains.

The state of Shri Rama represents a just, prosperous and harmonious society, where people live in peace, health and abundance, free from various forms of suffering and fear. It embodies an ideal state of existence, where the welfare and happiness of all are prioritized and realized.

न पर्यदेवन् विधवा न च व्यालकृतं भयम्।
न व्याधिजं भयं चासीद् रामे राज्यं प्रशसति ।।98।।

Na paryadevan vidhavā na ca vyālakṛtaṃ bhayam.
Na vyādhijaṃ bhayaṃ cāsīd rāme rājyaṃ praśasati ।।98।।[37]

The wailing of widows was unheard. There was no fear of snakes or other maleficent creatures, or of diseases.

निर्दस्युरभवल्लोको नानर्थं कश्चिदस्पृशत्।
न च स्म वृद्धा बालानां प्रेतकार्याणि कुर्वते ।।99।।

Nirdasyurabhavalloko nānarthaṃ kaścidaspṛśat.
Na ca sma vṛddhā bālānāṃ pretakāryāṇi kurvate ।।99।।[38]

The names of the thieves and marauders were not heard in the state. No one was engaged in harmful acts, and old people did not need to perform the last rites of youngsters.

The positive outcomes of a well-functioning law enforcement system, where criminal activities like theft and violence are nonexistent, lead to a sense of security, safety and peace among the population.

The absence of the need for last rites for infants and youngsters suggests that mortality within these age groups is nonexistent, likely due to a combination of factors such as good health resulting from nutritious food, socioeconomic development, improved healthcare and public health interventions.

सर्वं मुदितमेवासीत् सर्वो धर्मपरोऽभवत्।
राममेवानुपश्यन्तो नाभ्यहिंसन् परस्परम् ।।100।।

Sarvaṃ muditamevāsīt sarvo dharmaparo'bhavat.
Rāmamevānupaśyanto nābhyahiṃsan parasparam ।।100।।[39]

All people were always pleased. Everyone followed dharma, and they did not trouble one another.

नित्यमूला नित्यफलास्तरवस्तत्र पुष्पिताः ।।103।।

Nityamūlā nityaphalāstaravastatra puṣpitāḥ ।।103।।[40]

The trees were rooted and consistently bore flowers and fruits. Rain occurred regularly according to the season.

आसन् प्रजा धर्मपरा रामे शासति नानृताः।
सर्वे लक्षणसम्पन्नाः सर्वे धर्मपरायणाः ।।105।।

Āsan prajā dharmaparā rāme śāsati nānṛtāḥ.
Sarve lakṣaṇasampannāḥ sarve dharmaparāyaṇāḥ ।।105।।[41]

As long as Sri Rama ruled, people remained devoted to dharma, never lying, endowed with the highest qualities and all followed dharma.

The reign of Shri Rama, who ruled with compassion, justice and adherence to dharma, is often depicted as a time of peace, prosperity and moral integrity. It serves as a model for righteous governance and ethical living.

कच्चिच्चैत्यशतैर्जुष्टः सुनिविष्टजनाकुलः।
देवस्थानैः प्रपाभिश्च तटाकैश्चोपशोभितः ।।43।।
प्रहृष्टनरनारीकः समाजोत्सवशोभितः ।
सुकृष्टसीमापशुमान् हिंसाभिरभिवर्जितः ।।
अदेवमातृको रम्यः श्वापदैः परिवर्जितः ।
परित्यक्तो भयैः सर्वैः खनिभिश्चोपशोभितः ।।
विवर्जितो नरैः पापैर्मम पूर्वैः सुरक्षितः ।
कच्चिज्जनपदः स्फीतः सुखं वसति राघव ।।46।।

Kacciccaityaśatairjuṣṭaḥ sunivișṭajanākulaḥ.
Devasthānaiḥ prapābhiśca taṭākaiścopaśobhitaḥ ।।46।।
Prahṛṣṭanaranārīkaḥ samājotsavaśobhitaḥ.
Sukṛṣṭasīmāpaśumān hiṃsābhirabhivarjitaḥ.
Adevamātṛko ramyaḥ śvāpadaiḥ parivarjitaḥ.
Parityakto bhayaiḥ sarvaiḥ khanibhiścopaśobhitaḥ.
Vivarjito naraiḥ pāpairmama pūrvaiḥ surakṣitaḥ.
Kaccijjanapadaḥ sphītaḥ sukhaṃ vasati rāghava ।।46।।[42]

The state of Ayodhya is populated with well-established people, its temples adorned with water tanks and fountains. Men and women of Ayodhya are highly delighted, graced by cultural festivities, surrounded by well-cultivated fields and abundant in cattle. Furthermore, it is completely free from violence. The region doesn't depend exclusively on rains for agricultural produce; it boasts charming topography and is free of predatory beasts. Entirely devoid of fears, enriched with mines and minerals, Ayodhya thrives, protected by ancestors and presently free from sinful people. Consequently, the state thrives and prospers.

Ayodhya is described as being populated with well-established people, indicating a stable society. The temples adorned with water tanks and fountains suggest not only religious and cultural richness but also a level of sophistication in planning and infrastructure development. The men and women of Ayodhya are depicted as highly delighted, indicating a content and joyful populace. The mention of cultural festivities suggests a vibrant cultural life, likely characterized by music, dance and various celebrations, contributing to the overall happiness of the people. The region is surrounded by well-cultivated fields abundant in cattle, implying a flourishing agricultural economy that ensures food security and prosperity for the inhabitants. Ayodhya is portrayed as completely free from violence, indicating a peaceful and harmonious society where people can live without fear of conflict or aggression. The region is not exclusively dependent on rains for agricultural produce, suggesting advanced irrigation systems. The charming topography and absence of predatory beasts indicate a serene and safe environment conducive to both agriculture and human habitation. Ayodhya is described as devoid of fears and enriched with mines and minerals, suggesting wealth and natural resources that contribute to its prosperity. The state of Ayodhya is known for peace, prosperity, cultural richness and abundant natural resources, where its people live happily and harmoniously, enjoying the fruits of their labour in a nurturing environment.

Caring for the Weak

कच्चिदन्धांश्च मूकांश्च पङ्गून्व्यङ्गानबान्धवान्।
पितेव पासि धर्मज्ञ तथा प्रव्रजितानपि ।।125।।

kaccidandhāṃśca mūkāṃśca paṅgūnvyaṅgānabāndhavān|
piteva pāsi dharmajña tathā pravrajitānapi ||125||[43]

The state should provide support and care for weak and vulnerable individuals, including the blind, deaf, lame, disabled, those with limb loss, and wandering monks.

धर्मासनस्थः सद्भिः स स्त्रीबालातुरवृद्धकान्।।

Dharmāsanasthaḥ sadbhiḥ sa srībālāturavṛddhakān.[44]

The state takes care of good people, women, children, the sick and the elderly.

It reflects an ethos of social welfare and solidarity, where the state assumes responsibility for protecting, caring for and supporting the most vulnerable members of society, ensuring that their basic needs are met. This approach is often rooted in principles of societal care and well-being, aiming to enhance the overall quality of life for all individuals.

ववर्ष भगवान् देवः काले देशे यथेप्सितम्
निरामयं जगदभूत् क्षुत्पिपासे न किंचन ।।

Vavarṣa bhagavān devaḥ kāle deśe yathepsitam.
Nirāmayaṃ jagadabhūt kṣutpipāse na kiṃcana[45]

Adequate rainfall occurs in every part of the state, ensuring that people are free from hunger, disease and sorrow.

Adequate rainfall implies that there is enough precipitation throughout the state to meet the needs of agriculture, natural ecosystems and human consumption. Sufficient rainfall supports agricultural activities by providing moisture for crops to grow, leading to good crop yields and ensuring a steady food supply for the population. Regular rainfall helps maintain the water cycle, ensuring the availability of clean water sources for drinking and sanitation purposes. Additionally, adequate rainfall can help control the spread of vector-borne diseases. It can also provide economic stability and reduce stress related to crop failure and financial hardship, fostering a sense of security and well-being among the population.

Hastinapur under Bheeshma's Leadership

ऊर्ध्वसस्याभवद् भूमिः सस्यानि रसवन्ति च।
यथर्तुवर्षी पर्जन्यो बहुपुष्पफला द्रुमाः ।।2।।

Ūrdhvasasyābhavad bhūmiḥ sasyāni rasavanti ca.
Yathartuvarṣī parjanyo bahupuṣpaphalā drumāḥ ।।2।।[46]

The land yielded abundant harvests, with crops that were rich in nutrition. The clouds generously showered rain at the appropriate time, causing the trees to flourish with fruits and flowers.

It shows a harmonious relationship between nature and agriculture, wherein the land generously yields abundant, nutritious food for the people residing there. It underscores the significance of favourable environmental conditions for both successful farming and the sustenance of a thriving ecosystem.

वाहनानि प्रहृष्टानि मुदिता मृगपक्षिणः।
गन्धवन्ति च माल्यानि रसवन्ति फलानि च॥3॥

Vāhanāni prahṛṣṭāni muditā mṛgapakṣiṇaḥ.
Gandhavanti ca mālyāni rasavanti phalāni ca ॥3॥[47]

The horses and elephants that carried the vehicle remained healthy. Deer and birds enjoy life, while the flowers emit an extraordinary fragrance, and the fruits have become juicy.

The horses and elephants tasked with carrying a vehicle managed to maintain good health despite their exertion, implying proper care and attention. Meanwhile, the carefree existence of deer and birds, portrayed as enjoying life, suggests a natural state of harmony and contentment in their environment. Additionally, the description of the sensory delights of the surroundings highlights the extraordinary fragrance emitted by the flowers, indicating a lush and vibrant ecosystem where nature flourishes. Furthermore, the mention of the fruits becoming juicy suggests their ripeness and abundance, contributing to the overall richness of the environment—a thriving and harmonious natural setting where both flora and fauna coexist in health and abundance.

वणिग्भिश्चान्वकीर्यन्त नगराण्यथ शिल्पिभिः।
शूराश्च कृतविद्याश्च सन्तश्च सुखिनोऽभवन्॥4॥

vaṇigbhiścānvakīryanta nagarāṇyatha śilpibhiḥ.
śūrāśca kṛtavidyāśca santaśca sukhino'bhavan ॥4॥[48]

The cities bustled with merchants and artisans, bringing happiness to the brave, the learned and the holy.

In bustling cities, the streets throng with the lively presence of merchants and artisans, each contributing. Their presence brings not just economic activity but also a sense of joy and fulfilment to different segments of society. The brave souls find happiness in the opportunities and challenges, while the learned individuals find satisfaction amidst the intellectual ferment of the cities. Here, they can engage in lively discussions, access libraries and centres of knowledge and interact with fellow thinkers, fostering an environment conducive to intellectual growth and discovery. Amidst the bustling streets and marketplaces, they encounter opportunities for spiritual guidance and the devout spirituality of the community.

नाभवन् दस्यवः केचिन्नाधर्मरुचयो जनाः ।
प्रदेशेष्वपि राष्ट्राणां कृतं युगमवर्तत ।।5।।

Nābhavan dasyavaḥ kecinnādharmarucayo janāḥ.
Pradeśeṣvapi rāṣṭrāṇāṃ kṛtaṃ yugamavartata ।।5।।[49]

No person was a dacoit. Those interested in sin were nonexistent. The age of truth (Satyayuga) was casting its shadow over various parts of the state.

It collectively portrays the state where criminal behaviour is absent, immoral inclinations are nonexistent, and truth and righteousness are prevalent across different regions of a state. It is a society or community characterized by virtue and honesty.

धर्मक्रिया यज्ञशीलाः सत्यव्रतपरायणाः ।
अन्योन्यप्रीतिसंयुक्ता व्यवर्धन्त प्रजास्तदा ।।6।।

Dharmakriyā yajñaśīlāḥ satyavrataparāyaṇāḥ.
Anyonyaprītisaṃyuktā vyavardhanta prajāstadā ।।6।।[50]

The people there followed the work assigned to them according to dharma, abided by truth and engaged in performing yagya (sacred rituals). They were friendly with each other and contributed to the development and upward growth of society.

मानक्रोधविहीनाश्च नरा लोभविवर्जिताः।
अन्योन्यमभ्यनन्दन्त धर्मोत्तरमवर्तत।।7।।

Mānakrodhavihīnāśca narā lobhavivarjitāḥ.
Anyonyamabhyanandanta dharmottaramavartata ।।7।।[51]

People were free from ego, anger, aloofness and greed; everyone was friendly and pleasing with each other. The conduct of the people was predominantly dharmic.

तन्महोदधिवत् पूर्णं नगरं वै व्यरोचत।
द्वारतोरणनिर्यूहैर्युक्तमभ्रचयोपमैः ।।8।।

Tanmahodadhivat pūrṇaṃ nagaraṃ vai vyarocata.
Dvāratoraṇaniryūhairyuktamabhracayopamaiḥ ।।8।।[52]

प्रासादशतसम्बाधं महेन्द्रपुरसंनिभम्।
नदीषु वनखण्डेषु वापीपल्वलसानुषु।
काननेषु च रम्येषु विजह्रुर्मुदिता जनाः।।9।।

Prāsādaśatasambādhaṃ mahendrapurasaṃnibham.
Nadīṣu vanakhaṇḍeṣu vāpīpalvalasānuṣu.
Kānaneṣu ca ramyeṣu vijahrurmuditā janāḥ ।।9।।[53]

The city was as full and expansive as the wide ocean, adorned with huge doors, gates, arches and hundreds of palaces, as glorious as Amravati of Indra. The people there delighted in the rivers, lakes, water tanks, parks, beautiful groves and woods.

The city boasted vastness and abundance, exemplified by its grandeur and magnificence in architecture. Its impressive structures—doors, gates, arches and numerous palaces—evoked comparisons to Amravati, renowned for its splendour and opulence. Furthermore, the city offered natural beauty and recreational amenities, bringing joy to its inhabitants. It hinted at people finding pleasure in various water bodies like rivers, lakes and water tanks, along with parks, groves and woods, showcasing a harmonious relationship between the city's environment and its natural surroundings.

नाभवत्‌ कृपणः कश्चिन्नाभवन्‌ विधवाः स्त्रियः।
तस्मिञ्जनपदे रम्ये कुरुभिर्बहुलीकृते॥11॥

Nābhavat kṛpaṇaḥ kaścinnābhavan vidhavāḥ striyaḥ.
Tasmiñjanapade ramye kurubhirbahulīkṛte ॥11॥[54]

In that delightful country whose prosperity was thus increased by the Kurus, there were no misers or widows to be seen.

कृपारामसभावाप्यो ब्राह्मणावसथास्तथा।
बभूवुः सर्वर्द्धियुतास्तस्मिन्‌ राष्ट्रे सदोत्सवाः॥12॥

Kṛpārāmasabhāvāpyo brāhmaṇāvasathāstathā.
Babhūvuḥ sarvarddhiyutāstasmin rāṣṭre sadotsavāḥ ॥12॥[55]

The wells, fountains, gardens and assembly buildings overflowed with various types of prosperity, while new festivities were hosted regularly.

भीष्मेण धर्मतो राजन्‌ सर्वतः परिरक्षिते।
बभूव रमणीयश्च चैत्ययूपशताङ्कितः ॥13॥

Bhīṣmeṇa dharmato rājan sarvataḥ parirakṣite.
Babhūva ramaṇīyaśca caityayūpaśatāṅkitaḥ ॥13॥[56]

According to dharma, Bheeshma had secured the Kuru territory from all sides; it was marked by hundreds of sacred sites and attained immense glory.

According to the principles of dharma, Bheeshma ensured the protection and security of the Kuru territory from all directions. He implemented strategies and defences that safeguarded the land and its people. This territory was distinguished by the presence of numerous sacred sites, which held great religious and cultural significance.

भीष्मेण विहितं राष्ट्रे धर्मचक्रमवर्तत॥14॥

Bhīṣmeṇa vihitaṃ rāṣṭre dharmacakramavartata ॥14॥[57]

The state was moving relentlessly on the path of progress, with the dharma upheld by Bheeshma holding sway throughout.

The state's progress is closely tied to the adherence to principles of the rule of law, justice and their enforcement, symbolized by Bheeshma's commitment to dharma. It suggests that the state's advancement is not solely measured by material or economic growth but also by the ethical and moral foundations on which it is built.

Hastinapur under Yudhishthira's Reign

आधिर्नास्ति मनुष्याणां व्यसने नाभवन्मतिः।
ब्राह्मणप्रमुखा वर्णास्ते स्वधर्मोत्तराः शिवाः॥

Ādhirnāsti manuṣyāṇāṃ vyasane nābhavanmatiḥ.
Brāhmaṇapramukhā varṇāste svadharmottarāḥ śivāḥ.[58]

People do not suffer from mental illness, are not attracted to addiction, but follow their own dharma, leading to happiness for everyone.

Employment for the Public

अवृत्तिवृत्तिदानाद्यैर्यज्ञार्थैर्दीपितैरपि ।

Avṛttivṛttidānādyairyajñārthairdīpitairapi.[59]

The state ensures employment opportunities for the unemployed.

When the state ensures employment opportunities for the unemployed, it actively works to address the challenges of unemployment through policy interventions, support services and promoting economic growth. This helps individuals achieve financial independence, fosters social cohesion and strengthens the overall economy.

The Characteristics of the Highest Form of a Democratic State

न वै राज्यं न राजाऽऽसीन्न च दण्डो न दाण्डिकः।
धर्मेणैव प्रजाः सर्वा रक्षन्ति स्म परस्परम्॥14॥

Na vai rājyaṃ na rājā''sīnna ca daṇḍo na dāṇḍikaḥ.
Dharmeṇaiva prajāḥ sarvā rakṣanti sma parasparam ॥14॥[60]

Neither a kingdom nor a king or head of state existed; neither punishment nor its dispenser was present. Instead, all individuals protected one another by adhering to dharma.

न तत्र राजा राजेन्द्र न दण्डो न च दण्डिकः।
स्वधर्मेणैव धर्मज्ञास्ते रक्षन्ति परस्परम्॥39॥

Na tatra rājā rājendra na daṇḍo na ca daṇḍikaḥ.
Svadharmeṇaiva dharmajñāste rakṣanti parasparam ॥39॥[62]

The state where neither a king nor punishment exists, nor is there anyone designated to administer them. Its inhabitants are deeply versed in dharma, and through steadfast adherence to it, they mutually safeguard one another.

In a state where there is no centralized authority, such as a king or ruler, punitive measures enforced by a governing body become unnecessary. This absence signifies a profound level of self-governance and mutual respect among individuals. Inhabitants of such a state not only understand the moral and ethical principles governing their society but also deeply internalize them. They possess an innate understanding of right and wrong according to the principle of dharma. Instead of relying on external authority to maintain order, the society operates smoothly because its members unwaveringly adhere to the principles of dharma. This steadfast adherence ensures that individuals act in alignment with moral principles, collectively upholding societal harmony. It is a state where individuals embody virtue and self-discipline to such an extent that external governance becomes redundant. Within this community, people coexist harmoniously, guided solely by their inner moral compass and mutual respect for each other's rights and duties.

Republican States

सङ्घा हि संहतत्वादधृष्याः परेषाम्।।1।।

Saṅghā hi saṃhatatvādadhṛṣyāḥ pareṣām ।।1।।[63]

The sangha (republic) is organized, making them superior and therefore undefeatable by their enemies.

In 'the sangha (republic)', the decision-making process involves collective participation; meaning important choices are made through consensus rather than by a single authority. This collective decision-making fosters a deep sense of unity and organization within the society. When individuals come together to make decisions affecting their community, it strengthens their bonds and reinforces shared values and goals. This unity becomes a formidable force against any external threat or enemy. The cohesive nature of the society makes it resilient, capable of facing challenges with solidarity and determination. Therefore, in 'the sangha (republic)', the enemy faces a significant obstacle in attempting to defeat the community. The collective strength and unity of its people serve as a powerful defence mechanism, making it difficult for any adversary to undermine or conquer the society.

यथा गणाः प्रवर्धन्ते न भिद्यन्ते च भारत।
अरींश्च विजिगीषन्ते सुहृदः प्राप्नुवन्ति च।।7।।

Yathā gaṇāḥ pravardhante na bhidyante ca bhārata.
Arīṃśca vijigīṣante suhṛdaḥ prāpnuvanti ca ।।7।।[64]

In republican states, people progress without becoming divided. They unite to defeat their enemies and gather friends and supporters.

In states governed by republican principles, people advance without succumbing to division. When differences arise, they find common ground and unite to overcome challenges, particularly when facing adversaries. This unity helps in defeating opponents and expanding their circle of allies, friends and supporters. Together, they strengthen their bonds and work towards shared goals, fostering solidarity and collective progress.

प्राज्ञाञ्छूरान् महोत्साहान् कर्मसु स्थिरपौरुषान्।
मानयन्तः सदा युक्ता विवर्धन्ते गणा नृप॥20॥

Prājñāñśūrān mahotsāhān karmasu sthirapauruṣān.
Mānayantaḥ sadā yuktā vivardhante gaṇā nṛpa॥20॥[65]

Members of the republic rule collectively, always respecting individuals who are intelligent, brave, immensely enthusiastic and demonstrate determination in all endeavours. They remain industrious for the progress of the republic, thus advancing faster.

In a republic, power is vested in the hands of the people, either directly or through elected representatives, meaning governance decisions are made collectively. Within the republic, there is a culture of valuing certain qualities in individuals such as intelligence, bravery, enthusiasm and determination. These qualities are respected and admired because they contribute to the betterment of society as a whole.

The members of the republic are characterized by their industriousness, meaning they are hardworking, diligent and productive. Their collective efforts are directed towards advancing the republic and its interests. By working together and leveraging their intelligence, bravery, enthusiasm and determination, they are able to make progress at a faster pace compared to societies where these qualities are not as valued or cultivated.

ज्ञानवृद्धाः प्रशंसन्ति शुश्रूषन्तः परस्परम्।
विनिवृत्ताभि संधानाः सुखमेधन्ति सर्वशः॥16॥

Jñānavṛddhāḥ praśaṃsanti śuśrūṣantaḥ parasparam.
Vinivṛttābhi saṃdhānāḥ sukhamedhanti sarvaśaḥ।।16।।[66]

Learned and wise individuals praise the people of the sangha (republic) for their unity and integrity. They do not deceive one another but instead serve each other, fostering collective growth, progress, and, ultimately, shared happiness.

In the sangha (republic), people are united and uphold strong moral principles. They stand together, support one another and are committed to honesty and ethical behaviour. Deceit or fraudulent behaviour is absent among them; they do not exploit or take advantage of each other for personal gain. Instead, they engage in fair dealings and cultivate genuine relationships. The people prioritize serving each other, actively working towards the well-being of their community rather than focusing solely on individual interests. This service-oriented mindset fosters collective responsibility and mutual support. Through their unity, integrity and service to one another, they contribute to the growth and progress of their society. By working together towards common goals, they create opportunities for advancement and development that benefit everyone, leading to shared happiness. By prioritizing unity, integrity and service, the people establish a harmonious and prosperous environment where fulfilment and joy are shared by all.

धर्मिष्ठान् व्यवहारांश्च स्थापयन्तश्च शास्रतः।
यथावत् प्रतिपश्यन्तो विवर्धन्ते गणोत्तमाः।।17।।

Dharmiṣṭṭhān vyavahārāṃśca sthāpayantaśca śāsrataḥ.
Yathāvat pratipaśyanto vivardhante gaṇottamāḥ।।17।।[67]

The honest leaders of the sangha (republic) establish systems and constitutions based on dharma, ensuring mutual care and fostering growth, development and progress.

The honest leaders of the sangha (republic) are dedicated to establishing systems and constitutions rooted in dharma. By adhering to dharma, these leaders ensure that the foundation of their society is built upon values such as justice, fairness, compassion and integrity. Through the implementation of these systems and constitutions, they aim to foster an environment of mutual care and support among the people of the republic. They recognize the interconnectedness of all members of society and strive to create structures that prioritize the well-being of every individual, regardless of their background or status.

Furthermore, these systems and constitutions are designed to promote growth, development and progress on both individual and collective levels. They provide avenues for education, innovation and economic opportunity, empowering citizens to fulfil their potential and contribute meaningfully to the advancement of society as a whole. The honest leaders of the republic lay the groundwork for a just, prosperous and harmonious society where every individual can thrive and contribute to the greater good.

पुत्रान् भ्रातॄन् निगृह्णन्तो विनयन्तश्च तान् सदा।
विनीतांश्च प्रगृह्णन्तो विवर्धन्ते गणोत्तमाः।।18।।

Putrān bhrātṛn nigṛhanto vinayantaśca tān sadā.
Vinītāṃśca pragṛhanto vivardhante gaṇottamāḥ ।।18।।[68]

The leaders of the republic consistently provide their people with the finest education, ensuring proper training for integration into the republic's administrative system. These leaders also uphold justice by penalizing their own family members and relatives should they stray from the law. This commitment to discipline and education is what propels the exceptional progress of the republican state.

The leadership of a republic emphasizes providing the finest education, indicating their understanding of the importance of a well-educated populace for the efficient functioning of the administrative system. By ensuring proper training for their people, they equip them with the necessary skills and knowledge to contribute effectively to governance and development.

The commitment to upholding justice, even when it involves penalizing their own family members, demonstrates strong adherence to the rule of law and equality before it. This sends a powerful message that no one, regardless of familial ties or position, is above the law. By holding their own relatives accountable, the leaders set a precedent for fair and just governance, fostering trust and confidence among the population.

Together, these principles of discipline and education form the backbone of the republic's progress. By prioritizing these values, the leaders create a conducive environment for growth, innovation and social cohesion, ultimately contributing to the exceptional progress of the republic.

तस्मान्मानयितव्यास्ते गणमुख्याः प्रधानतः।
लोकयात्रा समायत्ता भूयसी तेषु पार्थिव।।23।।

Tasmānmānayitavyāste gaṇamukhyāḥ pradhānataḥ.
Lokayātrā samāyattā bhūyasī teṣu pārthiva ।।23।।[69]

The leaders of the republic always shoulder the responsibility of managing and administering it; therefore, they deserve respect and honour.

Managing and administering a republic entails a broad spectrum of tasks and responsibilities. These include formulating laws, executing policies, supervising governmental agencies, handling budgets, representing the nation in diplomatic affairs, and safeguarding the welfare and security of its populace. Leaders are entrusted with the effective execution of these duties to ensure the seamless operation of the republic.

The burden of managing and administering the republic falls squarely on the shoulders of its leaders; thus, they deserve respect and reverence. Demonstrating respect and reverence for leaders can take various forms, such as heeding their guidance and decisions, complying with the laws and regulations they enact, treating them with dignity and respect, recognizing their endeavours and contributions, and safeguarding their authority from unjustified attacks or criticisms.

आभ्यन्तरं भयं रक्ष्यमसारं बाह्यतो भयम्।।28।।
आभ्यन्तरं भयं राजन् सद्यो मूलानि कृन्तति।

Ābhyantaraṃ bhayaṃ rakṣyamasāraṃ bāhyato bhayam।।28।।
Ābhyantaraṃ bhayaṃ rājan sadyo mūlāni kṛntati.[70]

Protecting the republic entails dispelling internal threats to ensure its safety. An internal threat undermines the foundation of the republic. When the republic is united, external threats become irrelevant and cannot cause harm.

Protecting the republic involves safeguarding it from any dangers that may arise, whether they originate from within its borders or externally. Internal threats refer to challenges or dangers arising from within the society or government structure itself, such as corruption, abuse of power, erosion of democratic principles or social unrest.

The significance of addressing internal threats lies in their potential to destabilize the very foundation of the republic. If left unchecked, they can weaken institutions, erode public trust and undermine the rule of law, ultimately threatening the stability and longevity of the republic itself.

A united republic is better equipped to confront external threats. When the people and institutions of a republic are united, cohesive and work together towards common goals, external threats become less potent. Unity fosters strength and resilience, enabling the republic to defend itself against external pressures, whether economic, military or political.

By prioritizing the resolution of internal threats and fostering unity within the republic, its ability to withstand external challenges is greatly enhanced. This ensures the safety and longevity of the republic, allowing it to thrive and fulfil its purpose of serving the interests of its people.

अकस्मात् क्रोधमोहाभ्यां लोभाद् वापिस्वभावजात्।।29।।
अन्योन्यं नाभिभाषन्ते तत्पराभवलक्षणम्।

Akasmāt krodhamohābhyāṃ lobhād vāpisvabhāvajāt॥29॥
Anyonyaṃ nābhibhāṣante tatparābhavalakṣaṇam.[71]

When people in a republic cease communicating with one another due to sudden anger, attachment or innate greed, it is a symptom of defeat.

In a republic, where power is held by the people and their elected representatives, effective communication and collaboration are vital. When individuals within such a system stop communicating with each other due to sudden anger, attachment to personal interests or innate greed, it indicates a breakdown in the fundamental principles of a republic and democracy. When these negative traits manifest and cause individuals to cease communication with one another within a republic, it signals a failure to uphold the principles of democracy. Effective communication, cooperation and a commitment to the common good are essential for the functioning of a republic. When these principles are compromised, the fabric of a republic and democracy is weakened, leading to a sense of defeat for the ideals upon which the republic was founded.

भेदे गणा विनेशुर्हि भिन्नास्तु सुजयाः परैः।
तस्मात् संघातयोगेन प्रयतेरन् गणाः सदा॥14॥

Bhede gaṇā vineśurhi bhinnāstu sujayāḥ paraiḥ.
Tasmāt saṃghātayogena prayateran gaṇāḥ sadā ॥14॥[72]

Republics have been destroyed owing to disunity. Enemies defeat them easily on account of disunity. Therefore, republics should always be united.

Republican states are founded on principles of equality, justice and popular sovereignty; however, when internal divisions and disunity arise within a republic, they weaken the fabric of society. Disunity can manifest in various forms, such as political factions, social unrest or regional conflicts, making republics easy targets for external enemies. When a nation is fragmented internally, it becomes less capable of effectively organizing and mobilizing resources to defend itself against external aggression. Divided leadership, conflicting interests and a lack of solidarity weaken a republic's ability to respond cohesively to external challenges.

A united republic is better equipped to defend its sovereignty, uphold its values and safeguard the interests of its people. Throughout history, there have been numerous instances where disunity has led to the downfall of republics or democratic systems. By fostering internal cohesion and solidarity, republics can better withstand external pressures and preserve their autonomy and democratic principles.

The Strength of Democracy

राजा राष्ट्रं यथाऽऽपत्सु द्रव्यौघैरपि रक्षति।
राष्ट्रेण राजा व्यसने रक्षितव्यस्तथा भवेत्।।31।।

Rājā rāṣṭraṃ yathā''patsu dravyaughairapi rakṣati.
Rāṣṭreṇa rājā vyasane rakṣitavyastathā bhavet।।31।।[73]

Just as the state protects its people in a crisis by spending its wealth and resources, similarly, the people of the state should protect the state when it is in distress.

In times of crisis, such as natural disasters (floods, droughts, famines), pandemics or economic downturns, democratic states typically mobilize their resources and allocate significant funds to protect and support their people. This can involve various measures such as deploying emergency services, providing financial aid, implementing healthcare initiatives and ensuring public safety.

The state devotes its wealth and resources to protect its people; in turn, the people have a reciprocal duty to support and safeguard the state when it faces challenges. This support can take various forms, including compliance with government directives, participation in community resilience efforts, contributing to the collective welfare fund and engaging in voluntary service.

Both the state and its people have obligations to each other, particularly during times of crisis. While the state is responsible for ensuring the safety and well-being of its people, people, in turn, are expected to uphold the stability and integrity of the state.

When both the state and its people work together harmoniously, they can better navigate crises and emerge stronger as a community. The interdependence between the democratic state and its people highlights the importance of collective responsibility and mutual support in times of need.

Collective Decision-Making in a Democratic State

सर्वविद्यासु कुशलो नृपो ह्यपि सुमन्त्रवित्।
मन्त्रिभिस्तु विना मन्त्रं नैकोऽर्थं चिन्तयेत्क्वचित्।।2।।

Sarvavidyāsu kuśalo nṛpo hyapi sumantravit.
Mantribhistu vinā mantraṃ naiko'rthaṃ cintayetkvacit ।।2।।[74]

The head of state should refrain from making decisions in the absence of their ministers, even though they may be adept in all forms of knowledge and capable of discussing and deliberating.

सभ्याऽधिकारिप्रकृतिसभासत्सुमते स्थितः।
सर्वदा स्यान्नृपः प्राज्ञः स्वमते न कदाचन।।3।।

Sabhyā'dhikāriprakṛtisabhāsatsumate sthitaḥ.
Sarvadā syānnṛpaḥ prājñaḥ svamate na kadācana ।।3।।[75]

The learned head of state should always act in consensus with the ministers, members of his council and officials, never acting solely according to his own wishes.

बहुनामैकमत्यं हि नृपतेर्बलवत्तरम्।।398।।

Bahūnāmaikamatyaṃ hi nṛpaterbalavattaram।।398।।[76]

The collective advice of the council of ministers is undoubtedly more influential and significant than that of the head of state.

While the head of state may possess significant knowledge and capabilities, involving ministers in decision-making processes is essential for promoting effective governance, accountability and transparency. Harnessing the collective wisdom and expertise of the entire government leads to more well-informed and balanced decisions.

Even though the head of state may possess extensive knowledge and decision-making capabilities, they need to work collaboratively with their ministers when making decisions, ensuring diverse perspectives and expertise within the government. Involving them in decision-making ensures that a broader range of perspectives and interests are considered, leading to more well-rounded and informed decisions. Ministers often have specialized knowledge and expertise in their respective fields, which is crucial for making informed decisions.

While the head of state may have a broad understanding of various subjects, ministers can provide in-depth insights and analysis that contribute to better decision-making outcomes. Collaboration with ministers fosters a sense of trust and teamwork within the government, demonstrating that the head of state values the input and expertise of their colleagues. This enhances morale and productivity within the administration and ensures checks and balances.

Attributes of a Head of State

राजधर्मार्थकुशलो युक्तः सर्वगुणैर्वृतः।।15।।

Rājadharmārthakuśalo yuktaḥ sarvaguṇairvṛtaḥ ।।15।।[77]

One who is highly proficient and learned in rajdharma (politics and administration) and artha (economy) is adorned with all noble qualities.

जितेन्द्रियश्चात्मवांश्च मेधावी धर्मसेविता।
षड्वर्गजिन्महाबुद्धिर्नीतिशास्त्रविदुत्तमः।।16।।

Jitendriyaścātmavāṃśca medhāvī dharmasevitā.
Ṣaḍvargajinmahābuddhirnītiśāstraviduttamaḥ।।16।।[78]

One who has conquered their passions has control over their mind and has served the supreme intelligence and dharma. By overcoming the six enemies—sensual gratification, anger, greed, attachment, egotism and possessiveness—their intellect becomes expansive. They are regarded as supreme among intellectuals in the field of rajdharma (politics and administration).

विद्याविनीतो राजा हि प्रजानां विनये रतः।
अनन्यां पृथिवीं भुङ्क्ते सर्वभूतहिते रतः।।

Vidyāvinīto rājā hi prajānāṃ vinaye rataḥ.
Ananyāṃ pṛthivīṃ bhuṅkte sarvabhūtahite rataḥ.[79]

A qualified, learned and humble head of state stays focused on ensuring the welfare of all and actively engages in educating and governing the populace. Such a head of state is respected and governs effectively for an extended period.

रक्षन् राज्यं बुद्धिपूर्वं नयेन।।33।।

Rakṣan rājyaṃ buddhipūrvaṃ nayena।।33।।[80]

राष्ट्रं रक्षन् बुद्धिपूर्वं नयेन।।29।।

Rāṣṭraṃ rakṣan buddhipūrvaṃ nayena ।।29।।[81]

In accordance with dharma, the head of state should protect both its people and the state intelligently.

गुणवाञ्शीलवान् दान्तो मृदुर्धर्म्योजितेन्द्रियः।
सुदर्शः स्थूललक्ष्यश्च न भ्रश्येत सदा श्रियः।।18।।

Guṇavāñśīlavān dānto mṛdurdharmyojitendriyaḥ.
Sudarśaḥ sthūlalakṣyaśca na bhraśyeta sadā śriyaḥ।।18।।[82]

A head of state, whose character should embody good conduct, self-control, compassion and dharmic principles, and who has mastered their passion and senses while displaying a pleasing countenance, is a generous being and never loses prosperity.

तस्मान्नैव मृदुर्नित्यं तीक्ष्णो नैव भवेन्नृपः।
वासन्तार्क इव श्रीमान् न शीतो न च घर्मदः।।40।।

Tasmānnaiva mṛdurnityaṃ tīkṣṇo naiva bhavennṛpaḥ.
Vāsantārka iva śrīmān na śīto na ca gharmadaḥ।।40।।[83]

Just as the radiant spring sun is neither too cool nor too hot, similarly, the head of state should neither be too soft nor too harsh.

प्राज्ञस्त्यागगुणोपेतः पररन्ध्रेषु तत्परः।
सुदर्शः सर्ववर्णानां नयापनयवित् तथा।।30।।
क्षिप्रकारी जितक्रोधः सुप्रसादो महामनाः।
अरोषप्रकृतिर्युक्तः क्रियावानविकत्थनः।।31।।
आरब्धान्येव कार्याणि सुपर्यवसितानि च।
यस्य राज्ञः प्रदृश्यन्ति स राजा राजसत्तमः।।32।।

Prājñastyāgaguṇopetaḥ pararandhreṣu tatparaḥ.
Sudarśaḥ sarvavarṇānāṃ nayāpanayavit tathā।।30।।
Kṣiprakārī jitakrodhaḥ suprasādo mahāmanāḥ.
Aroṣaprakṛtiryuktaḥ kriyāvānavikatthanaḥ।।31।।
Ārabdhānyeva kāryāṇi suparyavasitāni ca.
Yasya rājñaḥ pradṛśyanti sa rājā rājasattamaḥ।।32।।[84]

A head of state should be intelligent and self-sacrificing, capable of discerning the shortcomings of foes, smart, understanding justice and injustice for all, prompt in work, with controlled anger, a deep thinker, gentle, industrious, committed to duty and shunning self-praise. By completing all initiated projects and work properly, such a head of state stands supreme.

अविजित्य य आत्मानममात्यान् विजिगीषते।
अमित्रान् वाजितामात्यः सोऽवशः परिहीयते।।28।।

Avijitya ya ātmānamamātyān vijigīṣate.
Amitrān vājitāmātyaḥ so'vaśaḥ parihīyate।।28।।[85]

आत्मा जेयः सदा राज्ञा ततो जेयाश्च शत्रवः।
अजितात्मा नरपतिर्विजयेत कथं रिपून्।।4।।

Ātmā jeyaḥ sadā rājñā tato jeyāśca śatravaḥ.
Ajitātmā narapatirvijayeta kathaṃ ripūn ।।4।।[86]

A head of state must first conquer his own mind, and then win over his ministers. Without gaining control over his mind and authority over ministers, he cannot triumph over his enemies. Failing to do so, he cannot achieve victory against his enemy.

षाड्गुण्यं च त्रिवर्गं च त्रिवर्गपरमं तथा।
यो वेत्ति पुरुषव्याघ्र स भुङ्क्ते पृथिवीमिमाम्।।66।।
षाड्गुण्यमिति यत् प्रोक्तं तन्निबोध युधिष्ठिर।
संधानासनमित्येव यात्रासंधानमेव च।।67।।
विगृह्यासनामित्येव यात्रां सम्परिगृह्य च।
द्वैधीभावस्तथान्येषां संश्रयोऽथ परस्य च।।68।।

Ṣāṅguṇyaṃ ca trivarge ca trivargaparamaṃ tathā.
Yo vetti puruṣavyāghra sa bhuṅkte pṛthivīmimām।।66।।
Ṣāḍguṇyamiti yat proktaṃ tannibodha yudhiṣṭhira.
Saṃdhānāsanamityeva yātrāsaṃdhānameva ca।।67।।
Vigṛhyāsanāmityeva yātrāṃ samparigṛhya ca.
Dvaidhībhāvastathānyeṣāṃ saṃśrayo'tha parasya ca।।67।।[87]

The head of state should be well-versed in Shadgunya (the Six Qualities Aggregate), Trivarga (the Grouping of Three: decline, positioning and growth) and Param Trivarga (the Highest Grouping of Three: dharma, artha and kama). The Six Qualities Aggregate encompasses various strategies, including negotiating with adversaries while maintaining an appearance of peace, advancing towards enemies, posturing to deceive foes after aggression, feigning attacks to intimidate opponents, dividing enemy forces and seeking refuge either in a fortified position or under the protection of an unbeatable ally. It is essential for the head of state to comprehend these concepts thoroughly and apply them judiciously. Such knowledge enables effective governance and contributes to prolonged leadership.

Thirty-six Attributes of an Effective Head of State

अयं गुणानां षट्त्रिंशत्षट्त्रिंशद्गुणसंयुतः।
यान् गुणांस्तु गुणोपेतः कुर्वन् गुणमवाप्नुयात्।।2।।

Ayaṃ guṇānāṃ ṣaṭtriṃśatṣaṭtriṃśadguṇasaṃyutaḥ.
Yān guṇāṃstu guṇopetaḥ kurvan guṇamavāpnuyāt ।।2।।[88]

There are thirty-six (36) attributes for a head of state. He should incorporate them into his conduct as they uplift and yield immense benefits. The head of state should strive to embody these attributes.

चरेद् धर्मानकटुको मुञ्चेत् स्नेहं न चास्तिकः।
अनुशंसश्चरेदर्थं चरेत् काममनुद्धतः।।3।।

Cared dharmānakaṭuko muñcet snehaṃ na cāstikaḥ.
Anuśaṃsaścaredarthaṃ caret kāmamanuddhataḥ।।3।।[89]

1) Act in accordance with dharma, avoiding bitterness.
2) While remaining a believer, do not forsake kindness towards others.
3) Accumulate wealth for the state treasury without resorting to cruelty.
4) Indulge with discipline intact.

प्रियं ब्रूयादकृपणः शूरः स्यादविकत्थनः।
दाता नापात्रवर्षी स्यात् प्रगल्भः स्यादनिष्ठुरः।।4।।

Priyaṃ brūyādakṛpaṇaḥ śūraḥ syādavikatthanaḥ.
Dātā nāpātravarṣī syāt pragalbhaḥ syādaniṣṭhuraḥ।।4।।[90]

5) Speak with cordiality, devoid of weakness. 6) Demonstrate bravery without resorting to boasting. 7) Donate generously, but not to the undeserving. 8) Display courage without descending into cruelty.

संदधीत न चानार्यैर्विंगृह्णीयान्न बन्धुभिः।
नाभक्तं चारयेच्चारं कुर्यात् कार्यमपीडया॥5॥

Saṃdadhīta na cānāryairviṃgṛhṇīyānna bandhubhiḥ.
Nābhaktaṃ cārayeccāraṃ kuryāt kāryamapīḍayā ॥5॥[91]

9) Do not make friends with the wicked. 10) Do not act unfriendly towards supporters. 11) Do not employ a person as a spy who is not a patriot. 12) Accomplish work without afflicting others.

अर्थं ब्रूयान्न चासत्सु गुणान् ब्रूयान्न चात्मनः।
आदद्यान्न च साधुभ्यो नासत्पुरुषमाश्रयेत्॥6॥

Arthaṃ brūyānna cāsatsu guṇān brūyānna cātmanaḥ.
Ādadyānna ca sādhubhyo nāsatpuruṣamāśrayet॥6॥[92]

13) Never inform the wicked about your own intended deeds.
14) Refrain from praising personal attributes.
15) Avoid appropriating the wealth of virtuous individuals.
16) Do not seek assistance from the wicked.

नापरीक्ष्य नयेद् दण्डं न च मन्त्रं प्रकाशयेत्।
विसृजेन्न च लुब्धेभ्यो विश्वसेन्नापकारिषु॥7॥

Nāparīkṣya nayed daṇḍaṃ na ca mantraṃ prakāśayet.
Visṛjenna ca lubdhebhyo viśvasennāpakāriṣu॥7॥[93]

17) Never inflict punishment on anyone without diligently investigating the offence. 18) Do not disclose secret counsel. 19) Do not give wealth to the greedy. 20) Do not trust those who have harmed you.

अनीर्षुर्गुप्तदारः स्याच्चोक्षः स्यादघृणी नृपः।
स्त्रियः सेवेत नात्यर्थे मृष्टं भुञ्जीत नाहितम्॥8॥

Anīrṣurguptadāraḥ syāccokṣaḥ syādaghṛṇī nṛpaḥ.
Striyaḥ seveta nātyarthe mṛṣṭaṃ bhuñjīta nāhitam॥8॥[94]

21) Without jealousy, protect own spouse. 22) To remain pure, one should avoid harbouring animosity towards anyone. 23) Refrain from pursuing excessive pleasure. 24) Consume wholesome, nutritious food and stay away from harmful substances.

अस्तब्धः पूजयेन्मान्यान् गुरून् सेवेदमायया।
अर्चेद् देवानदम्भेन श्रियमिच्छेदकुत्सिताम्।।9।।

Astabdhaḥ pūjayenmānyān gurūn sevedamāyayā.
Arced devānadambhena śriyamicchedakutsitām।।9।।[95]

25) Abandon indiscipline and show humble respect to esteemed persons. 26) Serve preceptors sincerely. 27) Worship sincerely, free from ego. 28) Pursue prosperity but refrain from using forbidden means.

सेवेत प्रणयं हित्वा दक्षः स्यान्न त्वकालवित्।
सान्त्वयेन्न च मोक्षाय अनुगृह्णन्न चाक्षिपेत्।।10।।

Seveta praṇayaṃ hitvā dakṣaḥ syānna tvakālavit.
Sāntvayenna ca mokṣāya anugṛhṇanna cākṣipet।।10।।[96]

29) Abandon stubbornness and embrace affectionate behaviour. 30) Excel in your work, but do not overlook the right opportunities or lack knowledge. 31) To free oneself, refrain from offering false reassurance to anyone. 32) While showing kindness to someone, avoid placing blame.

प्रहरेन्न त्वविज्ञाय हत्वा शत्रून् न शोचयेत्।
क्रोधं कुर्यान्न चाकस्मान्मृदुः स्यान्नापकारिषु।।11।।

Praharenna tvavijñāya hatvā śatrūn na śocayet.
Krodhaṃ kuryānna cākasmānmṛduḥ syānnāpakāriṣu।।11।।[97]

33) Never assault someone without proper knowledge. 34) After destroying the enemies, do not mourn. 35) Do not suddenly become angry. 36) Be soft, but never towards offenders.

प्रजाकार्यं तु तत्कार्यं प्रजासौख्यं तु तत्सुखम्।
प्रजाप्रियं प्रियं तस्य स्वहितं तु प्रजाहितम्।।
प्रजार्थं तस्य सर्वस्वमात्मार्थं न विधीयते।।

Prajākāryaṃ tu tatkāryaṃ prajāsaukhyaṃ tu tatsukham.
Prajāpriyaṃ priyaṃ tasya svahitaṃ tu prajāhitam.
Prajārthaṃ tasya sarvasvamātmārthaṃ na vidhīyate.[98]

The work of the people is synonymous with the work of the head of state; their happiness intertwines with his own. What holds significance for them holds equal importance for him, and their welfare is the cornerstone of his personal interests. Every possession he holds is devoted to the betterment of the people; nothing exists solely for his own benefit.

एवं चरति यो नित्यं राजा राष्ट्रहिते रतः।
तस्य राष्ट्रं धनं धर्मो यशः कीर्तिश्च वर्धते।।

Evaṃ carati yo nityaṃ rājā rāṣṭrahite rataḥ.
Tasya rāṣṭraṃ dhanaṃ dharmo yaśaḥ kīrtiśca vardhate.[99]

In the scenario where the head of state is always prepared to care for both the nation and the state, there is a continual expansion and flourishing of the state's area, wealth, prosperity, name and fame.

यस्यां भवन्ति भूतानि तद् विद्धि मनुजर्षभ।
एष एव परो धर्मो यद् राजा दण्डनीतिमान्।।104।।

Yasyāṃ bhavanti bhūtāni tad viddhi manujarṣabha.
Eṣa eva paro dharmo yad rājā daṇḍanītimān।।104।।[100]

The rule of law and justice, along with its enforcement, sustain a state and its people. The head of state should personally adhere to the enforcement of the rule of law and justice. It is proclaimed that the rule of law and justice, along with its enforcement, are the supreme dharma of the head of state.

दण्डनीतिं पुरस्कृत्य विजानन् क्षत्रियः सदा।
अनवाप्तं च लिप्सेत लब्धं च परिपालयेत्।।102।।

Daṇḍanītiṃ puraskṛtya vijānan kṣatriyaḥ sadā.
Anavāptaṃ ca lipseta labdhaṃ ca paripālayet।।102।।[101]

The head of state should utilize the rule of law and justice, along with its enforcement, to obtain what is needed and safeguard what has been attained. By employing these principles, the leader ensures the welfare of the people.

Not Qualified for the Position of Head of State

नापराधं हि क्षमते प्रदण्डो धनहारकः।
स्वदुर्गुणश्रवणतो लोकानां परिपीडकः।।129।।

Nāparādhaṃ hi kṣamate pradaṇḍo dhanahārakaḥ.
Svadurguṇaśravaṇato lokānāṃ paripīḍakaḥ।।129।।[102]

Someone who severely punishes their people and refuses to forgive them, steals and confiscates the wealth of the people and punishes those who criticize them.

स्वस्मात् पूर्वतरं राजा विनयत्येव वै प्रजाः।
अपहास्यो भवेत्तादृक् स्वदोषस्यानवेक्षणात्।।

Svasmāt pūrvataraṃ rājā vinayatyeva vai prajāḥ.
Apahāsyo bhavettādṛk svadoṣasyānavekṣaṇāt.[103]

A head of state who doesn't learn humility first and tries to teach his people about humility while ignoring his own faults and mistakes becomes an object of ridicule.

परोपदेशकुशलः केवलो न भवेन्नृपः।
प्रजाधिकारहीनः स्यात्सगुणोऽपि नृपः क्वचित्।।93।।

Paropadeśakuśalaḥ kevalo na bhavennṛpaḥ.
Prajādhikārahīnaḥ syātsaguṇo'pi nṛpaḥ kvacit||93||[104]

The head of state shouldn't merely be good at giving lectures to the populace; it's better if they remain humble. Sometimes, even a highly capable head of state, lacking humility, may lose their rightful authority over the people.

A head of state must embody both competence and humility. Competence encompasses effective governance, informed decision-making and leading the nation towards progress. Humility entails listening to others and recognizing limitations despite competence. Excelling in public speaking or communication is valuable, but not the sole requirement. Humility ensures the leader doesn't view themselves as superior, understanding leadership as service, not personal glory. Arrogance and entitlement can alienate, fostering resentment. Ignoring advice or refusing to admit mistakes leads to poor decisions, eroding trust. A leader disconnected from people risks losing legitimacy. Humility builds trust, empathy and collaboration, vital for governance. A humble leader listens, admits faults and seeks consensus, enhancing credibility and authority.

अकौशल्यं नृपस्यैतदनीतेर्यस्य सर्वदा||19||

Akauśalyaṃ nṛpasyaitadanīteryasya sarvadā||19||[105]

Disunity in the realm and the army, disagreement among ministers and their alignment with enemies—all indicate a lack of leadership, strategy and policy on the part of the head of state, as well as folly.

Importance of State Secrets, Their Confidentiality, and Ministerial Responsibility

मन्त्रिणां मन्त्रमूलं हि राज्ञो राष्ट्रं विवर्धते||48||

Mantriṇāṃ mantramūlaṃ hi rājño rāṣṭraṃ vivardhate||48||[106]

The minister's advice to the head of state is paramount for the development of the nation.

Ministers, as appointed officials overseeing governmental departments, wield substantial influence in policy formulation and decision-making. Advising the head of state, typically the highest-ranking official, their counsel carries significant weight. Chosen for their expertise and experience, ministers provide informed guidance rooted in deep sector knowledge, whether in finance, defence, education, health or other critical areas. They play a direct role in shaping national policies, spanning economic strategies to social welfare initiatives, aligning them with overarching goals.

Accountable to both the government and the public, ministers ensure that departmental performance reflects broader governance and public welfare concerns. The head of state relies on ministers for strategic navigation through challenges, crises and opportunities for growth. Serving as governmental representatives, ministers' advice echoes collective governmental wisdom, ensuring coherence in decision-making and fostering public trust.

Ministers' advice to the head of state not only influences policies and decisions but also signifies the government's dedication to national progress. It embodies collaborative governance efforts and underscores the need for strategic leadership in advancing the nation.

मन्त्रगूढा हि राज्यस्य मन्त्रिणो ये मनीषिणः।
मन्त्रसंहननो राजा मन्त्राङ्गानीतरे जनाः॥50॥

Mantragūḍhā hi rājyasya mantriṇo ye manīṣiṇaḥ.
Mantrasaṃhanano rājā mantrāṅgānītare janāḥ॥50॥[107]

Ministers engage in confidential discussions. An astute minister ensures the confidentiality of state secrets. The confidentiality of these secrets acts as a shield for the state.

Ministers, holding pivotal roles in government, regularly engage in private discussions concerning sensitive matters. These discussions encompass issues of national security, policy decisions, international relations, and other vital state affairs.

An astute minister demonstrates sharpness, discernment and prudence in actions. Within the realm of confidentiality, such a minister recognizes the significance of protecting state secrets, including classified information, strategic plans and confidential communications. Disclosure of these could potentially compromise national security or strategic interests.

Maintaining the secrecy of state secrets acts as a protective shield for the state itself. By safeguarding sensitive information, the government can thwart adversaries and unauthorized entities from acquiring knowledge that may jeopardize national interests. This metaphorical shield serves to fortify the state against various internal and external threats.

The interconnectedness of these aspects underscores the crucial role of ministers in preserving the confidentiality of state secrets. Their adeptness in this area enhances the security and stability of the state by averting unauthorized access to sensitive information, which could otherwise be exploited to the detriment of national interests.

संविनीय मदक्रोधौ मानमीर्ष्यो च निर्वृताः।
नित्यं पञ्चोपधातीतैर्मन्त्रयेत् सह मन्त्रिभिः।।52।।

Saṃvinīya madakrodhau mānamīrṣyo ca nirvṛtāḥ.
Nityaṃ pañcopadhātītairmantrayet saha mantribhiḥ।।52।।[108]

Only those ministers who have overcome their ego and anger, are devoid of pride and jealousy, and have transcended all forms of deception—whether by deed, mental, physical, verbal or intentional—are deemed qualified to discuss state secrets.

Ego and anger, if unchecked, can distort judgement, leading to decisions driven by personal emotions rather than the state's welfare. Ministers who have transcended these traits are more likely to make objective decisions in the best interest of the country.

Similarly, pride and jealousy can foster biases and internal conflicts among ministers. Those who are free from these emotions are better positioned to collaborate effectively and prioritize the common good over personal agendas.

Deception in any form—whether through actions, thoughts, physical means, words or intentions—erodes trust and can manipulate state affairs. Ministers who have risen above these tendencies are perceived as trustworthy and dependable.

Possessing these qualities—lack of ego, anger, pride, jealousy and deception—is essential for ministers involved in discussions concerning state secrets. State secrets, critical to national security and policymaking, demand integrity, objectivity and trustworthiness from those handling them.

These points underscore the significance of moral and ethical virtues in governance, particularly when dealing with state secrets. Competence in governance must be accompanied by a high standard of personal integrity and ethical conduct for ministers to effectively contribute to national security and the country's well-being.

Essential Attributes and Qualifications for a Minister

धर्मशास्त्रार्थतत्त्वज्ञः सांधिविग्रहिको भवेत्।
मतिमान् धृतिमान् ह्रीमान् रहस्यविनिगूहिता।।85/30।।
कुलीनः सत्त्वसम्पन्नः शुक्लोऽमात्यः प्रशस्यते।
एतैरेव गुणैर्युक्तस्तथा सेनापतिर्भवेत्।।31।।

Dharmaśāstrārthatattvajñaḥ sāṃdhivigrahiko bhavet.
Matimān dhṛtimān hrīmān rahasyavinigūhitā।।85/30।।
Kulīnaḥ sattvasampannaḥ śuklo'mātyaḥ praśasyate.
Etaireva guṇairyuktastathā senāpatirbhavet।।31।।[109]

The superior minister is one who discerns the opportune moments for war, peace and diplomacy, possesses domain knowledge of politics and administration, demonstrates intelligence, patience and decorum, maintains secrecy and possesses a brave and pure heart.

कुलीनं शिक्षितं प्राज्ञं ज्ञानविज्ञानपारगम्।
सर्वशास्त्रार्थतत्त्वज्ञं सहिष्णुं देशजं तथा।।7।।

कृतज्ञं बलवन्तं च क्षान्तं दान्तं जितेन्द्रियम्।
अलुब्धं लब्धसंतुष्टं स्वामिमित्रबुभूषकम्।।8।।
सचिवं देशकालज्ञं सत्त्वसंग्रहणे रतम्।
सततं युक्तमनसं हितैषिणमतन्द्रितम्।।9।।
युक्तचारं स्वविषये संधिविग्रहकोविदम्।
राज्ञस्त्रिवर्गवेत्तारं पौरजानपदप्रियम्।।10।।
खातकव्यूहतत्त्वज्ञं बलहर्षणकोविदम्।
इङ्गिताकारतत्त्वज्ञं यात्राज्ञानविशारदम्।।11।।
हस्तिशिक्षासु तत्त्वज्ञमहंकारविवर्वितम्।
प्रगल्भं दक्षिणं दान्तं बलिनं युक्तकारिणम्।।12।।
चौक्षं चौक्षजनाकीर्णे सुमुखं सुखदर्शनम्।
नाकं नीतिकुशलं गुणचेष्टासमन्वितम्।।13।।
अस्तब्धं प्रश्रितं श्लक्ष्णं मृदुवादिनमेव च।
धीरं शूरं महर्द्धिं च देशकालोपपादकम्।।14।।

Kulīnaṃ śikṣitaṃ prājñaṃ jñānavijñānapāragam.
Sarvaśāstrārthatattvajñaṃ sahiṣṇuṃ deśajaṃ tathā।।7।।
Kṛtajñaṃ balavantaṃ ca kṣāntaṃ dāntaṃ jitendriyam.
Alubdhaṃ labdhasaṃtuṣṭaṃ svāmimitrabubhūṣakam।।8।।
Sacivaṃ deśakālajñaṃ sattvasaṃgrahaṇe ratam.
Satataṃ yuktamanasaṃ hitaiṣiṇamatandritam।।9।।
Yuktacāraṃ svaviṣaye saṃdhivigrahakovidam.
Rājñastrivargavettāraṃ paurajānapadapriyam।।10।।
Khātakavyūhatattvajñaṃ balaharṣaṇakovidam.
Iṅgitākāratattvajñaṃ yātrājñānaviśāradam।।11।।
Hastiśikṣāsu tattvajñamahaṃkāravivarvitam.
Pragalbhaṃ dakṣiṇaṃ dāntaṃ balinaṃ yuktakāriṇam।।12।।
Caukṣaṃ caukṣajanākīrṇe sumukhaṃ sukhadarśanam.
Nākaṃ nītikuśalaṃ guṇaceṣṭāsamanvitam।।13।।
Astabdhaṃ praśritaṃ ślakṣṇaṃ mṛduvādinameva ca.
Dhīraṃ śūraṃ maharddhiṃ ca deśakālopapādakam।।14।।[110]

A person appointed as a minister by the state must possess a multitude of qualities:
Qualified and learned, with proficiency in science and technology, as well as knowledge of politics and administration. Demonstrates tolerance towards diverse perspectives and is a native resident of the state.

Gratitude for opportunities and support, possessing authority and leadership capability, showing forgiveness towards mistakes and shortcomings, maintaining control over their mind and senses, embracing freedom from greed and personal agendas, and finding contentment with available resources are all attributes of a balanced and virtuous minister.

A good minister exhibits a desire for the progress of the state and its constituents, coupled with a deep familiarity with geography, time dynamics and situational awareness. They are proactive in resource acquisition for the state's welfare and maintain consistent mental discipline. A service-oriented approach towards people and the head of state defines their qualities.

A minister should remain free from lethargy and complacency, adept at navigating through war, peace and diplomacy, facilitating the advancement of both dharma and artha of the state, appreciated by rural and urban people alike.

The minister should be skilled in planning war strategy, proficient in organizing and empowering their forces, adept at discerning intentions through demeanour, and particularly shrewd in identifying opportune moments for defensive and offensive strategies.

The minister should possess knowledge of cavalry training methods, exhibit humility and fearlessness, demonstrate generosity, maintain discipline, showcase dedication to their responsibilities, uphold purity in actions and thoughts, and exhibit a serene demeanour.

The minister should maintain a cheerful countenance, possess a pleasing appearance, excel in strategic planning, and demonstrate exemplary qualities and unwavering commitment.

The minister should avoid arrogance, exhibit modesty, radiate warmth and kindness, display courage and synchronize their actions with the needs of the era and the realm.

विद्याविनीता ह्रीमन्तः कुशला नियतेन्द्रियाः।।6।।
श्रीमन्तश्च महात्मानः शस्त्रज्ञा दृढविक्रमाः।
कीर्तिमन्तः प्रणिहिता यथावचनकारिणः।।7।।
तेजःक्षमायशःप्राप्ताः स्मितपूर्वाभिभाषिणः।
क्रोधात् कामार्थहेतोर्वा न ब्रूयुरनृतं वचः।।8।।

Vidyāvinītā hrīmantaḥ kuśalā niyatendriyāḥ।।6।।
Śrīmantaśca mahātmānaḥ śastrajñā dṛḍhavikramāḥ.
Kīrtimantaḥ praṇihitā yathāvacanakāriṇaḥ।।7।।
Tejaḥkṣamāyaśaḥprāptāḥ smitapūrvābhibhāṣiṇaḥ.
Krodhāt kāmārthahetorvā na brūyuranṛtaṃ vacaḥ।।8।।[111]

The minister should always maintain modesty, owing to their learning, expertise in their domain, mastery over their mind, purity of soul, and proficiency in military sciences. They ought to exhibit unrelenting valour, caution in governance and adherence to the directives of the head of state. Furthermore, they must refrain from falsehoods, particularly when influenced by anger or self-interest.

अवेक्ष्यमाणश्चारेण प्रजा धर्मेण रक्षयन्।
प्रजानां पालनं कुर्वन्नधर्मं परिवर्जयन्।।21।।

Avekṣyamāṇaścāreṇa prajā dharmeṇa rakṣayan.
Prajānāṃ pālanaṃ kurvannadharmaṃ parivarjayan।।21।।[112]

The minister should keep a close watch on the affairs of the enemy state, ensuring that people are taken care of in accordance with dharma and rule, and they should distance themselves from adharma (unrighteousness).

तेषामविदितं किंचित् स्वेषु नास्ति परेषु वा।
क्रियमाणं कृतं वापि चारेणापि चिकीर्षितम्।।9।।

Teṣāmaviditaṃ kiṃcit sveṣu nāsti pareṣu vā.
Kriyamāṇaṃ kṛtaṃ vāpi cāreṇāpi cikīrṣitam।।9।।[113]

The minister should always be aware of the surroundings and the neighbouring enemy state. Nothing should be hidden from them regarding the activities of the neighbouring enemy state. They should be aware of what the neighbouring state has done, is doing or intends to do.

Ministers need a nuanced grasp of the broader geopolitical landscape, encompassing political, social and economic dynamics within their country and neighbouring states, alongside factors like military presence, alliances and potential threats. They must possess comprehensive knowledge about neighbouring enemy states, including their leadership, government functioning, military capabilities and strategic objectives. Access to accurate and timely intelligence is crucial for informed decision-making. Ministers should track neighbouring states' past actions, current engagements and future plans through diplomatic channels, intelligence gathering and analysis. They play a critical role in understanding the surrounding geopolitical environment, particularly concerning neighbouring enemy states, to formulate effective strategies for safeguarding national interests and security.

कुशला व्यवहारेषु सौहृदेषु परीक्षिताः।
प्राप्तकालं यथा दण्डं धारयेयुः सुतेष्वपि।।10।।

Kuśalā vyavahāreṣu sauhṛdeṣu parīkṣitāḥ.
Prāptakālaṃ yathā daṇḍaṃ dhārayeyuḥ suteṣvapi।।10।।[114]

The minister should be cordial in dealing with the public and should be tested on numerous occasions to determine their effectiveness in doing so. They should not hesitate to administer punishment, even to their family members and relatives.

वीराश्च नियतोत्साहा राजशास्त्रमनुष्ठिताः।
शुचीनां रक्षितारश्च नित्यं विषयवासिनाम्।।12।।

Vīrāśca niyatotsāhā rājaśāstramanuṣṭhitāḥ.
Śucīnāṃ rakṣitāraśca nityaṃ viṣayavāsinām।।12।।[115]

The minister should always be filled with valour and enthusiasm. They should act in accordance with the ethics of politics and administration, always protecting the virtuous people residing in their state.

अभितो गुणवन्तश्च न चासन् गुणवर्जिताः।
संधिविग्रहतत्त्वज्ञाः प्रकृत्या सम्पदान्विताः।।18।।

Abhito guṇavantaśca na cāsan guṇavarjitāḥ.
Saṃdhivigrahatattvajñāḥ prakṛtyā sampadānvitāḥ।।18।।[116]

The minister should consistently demonstrate qualifications and merit across all areas, without lacking virtues. They must be proficient in matters of war, peace and diplomacy, while naturally possessing virtuous and meritorious qualities.

मन्त्रसंवरणे शक्ताः शक्ताः सूक्ष्मासु बुद्धिषु।
नीतिशास्त्रविशेषज्ञाः सततं प्रियवादिनः।।19।।

Mantrasaṃvaraṇe śaktāḥ śaktāḥ sūkṣmāsu buddhiṣu.
Nītiśāstraviśeṣajñāḥ satataṃ priyavādinaḥ।।19।।[117]

The minister should be fully capable of maintaining the secrecy of deliberations, while also being adept in sharp reasoning and possessing deep knowledge of politics and administration. Additionally, they should always maintain a soft-spoken demeanour.

कच्चिदात्मसमाः शूराः श्रुतवन्तो जितेन्द्रियाः।
कुलीनाश्चेङ्गितज्ञाश्च कृतास्ते तात मन्त्रिणः।।14।।

Kaccidātmasamāḥ śūrāḥ śrutavanto jitendriyāḥ.
Kulīnāśceṅgitajñāśca kṛtāste tāta mantriṇaḥ।।14।।[118]

The minister should be learned, self-controlled and valiant, able to gauge the mindset of others through their expressions.

एकोऽप्यमात्यो मेधावी शूरो दक्षो विचक्षणः।
राजानं राजपुत्रं वा प्रापयेन्महतीं श्रियम्।।24।।

Eko'pyamātyo medhāvī śūro dakṣo vicakṣaṇaḥ.
Rājānaṃ rājaputraṃ vā prāpayenmahatīṃ śriyam।।24।।[119]

A talented, valiant, intelligent minister, well-versed in strategizing, can acquire immense wealth and resources for the state.

येषां वैनयिकी बुद्धिः प्रकृतिश्चैव शोभना।
तेजो धैर्यं क्षमा शौचमनुरागः स्थितिधृतिः।।21।।
परीक्ष्य च गुणान् नित्यं प्रौढभावान् धुरंधरान्।
पञ्चोपधाव्यतीतांश्च कुर्याद् राजार्थकारिणः।।22।।

Yeṣāṃ vainayikī buddhiḥ prakṛtiścaiva śobhanā.
Tejo dhairyaṃ kṣamā śaucamanurāgaḥ sthitidhṛtiḥ।।21।।
Parīkṣya ca guṇān nityaṃ prauḍhabhāvān dhuraṃdharān.
Pañcopadhāvyatītāṃśca kuryād rājārthakāriṇaḥ।।22।।1[120]

Individuals possessing knowledge, wisdom, intelligence, bravery, forgiveness, purity and steadfastness should be evaluated for their suitability for state responsibilities. From this group, the head of state should select five mature and forthright individuals to appoint them as finance ministers.

A specific set of essential qualities is deemed necessary for individuals considered for state responsibilities, particularly as finance ministers. These qualities encompass a deep understanding gained through education, experience and continuous learning, focusing on economic principles, fiscal policies and financial markets.

They require the ability to apply knowledge judiciously, demonstrating sound judgement, foresight and the capacity to make informed decisions for the long-term benefit of the state. Cognitive abilities such as analytical skills and a knack for understanding complex issues are crucial, involving strategic thinking, problem solving and adaptability within financial contexts.

Moral courage plays a significant role, demanding the willingness to make tough but necessary decisions for the economic health of the state and to stand firm against challenges and criticism. It involves overcoming personal biases and focusing solely on the nation's financial well-being, learning from past errors to move forward constructively.

Integrity is paramount—commitment to ethical behaviour and transparency in financial matters ensures no conflict of interest interferes with public duties. Reliability and consistency are equally vital, necessitating perseverance in decision-making aligned with principles and goals despite external pressures.

Evaluation of individuals possessing these qualities is essential for state responsibilities, particularly as finance ministers. A recommended approach involves selecting five mature and forthright individuals who are emotionally and intellectually equipped to handle the complexities and pressures of public office with composure and stability.

These individuals are characterized by honesty, directness and transparency in actions and communications, fostering open dialogue on financial matters and policies for public accountability. Appointing such individuals as finance ministers is critical, as these roles demand not only technical expertise in finance and economics but also a strong ethical foundation and the ability to prioritize the country's best interests.

By prioritizing these qualities in the selection process, effective governance and responsible management of the state's financial affairs are ensured, contributing to overall national prosperity and stability.

Not Qualified for the Position of a Minister

अनभिज्ञाय शास्त्रार्थान् पुरुषाः पशुबुद्धयः।
प्रागल्भ्याद् वक्तुमिच्छन्ति मन्त्रिष्वभ्यन्तरीकृताः।।14।।

Anabhijñāya śāstrārthān puruṣāḥ paśubuddhayaḥ.
Prāgalbhyād vaktumicchanti mantriṣvabhyantarīkṛtāḥ।।14।।[121]

Individuals lacking qualifications, knowledge and wisdom, yet boastful, have somehow been included among the ministers, rendering them unsuitable for their ministerial roles.

In any government or administration, ministers shoulder significant responsibilities in shaping policies, making decisions and overseeing crucial sectors vital to the country's functioning. They are expected to possess specific qualifications, expertise and a profound understanding of their respective fields, encompassing economic principles, social dynamics, legal frameworks and administrative procedures.

Ministers lacking essential knowledge and expertise may struggle to grasp intricate issues and to make well-informed decisions. This, in turn, can result in ineffective governance and suboptimal policy outcomes, which detrimentally impact the country's progress and stability. Incompetence in ministerial roles can lead to mismanagement, inefficiencies, delays and potential harm to public interests.

Individuals assuming ministerial roles without requisite qualifications may prioritize personal ambitions or agendas at the expense of broader public welfare. This bias can manifest in decisions influenced by favouritism or divergence from national priorities.

The appointment of unqualified individuals to ministerial positions risks eroding public trust in the government's capacity to manage public affairs effectively. Such appointments often provoke skepticism, criticism and unrest among the populace, undermining confidence in governmental integrity and competence.

Therefore, ministers lacking the necessary qualifications should be promptly relieved of their ministerial responsibilities to safeguard effective governance and restore public trust in the government's credibility and commitment to sound governance practices.

अशास्त्रविदुषां तेषां कार्यं नाभिहितं वचः।'
अर्थशास्त्रनभिज्ञानां विपुलां श्रियमिच्छताम्।।15।।

Aśāstraviduṣāṃ teṣāṃ kāryaṃ nābhihitaṃ vacaḥ.
Arthaśāstranabhijñānāṃ vipulāṃ śriyamicchatām।।15।।[122]

Individuals lacking qualifications, knowledge and expertise in economics, politics and administration yet seeking immense wealth, should not be considered suitable for ministerial posts, and their advice should not be given any attention.

Individuals lacking qualifications, knowledge and expertise in economics, politics and administration yet driven primarily by the pursuit of immense wealth, are inherently unsuitable for ministerial positions in any government or administration. Ministerial roles necessitate a profound grasp of economic principles and dynamics, given that economic decisions profoundly impact a nation's prosperity, stability and welfare.

Without a solid foundation in economics, politics and administration, such individuals may struggle to grasp the complexities of economic issues, devise effective policies or make informed decisions that benefit society at large. Their motivations centred on personal gain rather than public welfare can result in biased decision-making, favouritism towards vested interests or policies prioritizing short-term gains over long-term economic sustainability.

Furthermore, advice from individuals lacking economics, politics and administration qualifications should not hold significant sway in governmental decision-making processes. Sound economics counsel is essential for crafting policies that foster economic growth, manage risks and ensure equitable resource distribution. Advice based on superficial understanding or influenced by personal financial interests can lead to misguided policies that undermine economic stability and worsen social inequalities. Such ministers should be removed from the government.

Rule of Law and Justice Are Paramount in the Superior State

दण्डे स्थिताः प्रजाः सर्वाः।।43।।

Daṇḍe sthitāḥ prajāḥ sarvāḥ ।।43।।[123]

The rule of law, justice and their enforcement uphold society.

The rule of law, justice and their enforcement form the backbone of a stable and orderly society. They provide a framework for resolving conflicts, protecting individual rights and promoting the common good. Without these principles and mechanisms in place, societies are susceptible to chaos, injustice and the arbitrary exercise of power.

दण्डे सर्वं प्रतिष्ठितम्।।1।।

Daṇḍe sarvaṃ pratiṣṭhitam।।1।।[124]

Everything is instituted within the rule of law, justice and its enforcement.

यस्माददान्तान् दमयत्यशिष्टान् दण्डयत्यपि।।8।।

Yasmādadāntān damayatyaśiṣṭān daṇḍayatyapi।।8।।[125]

The rule of law and justice, along with their enforcement, discipline the undisciplined and control and punish rogues in society.

The rule of law, when properly enforced, acts as a bulwark against chaos, ensuring that society operates in a manner that is fair, just and orderly. It disciplines those who would seek to disrupt this order and controls and punishes those who flout its principles, thereby safeguarding the rights and freedoms of all members of society.

सर्वो दण्डजितो लोको दुर्लभो हि शुचिर्जनः।।34।।

Sarvo daṇḍajito loko durlabho hi śucirjanaḥ।।34।।[126]

The rule of law and justice, along with their enforcement, discipline everyone to follow the right conduct.

दण्डः प्रजा रक्षति साधुः नीतः।।31।।

Daṇḍaḥ prajā rakṣati sādhuḥ nītaḥ।।31।।[127]

The proper application of the rule of law, justice and their enforcement protects the people of the state.

दण्डेन नीयते चेदं दण्डं नयति वा पुनः।।78।।

Daṇḍena nīyate cedaṃ daṇḍaṃ nayati vā punaḥ।।78।।[128]

According to the doctrine of the rule of law and justice, along with its enforcement, order and discipline are established in society.

दण्डः शास्ति प्रजाः सर्वा दण्ड एवाभिरक्षति।
दण्डः सुप्तेषु जागर्ति दण्डं धर्मं विदुर्बुधाः।।2।।

Daṇḍaḥ śāsti prajāḥ sarvā daṇḍa evābhirakṣati.
Daṇḍaḥ supteṣu jāgarti daṇḍaṃ dharmaṃ vidurbudhāḥ।।2।।[129]

The state should always protect its people through the rule of law and justice, ensuring their enforcement to safeguard everyone. Even while people sleep, the rule of law and justice remains active. Therefore, wise individuals have proclaimed that the rule of law and justice is the dharma of the state.

The state bears the responsibility of safeguarding rights, freedoms and overall welfare by applying laws equally to all individuals, including those in power, ensuring no one is above the law. It ensures predictability, fairness and accountability in governance. Justice involves fair treatment, ensuring individuals receive what is due according to the law, encompassing equality, access to legal remedies and protection from discrimination. Laws and justice must not merely exist on paper but be actively enforced to maintain order and protect citizens from harm or injustice.

The protection provided by the rule of law and justice is constant, even when people are not actively engaged in societal affairs, such as when they sleep, underscoring the state's commitment to upholding these principles unwaveringly and consistently. The dharma of the state emphasizes its moral obligation to uphold these principles for citizens' well-being and societal order. The state plays a vital role in ensuring the protection and well-being of its people through the consistent application and enforcement of laws and justice, framing this responsibility as a moral imperative inherent to governance.

दण्डः संरक्षते धर्मं तथैवार्थं जनाधिप।
कामं संरक्षते दण्डस्त्रिवर्गो दण्ड उच्यते।।3।।

Daṇḍaḥ saṃrakṣate dharmaṃ tathaivārthaṃ janādhipa.
Kāmaṃ saṃrakṣate daṇḍastrivargo daṇḍa ucyate।।3।।[130]

The rule of law and justice, along with their enforcement, protect dharma, artha and kama. It is said that the rule of law and justice, along with its enforcement, embodies the concept of trivarga, which consists of dharma, artha and kama.

The rule of law and justice serve to protect and uphold the principles of dharma, artha and kama within society. They ensure that individuals can pursue their dharma, as well as their material wealth and prosperity (artha) and desires (kama), without infringing upon the rights and well-being of others. In this way, they contribute to the overall balance and harmony of society.

दण्डनीत्यां यदा राजा सम्यक् कात्स्न्येंन वर्तते।
तदा कृतयुगं नाम कालसृष्टं प्रवर्तते।।80।।

Daṇḍanītyāṃ yadā rājā samyak kārtsnyena vartate.
Tadā kṛtayugaṃ nāma kālasṛṣṭaṃ pravartate।।80।।[131]

When the rule of law, justice and its enforcement are properly and fully applied in the state, the Satya Yuga (Age of Truth) commences in its full manifestation.

लोकस्य सीमन्तकरी मर्यादा लोकभाविनी।
सम्यङ्नीता दण्डनीतिर्यथा माता यथा पिता।।103।।

Lokasya sīmantakarī maryādā lokabhāvinī.
Samyaṅnītā daṇḍanītiryathā mātā yathā pitā।।103।।[132]

The rule of law and justice, along with their enforcement, are akin to a parent protecting their child. Similarly, they safeguard society and establish orderly discipline within it.

अन्धे तमसि मज्जेयुर्यदि दण्डो न पालयेत्।।7।।

Andhe tamasi majjeyuryadi daṇḍo na pālayet।।7।।[133]

Without the rule of law, justice and enforcement in the state,
society will descend into lawlessness,
causing chaos for its inhabitants.

When the rule of law, justice and their enforcement are absent or weak within a state, society becomes vulnerable to lawlessness. Without the rule of law, justice and effective enforcement, there's little to prevent chaos and disorder from taking hold. This can manifest in various forms, including rampant crime, corruption, violence and an erosion of trust in institutions. Ultimately, the stability and well-being of society depend on these fundamental pillars—the rule of law, justice and their enforcement—being firmly in place.

शिष्ट्यर्थं विहितो दण्डो न वधार्थं विधीयते।
ये च शिष्टान्प्रबाधन्ते धर्मस्तेषां वधः स्मृतः।।20।।

śiṣṭyarthaṃ vihito daṇḍo na vadhārthaṃ vidhīyate|
ye ca śiṣṭānprabādhante dharmasteṣāṃ vadhaḥ smṛtaḥ ||20||[134]

The rule of law and its enforcement are intended for the wicked and rogue, not for the purpose of accumulating wealth for the state. Those who torment the righteous deserve the ultimate punishment, including death.

Ensuring Non-Corruption of the Rule of Law and the Justice System Is Imperative for a Fair and Just Society

व्यसने कच्चिदाढ्यस्य दुर्बलस्य च राघव।
अर्थं विरागाः पश्यन्ति तवामात्या बहुश्रुताः।।58।।

Vyasane kaccidāḍhyasya durbalasya ca rāghava.
Arthaṃ virāgāḥ paśyanti tavāmātyā bahuśrutāḥ।।58।।[135]

In the event of a dispute between a wealthy individual and a poor and weak one, which is brought before the court or justice system for resolution, learned judges, forsaking greed for wealth and disregarding bribes, should impartially deliberate on the matter.

In the scenario where two parties, one wealthy and the other poor and weak, are embroiled in conflict and seek resolution through the legal system, the significance of judges being impartial and unbiased in their decision-making process cannot be overstated. Irrespective of the social status or wealth of the parties involved, judges are anticipated to apply the law objectively and fairly. It is imperative for judges to resist any external influences that could sway their judgement, such as bribery or personal gain. They are entrusted with the responsibility of upholding the law and administering justice without being influenced by monetary incentives or personal interests. This underscores the principle of equality before the law, regardless of socioeconomic status, and emphasizes the importance of integrity and impartiality in the judiciary to ensure a fair and just legal system.

The State Should Prioritize and Ensure the Well-being of Its People

गुणसाधनसंदक्षः स्वप्रजायाः पिता यथा।
क्षमयित्र्यपराधानां माता पुष्टिविधायिनी।।78।।

Guṇasādhanasaṃdakṣaḥ svaprajāyāḥ pitā yathā.
Kṣamayitryaparādhānāṃ mātā puṣṭividhāyinī।।78।।[136]

The parents excel in guiding their children towards excellence. Similarly, the state should be proficient and capable of nurturing excellence among its populace. The state should emulate a caring mother who forgives her children's minor mistakes and nurtures them.

Parents play a pivotal role in shaping their children's character, values and skills, providing guidance, support and encouragement for excellence in various life aspects. Similarly, the state should foster an environment conducive to its people's growth and development, offering quality education, healthcare, infrastructure and opportunities for personal and professional advancement. Embracing a nurturing stance akin to that of a caring mother, the state should refrain from employing excessive punitive measures for minor infractions, prioritizing rehabilitation, education and empowerment to deter future mistakes and encourage positive conduct. Actively nurturing growth, development and well-being, the state ought to invest in policies and programmes empowering individuals to realize their full potential, fulfil aspirations and contribute meaningfully to society.

परचक्राटवीग्रस्तं व्याधिदुर्भिक्षपीडितम्।

Paracakrāṭavīgrastaṃ vyādhidurbhikṣapīḍitam.[137]

The head of state should strive to protect their nation from enemies, rogue individuals, diseases, famines and predatory animals.

The head of state bears the responsibility of safeguarding the nation against external threats emanating from hostile nations, terrorist organizations or entities aiming to undermine stability, security or sovereignty. Simultaneously, they must address internal threats posed by individuals engaged in criminal activities such as terrorism or organized crime. Collaborating with law enforcement agencies, the head of state ensures the maintenance of law and order and the apprehension of rogue elements to forestall harm to the state and its people.

Disease outbreaks, including pandemics, present substantial challenges to public health with far-reaching social and economic ramifications. Therefore, prioritizing preventative detection and response measures becomes imperative for the head of state. Famine, often resulting from drought, crop failure or conflict, can trigger widespread hunger and malnutrition. It is incumbent upon the head of state to implement policies ensuring food security through measures such as food distribution programmes and humanitarian aid.

Furthermore, in certain regions, predatory animals threaten human lives, livestock and agricultural endeavours. To mitigate these risks, the head of state should endorse strategies for managing human–wildlife conflicts, including wildlife conservation, habitat preservation, community-based initiatives and compensation schemes for affected farmers.

The State Should Protect Its People and Prevent Them from Developing or Falling into Harmful Habits

देशं परिहरेद्राजा व्ययक्रीडाश्च वारयेत्।।

Deśaṃ pariharedrājā vyayakrīḍāśca vārayet.[138]

The head of state should strive to discourage unnecessary and unproductive games, sports activities and superfluous luxury that waste time and resources.

National leaders should prioritize their country's well-being and prosperity, discouraging activities they deem wasteful or harmful. They should advocate against squandering time and resources on unproductive games and sports, and intervene to prevent such misuse. Leaders must also discourage unnecessary luxury and hedonism, which can detract from meaningful pursuits and exacerbate social inequalities. By protecting the people from overindulgence in unproductive leisure activities, leaders emphasize the importance of focusing on the nation's long-term prosperity and well-being.

The State Should Care for the Helpless, Women and Children

विधवानाथविकलान् कृपणांश्च बभार सः।।11।।

Vidhavānāthavikalān kṛpaṇāṃśca babhāra saḥ।।11।।[139]

The state should take care of widows, orphans, the disabled, and the destitute.

The state bears the responsibility of providing support and assistance to vulnerable segments of society. Widows, who are often financially reliant on their spouses, encounter social and economic hurdles alongside the loss of income and support networks. In response, the state can extend aid through financial assistance, social services and programmes facilitating their reintegration.

Children, who have been orphaned and lack parental care, face significant vulnerability. The state plays a pivotal role in securing their fundamental needs such as shelter, food, education and healthcare, alongside additional support services to aid in their adjustment.

Individuals with disabilities encounter various impairments that inhibit full societal engagement. The state must ensure their equal access to resources, spanning employment, education, healthcare, transportation and social services. This entails enacting anti-discrimination legislation, offering disability benefits, enhancing public space accessibility and fostering inclusive policies.

The destitute, encompassing the severely impoverished, lack necessities like food, shelter and clothing, potentially due to homelessness, unemployment or marginalization. Addressing poverty and social inequity, the state implements policies and programmes to alleviate hardship, furnish social safety nets and stimulate economic prospects. Welfare aid, affordable housing endeavours, job training initiatives and measures addressing poverty's root causes, such as educational and healthcare disparities, feature in this approach.

The overarching principle asserts the state as a safety net, ensuring no one is neglected, and all individuals have access to the support essential for a dignified living and holistic community participation.

अभृतानां च भरणं भृतानां चान्ववेक्षणम्।
अर्थस्य काले दानं च व्यसने चाप्रसङ्गिता।।54।।

Abhṛtānāṃ ca bharaṇaṃ bhṛtānāṃ cānvavekṣaṇam.
Arthasya kāle dānaṃ ca vyasane cāprasaṅgitā।।54।।[140]

The state should make arrangements for the subsistence of those without means, while also providing support to those whose subsistence is arranged by the state. Additionally, the state should donate wealth periodically to people who rely on state-provided subsistence. Furthermore, preventive measures should be taken to ensure that individuals do not become addicts.

The state has a responsibility to ensure that basic needs such as food, shelter and healthcare are provided for individuals who are unable to afford them on their own. This could include programmes such as welfare, free food, public housing and healthcare subsidies. Even those who receive assistance from the state should be supported further, possibly through additional services or resources to help them improve their quality of life beyond mere subsistence. This could include job training programmes, educational opportunities and other necessary services.

The state periodically provides financial assistance to individuals who rely on state-provided subsistence, helping to alleviate financial strain or provide opportunities for advancement. It emphasizes the importance of addressing social issues such as addiction before they become pervasive problems. This could involve education and awareness campaigns, access to addiction treatment programmes and regulations on substances such as alcohol and drugs.

This approach reflects a commitment to ensuring social justice and equity by providing support to those in need, while also addressing underlying issues that perpetuate poverty and inequality. It underscores the importance of both individual and collective responsibility in creating a more just society.

वृद्धबालधनं रक्ष्यमन्धस्य कृपणस्य च।
न खातपूर्वं कुर्वीत न रुदन्ती धनं हरेत्।।25।।

Vṛddhabāladhanaṃ rakṣyamandhasya kṛpaṇasya ca.
Na khātapūrvaṃ kurvīta na rudantī dhanaṃ haret।।25।।[141]

The state should protect the wealth of the elderly, minors, weak, indigent and blind individuals. It should not take their wealth. When there is no rainfall and people dig wells and somehow irrigate to grow grain and thereby survive, the state should not take their wealth, nor should it take wealth from a crying woman in distress.

The state has a duty to safeguard the wealth and well-being of those who are particularly vulnerable—specifically the old, young, weak, indigent (poor) and blind individuals. These groups are often more susceptible to exploitation or neglect, so the state should ensure they are not deprived of their wealth or resources. A crying woman in distress signifies a broader commitment to protecting the vulnerable and ensuring that their wealth or resources are not unjustly taken away.

During times of adversity, such as droughts when there is no rainfall, people may resort to digging wells and irrigating their land to grow crops like grain to survive. In such situations, the state should refrain from taking away the wealth or resources these individuals have managed to gather through their own efforts. This underscores the principle that self-sufficiency efforts should be respected and not undermined by state intervention.

A state that acts as a guardian of social justice, protecting those who are at risk or facing hardship, and refraining from actions that would exacerbate their plight or undermine their efforts to sustain themselves, reflects a moral stance on the responsibilities of governance towards its most vulnerable citizens.

हृतं कृपणवित्तं हि राष्ट्रं हन्ति नृपश्रियम्।
दद्याच्च महतो भोगान् क्षुद्भयं प्रणुदेत् सताम्।।26।।

Hṛtaṃ kṛpaṇavittaṃ hi rāṣṭraṃ hanti nṛpaśriyam.
Dadyācca mahato bhogān kṣudbhayaṃ praṇudet satām।।26।।[142]

The state should not confiscate the wealth of indigent persons. Instead, it should provide them with adequate provisions and commodities and ensure that no one experiences the pain of hunger.

The role of the state in supporting its most vulnerable members, particularly those who are indigent or impoverished, hinges on a fundamental responsibility to protect and uplift them rather than stripping away whatever meagre wealth or resources they may possess. The state's duty lies in safeguarding and assisting these individuals, ensuring they have access to essential goods and services necessary for a decent standard of living, including adequate nutrition to prevent hunger.

Moreover, this necessitates comprehensive social welfare policies that extend beyond mere sustenance to encompass essentials like shelter, healthcare and education. These measures aim not only to alleviate immediate needs but also to empower individuals, enabling them to escape the cycle of poverty.

By meeting these basic needs, the state not only restores dignity to those in poverty but also fosters their fuller participation in society. This approach advocates for a compassionate and proactive role for the state in combating poverty and inequality, prioritizing the assurance of basic necessities over mere redistribution of minimal individual resources.

Oppression of People by the State Is Forbidden

कच्चिन्नोग्रेण दण्डेन भृशमुद्विजसे प्रजाः।
राष्ट्रं तवानुशासन्ति मन्त्रिणो भरतर्षभ॥45॥

Kaccinnogreṇa daṇḍena bhṛśamudvijase prajāḥ.
Rāṣṭraṃ tavānuśāsanti mantriṇo bharatarṣabha॥45॥[143]

कच्चिन्नोग्रेण दण्डेन भृशमुद्वेजिताः प्रजाः।
राष्ट्रे तवावजानन्ति मन्त्रिणः कैकयीसुत॥27॥

Kaccinnogreṇa daṇḍena bhṛśamudvejitāḥ prajāḥ.
Rāṣṭre tavāvajānanti mantriṇaḥ kaikayīsuta॥27॥[144]

The state should not oppress its people through harsh punishment.
Ministers should govern the state with fairness and justice.

The state should refrain from using excessive or disproportionate force or punishment against its people. Historically, oppressive regimes have employed brutal methods such as torture, executions or imprisonment to control dissent or maintain power. However, this approach not only violates human rights but also undermines social cohesion and stability. Instead, a just and humane approach to law enforcement and punishment is advocated, which focuses on rehabilitation, accountability and respect for human dignity.

The importance of governance based on principles of fairness, equality and justice is paramount. Ministers, as representatives of the government, are entrusted with the responsibility of upholding the rule of law and ensuring that all citizens are treated equitably. Fair governance involves impartiality, transparency and accountability in decision-making processes, as well as the protection of individual rights and freedoms. Justice entails not only the fair application of laws but also addressing systemic inequalities and meeting the needs of marginalized or disadvantaged groups within society.

Together, these principles advocate for a form of governance that respects the rights and dignity of individuals, promotes social harmony and fosters trust and cooperation between the state and its people. By upholding fairness, justice and respect for human rights, governments can build stronger, more inclusive societies and contribute to the well-being and prosperity of all members of the community.

अर्थमूलोऽपि हिंसां च कुरुते स्वयमात्मनः।
करैरशास्त्रदृष्टैर्हि मोहात् सम्पीडयन् प्रजाः।।5।।

Arthamūlo'pi hiṃsāṃ ca kurute svayamātmanaḥ.
Karairaśāstradṛṣṭairhi mohāt sampīḍayan prajāḥ।।5।।[145]

The state should not oppress its people by extracting excessive taxes, as this undermines the prescribed rules and ultimately leads to the destruction of the state.

Taxes are crucial for financing defence and essential services such as education, healthcare and infrastructure. However, when state authority is exercised unjustly through oppressive and unfair tax policies, it contradicts established societal principles and legal frameworks, including constitutions. Excessive taxation can erode public trust in the government, lead to economic stagnation and provoke social unrest, ultimately weakening or collapsing the state. When people feel excessively burdened by taxes without seeing corresponding benefits, or when taxes are perceived as unfair, it undermines the stability and legitimacy of the government. While taxation is necessary for a state's functioning, it must be fair and reasonable. Excessive taxation that oppresses the people violates governance rules and can have detrimental consequences for the state's stability and longevity.

व्यङ्गत्वं च शरीरस्य वधो नाल्पस्य कारणात्।
शरीरपीडास्तास्ताश्च देहत्यागो विवासनम्।।41।।

Vyaṅgatvaṃ ca śarīrasya vadho nālpasya kāraṇāt.
Śarīrapīḍāstāstāśca dehatyāgo vivāsanam।।41।।[146]

For minor mistakes made by its people, a state should not resort to mutilation, execution or various forms of torture. Furthermore, compelling someone to give up their life or expelling them from the state is entirely unacceptable.

The principle of proportionality and humane treatment within a state's justice system dictates that punishments for minor infractions should be appropriate and not excessive. Extreme forms of punishment, such as mutilation, execution or torture, violate basic human rights and dignity and should never be used by the state for minor infractions. Forcing individuals into situations that endanger their lives is both morally and ethically wrong. This principle also applies to the unjust practice of forcibly removing citizens from their homes without compelling reasons, which deprives them of their right to belong to a community or nation. Advocates call for a justice system that is fair, proportionate and respectful of individuals' inherent dignity and rights, even when addressing their mistakes or offences. Such a system aims to correct behaviour and uphold justice without resorting to extreme and inhumane measures.

The State Should Appropriately Reward Its Employees

कच्चित् पुरुषकारेण पुरुषः कर्म शोभयन्।
लभते मानमधिकं भूयो वा भक्तवेतनम्।।53।।

Kaccit puruṣakāreṇa puruṣaḥ karma śobhayan.
Labhate mānamadhikaṃ bhūyo vā bhaktavetanam।।53।।[147]

Given the exceptional merit of the employee in his responsibilities and accomplishments, he should be rewarded by the state with an increased salary and additional bonuses.

कच्चिद् दारान्मनुष्याणां तवार्थे मृत्युमीयुषाम्।
व्यसनं चाभ्युपेतानां बिभर्षि भरतर्षभ।।55।।

Kaccid dārānmanuṣyāṇāṃ tavārthe mṛtyumīyuṣām.
Vyasanaṃ cābhyupetānāṃ bibharṣi bharatarṣabha।।55।।[148]

The state should protect the wives and children of employees who have sacrificed their lives or encountered trouble while serving the state.

The state bears the responsibility of providing support and protection to the families of individuals who have dedicated their lives to serving it and have either lost their lives or encountered significant trouble in the line of duty. It acknowledges that the families of these employees, particularly their spouses and children, may face challenges and vulnerabilities as a result of their loved one's service-related sacrifices or troubles. Thus, the state should offer assistance, care and resources to these families. This assistance can encompass financial aid, educational benefits, healthcare coverage, housing assistance and other forms of support aimed at helping them cope with their loss or overcome the challenges they encounter. It is a moral obligation and a social contract between the state and its employees, recognizing and honouring their sacrifices by ensuring that their families are cared for and protected in times of need.

The State Should Provide Appropriate Salaries to Its Employees

कच्चिते सम्भृता भृत्याः कच्चित् तिष्ठन्ति शासने।।8।।

Kaccite sambhṛtā bhṛtyāḥ kaccit tiṣṭhanti śāsane।।8।।[149]

The state should ensure that employees' salaries are paid in a timely and accurate manner.

अवश्यपोष्यवर्गस्य भरणं भृतकाद्भवेत्।
तथा भृतिस्तु संयोज्या यद्योग्या भृतकाय वै।।382।।

Avaśyapoṣyavargasya bharaṇaṃ bhṛtakādbhavet.
Tathā bhṛtistu saṃyojyā yadyogyā bhṛtakāya vai।।382।।[150]

Employees should receive salaries that enable them to care for their parents and other family members.

Ensuring that employees receive salaries that enable them to care for their parents and other family members is fundamentally about recognizing and supporting the holistic well-being of individuals within the workforce. Adequate salaries are essential for providing financial stability not only for the employees but also for their dependents. A salary that covers basic needs, healthcare expenses and additional costs associated with caring for family members is crucial for alleviating financial stress and ensuring the employees can fulfil their familial obligations without sacrificing their own well-being.

यथा यथा तु गुणवान् भृतकस्तद् भृतिस्तथा।
संयोज्या तु प्रयत्नेन नृपेणात्महिताय वै।।381।।

Yathā yathā tu guṇavān bhṛtakastad bhṛtistathā.
Saṃyojyā tu prayatnena nṛpeṇātmahitāya vai।।381।।[151]

The state should strive to increase the wages of employees as soon as they demonstrate merit or pay them according to their abilities.

अष्टमांशं पारितोष्यं दद्याद् भृत्याय वत्सरे।
कार्याष्टमांशं वा दद्यात्कार्यं द्रागधिकं कृतम्।।395।।

Aṣṭamāṃśaṃ pāritoṣyaṃ dadyād bhṛtyāya vatsare.
Kāryāṣṭamāṃśaṃ vā dadyātkāryaṃ drāgadhikaṃ kṛtam।।395।।[152]

The state should provide an annual bonus equivalent to one-eighth of the employee's wages. Moreover, if the employee efficiently completes additional work, they should be entitled to one-eighth of their wages as a reward for their diligence.

Preference for Qualified and Knowledgeable Individuals

कच्चित् सहस्त्रैर्मूर्खाणामेकमिच्छसि पण्डितम्।
पण्डितो ह्यर्थकृच्छ्रेषु कुर्यान्निःश्रेयसं महत्।।22।।

Kaccit sahastrairmūrkhāṇāmekamicchasi paṇḍitam.
Paṇḍito hyarthakṛcchreṣu kuryānniḥśreyasaṃ mahat।।22।।[153]

The state should prioritize a single learned and knowledgeable individual over thousands of illiterate fools, as such individuals can greatly contribute during an economic crisis.

The state should prioritize the expertise and knowledge of individuals over the collective ignorance of many. Instead of relying on the opinions of a large number of uneducated or ill-informed people, the emphasis should be on individuals who possess knowledge, expertise and education. Educated individuals can propel innovation, economic growth and social progress, ultimately benefiting the state and its people in various ways beyond crisis management. The significance of prioritizing knowledge and expertise in governance, particularly in managing crises, where informed decision-making is crucial for effective response and recovery, cannot be overstated.

State: A Complex and Massive Structure

राज्यं हि सुमहत् तन्त्रं धार्यते नाकृतात्मभिः।
न शक्यं मृदुना वोढुमायासस्थानमुत्तमम्॥21॥

Rājyaṃ hi sumahat tantraṃ dhāryate nākṛtātmabhiḥ.
Na śakyaṃ mṛdunā voḍhumāyāsasthānamuttamam॥21॥[154]

The state is a massive establishment. Ministers lacking self-control cannot effectively manage such an extensive institution. Similarly, those who are soft natured cannot withstand its immense pressure; governance becomes an overwhelming entanglement for them.

The state, encompassing various institutions, departments and branches responsible for governance, is often described as 'massive' due to its complexity and multitude of responsibilities. Without self-control, ministers may succumb to impulses, emotions or external influences, leading to erratic or inconsistent decision-making. Such lack of control within the context of managing a vast establishment like the state can result in chaos, inefficiency or even corruption.

While soft-natured individuals possess valuable qualities in interpersonal relationships, they may not always be well suited for the rigours of governance within a large government system. The immense pressure and complexity of the state can easily overwhelm those who are too gentle or emotionally vulnerable. The complexities, challenges and demands of governance become excessively burdensome for individuals lacking the necessary toughness, assertiveness or resilience, leaving them entangled in political maneuvering or unable to meet the demands of various stakeholders effectively.

The importance of leaders in government possessing a balanced set of qualities is paramount: self-control to manage themselves and the institutions they oversee effectively, and resilience to withstand the pressures and challenges inherent in governing a vast and complex entity like the state.

राज्यं सर्वामिषं नित्यमार्जवेनेह धार्यते।।22।।

Rājyaṃ sarvāmiṣaṃ nityamārjaveneha dhāryate।।22।।[155]

The state exists for the benefit of everyone. It can only be managed effectively through humility.

The fundamental principle of states and their governance is through institutions comprising legislatures, executives, judiciaries and administration. The state formulates and enforces laws and policies to serve the interests and well-being of its people, ensuring safety, security, justice and the promotion of the common good. All individuals within the state's jurisdiction, irrespective of their social status or ethnicity, are entitled to equal treatment. The state's actions and policies should aim to benefit all members of society equally, without discrimination or favouritism, balancing the protection of individual rights and freedoms with the promotion of the common good. This involves navigating complex ethical and political dilemmas to achieve a just and equitable society.

Governance involves complex decision-making processes that impact diverse segments of society. Humility in governance acknowledges the limitations of individual understanding and the complexity of societal issues. It requires leaders to approach their roles with a sense of modesty, recognizing that they do not possess all the answers or solutions. Instead, they must listen to diverse perspectives, learn from the experiences of others and be open to feedback and criticism. Humble leadership fosters collaboration, inclusivity and a willingness to adapt in the face of changing circumstances.

अमात्या बुद्धिसम्पन्ना राष्ट्रं बहुजनप्रियम्।
दुराधर्षे पुरश्रेष्ठं कोशः कृच्छ्रसहः स्मृतः।।
अनुरक्तं बलं साम्नामद्वैधं मित्रमेव च।
एताः प्रकृतयः स्वेषु स्वामी विनयतत्त्ववित्।।

Amātyā buddhisampannā rāṣṭraṃ bahujanapriyam.
Durādharṣe puraśreṣṭhaṃ kośaḥ kṛcchrasahaḥ smṛtaḥ.

Anuraktaṃ balaṃ sāmnāmadvaidhaṃ mitrameva ca.
Etāḥ prakṛtayaḥ sveṣu svāmī vinayatattvavit.[156]

स्वाम्यमात्यसुहृत्कोशराष्ट्रदुर्गबलानि च।
सप्ताङ्गमुच्यते राज्यं तत्र मूर्धा नृपः स्मृतः।।61।।
दृगमात्यः सुहृच्छोत्रं मुखं कोशो बलं मनः।
हस्तौ पादौ दुर्गराष्ट्रौ राज्याङ्गानि स्मृतानि हि।।62।।

Svāmyamātyasuhṛtkośarāṣṭradurgabalāni ca.
Saptāṅgamucyate rājyaṃ tatra mūrdhā nṛpaḥ smṛtaḥ।।61।।
Dṛgamātyaḥ suhṛcchotraṃ mukhaṃ kośo balaṃ manaḥ.
Hastau pādau durgarāṣṭrau rājyāṅgāni smṛtāni hi।।62।।[157]

Seven important aspects for states include: a country beloved by patriots, wise ministers, a treasury that proves useful in crises, a committed army always ready to defend the state, well-fortified defences, friendly states that stand in support without hesitation in any circumstance, and a head of state who understands the principle of humility and is committed to the state's betterment.

Seven Crucial Elements Contribute to the Strength and Stability of a State or Nation

A populace deeply committed and loyal to their nation fosters patriotism, unity, resilience and a sense of belonging among people, which are vital for the overall well-being of the state.

Wise and capable ministers in positions of authority play a pivotal role in governing the state effectively. They are responsible for making sound decisions, formulating policies and providing guidance in times of both peace and crisis.

A well-managed treasury with sufficient reserves is essential for handling unexpected challenges and crises. It enables the government to provide essential services, support the economy and respond effectively to emergencies without resorting to drastic measures that could destabilize the state.

A strong and dedicated military is crucial for safeguarding the sovereignty and security of the state. A well-trained and disciplined army serves as a deterrent against external threats and ensures the protection of the nation.

In addition to a capable military, robust defence infrastructure—including fortified borders, border infrastructure and strategic installations—is essential for deterring potential aggressors and safeguarding the state's territorial integrity.

Friendly states and their support, alliances and partnerships can provide valuable solidarity during times of need. Building strong relationships with friendly states fosters cooperation, mutual assistance and collective security, enhancing the state's resilience and influence on the global stage.

Humility and a genuine commitment to the welfare and progress of the state are qualities that define effective leadership. A humble head of state prioritizes the needs of the people over personal ambitions, fosters unity and inclusivity and works tirelessly to promote the common good and prosperity of the nation. Such leadership inspires trust, confidence and loyalty among people, contributing to the overall stability and success of the state.

Table 1: Seven Parts of the State

1.	Head of State	Head
2.	Council of Minister	Eye
3.	Friendly Country	Ear
4.	Treasury	Mouth
5.	Military	Mind
6.	Defence Fortification	Hand
7.	Country (Territory)	Leg

Dividing State into Smaller Divisions Not Recommended as It Goes against State's Interest

राज्यविभाजनाच्छ्रेयो न भूपानां भवेत्खलु।।347।।
अल्पीकृतं विभागेन राज्यं शत्रुर्जिघृक्षति।

Rājyavibhājanācchreyo na bhūpānāṃ bhavetkhalu।।347।।
Alpīkṛtaṃ vibhāgena rājyaṃ śatrurjighṛkṣati.[158]

The state should not be divided into smaller divisions as these smaller units are easily captured by the enemy.

Reflecting a strategic or geopolitical perspective, advocating for the unity and integrity of a state or nation is crucial. When a state is unnecessarily divided into smaller divisions, such as provinces or regions, it can become more vulnerable to external threats, including invasion or capture by hostile forces. Furthermore, dividing a state can create internal fragmentation and discord, potentially leading to conflicts between different regions or groups vying for control or independence. These internal divisions weaken the overall strength and stability of the state, making it easier for external enemies to exploit vulnerabilities and exert influence. On the contrary, maintaining the unity and integrity of a state can enhance its ability to defend itself.

Wealth of the State

राज्ञः कोशबलं मूलं कोशमूलं पुनर्बलम्।
तन्मूलं सर्वधर्माणां धर्ममूलाः पुनः प्रजाः।।35।।

Rājñaḥ kośabalaṃ mūlaṃ kośamūlaṃ punarbalam.
Tanmūlaṃ sarvadharmāṇāṃ dharmamūlāḥ punaḥ prajāḥ।।35।।[159]

The state is grounded in its army and treasury. Within this treasury lies the strength of the army, which is the primary safeguard for all people and their dharmas.

It is a fundamental principle often observed in political philosophy and historical analysis that the foundation of a state's power and stability rests upon two pillars: its military force and its financial resources. The 'military' represents the physical strength and ability to enforce laws, protect borders and maintain order, while the 'treasury' represents the economic resources necessary to sustain the state, including funding for the military, infrastructure, social programmes, etc.

The effectiveness and capability of the military are directly tied to the financial resources available to it. A well-funded military can afford better training, equipment and support services, which in turn enhance its ability to fulfil its duties effectively. The protection and defence provided by the military ensure the safety and security of the population.

A strong military, supported by a robust treasury, plays a crucial role in upholding societal order, protecting people, defending sovereignty from external threats and preserving the moral and ethical values inherent in society's fabric. It highlights the interdependence between military power, economic stability and societal well-being within a state.

कोशस्योपार्जनरतिर्यमवैश्रवणोपमः।
वेत्ता च दशवर्गस्य स्थानवृद्धिक्षयात्मनः।।18।।

Kośasyopārjanaratiryamavaiśravaṇopamaḥ.
Vettā ca daśavargasya sthānavṛddhikṣayātmanaḥ।।18।।[160]

It is appropriate for the head of state to always strive to accumulate wealth for the state and to maintain a full treasury.

A full treasury ensures financial stability for a country, enabling the government to meet its financial obligations such as paying salaries, investing in infrastructure, social welfare programmes, education, healthcare and other essential services. A stable financial situation can foster economic growth and attract investment. A well-funded treasury provides a buffer against economic downturns, war or unexpected crises. In times of need, having reserves enables the government to implement support programmes. A responsible head of state should prioritize managing the treasury efficiently to ensure that public funds are used wisely and transparently. Constantly striving to maintain a full treasury reflects a commitment to fiscal responsibility.

आददीत बलिं चापि प्रजाभ्यः कुरुनन्दन।
स षड्भागमपि प्राज्ञस्तासामेवाभिगुप्तये।।25।।

Ādadīta baliṃ cāpi prajābhyaḥ kurunandana.
Sa ṣaḍbhāgamapi prājñastāsāmevābhiguptaye।।25।।[161]

The state should collect one-sixth of its people's income as taxes to fulfil its duties and responsibilities for their welfare and protection.

The purpose of collecting taxes is to enrich the treasury and enable the government to carry out its duties and responsibilities effectively.

Characteristics of a Failed State

क्रोशन्त्यो यस्य वै राष्ट्राद्ध्रियन्ते तरसा स्त्रियः।
क्रोशतां पतिपुत्राणां मृतोऽसौ न च जीवति।।31।।

Krośantyo yasya vai rāṣṭrāddhriyante tarasā striyaḥ.
Krośatāṃ patiputrāṇāṃ mṛto'sau na ca jīvati।।31।।[162]

In a state where women are forcibly abducted, leaving their husbands and children to cry and lament, it is deemed a failed one. Even though a head of state is alive, they resemble a lifeless corpse.

The forcible abduction of women represents a poignant critique of a state's failure to protect the rights and safety of its people, particularly women. It showcases a breakdown in law and order, where women are taken against their will, likely for nefarious purposes, indicating a lack of security and protection for vulnerable members of society. Families are torn apart, with husbands losing their wives and children losing their mothers, leading to profound grief and despair. Despite the head of state being physically alive, their leadership is ineffective and lacks vitality. They are unable or unwilling to address the crises facing their country, appearing inert and unresponsive to the suffering of their people. A state's primary responsibility is to ensure the safety and well-being of its people, and when it fails to do so, it can be considered a failed state.

न च पापैर्न चानर्थैर्युज्यते स नराधिपः।।
षड्भागमुपयुञ्जन् यः प्रजा राजा न रक्षति।।
स्वचक्रपरचक्राभ्यां धर्मैर्वा विक्रमेण वा।
निरुद्योगो नृपो यश्च परराष्ट्रविघातने।।
स्वराष्ट्रं निष्प्रतापस्य परचक्रेण हन्यते।।

Na ca pāpairna cānarthairyujyate sa narādhipaḥ.
Ṣaḍbhāgamupayuñjan yaḥ prajā rājā na rakṣati.
Svacakraparacakrābhyāṃ dharmairvā vikrameṇa vā.
Nirudyogo nṛpo yaśca pararāṣṭravighātane.
Svarāṣṭraṃ niṣpratāpasya paracakreṇa hanyate.[163]

The state is considered a failed state if, despite collecting and utilizing one-sixth of its people's income as tax, it fails to protect them from individuals within the government or the enemy. Such a state is easily destroyed by the enemy.

A state that has essentially collapsed or lost control over its territory and population is commonly referred to as a failed state. This term denotes a government's incapacity to ensure safety, security and basic public services for its populace. Despite collecting taxes, such a state is incapable of shielding its people from threats, be they emanating from within the government itself (such as corruption or abuse of power) or from external adversaries (including armed groups or foreign invaders). This failure to provide security undermines both the state and its people, resulting in a loss of legitimacy and trust in the government. Consequently, such a state becomes vulnerable to destruction by its enemies due to its internal vulnerabilities.

भिन्नं राष्ट्रं बलं भिन्नं भिन्नोऽमात्यादिको गणः।।19।।

Bhinnaṃ rāṣṭraṃ balaṃ bhinnaṃ bhinno'mātyādiko gaṇaḥ।।19।।[164]

Disunity within both the state and the military, coupled with disagreements among ministers, are characteristics of a failed state.

A cohesive state typically has a unified vision, where its people, leaders and institutions work towards common goals. Disunity within the state government and key institutions such as the military and administration can hinder progress. In a functional government, ministers or cabinet members are expected to work together cohesively to formulate and implement policies that serve the interests of the state and its people. Disagreements among ministers can arise due to differences in ideology, personal ambitions or policy priorities. When these disagreements are frequent or severe, they can lead to gridlock, dysfunction or even paralysis within the government, preventing it from effectively addressing key issues or responding to crises. A state characterized by disunity and dysfunction is often perceived as a failed or failing state, unable to fulfil its basic functions of maintaining order, providing services and protecting its people.

Dictatorship in a State Leads to Its Destruction

प्रभुः स्वातन्त्र्यमापन्नो ह्यनर्थायैव कल्पते।
भिन्नराष्ट्रो भवेत्सद्यो भिन्नप्रकृतिरेव च।।4।।

Prabhuḥ svātantryamāpanno hyanarthāyaiva kalpate.
Bhinnarāṣṭro bhavetsadyo bhinnaprakṛtireva ca।।4।।[165]

The state's dictator is capable of wrongdoing, and essential components of the state, such as ministers, the administration and the army, can become divided, ultimately leading to the destruction of the state.

The leader of a state, wielding dictatorial power, perpetrates wrongdoing, causing fragmentation among essential components like ministers, the administration and the army. This division can precipitate the state's downfall or destruction.

Dictators, exercising absolute authority, often act without accountability or oversight, significantly impacting the state's trajectory and stability. Unconstrained by ethical or legal boundaries, they engage in harmful, unjust or corrupt behaviours.

The dictator's misconduct typically fosters dissent within these crucial components. Ministers and the administration may disagree on how to respond to the dictator's actions, while the military's loyalties may become divided.

Ultimately, the conflict among these key components can spell the state's demise, leading to civil unrest and internal strife. When a dictator abuses power and fractures the state's essential institutions, the consequences can be catastrophic, potentially culminating in its collapse or destruction.

Responsibilities of the People in a Dictatorship Scenario

अरक्षितारं हर्तारं विलोप्तारमनायकम्।
तं वै राजकलिं हन्युः प्रजाः सन्नह्य निर्घृणम्।।32।।

Arakṣitāraṃ hartāraṃ viloptāramanāyakam.
Taṃ vai rājakaliṃ hanyuḥ prajāḥ sannahya nirghṛṇam।।32।।[166]

The head of state that fails to protect the people, instead plundering their wealth, and lacks a minister to serve as a leader, is deemed the most sinful of heads of state, resembling a dictator. All people should revolt against such a dictator, striving to dismantle and overthrow their regime.

The head of state, instead of fulfilling their duty to protect and serve the people, engages in corruption, oppression and exploitation. Revolting against a dictator or an oppressive regime is often seen as a last resort, suggesting that overthrowing such a regime is not only justified but necessary for the well-being and freedom of the people. This situation calls for collective action to dismantle such regimes and replace them with governments that genuinely serve the interests of both the people and the state.

APPENDIX

Excerpts from *Hindu Polity*

The following are excerpts from *Hindu Polity* by K.P. Jayaswal

The Election of Kings [Heads of State]

समानो मन्त्रः समितिः समानी समानं व्रतं सह चित्तमेषाम्॥2॥

Samāno mantraḥ samitiḥ samānī samānaṃ vrataṃ saha cittameṣām॥2॥ Atharvaveda, Kanda – 6, Sukta – 64

समानो मन्त्रः समितिः समानी समानं मनः सह चित्तमेषाम्॥3॥

Samāno mantraḥ samitiḥ samānī samānaṃ mana: sahacittameṣām॥3॥ Rigveda, Mandal – 10, Sukta – 191

The greatest institution of this nature was the Samiti of our Vedic forefathers. The word Samiti (sam+iti) means 'meeting together', i.e., in assembly. The Samiti was the national assembly of the whole people or visah (विशः) for we find the whole people or Samiti in the alternative, electing and re-electing the Rajan (राजा) or King विशस्त्वा सर्वा वाञ्छन्तु। viśastvā sarvā vāñchantu| Rig-Veda, Mandal – 10, Sukta – 173, Atharva-Veda, Mandal – 6, Sukta – 87 ध्रुवाय ते समितिः कल्पतामिह। rdhruvāya te samitiḥ kalpatāmiha| Atharva-Veda, Kanda – 6, Sukta – 88 त्वां विशो वृणतां राज्याय। tvāṃ viśo vṛṇatāṃ rājyāya| Atharva-Veda, Kanda – 3, Sukta – 4. The whole people were supposed to be present in the assembly.

The functions of the Samiti may be gathered from different references. We have already noticed the most important business of the Samiti, to wit, electing the Rajan नास्मै समितिः कल्पते ॥15॥ Nāsmai samitiḥ kalpate ॥15॥ Atharvaveda, Kanda – 5, Sukta – 19. It could also re-elect a king who had been banished. They were thus a sovereign body from the constitutional point of view. In the Atharva-Veda, Kanda – 6, Sukta – 64, which is a prayer–hymn for union and concord, and also in the Rig-Veda Mandal – 10, Sukta – 191, Mantra 3, we have a prayer for a common Samiti and common policy of state समानो मन्त्रः समितिः समानी (Samāno mantraḥ samitiḥ samānī) a common aim and a common mind. समानं व्रतं सह चित्तमेषाम् (Samānaṃ vrataṃ saha cittameṣām) This indicates that matters of state (Mantra) were discussed in the Samiti. The king attended the Samiti, and it was thought necessary that he should do so. The Rigveda has like a true king going to the Samiti. (राजा न सत्यः समितिरियानः) (Rājā na satyaḥ samitiriyānaḥ) Rigveda Mandal – 09, Sukta – 92, Mantra 6.[167]

***

Vedic King and His Election

The King was elected by the people assembled in the Samiti. The people assembled are said to elect him to rularship unanimously. The samiti appoints him. He is asked to hold the state. It is hoped that he would not fall from his office. He is expected to crush the enemies. Here it is a complete song of Election.

आ त्वाहार्षमन्तरभूर्ध्रुवस्तिष्ठाविचाचलत्।
विशस्त्वा सर्वा वाञ्छन्तु मा त्वद्राष्ट्रमधि भ्रशत्॥1॥

Ā tvāhārṣamantarabhūrdhruvastiṣṭhāvicācalat.
Viśastvā sarvā vāñchantu mā tvadrāṣṭramadhi bhraśat॥1॥
Atharvaveda, Kanda – 6, Sukta – 87

Gladly you come among us; remain firmly without faltering; all the people want you; may you not fall off the State.

इहैवैधि माप च्योष्ठाः पर्वत इवाविचाचलत्।
इन्द्रे इहैव ध्रुवस्तिष्ठेह राष्ट्रमु धारय॥2॥

Ihaivaidhi māpa cyoṣṭṭhāḥ parvata ivāvicācalat.
Indre ihaiva dhruvastiṣṭheha rāṣṭramu dhāraya॥2॥ Atharvaveda, Kanda – 6, Sukta – 87

Here be you firm like the mountain and may you not come down. Be you firm here like Indra; remain you here and hold the state.

इन्द्र एतमदीधरत्ध्रुवं ध्रुवेण हविषा ।
तस्मै सोमो अधि ब्रवदयं च ब्रह्मणस्पतिः॥3॥

Indra etamadīdharatdhruvaṃ dhruveṇa haviṣā.
Tasmai somo adhi bravadayaṃ ca brahmaṇaspatiḥ॥3॥
Atharvaveda, Kanda – 6, Sukta – 87

Indra has held it (the state) firm on account of the firm Havi offering; for it Soma as well as the Brahmanaspati has said the same.

ध्रुवा द्यौर्ध्रुवा पृथिवी ध्रुवं विश्वमिदं जगत्।
ध्रुवासः पर्वता इमे ध्रुवो राजा विशामयम्॥1॥

Dhruvā dyaurdhruvā pṛthivī dhruvaṃ viśvamidaṃ jagat.
Dhruvāsaḥ parvatā ime dhruvo rājā viśāmayam॥1॥ Atharvaveda, Kanda – 6, Sukta – 88

Firm (as) the heaven, firm (as) the earth, firm (as) the universe, firm (as) the mountains, let this raja of the people be firm.

ध्रुवं ते राजा वरुणो ध्रुवं देवो बृहस्पतिः ।
ध्रुवं त इन्द्रश्चाग्निश्च राष्ट्रं धारयतां ध्रुवम्॥2॥

Dhruvaṃ te rājā varuṇo dhruvaṃ devo bṛhaspatiḥ.
Dhruvaṃ ta indraścāgniśca rāṣṭraṃ dhārayatāṃ dhruvam॥2॥
Atharvaveda, Kanda – 6, Sukta – 88

Let the State be held by you, be made firm by the raja Varuna, the God Brihaspati, Indra and also Agni.

ध्रुवोऽच्युतः प्र मृणीहि शत्रून् छत्रूयतोऽधरान् पादयस्व ।
सर्वा दिशः संमनसः सध्रीचीर्ध्रुवाय ते समितिः कल्पतामिह॥3॥

Dhruvo'cyutaḥ pra mṛṇīhi śatrūn chatrūyato'dharān pādayasva.
Sarvā diśaḥ saṃmanasaḥ sadhrīcīrdhruvāya te samitiḥ kalpatāmiha॥3॥ Atharvaveda, Kanda – 6, Sukta – 88

Vanquish you firmly, without falling, the enemies, and those behaving like enemies crush you under your feet. All the quarters unanimously honour you, and for firmness the assembly here creates (appoints) you.[168]

अग्र एति युवतिरह्रयाणा[1]

Agra eti yuvatirahrayāṇā

CHAPTER 5

Highest Respect for Women

The progress and advancement of any civilization, nation or society are measured by their respect for women and their commitment to ensuring women's safety and security. Furthermore, it is also determined by the extent of women's involvement in decision-making processes within a nation and society.

Hindu ancestors placed great importance on respecting women and ensuring their safety and security. Women are regarded as the *mukut mani* (the crest jewel—not in material terms, but as a symbol of honour) of Hindu society. Ensuring their safety is considered essential to upholding the rule of law, enabling them to move freely and fearlessly, adorned with beautiful ornaments.

Hindu women have displayed brilliance in various spheres of life from the Vedic ages to the present times. They have played and continue to play an increasingly significant role globally in numerous fields, including business, science, politics and culture. Therefore, the fifth Hindu Sutra is 'अग्र एति युवतिरह्रयाणा' (*Agra eti yuvatirahrayāṇā*)—highest respect for women.

Highest and Profound Respect for Women

Women as Rishis in the Rigveda

घोषा गोधा विश्ववारा अपालोपनिषन्निषद् ।
ब्रह्मजाया जुहुर्नाम अगस्त्यस्य स्वसादितिः ।।
इन्द्राणी चेन्द्रमाता च सरमा रोमशोर्वशी ।
लोपामुद्रा च नद्यश्च यमी नारी च शश्वती ।।
श्रीर्लाक्षा सार्पराज्ञी वाक् श्रद्धा मेधा च दक्षिणा ।
रात्री सूर्या च सावित्री ब्रह्मवादिन्य ईरिता: ।।

ghoṣā godhā viśvavārā apālopaniṣanniṣad |
brahmajāyā juhūrnāma agastyasya svasāditiḥ ||
indrāṇī cendramātā ca saramā romaśorvaśī |
lopāmudrā ca nadyaśca yamī nārī ca śaśvatī ||
śrīrlākṣā sārparājñī vāk śraddhā medhā ca dakṣiṇā |
rātrī sūryā ca sāvitrī brahmavādinya īritā: ||[2]

Goṣā, Godhā, Viśvavarā, Apālā, Upaniṣad, Niṣad, the Brahmajaya named Juhū, the sister of Agastya, Aditi, Indrāṇī and the mother of Indra, Śaramā, Romaśā, Urvaśī and Lopāmudrā, and the Nadi, Yamī and the wife Śaśvatī, Śrī, Lākṣā, Sārparājñī, Vāk, Śraddhā, Medhā, Dākṣiṇā, Rātri, Sūryā and Sāvitrī, all of them are referred to as Brahmavādinī.

Brahmavādinī Rishi (ब्रह्मवादिनी ऋषि): The woman rishi who expounds on the ultimate reality, Brahman, represents a female figure associated with the highest level of wisdom and spiritual knowledge. In the *Rigveda*, there are a total of 28 Brahmavadini rishis (female sages). Out of the 28 Brahmavadini rishis mentioned in *Brihat Devat*a, 23 are found in the *Rigveda* Samhita, one in the *Rigveda* Parishishta Sukta, and another in the *Taittiriya Aranyaka*. The remaining three rishis are not traceable.

In Hindu society, rishihood is considered the highest position. The presence of Brahmavadini rishis in the *Rigveda* signifies that women are respected and honoured as rishis within Hindu Dharma and its most revered scripture. This concept embodies the pinnacle of spiritual and intellectual achievement. Rishis, revered sages endowed with profound wisdom and insight, are known as Mantradrashta (मन्त्रद्रष्टा). Their teachings go beyond mere academic knowledge.

The existence of Brahmavadini rishis in the *Rigveda* is particularly significant in illustrating the role of women in Hindu society. These women attained a high level of spiritual realization and are recognized as authoritative figures of wisdom and spiritual knowledge concerning the Vedas. This acknowledgement underscores the respect and honour afforded to women within Hindu Dharma.

The recognition of women as rishis illustrates their equality in spiritual pursuits, challenging contemporary narratives that suggest marginalization in ancient Hindu society. It establishes that women held spiritual authority, actively contributing to the discourse of spiritual knowledge rather than being mere followers. This acknowledgement also attests to the principle that both men and women can attain the highest spiritual truths and enhance the collective understanding of the divine.

The presence of female rishis in the *Rigveda* reflects a rich cultural legacy that values the contributions of women in spiritual and intellectual spheres. The 28 Brahmavadini rishis stand as a powerful testament to the respect and honour bestowed upon women in Hindu Dharma, affirming that spirituality knows no gender boundaries. Both men and women can reach the highest levels of spiritual wisdom, contributing to the rich tapestry of Hindu thought and practice.

The *Rigveda* suktas and mantras associated with the Brahmavadini rishis are given here to highlight the significance and breadth of their contributions to the *Rigveda*.

Romesha (रोमशा) Mandal 1, Sukta 126
Lopāmudrā (लोपामुद्रा) Mandal 1, Sukta 179
Nadi (नदी) Mandal 3, Sukta 33
Vishwavara (विश्ववारा) Mandal 5, Sukta 28
Shashwati (शश्वती) Mandal 8, Sukta 1
Apala (अपाला) Mandal 8, Sukta 91
Yami (यमी) Mandal 10, Sukta 10
Ghosha (घोषा) Mandal 10, Suktas 39 and 40
Agastya (अगस्त्या) Mandal 10, Sukta 60
Aditi (अदिति) Mandal 10, Sukta 72
Surya (सूर्या) and Savitri (सावित्री) Mandal 10, Sukta 85
Indrani (इन्द्राणी) Mandal 10, Suktas 86 and 145
Urvashi (उर्वशी) Mandal 10, Sukta 95
Dakshina (दक्षिणा) Mandal 10, Sukta 107
Sarma (सरमा) Mandal 10, Sukta 108
Juhu (जुहु) Mandal 10, Sukta 109
Vak (वाक्) Mandal 10, Sukta 125
Ratri (रात्रि) Mandal 10, Sukta 127
Godha (गोधा) Mandal 10, Sukta 134

Shradha (श्रद्धा) Mandal 10, Sukta 151
Indramata (इन्द्रमाता) Mandal 10, Sukta 153
Saarprajni (सार्पराज्ञी) Mandal 10, Sukta 189
Shree (श्री) *Rigveda*, Parishisht Sukta 10
Medha (मेधा) *Taittiriya Aranyaka* 4, Prapataka 10: Anuvaks 41–44

All the suktas and mantras of the *Rigveda* associated with the Brahmavadini rishis are included in the appendix of this chapter.

Daughters and Sons Are Equal and They Are Valued and Treated with Equal Care

यथैवात्मा तथा पुत्रः पुत्रेण दुहिता समा।।11।।

Yathaivātmā tathā putraḥ putreṇa duhitā samā।।11।।[3]

The son is like oneself, and the daughter is like the son.

Both sons and daughters are valued equally, and the love, care and support given to them are also equal. This further reinforces the notion of equality by highlighting the similarities between a son and a daughter. It implies that a daughter should be regarded with the same level of importance, respect and affection as a son. By equating the daughter to the son, it emphasizes that gender should not determine how children are treated or perceived within the family or society. In essence, both sons and daughters are equally valuable members of the family, deserving of equal opportunities, rights and love.

एका च मम कन्येयं कुलस्योत्पादनी भृशम्।
पुत्रो ममायमिति मे भावना पुरुषर्षभ।।23।।

ekā ca mama kanyeyaṃ kulasyotpādanī bhṛśam|
putro mamāyamiti me bhāvanā puruṣarṣabha||23||[4]

A daughter is like a son; she will be the one to carry forward the family lineage.

A daughter embodies the strength and qualities of the family. Lineage is about the values, traditions and legacy that one generation passes down to the next. A daughter possesses incredible resilience, wisdom and leadership, making her the perfect custodian of the family's heritage.

She understands the importance of family history, culture and the principles that have guided the family. A daughter carries with her the hopes and dreams of the family, embracing her role in continuing the lineage with pride and grace.

नीलस्य राज्ञो दुहिता बभूवतातीव शोभना।
साऽग्निहोत्रमुपातिष्ठद्बोधनाय पितुः सदा।।28।।

nīlasya rājño duhitā babhūvatātīva śobhanā|
sā'gnihotramupātiṣṭhadbodhanāya pituḥ sadā||28||[5]

King Neel of Mahismati has an extraordinarily beautiful daughter who always helps her father light the fire and perform the Agnihotra yajna (sacred ritual).

Respect of the Highest Order for Women

अर्धं भार्या मनुष्यस्य भार्या श्रेष्ठतमः सखा।
भार्या मूलं त्रिवर्गस्य भार्या मूलं तरिष्यतः।।41।।

Ardhaṃ bhāryā manuṣyasya bhāryā śreṣṭhatamaḥ sakhā.
Bhāryā mūlaṃ trivargasya bhāryā mūlaṃ tariṣyataḥ।।41।।[6]

The wife is one half of a man; she is his supreme friend. She is the source of dharma, artha and kama. For a man who wishes to navigate the ocean of life, the wife is his chief navigator.

In Hindu tradition, a man (grihastha—householder) is considered incomplete without his wife. The concept of unity and partnership within marriage portrays both husband and wife as integral parts of a whole. The wife and husband are not only life partners but also each other's closest and most trusted companions. Their relationship is revered as one of deep friendship, where they mutually support and rely on each other in all aspects of life.

It is believed that a wife plays a vital role in guiding her husband towards his goals by supporting him in dharma, assisting him in achieving material success (artha) and fulfilling his desires (kama). Life is often perceived as a vast and challenging ocean filled with obstacles and uncertainties. In this journey, the wife serves as a skilled navigator, helping her husband chart his course through life's challenges and reach their shared objectives. She provides him with emotional strength, companionship and practical assistance, empowering him to overcome difficulties and achieve success in both worldly and spiritual pursuits.

आत्मनोऽर्धमिति श्रौतं सा रक्षति धनं प्रजाः।
शरीरं लोकयात्रां वै धर्मं स्वर्गमृषीन् पितॄन्।।

Ātmano'rdhamiti śrautaṃ sā rakṣati dhanaṃ prajāḥ.
Śarīraṃ lokayātrāṃ vai dharmaṃ svargamṛṣīn pitṛn.[7]

As per the Shruti (the Vedas), the wife is regarded as one's better half, safeguarding wealth, progeny, the body, the journey of life, dharma, heaven, rishis and ancestors.

भार्यावन्तः क्रियावन्तः सभार्या गृहमेधिनः।
भार्यावन्तः प्रमोदन्ते भार्यावन्तः श्रियान्विताः।।42।।

Bhāryāvantaḥ kriyāvantaḥ sabhāryā gṛhamedhinaḥ.
Bhāryāvantaḥ pramodante bhāryāvantaḥ śriyānvitaḥ।।42।।[8]

A man who has a wife is eligible to perform yajna (sacred rituals); such a man is considered a true householder and deemed a happy person. For those blessed with wives, it is as if they have Lakshmi as a wife, who is considered the embodiment of prosperity in the home.

In Hindu tradition, an unmarried individual is not eligible or qualified to perform all types of sacred rituals (yajna), except for daily routine rituals. Only married couples are qualified to perform all types of rituals.

सखायः प्रविविक्तेषु भवन्त्येताः प्रियंवदाः।
पितरो धर्मकार्येषु भवन्त्यार्तस्य मातरः।।43।।

Sakhāyaḥ praviviktesu bhavantyetāḥ priyaṃvadāḥ.
Pitaro dharmakāryeṣu bhavantyārtasya mātaraḥ।।43।।[9]

The wife is a companion who speaks congenial words. They are well-wishers, acting as a father in public activities and as a mother in times of distress, sharing sorrows and endeavouring to alleviate suffering.

आत्माऽऽत्मनैव जनितः पुत्र इत्युच्यते बुधैः।
तस्माद् भार्यो नरः पश्येन्मातृवत् पुत्रमातरम्।।48।।

Ātmā"tmanaiva janitaḥ putra ityucyate budhaiḥ.
Tasmād bhāryo naraḥ paśyenmātṛvat putramātaram।।48।।[10]

Learned men say that the soul born from the womb of a wife is considered to be her child (son or daughter). Consequently, a man should regard his wife, who has borne his child, as he would regard his mother.

आत्मनो जन्मनः क्षेत्रं पुण्यं रामाः सनातनम्।
ऋषीणामपि का शक्तिः स्रष्टुं रामामृते प्रजाम्।।52।।

Ātmano janmanaḥ kṣetraṃ puṇyaṃ rāmāḥ sanātanam.
Rṣīṇāmapi kā śaktiḥ sraṣṭuṃ rāmāmṛte prajām।।52।।[11]

Wives are the timeless sanctum of creation, wherein husbands' souls are born. Even rishis (sages) don't have the power to create progeny without a wife.

A spiritually advanced person, such as a sage, cannot bring forth offspring without a wife. This reflects the biological reality that reproduction typically involves both male and female coming together to create offspring.

सुसंरब्धोऽपि रामाणां न कुर्यादप्रियं नरः।।15।।

Susaṃrabdho'pi rāmāṇāṃ na kuryādapriyaṃ naraḥ।।15।।[12]

Even when angry, a man should refrain from misbehaving with his wife. It's important to keep in mind that love, affection and dharma depend on the wife.

A man should always treat his wife with respect and refrain from any form of mistreatment, verbal or physical, even when experiencing strong emotions like anger. Respect and healthy communication in marital relationships are crucial, even during moments of anger or conflict. It promotes a mindset of mutual understanding and cooperation, which is essential for the longevity and happiness of a marriage.

सहधर्मचरीं दान्तां नित्यं मातृसमां मम।
सखायं विहितां देवैर्नित्यं परमिकां गतिम्।।156/31।।

Sahadharmacarīṃ dāntāṃ nityaṃ mātṛsamāṃ mama.
Sakhāyaṃ vihitāṃ devairnityaṃ paramikāṃ gatim।।156/31।।[13]

The wife, as a partner in dharma, maintains discipline and perpetually cares for her husband with a motherly touch. The gods have ordained the wife and husband as companions, and she remains the supreme support throughout their spiritual journey.

इयं हि नः प्रिया भार्या प्राणेभ्योऽपि गरीयसी।
मातेव परिपाल्या च पूज्या ज्येष्ठेव च स्वसा।।14।।

Iyaṃ hi naḥ priyā bhāryā prāṇebhyo'pi garīyasī.
Māteva paripālyā ca pūjyā jyeṣṭheva ca svasā।।14।।[14]

Yudhisthira said that Draupadi is our beloved wife, more precious to us than life itself. She deserves to be cared for like a mother and cherished like an elder sister.

प्रिया च दर्शनीया च पण्डिता च पतिव्रता।।2।।

priyā ca darśanīyā ca paṇḍitā ca pativratā।।2।।[15]

Draupadi, the beloved wife of the Pandavas, was admirable, intellectual and learned.

स्त्रीरत्नं दुष्कुलाच्चापि विषादप्यमृतं पिबेत्।
अदूष्या हि स्त्रियो रत्नमाप इत्येव धर्मतः।।32।।

Strīratnaṃ duṣkulāccāpi viṣādapyamṛtaṃ pibet.
Adūṣyā hi striyo ratnamāpa ityeva dharmataḥ।।32।।[16]

न स्त्रीरत्नसमं रत्नम्।।313।।

Na strīratnasamaṃ ratnam।।313।।[17]

Women are like crest jewels; accept them as wives, even if they come from less esteemed family lineages. According to dharma, women, jewels and water are not impure.

Women are akin to *mukut mani* (the crest jewel—not in material terms, but as a symbol of honour); they deserve to be treated with care, respect and appreciation. It is important to embrace women as partners in marriage, regardless of their familial background or social standing. Women, like jewels and water, possess inherent purity, underscoring that societal status or birth should not diminish their worth.

पृथिवी सर्वभूतानां जनित्री तद्विधाः स्त्रियः।

Pṛthivī sarvabhūtānāṃ janitrī tadvidhāḥ striyaḥ.[18]

The Earth is the mother of all beings, and similarly, women worldwide are mothers to all offspring.

Earth serves as a mother, providing sustenance, shelter and life to all living beings. Similarly, women, irrespective of nationality, ethnicity or culture, play a fundamental role in nurturing and caring for their offspring. The role of motherhood is universal, transcending boundaries and differences, acknowledging the vital role women play in the continuation and well-being of humanity. They bring new life into the world and provide care, love and support to children.

सर्वान् कामयते यस्मात् कमेर्धातोश्च भाविनि।
तस्मात् कन्येह सुश्रोणि स्वतन्त्रा वरवर्णिनि।।13।।

Sarvān kāmayate yasmāt kamerdhātośca bhāvini.
Tasmāt kanyeha suśroṇi svatantrā varavarṇini।।13।।[19]

The term 'kanya' originates from the Sanskrit roots 'kame', meaning 'to desire', and is applied to a maiden. It signifies her desire, as in the tradition of Swayamvara, where she has the freedom to choose her husband from among the suitors who attend the event.

The tradition of Swayamvara, deeply entrenched in ancient Hindu culture, epitomizes profound principles of autonomy and choice. The term 'Swayamvara' translates to 'self-choice' or 'self-selection', portraying a Hindu custom where a woman holds the autonomy to select her life partner from a gathering of eligible suitors convened at the Swayamvara event. This event serves as a reflection of the values and virtues cherished by the prospective bride in a partner. It offers her a unique opportunity to firsthand observe the qualities, character and capabilities of the suitors, enabling her to make an informed decision regarding her future spouse. Crucially, the essence of the Swayamvara tradition resides in the empowerment of women to exercise their agency, making choices based on their preferences rather than being subject to the dictates of others. This fundamental aspect underscores the significance of consent, mutual respect and partnership within the institution of marriage. The tradition of Swayamvara encapsulates themes of autonomy, agency and the celebration of individual choice, serving as a timeless emblem of love, romance and the pursuit of happiness in Hindu culture.

नित्यं निवसते लक्ष्मीः कन्यकासु प्रतिष्ठिता।
शोभना शुभयोग्या च पूज्या मङ्गलकर्मसु।।

Nityaṃ nivasate lakṣmīḥ kanyakāsu pratiṣṭhitā.
Śobhanā śubhayogyā ca pūjyā maṅgalakarmasu.[20]

Lakshmi, the Goddess of wealth, prosperity and abundance, eternally dwells within girls (kanya). She perpetually manifests within every girl. Each girl is inherently splendid, glorious, worthy of auspicious karma and is worshipped in auspicious works.

Lakshmi, the Goddess of wealth, prosperity and abundance, embodies the divine essence perpetually residing within every girl. This symbolic recognition underscores the inherent value, purity and potential of femininity, fostering reverence and respect towards women and girls. Each girl is inherently splendid and glorious, highlighting the intrinsic value and dignity of every individual regardless of external factors like social status or material wealth. This perspective fosters a sense of self-worth and empowerment among girls and women. Girls are inherently deserving of respect for their potential to positively contribute to society. This worldview celebrates the divine feminine, recognizes the inherent worth of every individual and underscores the importance of treating girls and women with respect, honour and dignity. It reflects cultural values that shape attitudes towards gender and femininity in Hindu society.

आकरस्थं यथा रत्नं सर्वकामफलोपगम्।
तथा कन्या महालक्ष्मीः सर्वलोकस्य मङ्गलम्।।

Ākarasthaṃ yathā ratnaṃ sarvakāmaphalopagam.
Tathā kanyā mahālakṣmīḥ sarvalokasya maṅgalam.[21]

Just as gems embedded in a mine fulfil all desires and bestow all fruits, the girl, embodying the form of Mahalakshmi, brings auspiciousness to the whole world.

एवं कन्या परा लक्ष्मी रतिस्तोषश्च देहिनाम्।

Evaṃ kanyā parā lakṣmī ratistoṣaśca dehinām.[22]

The girl represents the quintessential form of Lakshmi, from whom living beings attain happiness and contentment.

Ensuring the Safety and Security of Women Is a Paramount and Crucial Parameter for Upholding Law and Order as well as for Maintaining the Overall Standing of the State

स्त्रियश्चापुरुषा मार्गे सर्वालङ्कारभूषिताः।
निर्भयाः प्रतिपद्यन्ते यदि रक्षति भूमिपः।।32।।

Striyaścāpuruṣā mārge sarvālaṅkārabhūṣitāḥ.
Nirbhayāḥ pratipadyante yadi rakṣati bhūmipaḥ।।32।।[23]

When the state administration ensures the maintenance of the rule of law, oversees the implementation of justice and protects its people, women adorned with beautiful ornaments can move around fearlessly even when alone.

The responsibility of maintaining the rule of law, including enforcing laws, preventing crime and facilitating smooth societal functioning without chaos or unrest, falls upon the state administration. Additionally, they oversee the justice system to ensure its fair and impartial operation. One fundamental duty of an administration is to protect the people of their country. When women in society feel safe and confident, moving around fearlessly alone, adorned with beautiful ornaments, it signifies a sense of freedom and security. This indicates the highest form of safety and security in the state, making the safety and security of women crucial parameters for maintaining law and order.

Ensuring Care and Protection for Women

गतिरेका पतिर्नार्या द्वितीया गतिरात्मजः।
तृतीया ज्ञातयो राजंश्चतुर्थी नैव विद्यते।।24।।

Gatirekā patirnāryā dvitīyā gatirātmajaḥ.
Tṛtīyā jñātayo rājaṃścaturthī naiva vidyate।।24।।[24]

The first support for a woman is her husband, followed by her children and then by her father, brother, sister and other close relatives.

Women are capable of looking after themselves, but in terms of support systems, a woman's primary resource is often her husband, who provides emotional and practical assistance in navigating various aspects of life. Following her husband, children are commonly seen as the next layer of support, offering both assistance and emotional support to their mother. Beyond the immediate family unit of husband and children, a woman may also rely on support from her own parents, siblings and other close extended family members during times of need.

योषितो हि सदा रक्ष्याः स्वापराद्धापि नित्यशः।।12।।

Yoṣito hi sadā rakṣyāḥ svāparāddhāpi nityaśaḥ।।12।।[25]

Even if women make mistakes, men should still care for and protect them.

सद् भार्यां परिरक्षन्ति भर्तारोऽल्पबला अपि।।12/68।।

Sad bhāryāṃ parirakṣanti bhartāro'lpabalā api।।12/68।।[26]

Even a husband who is perceived as weak should still protect his wife.

भार्यायां रक्ष्यमाणायां प्रजा भवति रक्षिता।।69।।

Bhāryāyāṃ rakṣyamāṇāyāṃ prajā bhavati rakṣitā।।69।।[27]

Protecting one's wife provides protection for their offspring.

भर्तव्या रक्षणीया च पत्नी पत्या हि सर्वदा।।41।।

Bhartavyā rakṣaṇīyā ca patnī patyā hi sarvadā।।41।।[28]

It is appropriate for the husband to consistently uphold and safeguard his wife.

पुत्रदारमप्रतिविधाय प्रव्रजतः पूर्वः साहसदण्डः।।3।।

Putradāramapratividhāya pravrajataḥ pūrvaḥ sāhasadaṇḍaḥ।।3।।[29]

If a man chooses to become a sanyasi (renunciant) without ensuring the financial well-being of his wife and children, the state should hold him accountable and impose punishment.

The responsibilities of individuals, particularly husbands and fathers, towards their families when making significant life decisions like becoming a renunciate encompass the obligation a man has towards providing for the financial stability and security of his family, specifically his wife and children. This includes ensuring they have access to necessities such as food, shelter, education and healthcare. If a man decides to become a renunciate without fulfilling his financial responsibilities towards his family, the state should intervene. This intervention might involve holding the man legally accountable for neglecting his familial duties and imposing punishment as a consequence. It reflects a perspective on the balance between individual freedom and societal expectations, particularly regarding familial obligations, and the role of the state in upholding these expectations through legal means.

Woman Exempt from Death

अवध्यां स्त्रियमित्याहुर्धर्मज्ञा धर्मनिश्चये।।31।।

Avadhyāṃ striyamityāhurdharmajñā dharmaniścaye।।31।।[30]

According to dharma, it is considered unacceptable to kill women, as they are exempt from being killed.

सर्वथा स्त्री न हन्तव्या।।14।।

Sarvathā strī na hantavyā।।14।।[31]

One should never, under any circumstances, kill a woman.

मा वधीस्त्वं स्त्रियम्।।13।।

Mā vadhīstvaṃ striyam।।13।।[32]

Women are not subject to being killed. The killing of women is forbidden.

अवध्यास्तु स्त्रियः सृष्टा मन्यन्ते धर्मचारिणः।।4।।

Avadhyāstu striyaḥ sṛṣṭā manyante dharmacāriṇaḥ।।4।।[33]

According to learned individuals, women are deemed exempt from being killed.

स्त्रियश्चैव न हन्तव्या।।

Striyaścaiva na hantavyā.[34]

Women must not be killed.

स्त्रियो ह्यवध्याः।।46।।

Striyo hyavadhyāḥ।।46।।[35]

Women are exempt from being killed.

अवध्याः सर्वभूतानां प्रमदाः क्षम्यतामिति।।21।।

Avadhyāḥ sarvabhūtānāṃ pramadāḥ kṣamyatāmiti।।21।।[36]

Women are exempt from being killed and should be forgiven.

The Sale of Girls Is Condemned and Prohibited

यो मनुष्यः स्वकं पुत्रं विक्रीय धनमिच्छति।
कन्यां वा जीवितार्थाय यः शुल्केन प्रयच्छति।।18।।
सप्तावरे महाघोरे निरये कालसाह्वये।
स्वेदं मूत्रं पुरीषं च तस्मिन् मूढः समश्नुते।।19।।

Yo manuṣyaḥ svakaṃ putraṃ vikrīya dhanamicchati.
Kanyāṃ vā jīvitārthāya yaḥ śulkena prayacchati||18||
saptāvare mahāghore niraye kālasāhvaye |
svedaṃ mūtraṃ purīṣaṃ ca tasmin mūḍhaḥ samaśnute||19||[37]

A man who gains wealth by selling his son, and seeks wealth by selling his daughter, using her value for his own livelihood, is condemned and will fall into the unfathomable hell.

A man who seeks wealth by selling his daughter and exploiting her for personal gain is condemned to severe moral and spiritual consequences. His actions are profoundly unethical and corrupt, demonstrating a complete disregard for human dignity and familial responsibility. Such behaviour constitutes a grave violation of ethical and moral principles, leading to a state of suffering and punishment so extreme and incomprehensible that it transcends conventional measures of agony, representing the most severe form of punishment both morally and spiritually as 'unfathomable hell'.

Learned and Qualified Women

अभिज्ञा राजधर्माणां राजपुत्री प्रतीक्षति।।4।।

Abhijñā rājadharmāṇāṃ rājaputrī pratīkṣati||4||[38]

Sita is well versed in administration, governance and politics.

Bali's wife Tara is a learned woman

ततः स्वस्त्ययनं कृत्वा मन्त्रविद् विजयैषिणी।।12।।

Tataḥ svastyayanaṃ kṛtvā mantravid vijayaiṣiṇī||12||[39]

Tara desired victory for her husband, Bali; she possessed knowledge of mantras and their meanings. With a positive resolve for Bali, she performed Svastivachan, an auspicious invocation.

तारया वाक्यमुक्तोऽहं सत्यं सर्वज्ञया हितम्।।41।।

Tārayā vākyamukto'haṃ satyaṃ sarvajñayā hitam।।41।।[40]

Bali said, 'My wife, Tara, knows everything she has told me about truth and my well-being'.

तस्माच्छुभं हि कर्तव्यं पण्डितेनेह लौकिकम्।।5।।

Tasmācchubhaṃ hi kartavyaṃ paṇḍiteneha laukikam।।5।।[41]

Hanuman said to Tara, 'Devi, you are a learned woman.'

सुषेणदुहिता चेयमर्थसूक्ष्मविनिश्चये।।13।।

Suṣeṇaduhitā ceyamarthasūkṣmaviniścaye।।13।।[42]

It is stated that Tara, Sushena's daughter, is learned and discerning in the most profound matters.

यदैव नो विद्यापरिग्रहाय नानादिगन्तवासिनां साहचर्यमासीत्।
तदैव चास्मत्सौदामिनीसमक्षमनयोर्भूरिवसुदेवरातयो प्रवृत्तेयं प्रतिज्ञा।।

yadaiva no vidyāparigrahāya nānādigantavāsināṃ sāhacaryamāsīt|
tadaiva cāsmatsaudāminīsamakṣamanayorbhūrivasudevarātayo pravṛtteyaṃ pratijñā||[43]

Kamandaki (female) told her disciple, Avalokita (female), that she, along with Saudamini (female), Bhurivasu (male) and Devrat (male), had all been students of the same teacher and studied together. She mentioned that they had come from different places to pursue higher studies under this teacher. Notably, after completing their studies, Bhurivasu became a minister in the State of Padmavati, while Devrat became a minister in the State of Vidarbha.

Women's Involvement in Decision-making

सर्वं राज्ञः समुदायमायं च व्ययमेव च।
एकाहं वेद्मि कल्याणि पाण्डवानां यशस्विनि।।53।।

Sarvaṃ rājñaḥ samudāyamāyaṃ ca vyayameva ca.
Ekāhaṃ vedmi kalyāṇi pāṇḍavānāṃ yaśasvini।।53।।[44]

Draupadi told Satyabhama that she manages the accounting, income, expenditure and savings of the Pandavas' states.

धर्मार्थकुशला चैव द्रौपदी धर्मचारिणी।।11।।

Dharmārthakuśalā caiva draupadī dharmacāriṇī।।11।।[45]

Vidura said to the Pandavas, 'Draupadi is learned, versatile and knowledgeable in dharma and artha (economy and administration).'

Draupadi is renowned for her profound learning and versatility. Her knowledge extends beyond traditional wisdom to encompass a deep understanding of dharma and artha (economy and administration). Her insights into these areas make her a figure of considerable intellect and expertise. She demonstrates a comprehensive grasp of the principles that govern both moral conduct and practical matters, embodying a balanced perspective on ethical and economic aspects of life.

Women Are Naturally Nurturing and Often Take on the Role of Caring for Everyone around Them

अभुक्तं भुक्तवद् वापि सर्वमाकुब्जवामनम्।
अभुञ्जाना याज्ञसेनी प्रत्यवैक्षद् विशाम्पते।।48।।

Abhuktaṃ bhuktavad vāpi sarvamākubjavāmanam.
Abhuñjānā yājñasenī pratyavaikṣad viśāmpate।।48।।[46]

During the Rajasuya yajna, Draupadi would attend to the daily concern of determining who among the attendees, including hunchbacked individuals and dwarfs, had eaten and who had not, without partaking herself.

Draupadi, renowned for her intelligence and strength, demonstrates her keen observation and sense of care through her role in determining who among the attendees had eaten. Portrayed as a character with a strong moral compass, she often acts as a moral guide for those around her. Her task ensures that everyone present receives a fair share of care and food, irrespective of their social status or physical appearance. She attends to all attendees, including hunchbacked individuals and dwarfs, regardless of their physical condition or societal standing, ensuring that no one is overlooked. Attending to this task without partaking herself underscores her selflessness and dedication to her duties. Prioritizing the well-being of others over her own needs, Draupadi showcases her compassion and altruism.

Women Provide Solace and Support as Wives

क्रोधाविष्टेषु पार्थेषु धार्तराष्ट्रेषु चाप्यति।
द्रौपदी पाण्डुपुत्राणां कृष्णा शान्तिरिहाभवत्।।2।।

Krodhāviṣṭeṣu pārtheṣu dhārtarāṣṭreṣu cāpyati.
Draupadī pāṇḍuputrāṇāṃ kṛṣṇā śāntirihābhavat।।2।।[47]

Kunti's sons and Dhritarashtra's sons were all filled with anger towards each other. During this period, Draupadi became the provider of supreme peace to the Pandavas.

अप्लवेऽम्भसि मग्नानामप्रतिष्ठे निमज्जताम्।
पाञ्चाली पाण्डुपुत्राणां नौरेषा पारगाभवत्।।3।।

Aplave'mbhasi magnānāmapratiṣṭhe nimajjatām.
Pāñcālī pāṇḍuputrāṇāṃ naureṣā pāragābhavat।।3।।[48]

The Pandava brothers were drowning in a sea of problems, but Panchali (Draupadi) became the boat that helped them cross over.

Draupadi was renowned for her intelligence, courage and strength of character. In times of crisis, she played a pivotal role in supporting the Pandavas and guiding them through their overwhelming difficulties and obstacles. These challenges threatened to engulf them, leaving them feeling helpless and powerless. However, Draupadi, with her wisdom, resilience and unwavering support, acted as a beacon of hope and strength for the Pandavas. She provided them with stability, guidance and direction in navigating through their troubles. Her role as a supportive companion, advisor and moral anchor was instrumental in helping the Pandavas overcome their adversities and emerge victorious in their struggles.

न च भार्यासमं किंचिद् विद्यते भिषजां मतम्।
औषधं सर्वदुःखेषु सत्यमेतद् ब्रवीमि ते।।29।।

Na ca bhāryāsamaṃ kiṃcid vidyate bhiṣajāṃ matam.
Auṣadhaṃ sarvaduḥkheṣu satyametad bravīmi te।।29।।[49]

I am speaking the truth. Physicians assert that there is no better cure for soothing all sorrows than having a supportive wife.

The healing value of having a loving and supportive spouse, especially during difficult times, is not just specific to ancient times but has been echoed throughout literature and even in contemporary psychology. The support, understanding and companionship of a spouse can indeed provide immense comfort and help alleviate various kinds of sorrows and stresses in life.

भार्या मित्रं गृहे सतः।।64।।

Bhāryā mitraṃ gṛhe sataḥ।।64।।[50]

Yudhisthira responded to Yaksha, stating that the wife is the friend of the householder.

भार्या दैवकृतः सखा॥72॥

Bhāryā daivakṛtaḥ sakhā॥72॥[51]

Yudhisthira responded to the Yaksha by saying, 'A wife is a preordained companion.'

In the household, the role of a wife is pivotal. She is not merely a partner but also a confidante, advisor and companion to her husband, offering emotional support and sharing in his joys and sorrows. This contribution greatly enhances the overall well-being of the household. The relationship between husband and wife should be close and supportive, fostering a deep connection that underscores their shared journey in life. Spouses are seen as destined companions, imbuing the marital bond with purpose and significance. This perspective emphasizes the dedication and devotion required to fulfil their respective roles. There exists a deep reverence for the institution of marriage, acknowledging the wife's crucial role in providing companionship, support and stability within the household.

पुत्रपौत्रवधूभृत्यैराकीर्णमपि सर्वतः।
भार्याहीनं गृहस्थस्य शून्यमेव गृहं भवेत्॥5॥

Putrapautravadhūbhṛtyairākīrṇamapi sarvataḥ.
Bhāryāhīnaṃ gṛhasthasya śūnyameva gṛhaṃ bhavet॥5॥[52]

Even with sons, grandsons and worthy relatives filling a householder's home, it remains empty without the presence of a wife.

Despite the presence of these family members, the household is considered 'empty' without a wife due to the unique role and significance attributed to her within the family structure. A wife is seen as essential for the functioning and completeness of the household, often regarded as the primary caregiver, homemaker and emotional pillar of the family. She plays a central role in maintaining harmony, nurturing relationships and managing domestic affairs. Therefore, the absence of a wife can be perceived as leaving a void in the household's dynamics and emotional atmosphere.

Women Should Never Be Insulted under Any Circumstances

न च ग्राह्या बलात्स्त्रियः।।13।।

na ca grāhyā balātstriyaḥ||13||[53]

A woman should never be forcibly grabbed or restrained.

A woman should never be forcibly grabbed or restrained, as this violates her autonomy and personal space. Forcibly grabbing or restraining a woman can cause physical harm, emotional trauma and a profound sense of fear and helplessness, and it insults women. It is essential to foster an environment where respect for women's dignity is upheld, allowing them to feel safe and empowered to express themselves freely.

न च ते गर्हणीयाऽहं गर्हितव्याः स्त्रियः क्वचित्।।16।।

na ca te garhaṇīyā'haṃ garhitavyāḥ striyaḥ kvacit||16||[54]

Women should never be treated with contempt under any circumstances.

Women should never be treated with contempt under any circumstances as such attitudes undermine their inherent dignity and worth as human beings. Contempt breeds disrespect, which can manifest in various forms, including verbal abuse, discrimination and social exclusion. Every woman deserves to be treated with kindness, dignity, respect and equality, regardless of her background or circumstances.

Treating women with contempt not only harms individuals but also perpetuates harmful societal norms. It is essential to foster a culture that values and uplifts women while recognizing their contributions. By promoting respect and understanding, society can create an environment where women feel empowered to participate fully in all aspects of life, free from judgement and disdain.

न प्रियो मम कृष्णाया बीभत्सुर्न युधिष्ठिरः।
भीमसेनो यमौ वापि यदपश्यं सभागताम्।।49।।

Na priyo mama kṛṣṇāyā bībhatsurna yudhiṣṭhiraḥ.
Bhīmaseno yamau vāpi yadapaśyaṃ sabhāgatām।।49।।[55]

Kunti conveyed to Krishna that Yudhisthira, Bhim, Arjun, Nakula and Sahadeva are not as dear to her as Draupadi. I witnessed Draupadi being brought to the assembly. Never before have I experienced such profound sorrow.

यत्र सा बृहती श्यामा सभायां रुदती तदा।
अश्रौषीत् परुषा वाचस्तन्मे दुःखतरं महत्।।18।।

Yatra sā bṛhatī śyāmā sabhāyāṃ rudatī tadā.
Aśrauṣīt paruṣā vācastanme duḥkhataraṃ mahat।।18।।[56]

I'm not terribly saddened by the loss of the kingdom and being exiled. However, what truly grieve me are the bitter words uttered to my esteemed daughter-in-law, Draupadi, as she wept in front of the entire assembly.

औरसीं भगिनीं वापि भार्यां वाप्यनुजस्य यः।।22।।
प्रचरेत नरः कामात् तस्य दण्डो वधः स्मृतः।

Aurasīṃ bhaginīṃ vāpi bhāryāṃ vāpyanujasya yaḥ।।22।।
Pracareta naraḥ kāmāt tasya daṇḍo vadhaḥ smṛtaḥ.[57]

Shri Rama declared to Bali, 'Any man who approaches his own daughter, sister or the wife of his younger brothers with lust should face the punishment of death.'

Lustful behaviour directed towards women who are daughters, sisters or wives of younger brothers, particularly within close familial relationships, is condemned. This encompasses all forms of sexual advances or desires.

The emphasis lies in respecting familial bonds and refraining from inappropriate conduct.

The severity of the punishment underscores the gravity with which such actions are viewed. Punishments for serious offences were often portrayed as stringent to discourage such behaviour and uphold societal norms and values.

Any breach of these principles through lustful actions is deemed deserving of the severest punishment.

Utmost Respect Is Given to Women as Mothers

नास्ति मातृसमा छाया नास्ति मातृसमा गतिः।
नास्ति मातृसमं त्राणं नास्ति मातृसमा प्रिया॥31॥

Nāsti mātṛsamā chāyā nāsti mātṛsamā gatiḥ.
Nāsti mātṛsamaṃ trāṇaṃ nāsti mātṛsamā priyā॥31॥[58]

There is no refuge quite like a mother; her shelter embodies happiness, and there's no support like a mother's. And there is no protector comparable to a mother. For a child, nothing surpasses the endearment of a mother.

The unique and unparalleled role that mothers play in our lives extends beyond measure. A mother's love and care provide a sense of safety and security incomparable to any other. In her embrace, a child finds solace, comfort and joy, making a mother's presence itself a haven where one can find respite from life's storms. Mothers are often our greatest supporters, offering words of encouragement or simply being there to lend a listening ear. Their support is unwavering and unconditional, standing by us through thick and thin, offering guidance and strength whenever needed most.

A mother's instinct to protect her child is fierce and unyielding, leading her to go to great lengths to ensure their safety and well-being, shielding them from harm and danger. Her love is a powerful force, serving as a shield against the uncertainties of the world. The love and affection bestowed by a mother upon her child are unmatched, a bond forged through countless moments of care, sacrifice and devotion. In the eyes of a child, their mother's love is the purest and most cherished form of affection, surpassing all else in depth and significance.

देवतानां समावायमेकस्थं पितरं विदुः।
मर्त्यानां देवतानां च स्नेहादभ्येति मातरम्।।43।।

Devatānāṃ samāvāyamekasthaṃ pitaraṃ viduḥ.
Martyānāṃ devatānāṃ ca snehādabhyeti mātaram।।43।।[59]

Learned and wise individuals understand that the father symbolizes the culmination of all gods, situated in one place. Within the mother, affection resides for the entire humanity, encompassing the collective essence of all gods. Consequently, the glory of the mother surpasses that of the father.

The glory or greatness of the mother surpasses that of the father, as the nurturing and compassionate aspect represented by the mother is deemed more significant or powerful than the paternal aspect represented by the father.

उपाध्यायाद् दशाचार्य आचार्याणां शतं पिता।
पितुः शतगुणं माता गौरवेणातिरिच्यते।।

Upādhyāyād daśācārya ācāryāṇāṃ śataṃ pitā.
Pituḥ śataguṇaṃ mātā gauraveṇātiricyate.[60]

In terms of glory, a principal (acharya) is superior to ten teachers. A father is superior to a hundred principals, and a mother is superior to thousands of fathers.

The mother's influence and significance surpass that of teachers, principals and fathers many times over. This sentiment is deeply rooted in the nurturing and caregiving role traditionally associated with mothers. Mothers are often viewed as the primary caregivers, providing unconditional love, emotional support and guidance to their children. Their sacrifices and contributions to their children's lives are often considered immeasurable and unparalleled.

नास्ति मातृसमो गुरुः॥92॥

Nāsti mātṛsamo guruḥ॥92॥[61]

There is no teacher equal to a mother.

Mothers occupy a unique and profound role in a child's life, often serving as their first and most influential teacher. From the moment of birth, mothers nurture, guide and educate their children, instilling in them both basic as well as more complex lessons as they mature. This teaching is always accompanied by a deep sense of love, care and understanding, creating a safe environment where children can comfortably explore and learn. Mothers possess a unique ability to empathize with their children, comprehending their needs and emotions even when unspoken.

While formal education holds significance, a mother's teachings transcend mere academic lessons. They impart invaluable life skills, moral values and emotional intelligence that mould a child's character and future interactions with the world. Through their own actions, mothers exemplify qualities such as patience, resilience, kindness and empathy. A mother's teaching is not bound by a classroom or specific timeframe but rather is a lifelong, continuous process. Even as children mature into adults, mothers persist in offering support, guidance and wisdom, drawing upon their own experiences and acquired knowledge.

Mothers tailor their teaching methods to suit the individual needs and personalities of each child, recognizing and accommodating their uniqueness. This adaptability enables them to customize their approach to best foster each child's growth and development. The unparalleled influence and significance of a mother's role in shaping her children's lives are celebrated, acknowledging the profound impact of her love, guidance and teachings, which extend well beyond the confines of traditional education.

Maidens and Women: The Coronation of Female Rulers

स्योनासि सुषदासि क्षत्रस्य योनिरसि। स्योनामासीद
सुषदामासीद क्षत्रस्य योनिमासीद॥26॥

syonāsi suṣadāsi kṣatrasya yonirasi| syonāmāsīda suṣadāmāsīda
kṣatrasya yonimāsīda ||26||[62]

Women give birth to the protectors and defenders of the nation. They should occupy thrones of power and govern the state.

कन्यास्तत्राभिषेचय।।45।।

Kanyāstatrābhiṣecaya।।45।।[63]

The daughter should be installed as the ruler.

आत्मा हि दाराः सर्वेषां दारसंग्रहवर्तिनाम्।
आत्मेयमिति रामस्य पालयिष्यति मेदिनीम्॥ 24॥

ātmā hi dārāḥ sarveṣāṃ dārasaṃgrahavartinām|
ātmeyamiti rāmasya pālayiṣyati medinīm||24||[64]

The wives are the better half of their husbands.
Following this principle,
Sita represents Shri Rama. Therefore, in his absence,
Sita will rule the state of Ayodhya.

The Culprit Is the Man, Not the Woman

पाणिबन्धं स्वयं कृत्वा सह धर्ममुपेत्य च।
यदा यास्यन्ति पुरुषाः स्त्रियो नार्हन्ति वाच्यताम्।।36।।

Pāṇibandhaṃ svayaṃ kṛtvā saha dharmamupetya ca.
Yadā yāsyanti puruṣāḥ striyo nārhanti vācyatām||36||[65]

If a man, after entering into marriage and pledging to be honest and faithful, proceeds to engage in sexual misconduct with other men's wives, women cannot be held responsible for his actions.

एवं स्त्री नापराध्नोति नर एवापराध्यति।
व्युच्चरंश्च महादोषं नर एवापराध्यति।।38।।

Evaṃ strī nāparādhnoti nara evāparādhyati.
Vyuccaraṃśca mahādoṣaṃ nara evāparādhyati||38||[66]

In reality, the woman commits no offence; it is solely the men who commit offences. A man commits the grievous sin of adultery alone; thus, he is the offender.

नापराधोऽस्ति नारीणां नर एवापराध्यति।
सर्वकार्यापराध्यत्वान्नापराध्यन्ति चाङ्गनाः।।40।।

Nāparādho'sti nārīṇāṃ nara evāparādhyati.
Sarvakāryāparādhyatvānnāparādhyanti cāṅganāḥ||40||[67]

Women cannot commit sins; it is men who become the culprits and sinners. Due to being forced into submission and exploited due to their vulnerability, women cannot be deemed offenders.

The Marriage of Girls Should Be Carefully Considered to Ensure Their Well-being and Future Happiness

प्रीत्यारोपणमप्रतिषिद्धम्।

Prītyāropaṇamapratiṣiddham.[68]

Kautilya emphasizes that 'affection between a man and woman is essential in all marriages'.

यत्रेष्टं तत्र देया स्यान्नात्र कार्या विचारणा।।51।।

Yatreṣṭaṃ tatra deyā syānnātra kāryā vicāraṇā।।51।।[69]

The maiden should be given to the best groom available. Decent men ensure that the girl is married off to a suitable groom.

Respectable or honourable men will take on the responsibility of arranging a suitable marriage for the maiden. This implies a duty for the community or family members to ensure that the maiden does not marry someone unsuitable or unworthy. The term 'suitable groom' likely refers to someone who meets certain criteria deemed important by society or the family, such as being morally upright, financially secure and having good prospects for the future.

नानिष्टाय प्रदातव्या कन्या इत्यृषिचोदितम्।
तन्मूलं काममूलस्य प्रजनस्येति मे मतिः।।36।।

Nāniṣṭāya pradātavyā kanyā ityṛṣicoditam.
Tanmūlaṃ kāmamūlasya prajanasyeti me matiḥ।।36।।[70]

The perspective of the rishis is that a maiden should never be given to unworthy grooms. They believe that marrying a girl to a deserving man leads to fulfilment of amorous desires and the birth of worthy offspring.

A woman's hand in marriage should be bestowed upon a man deemed worthy by certain standards, encompassing moral character, physical personality, financial stability, social standing and compatibility with the woman in question. This ensures she thrives in a suitable environment and garners respect.

Marriage to a deserving man leads to sensual fulfillment, encompassing emotional, psychological and marital satisfaction. The notion is that when a woman is married to a man who respects, cherishes and fulfils her needs, she experiences a deeper level of fulfilment in her life, including her intimate relationship.

The quality of the marriage extends beyond the couple themselves and impacts future generations. By marrying a deserving man, the couple is believed to be more likely to raise children embodying virtues, morals and esteemed qualities, contributing positively to the community and the world.

The importance of careful consideration and discernment in marriage is highlighted, emphasizing potential long-term consequences for individuals and society as a whole. It underscores the belief that marriage is not merely a union between two individuals but also a significant institution with far-reaching implications.

न चैतेभ्यः प्रदातव्या न वोढव्या तथाविधा।
न ह्येव भार्या क्रेतव्या न विक्रय्या कथंचन।।46।।

Na caitebhyaḥ pradātavyā na voḍhavyā tathāvidhā.
Na hyeva bhāryā kretavyā na vikrayyā kathaṃcana।।46।।[71]

Do not give maidens to individuals involved in the sale and purchase of girls, and refrain from marrying a maiden who is being sold, because a wife is not a commodity to be bought or sold in any manner.

It is a clear denouncement of the sale and purchase of girls. It discourages marrying off maidens to individuals involved in such practices, emphasizing that a wife should not be treated as a commodity. This aligns with the ethical stance against human trafficking and the exploitation of women.

Women as Warriors and Companions in Warfare

सि॒ꣳह्यसि सपत्नसा॒ही दे॒वेभ्यः॑ शु॒न्धस्व।
सि॒ꣳह्यसि सपत्नसा॒ही दे॒वेभ्यः॑ शु॒म्भस्व॥10॥

siꣳhyasi sapatnasāhī devebhyaḥ śundhasva|
siꣳhyasi sapatnasāhī devebhyaḥ śumbhasva ||10||[72]

Women, like lionesses, possess the strength and capability to defeat any enemy.

तत्राकरोन्महायुद्धं राजा दशरथस्तदा।
असुरैश्च महाबाहुः शस्त्रैश्च शकलीकृतः।।15।।

Tatrākaronmahāyuddhaṃ rājā daśarathastadā.
Asuraiśca mahābāhuḥ śastraiśca śakalīkṛtaḥ।।15।।[73]

अपवाह्य त्वया देवि संग्रामान्नष्टचेतनः।
तत्रापि विक्षतः शस्त्रैः पतिस्ते रक्षितस्त्वया।।16।।

Apavāhya tvayā devi saṃgrāmānnaṣṭacetanaḥ.
Tatrāpi vikṣataḥ śastraiḥ patiste rakṣitastvayā।।16।।[74]

King Dashrath fought a terrible battle with the Asuras,
during which they lacerated his body with their weapons.
When the King became unconscious, Kaikeyi served as his charioteer,
moving him far from the battlefield to protect him. Again, when he was
injured by Asura weapons, Kaikeyi once more shielded him
by taking him to a safe place.

Women's Rights in the Dissolution of Marriage

नीचत्वं परदेशं वा प्रस्थितो राजकिल्बिषी।
प्राणाभिहन्ता पतितस्त्याज्यः क्लीबोऽपि वा पतिः।।

nīcatvaṃ paradeśaṃ vā prasthito rājakilbiṣī.
prāṇābhihantā patitastyājyaḥ klībo'pi vā patiḥ.[75]

The wife has the right to dissolve her marriage if her husband is
considered unworthy due to factors such as his low character,
residence in a foreign country, disloyalty to the nation,
involvement in criminal activities like murder, departure from moral
principles, lack of integrity, impotence or unmanliness.

Capital Punishment for Rapists

सवर्णामप्राप्तफलां कन्यां प्रकुर्वतो हस्तवधश्चतुःशतो वा दण्डः। मृतायां वधः।

Savarṇāmaprāptaphalāṃ kanyāṃ prakurvato hastavadhaścatuḥśato vā daṇḍaḥ. mṛtāyāṃ vadhaḥ.[76]

Kautilya emphasized that the death penalty should be imposed on any man who violates a maiden.

APPENDIX

Suktas and Mantras of the Brahmavadini Rishis in the *Rigveda*

Romesha (रोमशा), Mandal 1, Sukta 126

उपो॑प मे॒ परा॑ मृश॒ मा मे॑ द॒भ्राणि॑ मन्यथाः ।
सर्वा॒हम॑स्मि रोम॒शा ग॒न्धारी॑णामिवावि॒का ॥1॥

Lopāmudrā (लोपामुद्रा), Mandal 1, Sukta 179

पू॒र्वीर॒हं श॒रदः॑ शश्रमा॒णा दो॒षा वस्तो॑रु॒षसो॑ ज॒रय॑न्तीः ।
मि॒नाति॒ श्रियं॑ जरि॒मा त॒नूना॒मप्यू॒ नु पत्नी॒र्वृष॑णो जगम्युः ॥1॥
ये चि॒द्धि पूर्व॑ ऋत॒साप॒ आस॑न्सा॒कं दे॒वेभि॒रव॑दन्नृ॒तानि॑ ।
ते चि॒दवा॑सु॒र्नह्य॑न्त॒मा॒पुः समू॒ नु पत्नी॒र्वृष॑भिर्जगम्युः ॥2॥
न मृषा॑ श्रा॒न्तं यदव॑न्ति दे॒वा विश्वा॒ इत्स्पृधो॑ अ॒भ्य॑श्नवाव ।
जया॒वेदत्र॑ श॒तनी॑थमा॒जिं यत्स॒म्यञ्चा॑ मिथु॒नाव॒भ्यजा॑व ॥3॥
न॒दस्य॑ मा रुध॒तः काम॒ आग॑न्नि॒त आजा॑तो अ॒मुतः॒ कुत॑श्चित् ।
लोपा॑मुद्रा॒ वृष॑णं॒ नी रि॑णाति॒ धीर॒मधी॑रा धयति श्व॒सन्त॑म् ॥4॥
इ॒मं नु सोम॒मन्ति॑तो हृ॒त्सु पी॒तमुप॑ ब्रुवे ।
यत्सी॒माग॑श्चकृ॒मा तत्सु मृ॑ळतु पुलु॒कामो॒ हि मर्त्यः॑ ॥5॥
अ॒गस्त्यः॒ खन॑मानः ख॒नित्रैः॑ प्र॒जामप॑त्यं॒ बल॑मि॒च्छमा॑नः ।
उ॒भौ वर्णा॒वृषि॑रु॒ग्रः पु॑पोष स॒त्या दे॒वेष्वा॒शिषो॑ जगाम ॥6॥

Nadi (नदी), Mandal 3, Sukta 33

प्र पर्व॑ताना॒मुश॒ती उ॒पस्था॒दश्वे॑ इव॒ विषि॑ते॒ हास॑माने ।
गावे॑व शु॒भ्रे मा॒तरा॑ रिहा॒णे विपा॑ट्छु॒तुद्री॒ पय॑सा जवेते ॥1॥
इन्द्रे॑षिते प्रस॒वं भिक्ष॑माणे॒ अच्छा॑ समु॒द्रं र॒थ्ये॑व याथः ।
स॒मा॒रा॒णे ऊ॒र्मिभिः॒ पिन्व॑माने अ॒न्या वा॑म॒न्यामप्ये॑ति शुभ्रे ॥2॥
अच्छा॒ सिन्धुं॑ मा॒तृत॑मामयासं॒ विपा॑शमु॒र्वीं सु॒भगा॑मगन्म ।
व॒त्समि॑व मा॒तरा॑ संरिहा॒णे स॑मा॒नं योनि॒मनु॑ सं॒चर॑न्ती ॥3॥
ए॒ना व॒यं पय॑सा॒ पिन्व॑माना॒ अनु॒ योनिं॑ दे॒वकृ॑तं॒ चर॑न्तीः ।

न वर्त॑वे प्रस॒वः सर्ग॑तक्तः कि॒ंयु॒र्विप्रो॑ न॒द्यो॑ जोहवीति ॥4॥
रम॑ध्वं मे॒ वच॑से सो॒म्याय॒ ऋता॑वरी॒रुप॑ मु॒हु॒र्तमेवैः ।
प्र सिन्धु॒मच्छा॑ बृह॒ती म॑नी॒षाव॒स्युर॑ह्वे कु॒शि॒कस्य॑ सू॒नुः ॥5॥
इन्द्रो॑ अ॒स्माँ अ॑रद॒द्वज्र॑बाहु॒रपा॑हन्वृ॒त्रं प॑रि॒धिं न॒दीना॑म् ।
दे॒वो॑ऽनयत्सवि॒ता सु॑पा॒णिस्तस्य॑ व॒यं प्र॑स॒वे या॑म उ॒र्वीः ॥6॥
प्र॒वाच्यं॑ शश्व॒धा वी॒र्यं१ तदिन्द्र॑स्य॒ कर्म॒ यदहिं॑ विवृ॒श्चत् ।
वि वज्रे॑ण परि॒षदो॑ जघा॒नाय॒न्नापो॑ऽय॑नमि॒च्छमा॑नाः ॥7॥
ए॒तद्वचो॑ जरित॒र्मापि॑ मृष्ठा॒ आ यत्ते॒ घोषा॒नुत्त॑रा यु॒गानि॑ ।
उ॒क्थेषु॑ कारो॒ प्रति॑ नो जुषस्व॒ मा नो॒ नि कः॑ पुरुष॒त्रा नम॑स्ते ॥8॥
ओ षु स्व॑सारः का॒रवे॑ शृणोत य॒यौ वो॑ दू॒रादन॑सा॒ रथे॑न ।
नि षू न॑मध्वं॒ भव॑ता सु॒पा॒रा अ॑धोअ॒क्षाः सि॑न्धवः स्रो॒त्याभिः॑ ॥9॥
आ ते॑ कारो शृणवामा॒ वचां॑सि य॒याथ॑ दू॒रादन॑सा॒ रथे॑न ।
नि ते॑ नंसै पीप्या॒नेव॒ योषा॒ मर्या॑येव क॒न्या॑ शश्व॒चै॑ ते ॥10॥
यद॒ङ्ग त्वा॑ भर॒ताः सं॒तरे॑युर्ग॒व्यन्ग्राम॑ इषि॒त इन्द्र॑जूतः ।
अर्षा॒दह॑ प्रस॒वः सर्ग॑तक्त॒ आ वो॑ वृणे सु॒म॒तिं य॒ज्ञिया॑नाम् ॥11॥
अता॑रिषुर्भर॒ता ग॒व्यवः॒ सम॑भक्त॒ विप्रः॑ सु॒म॒तिं न॒दीना॑म् ।
प्र पि॑न्वध्वमि॒षय॑न्तीः सु॒राधा॒ आ व॒क्षणाः॑ पृ॒णध्वं॑ या॒त शीभ॑म् ॥12॥
उद्व॑ ऊ॒र्मिः शम्या॑ ह॒न्त्वापो॒ योक्त्रा॑णि मु॒ञ्चत ।
मादु॑ष्कृ॒तौ व्ये॑नसा॒घ्न्यौ शून॒मार॑ताम् ॥13॥

Vishwavara (विश्ववारा), Mandal 5, Sukta 28

समि॑द्धो अ॒ग्निर्दि॒वि शो॒चिर॑श्रेत्प्र॒त्यङ्ङु॒षस॑मुर्वि॒या वि भा॑ति ।
एति॒ प्राची॑ वि॒श्ववा॑रा॒ नमो॑भिर्दे॒वाँ ईळा॑ना ह॒विषा॑ घृ॒ताची॑ ॥1॥
स॒मि॒ध्यमा॑नो अ॒मृत॑स्य राजसि ह॒विष्कृ॒ण्वन्तं॑ सचसे स्व॒स्तये॑ ।
विश्वं॒ स ध॑त्ते॒ द्रवि॑णं॒ यमिन्व॑स्याति॒थ्यम॑ग्ने॒ नि च॑ धत्त॒ इत्पु॒रः ॥2॥
अग्ने॒ शर्ध॑ मह॒ते सौभ॑गाय॒ तव॑ द्यु॒म्नान्यु॑त्त॒मानि॑ सन्तु ।
सं जा॑स्प॒त्यं सु॒यम॒मा कृ॑णुष्व शत्रूय॒ताम॒भि ति॑ष्ठा॒ महां॑सि ॥3॥
समि॑द्धस्य॒ प्रम॑ह॒सोऽग्ने॒ वन्दे॒ तव॒ श्रिय॑म् ।
वृ॒ष॒भो द्यु॒म्नवा॑ँ॒ असि॒ सम॑ध्व॒रेष्वि॑ध्यसे ॥4॥
समि॑द्धो अग्न आहुत दे॒वान्य॑क्षि स्वध्वर ।
त्वं हि ह॑व्य॒वाळसि॑ ॥5॥
आ जु॑होता दुव॒स्यता॒ग्निं प्र॑य॒त्य॑ध्व॒रे ।
वृ॒णी॒ध्वं ह॑व्य॒वाह॑नम् ॥6॥

Shashwati (शश्वती), Mandal 8, Sukta 1

अन्व॑स्य स्थू॒रं द॑दृशे पु॒रस्ता॑दन॒स्थ ऊ॒रुर॑व॒रम्ब॑माणः ।
शश्व॑ती॒ नार्य॑भि॒चक्ष्या॑ह॒ सुभ॑द्रमर्य॒ भोज॑नं बिभर्षि ॥1॥

Apala (अपाला), Mandal 8, Sukta 91

कन्या॒३ वार॑वाय॒ती सोम॒मपि॑ स्रु॒तावि॑दत्।
अस्तं॒ भर॑न्त्यब्रवी॒दिन्द्रा॑य सुनवै त्वा श॒क्राय॑ सुनवै त्वा ॥1॥
अ॒सौ य एषि॑ वीर॒को गृ॒हंगृ॑हं वि॒चाक॑शद्।
इ॒मं जम्भ॑सुतं पिब धा॒नाव॑न्तं कर॒म्भिण॑मपू॒पव॑न्तमु॒क्थिन॑म् ॥2॥
आ च॒न त्वा॑ चिकित्सा॒मोऽधि॑ च॒न त्वा॒ नेम॑सि।
शनै॑रिव शन॒कैरि॒वेन्द्रा॑येन्दो॒ परि॑ स्रव ॥3॥
कु॒विच्छक॑त्कु॒वित्कर॑त्कु॒विन्नो॒ वस्य॑स॒स्कर॑त्।
कु॒वित्प॑ति॒द्विषो॑ य॒तीरिन्द्रे॑ण सं॒गमा॑महै ॥4॥
इ॒मानि॒ त्रीणि॑ वि॒ष्टपा॒ तानी॑न्द्र॒ वि रो॑हय।
शिर॑स्त॒तस्यो॒र्वरा॒मादि॒दं म॒ उपो॒दरे॑ ॥5॥
अ॒सौ च॒ या न॑ उ॒र्वरादि॒मां त॒न्व१ं मम॑।
अथो॑ त॒तस्य॒ यच्छिरः॒ सर्वा॒ ता रो॑म॒शा कृ॑धि ॥6॥
खे रथ॑स्य॒ खेऽन॑सः॒ खे यु॒गस्य॑ शतक्रतो।
अ॒पाला॑मिन्द्र॒ त्रिष्पू॒त्व्यकृ॑णोः॒ सूर्य॑त्वचम् ॥7॥

Yami (यमी), Mandal 10, Sukta 10

ओ चि॒त्सखा॑यं स॒ख्या व॑वृत्यां ति॒रः पु॒रू चि॑दर्ण॒वं ज॑ग॒न्वान्।
पि॒तुर्नपा॑त॒मा द॑धीत वे॒धा अधि॒ क्षमि॑ प्रत॒रं दीध्या॑नः ॥1॥
न ते॒ सखा॑ स॒ख्यं व॑ष्ट्ये॒तत्सल॑क्ष्मा॒ यद्विषु॑रूपा॒ भवा॑ति।
म॒हस्पु॒त्रासो॒ असु॑रस्य वी॒रा दि॒वो ध॒र्तार॑ उर्वि॒या परि॑ ख्यन् ॥2॥
उ॒शन्ति॑ घा॒ ते अ॒मृता॑स ए॒तदेक॑स्य चित्त्य॒जसं॒ मर्त्य॑स्य।
नि ते॒ मनो॒ मन॑सि धाय्य॒स्मे जन्युः॒ पति॑स्त॒न्व१मा वि॑विश्याः ॥3॥
न यत्पु॒रा च॑कृ॒मा कद्ध॑ नू॒नमृ॒ता वद॑न्तो॒ अनृ॑तं रपेम।
ग॒न्ध॒र्वो अ॒प्स्वप्या॑ च॒ योषा॒ सा नो॒ नाभिः॑ पर॒मं जा॒मि तन्नौ॑ ॥4॥
गर्भे॒ नु नौ॑ जनि॒ता दम्प॑ती कर्दे॒वस्त्वष्टा॑ सवि॒ता वि॒श्वरू॑पः।
नकि॑रस्य॒ प्र मि॑नन्ति व्र॒तानि॒ वेद॑ नावस्य पृथि॒वी उ॒त द्यौः ॥5॥
को अ॒स्य वे॑द प्रथ॒मस्याह्नः॒ क ईं॑ ददर्श॒ क इ॒ह प्र वो॑चत्।
बृ॒हन्मि॒त्रस्य॒ वरु॑णस्य॒ धाम॒ कदु॑ ब्रव आहनो॒ वीच्या॒ नॄन् ॥6॥
य॒मस्य॑ मा य॒म्य१ं काम॒ आग॑न्त्समा॒ने योनौ॑ सह॒शेय्या॑य।
जा॒येव॒ पत्ये॑ त॒न्वं॑ रिरिच्यां॒ वि चि॑द्वृहेव॒ रथ्ये॑व च॒क्रा ॥7॥
न ति॑ष्ठन्ति॒ न नि मि॑षन्त्ये॒ते दे॒वानां॒ स्पश॑ इ॒ह ये चर॑न्ति।
अ॒न्येन॒ मदा॑हनो याहि॒ तूयं॒ तेन॒ वि वृ॑ह॒ रथ्ये॑व च॒क्रा ॥8॥
रात्री॑भिरस्मा॒ अह॑भिर्दशस्ये॒त्सूर्य॑स्य॒ चक्षु॒र्मुहु॒रुन्मि॑मीयात्।
दि॒वा पृ॑थि॒व्या मि॑थु॒ना सब॑न्धू य॒मीर्य॒मस्य॑ बिभृया॒दजा॑मि ॥9॥
आ घा॒ ता ग॑च्छा॒नुत्त॑रा यु॒गानि॒ यत्र॑ जा॒मयः॑ कृ॒णव॒न्नजा॑मि।
उप॑ बर्बृहि वृष॒भाय॑ बा॒हुम॒न्यमि॑च्छस्व सुभगे॒ पतिं॒ मत् ॥10॥

किं भ्रातासद्यदनाथं भवाति किमु स्वसा यन्निर्ऋतिर्निगच्छात्।
काममूता बह्वे३तद्रपामि तन्वा मे तन्वं१ सं पिपृग्धि ॥11॥
न वा उ ते तन्वा तन्वं१ सं पपृच्यां पापमाहुर्यः स्वसारं निगच्छात्।
अन्येन मत्प्रमुदः कल्पयस्व न ते भ्राता सुभगे वष्ट्येतत् ॥12॥
बतो बतासि यम नैव ते मनो हृदयं चाविदाम।
अन्या किल त्वां कक्ष्येव युक्तं परि ष्वजाते लिबुजेव वृक्षम् ॥13॥
अन्यमू षु त्वं यम्यन्य उ त्वां परि ष्वजाते लिबुजेव वृक्षम्।
तस्य वा त्वं मन इच्छा स वा तवाधा कृणुष्व संविदं सुभद्राम् ॥14॥

Ghosha (घोषा), Mandal 10, Suktas 39 and 40

यो वां परिज्मा सुवृदश्विना रथो दोषामुषासो हव्यो हविष्मता।
शश्वत्तमासस्तमु वामिदं वयं पितुर्न नाम सुहवं हवामहे ॥1॥
चोदयतं सूनृताः पिन्वतं धिय उत्पुरंधीरीरयतं तदुश्मसि।
यशसं भागं कृणुतं नो अश्विना सोमं न चारुं मघवत्सु नस्कृतम् ॥2॥
अमाजुरश्चिद्भवथो युवं भगोऽनाशोश्चिदवितारापमस्य चित्।
अन्धस्य चिन्नासत्या कृशस्य चिद्युवामिदाहुर्भिषजा रुतस्य चित् ॥3॥
युवं च्यवानं सनयं यथा रथं पुनर्युवानं चरथाय तक्षथुः।
निष्टौग्र्यमूहथुरद्भ्यस्परि विश्वेत्ता वां सवनेषु प्रवाच्या ॥4॥
पुराणा वां वीर्या३ प्र ब्रवा जनेऽथो हासथुर्भिषजा मयोभुवा।
ता वां नु नव्याववसे करामहेऽयं नासत्या श्रदरिर्यथा दधत् ॥5॥
इयं वामह्वे शृणुतं मे अश्विना पुत्रायेव पितरा मह्यं शिक्षतम्।
अनापिरज्ञा असजात्यामतिः पुरा तस्या अभिशस्तेरव स्पृतम् ॥6॥
युवं रथेन विमदाय शुन्ध्युवं न्यूहथुः पुरुमित्रस्य योषणाम्।
युवं हवं वध्रिमत्या अगच्छतं युवं सुषुतिं चक्रथुः पुरंधये ॥7॥
युवं विप्रस्य जरणामुपेयुषः पुनः कलेरकृणुतं युवद्वयः।
युवं वन्दनमृश्यदादुदूपथुर्युवं सद्यो विश्पलामेतवे कृथः ॥8॥
युवं ह रेभं वृषणा गुहा हितमुदैरयतं ममृवांसमश्विना।
युवमृबीसमुत तप्तमत्रय ओमन्वन्तं चक्रथुः सप्तवध्रये ॥9॥
युवं श्वेतं पेदवेऽश्विनाश्वं नवभिर्वाजैर्नवती च वाजिनम्।
चर्कृत्यं ददथुर्द्रावयत्सखं भगं न नृभ्यो हव्यं मयोभुवम् ॥10॥
न तं राजानावदिते कुतश्चन नांहो अश्नोति दुरितं नकिर्भयम्।
यमश्विना सुहवा रुद्रवर्तनी पुरोरथं कृणुथः पत्न्या सह ॥11॥
आ तेन यातं मनसो जवीयसा रथं यं वामृभवश्चक्रुरश्विना।
यस्य योगे दुहिता जायते दिव उभे अहनी सुदिने विवस्वतः ॥12॥
ता वर्तिर्यातं जयुषा वि पर्वतमपिन्वतं शयवे धेनुमश्विना।
वृकस्य चिद्वर्तिकामन्तरास्याद्युवं शचीभिर्ग्रसिताममुञ्चतम् ॥13॥
एतं वां स्तोममश्विनावकर्मातक्षाम भृगवो न रथम्।

न्य॑मृक्षाम॒ योष॑णां॒ न मर्ये॒ नित्यं॒ न सू॒नुं तन॑यं॒ दधा॑नाः ॥14॥
रथं॒ यान्तं॒ कुह॒ को ह॑ वां नरा॒ प्रति॑ द्युमन्तं॑ सुवि॒ताय॑ भूषति ।
प्रा॒त॒र्यावा॑णं वि॒भ्वं॑ वि॒शेवि॑शे॒ वस्तो॑र्वस्तो॒र्वह॑मानं धि॒या शमि॑ ॥1॥
कुह॑ स्वि॒द्दोषा कुह॒ वस्तो॑र॒श्विना॒ कुहा॑भिपि॒त्वं क॑रत॒: कुहो॑षतुः ।
को वां॑ शयु॒त्रा वि॒धवे॑व दे॒वरं॒ मर्यं॒ न योषा॑ कृणु॒ते स॒धस्थ॒ आ ॥2॥
प्रा॒तर्ज॑रेथे जर॒णेव॒ काप॑या॒ वस्तो॑र्वस्तोर्यज॒ता ग॑च्छथो गृ॒हम् ।
कस्य॑ ध्व॒स्रा भ॑वथ॒: कस्य॑ वा नरा राजपु॒त्रेव॒ सव॒नाव॑ गच्छथः ॥3॥
यु॒वां मृ॒गेव॑ वार॒णा मृ॑ग॒ण्यवो॑ दो॒षा वस्तो॑र्ह॒विषा॒ नि ह्व॑यामहे ।
यु॒वं होत्रा॑मृतु॒था जुह्व॑ते न॒रेषं॒ जना॑य वहथः शुभस्पती ॥4॥
यु॒वां ह॒ घोषा॒ पर्य॑श्विना य॒ती राज्ञ॑ ऊचे दुहि॒ता पृ॒च्छे वां॑ नरा ।
भू॒तं मे॒ अह्न॑ उ॒त भू॑तम॒क्तवेऽश्वा॑वते र॒थिने॑ शक्त॒मर्व॑ते ॥5॥
यु॒वं क॒वी ष्ठ॒: पर्य॑श्विना॒ रथं॒ विशो॒ न कुत्सो॑ जरि॒तुर्न॑शायथः ।
यु॒वोर्ह॒ मक्षा॒ पर्य॑श्विना॒ मध्वा॒सा भ॑रत निष्कृ॒तं न योष॑णा ॥6॥
यु॒वं ह॑ भु॒ज्युं यु॒वम॑श्विना॒ वशं॑ यु॒वं शि॒ञ्जार॑मु॒शना॒मुपा॑रथुः ।
यु॒वो ररा॑वा॒ परि॑ स॒ख्यमा॑सते यु॒वोर॒हमव॑सा सु॒म्नमा च॑के ॥7॥
यु॒वं ह॑ कृ॒शं यु॒वम॑श्विना श॒युं यु॒वं वि॒धन्तं॑ वि॒धवा॑मुरुष्यथः ।
यु॒वं स॒निभ्य॑: स्त॒नय॑न्तमश्वि॒नाप॑ व्र॒जमू॑र्णु॒थः स॒प्तास्य॑म् ॥8॥
जनि॑ष्ट॒ योषा॑ प॒तय॑त्कनीन॒को वि चारु॑हन्वी॒रुधो॑ दं॒सना॒ अनु॑ ।
आस्मै॑ रीयन्ते निव॒नेव॒ सिन्ध॑वो॒ऽस्मा अह्ने॑ भवति॒ तत्प॑तित्व॒नम् ॥9॥
जी॒वं रु॑दन्ति॒ वि म॑यन्ते अध्व॒रे दी॒र्घामनु॒ प्रसि॑तिं दीधियु॒र्नर॑: ।
वा॒मं पि॒तृभ्यो॒ य इ॒दं स॑मेरि॒रे मय॒: पति॑भ्यो॒ जन॑यः परि॒ष्वजे॑ ॥10॥
न तस्य॑ विद्म॒ तदु॒ षु प्र वो॑चत॒ युवा॑ ह॒ यद्यु॑व॒त्याः क्षेति॒ योनि॑षु ।
प्रि॒योस्रि॑यस्य वृष॒भस्य॑ रे॒तिनो॑ गृ॒हं ग॑मेमाश्विना॒ तदु॑श्मसि ॥11॥
आ वा॑मगन्सुम॒तिर्वा॑जिनीवसू॒ न्य॑श्विना हृ॒त्सु कामा॑ अयंसत ।
अभू॑तं गो॒पा मि॑थु॒ना शु॑भस्पती प्रि॒या अ॑र्य॒म्णो दुर्या॑ अशीमहि ॥12॥
ता म॑न्दसा॒ना मनु॑षो दुरो॒ण आ ध॒त्तं र॒यिं स॒हवी॑रं वच॒स्यवे॑ ।
कृ॒तं ती॒र्थं सु॑प्रपा॒णं शु॑भस्पती स्था॒णुं प॑थे॒ष्ठामप॑ दुर्म॒तिं ह॑तम् ॥13॥
क्व॑ स्वि॒दद्य क॑त॒मास्व॒श्विना॑ वि॒क्षु द॒स्रा मा॑दयेते शु॒भस्पती॑ ।
क ईं॒ नि ये॑मे कत॒मस्य॑ जग्मतु॒र्विप्र॑स्य वा॒ यज॑मानस्य वा गृ॒हम् ॥14॥

Agastya (अगस्त्या), Mandal 10, Sukta 60

अ॒गस्त्य॑स्य॒ नद्भ्य॒: सप्ती॑ युनक्षि॒ रोहि॑ता ।
प॒णीन्न्य॑क्रमीर॒भि विश्वा॑न्राजन्नरा॒धस॑: ॥6॥

Aditi (अदिति) Mandal 10, Sukta 72

दे॒वानां॒ नु व॒यं जाना॒ प्र वो॑चाम विप॒न्यया॑ ।
उ॒क्थेषु॑ श॒स्यमा॑नेषु॒ यः पश्या॒दुत्त॑रे यु॒गे ॥1॥

देवानां पूर्व्ये युगेऽसतः सदजायत ॥2॥
देवानां युगे प्रथमेऽसतः सदजायत ।
तदाशा अन्वजायन्त तदुत्तानपदस्परि ॥3॥
भूर्जज्ञ उत्तानपदो भुव आशा अजायन्त ।
अदितेर्दक्षो अजायत दक्षाद्वदितिः परि ॥4॥
अदितिर्ह्यजनिष्ट दक्ष या दुहिता तव ।
तां देवा अन्वजायन्त भद्रा अमृतबन्धवः ॥5॥
यद्देवा अदः सलिले सुसंरब्धा अतिष्ठत ।
अत्रा वो नृत्यतामिव तीव्रो रेणुरपायत ॥6॥
यद्देवा यतयो यथा भुवनान्यपिन्वत ।
अत्रा समुद्र आ गूळहमा सूर्यमजभर्तन ॥7॥
अष्टौ पुत्रासो अदितेर्ये जातास्तन्वस्परि ।
देवाँ उप प्रैत्सप्तभिः परा मार्ताण्डमास्यत् ॥8॥
सप्तभिः पुत्रैरदितिरुप प्रैत्पूर्व्यं युगम् ।
प्रजायै मृत्यवे त्वत्पुनर्मार्ताण्डमाभरत् ॥9॥

Surya (सूर्या) and Savitri (सावित्री), Mandal 10, Sukta 85

सत्येनोत्तभिता भूमिः सूर्येणोत्तभिता द्यौः ।
ऋतेनादित्यास्तिष्ठन्ति दिवि सोमो अधि श्रितः ॥1॥
सोमेनादित्या बलिनः सोमेन पृथिवी मही ।
अथो नक्षत्राणामेषामुपस्थे सोम आहितः ॥2॥
सोमं मन्यते पपिवान्यत्सम्पिंषन्त्योषधिम् ।
सोमं यं ब्रह्माणो विदुर्न तस्याश्नाति कश्चन ॥3॥
आच्छद्विधानैर्गुपितो बार्हतैः सोम रक्षितः ।
ग्राव्णामिच्छृण्वन्तिष्ठसि न ते अश्नाति पार्थिवः ॥4॥
यत्त्वा देव प्रपिबन्ति तत आ प्यायसे पुनः ।
वायुः सोमस्य रक्षिता समानां मास आकृतिः ॥5॥
रैभ्यासीदनुदेयी नाराशंसी न्योचनी ।
सूर्याया भद्रमिद्वासो गाथयैति परिष्कृतम् ॥6॥
चित्तिरा उपबर्हणं चक्षुरा अभ्यञ्जनम् ।
द्यौर्भूमिः कोश आसीद्यदयात्सूर्या पतिम् ॥7॥
स्तोमा आसन्प्रतिधयः कुरीरं छन्द ओपशः ।
सूर्याया अश्विना वराग्निरासीत्पुरोगवः ॥8॥
सोमो वधूयुरभवदश्विनास्तामुभा वरा ।
सूर्यां यत्पत्ये शंसन्तीं मनसा सविताददात् ॥9॥
मनो अस्या अन आसीद्द्यौरासीदुत च्छदिः ।

शुक्रावनड्वाहावास्तां यदयात्सूर्या गृहम् ॥10॥
ऋक्सामाभ्यामभिहितौ गावौ ते सामनावितः ।
श्रोत्रं ते चक्रे आस्तां दिवि पन्थाश्चराचारः ॥11॥
शुची ते चक्रे यात्या व्यानो अक्ष आहतः ।
अनो मनस्मयं सूर्यारोहत्प्रयती पतिम् ॥12॥
सूर्याया वहतुः प्रागात्सविता यमवासृजत् ।
अघासु हन्यन्ते गावोऽर्जुन्योः पर्युह्यते ॥13॥
यदश्विना पृच्छमानावयातं त्रिचक्रेण वहतुं सूर्यायाः ।
विश्वे देवा अनु तद्वामजानन्पुत्रः पितराववृणीत पूषा ॥14॥
यदयातं शुभस्पती वरेयं सूर्यामुप ।
क्वैकं चक्रं वामासीत्क्व देष्ट्राय तस्थथुः ॥15॥
द्वे ते चक्रे सूर्ये ब्रह्माण ऋतुथा विदुः ।
अथैकं चक्रं यद्गुहा तदद्धातय इद्विदुः ॥16॥
सूर्यायै देवेभ्यो मित्राय वरुणाय च ।
ये भूतस्य प्रचेतस इदं तेभ्योऽकरं नमः ॥17॥
पूर्वापरं चरतो माययैतौ शिशू क्रीळन्तौ परि यातो अध्वरम् ।
विश्वान्यन्यो भुवनाभिचष्ट ऋतूँरन्यो विदधज्जायते पुनः ॥18॥
नवोनवो भवति जायमानोऽह्नां केतुरुषसामेत्यग्रम् ।
भागं देवेभ्यो वि दधात्यायन्प्र चन्द्रमास्तिरते दीर्घमायुः ॥19॥
सुकिंशुकं शल्मलिं विश्वरूपं हिरण्यवर्णं सुवृतं सुचक्रम् ।
आ रोह सूर्ये अमृतस्य लोकं स्योनं पत्ये वहतुं कृणुष्व ॥20॥
उदीर्ष्वातः पतिवती ह्येषा विश्वावसुं नमसा गीर्भिरीळे ।
अन्यामिच्छ पितृषदं व्यक्तां स ते भागो जनुषा तस्य विद्धि ॥21॥
उदीर्ष्वातो विश्वावसो नमसेळा महे त्वा ।
अन्यामिच्छ प्रफर्व्यँ१ सं जायां पत्या सृज ॥22॥
अनृक्षरा ऋजवः सन्तु पन्था येभिः सखायो यन्ति नो वरेयम् ।
समर्यमा सं भगो नो निनीयात्सं जास्पत्यं सुयममस्तु देवाः ॥23॥
प्र त्वा मुञ्चामि वरुणस्य पाशाद्येन त्वाबध्नात्सविता सुशेवः ।
ऋतस्य योनौ सुकृतस्य लोकेऽरिष्टां त्वा सह पत्या दधामि ॥24॥
प्रेतो मुञ्चामि नामुतः सुबद्धाममुतस्करम् ।
यथेयमिन्द्र मीढ्वः सुपुत्रा सुभगासति ॥25॥
पूषा त्वेतो नयतु हस्तगृह्याश्विना त्वा प्र वहतां रथेन ।
गृहान्गच्छ गृहपत्नी यथासो वशिनी त्वं विदथमा वदासि ॥26॥
इह प्रियं प्रजया ते समृध्यतामस्मिन्गृहे गार्हपत्याय जागृहि ।
एना पत्या तन्वं१ सं सृजस्वाधा जिव्री विदथमा वदाथः ॥27॥
नीललोहितं भवति कृत्यासक्तिर्व्यज्यते ।

एधन्ते अस्या ज्ञातयः पतिर्बन्धेषु बध्यते ॥28॥
परा देहि शामुल्यं ब्रह्मभ्यो वि भजा वसु ।
कृत्यैषा पद्वती भूत्वा जाया विशते पतिम् ॥29॥
अश्रीरा तनूर्भवति रुशती पापयामुया ।
पतिर्यद्वध्वो३ वाससा स्वमङ्गमभिधित्सते ॥30॥
ये वध्वश्चन्द्रं वहतुं यक्ष्मा यन्ति जनादनु ।
पुनस्तान्यज्ञिया देवा नयन्तु यत आगताः ॥31॥
मा विदन्परिपन्थिनो य आसीदन्ति दम्पती ।
सुगेभिर्दुर्गमतीतामप द्रान्त्वरातयः ॥32॥
सुमङ्गलीरियं वधूरिमां समेत पश्यत ।
सौभाग्यमस्यै दत्त्वायाथास्तं वि परेतन ॥33॥
तृष्टमेतत्कटुकमेतदपाष्ठवद्विषवन्नैतदत्तवे ।
सूर्यां यो ब्रह्मा विद्यात्स इद्वाधूयमर्हति ॥34॥
आशसनं विशसनमथो अधिविकर्तनम् ।
सूर्यायाः पश्य रूपाणि तानि ब्रह्मा तु शुन्धति ॥35॥
गृभ्णामि ते सौभगत्वाय हस्तं मया पत्या जरदष्टिर्यथासः ।
भगो अर्यमा सविता पुरंधिर्मह्यं त्वादुर्गार्हपत्याय देवाः ॥36॥
तां पूषञ्छिवतमामेरयस्व यस्यां बीजं मनुष्या वपन्ति ।
या न ऊरू उशती विश्रयाते यस्यामुशन्तः प्रहराम शेपम् ॥37॥
तुभ्यमग्रे पर्यवहन्सूर्यां वहतुना सह ।
पुनः पतिभ्यो जायां दा अग्ने प्रजया सह ॥38॥
पुनः पत्नीमग्निरदादायुषा सह वर्चसा ।
दीर्घायुरस्या यः पतिर्जीवाति शरदः शतम् ॥39॥
सोमः प्रथमो विविदे गन्धर्वो विविद उत्तरः ।
तृतीयो अग्निष्टे पतिस्तुरीयस्ते मनुष्यजाः ॥40॥
सोमो ददद्गन्धर्वाय गन्धर्वो दददग्नये ।
रयिं च पुत्राँश्चादादग्निर्मह्यमथो इमाम् ॥41॥
इहैव स्तं मा वि यौष्टं विश्वमायुर्व्यश्नुतम् ।
क्रीळन्तौ पुत्रैर्नप्तृभिर्मोदमानौ स्वे गृहे ॥42॥
आ नः प्रजां जनयतु प्रजापतिराजरसाय समनक्त्वर्यमा ।
अदुर्मङ्गलीः पतिलोकमा विश शं नो भव द्विपदे शं चतुष्पदे ॥43॥
अघोरचक्षुरपतिघ्न्येधि शिवा पशुभ्यः सुमनाः सुवर्चाः ।
वीरसूर्देवकामा स्योना शं नो भव द्विपदे शं चतुष्पदे ॥44॥
इमां त्वमिन्द्र मीढ्वः सुपुत्रां सुभगां कृणु ।
दशास्यां पुत्राना धेहि पतिमेकादशं कृधि ॥45॥
सम्राज्ञी श्वशुरे भव सम्राज्ञी श्वश्र्वां भव ।

ननान्दरि सम्राज्ञी भव सम्राज्ञी अधि देवृषु ॥46॥
समञ्जन्तु विश्वे देवाः समापो हृदयानि नौ ।
सं मातरिश्वा सं धाता समु देष्ट्री दधातु नौ ॥47॥

Indrani (इन्द्राणी), Mandal 10, Suktas 86 and 145

वि हि सोतोरसृक्षत नेन्द्रं देवममंसत ।
यत्रामदद्वृषाकपिरर्यः पुष्टेषु मत्सखा विश्वस्मादिन्द्र उत्तरः ॥1॥
परा हीन्द्र धावसि वृषाकपेरति व्यथिः ।
नो अह प्र विन्दस्यन्यत्र सोमपीतये विश्वस्मादिन्द्र उत्तरः ॥2॥
किमयं त्वां वृषाकपिश्चकार हरितो मृगः ।
यस्मा इरस्यसीदु न्वर्यो वा पुष्टिमद्वसु विश्वस्मादिन्द्र उत्तरः ॥3॥
यमिमं त्वं वृषाकपिं प्रियमिन्द्राभिरक्षसि ।
श्वा न्वस्य जम्भिषदपि कर्णे वराहयुर्विश्वस्मादिन्द्र उत्तरः ॥4॥
प्रिया तष्टानि मे कपिर्व्यक्ता व्यदूदुषत् ।
शिरो न्वस्य राविषं न सुगं दुष्कृते भुवं विश्वस्मादिन्द्र उत्तरः ॥5॥
न मत्स्त्री सुभसत्तरा न सुयाशुतरा भुवत् ।
न मत्प्रतिच्यवीयसी न सक्थ्युद्यमीयसी विश्वस्मादिन्द्र उत्तरः ॥6॥
उवे अम्ब सुलाभिके यथेवाङ्ग भविष्यति ।
भसन्मे अम्ब सक्थि मे शिरो मे वीव हृष्यति विश्वस्मादिन्द्र उत्तरः ॥7॥
किं सुबाहो स्वङ्गुरे पृथुष्टो पृथुजाघने ।
किं शूरपत्नि नस्त्वमभ्यमीषि वृषाकपिं विश्वस्मादिन्द्र उत्तरः ॥8॥
अवीरामिव मामयं शरारुरभि मन्यते ।
उताहमस्मि वीरिणीन्द्रपत्नी मरुत्सखा विश्वस्मादिन्द्र उत्तरः ॥9॥
संहोत्रं स्म पुरा नारी समनं वाव गच्छति ।
वेधा ऋतस्य वीरिणीन्द्रपत्नी महीयते विश्वस्मादिन्द्र उत्तरः ॥10॥
इन्द्राणीमासु नारिषु सुभगामहमश्रवम् ।
नह्यस्या अपरं चन जरसा मरते पतिर्विश्वस्मादिन्द्र उत्तरः ॥11॥
नाहमिन्द्राणि रारण सख्युर्वृषाकपेर्ऋते ।
यस्येदमप्यं हविः प्रियं देवेषु गच्छति विश्वस्मादिन्द्र उत्तरः ॥12॥
वृषाकपायि रेवति सुपुत्र आदु सुस्नुषे ।
घसत्त इन्द्र उक्षणः प्रियं काचित्करं हविर्विश्वस्मादिन्द्र उत्तरः ॥13॥
उक्ष्णो हि मे पञ्चदश साकं पचन्ति विंशतिम् ।
उताहमद्मि पीव इदुभा कुक्षी पृणन्ति मे विश्वस्मादिन्द्र उत्तरः ॥14॥
वृषभो न तिग्मशृङ्गोऽन्तर्यूथेषु रोरुवत् ।श्
मन्थस्त इन्द्र शं हृदे यं ते सुनोति भावयुर्विश्वस्मादिन्द्र उत्तरः ॥15॥
न सेशे यस्य रम्बतेऽन्तरा सक्थ्या३ कपृत् ।

सेदीशे यस्य रोमशं निषेदुषो विजृम्भते विश्वस्मादिन्द्र उत्तरः ॥16॥
न सेशे यस्य रोमशं निषेदुषो विजृम्भते ।
सेदीशे यस्य रम्बतेऽन्तरा सक्थ्या३ कपृद्विश्वस्मादिन्द्र उत्तरः ॥17॥
अयमिन्द्र वृषाकपिः परस्वन्तं हतं विदत् ।
असिं सूनां नवं चरुमादेधस्यान आचितं विश्वस्मादिन्द्र उत्तरः ॥18॥
अयमेमि विचाकशद्विचिन्वन्दासमार्यम् ।
पिबामि पाकसुत्वनोऽभि धीरमचाकशं विश्वस्मादिन्द्र उत्तरः ॥19॥
धन्व च यत्कृन्तत्रं च कति स्वित्ता वि योजना ।
नेदीयसो वृषाकपेऽस्तमेहि गृहाँ उप विश्वस्मादिन्द्र उत्तरः ॥20॥
पुनरेहि वृषाकपे सुविता कल्पयावहै ।
य एष स्वप्ननंशनोऽस्तमेषि पथा पुनर्विश्वस्मादिन्द्र उत्तरः ॥21॥
यदुदञ्चो वृषाकपे गृहमिन्द्राजगन्तन ।
क्व१ स्य पुल्वघो मृगः कमगञ्जनयोपनो विश्वस्मादिन्द्र उत्तरः ॥22॥
पर्शुर्ह नाम मानवी साकं ससूव विंशतिम् ।
भद्रं भल त्यस्या अभूद्यस्या उदरमामयद्विश्वस्मादिन्द्र उत्तरः ॥23॥
इमां खनाम्योषधिं वीरुधं बलवत्तमाम् ।
यया सपत्नीं बाधते यया संविन्दते पतिम् ॥1॥
उत्तानपर्णे सुभगे देवजूते सहस्वति ।
सपत्नीं मे परा धम पतिं मे केवलं कुरु ॥2॥
उत्तराहमुत्तर उत्तरेदुत्तराभ्यः ।
अथा सपत्नी या ममाधरा साधराभ्यः ॥3॥
नह्यस्या नाम गृभ्णामि नो अस्मिन्रमते जने ।
परामेव परावतं सपत्नीं गमयामसि ॥4॥
अहमस्मि सहमानाथ त्वमसि सासहिः ।
उभे सहस्वती भूत्वी सपत्नीं मे सहावहै ॥5॥
उप तेऽधां सहमानामभि त्वाधां सहीयसा ।
मामनु प्र ते मनो वत्सं गौरिव धावतु पथा वारिव धावतु ॥6॥

Urvashi (उर्वशी), Mandal 10, Sukta 95

हये जाये मनसा तिष्ठ घोरे वचांसि मिश्रा कृणवावहै नु ।
न नौ मन्त्रा अनुदितास एते मयस्करन्परतरे चनाहन् ॥1॥
किमेता वाचा कृणवा तवाहं प्राक्रमिषमुषसामग्रियेव ।
पुरूरवः पुनरस्तं परेहि दुरापना वात इवाहमस्मि ॥2॥
इषुर्न श्रिय इषुधेरसना गोषाः शतसा न रंहिः ।
अवीरे क्रतौ वि दविद्युतन्नोरा न मायुं चितयन्त धुनयः ॥3॥
सा वसु दधती श्वशुराय वय उषो यदि वष्ट्यन्तिगृहात् ।

अस्तं॑ ननक्षे॒ यस्मि॑ञ्चा॒कन्दिवा॒ नक्तं॑ श्नथि॒ता वै॑त॒सेन॑ ॥4॥
त्रिः स्म॒ माह्नः॑ श्नथयो वैत॒सेनो॒त स्म॒ मेऽव्यं॑त्यै पृणासि ।
पुरू॑र॒वोऽनु॑ ते॒ केत॑माय॒ राजा॑ मे वीर त॒न्व१स्तदा॑सीः ॥5॥
या सु॑जू॒र्णिः श्रेणिः॑ सु॒म्नापि॑र्ह्र॒देच॑क्षु॒र्न ग्र॒न्थिनी॑ चर॒ण्युः ।
ता अ॒ञ्जयो॑ऽरु॒णयो॒ न स॑स्रुः श्रि॒ये गावो॒ न धे॒नवो॑ऽनवन्त ॥6॥
सम॑स्मि॒ञ्जाय॑मान आसत॒ ग्ना उ॒तेम॑वर्धन्न॒द्य१ स्वगू॑र्ताः ।
म॒हे यत्त्वा॑ पुरूरवो॒ रणा॒याव॑र्धयन्दस्यु॒हत्या॑य दे॒वाः ॥7॥
सचा॒ यदा॑सु॒ जह॑ती॒ष्वत्क॒ममा॑नुषीषु॒ मानु॑षो नि॒षेवे॑ ।
अप॑ स्म॒ मत्त॒रसं॑न्ती॒ न भु॒ज्युस्ता अ॑त्रसन्रथ॒स्पृशो॒ नाश्वाः॑ ॥8॥
यदा॑सु॒ मर्तो॑ अ॒मृता॑सु नि॒स्पृक्सं क्षो॒णीभिः॒ क्रतु॑भि॒र्न पृ॒ङ्क्ते ।
ता आ॒तयो॒ न त॒न्वः॑ शुम्भत॒ स्वा अश्वा॑सो॒ न क्री॒ळयो॒ दन्द॑शानाः ॥9॥
वि॒द्युन्न या पत॑न्ती॒ दवि॑द्यो॒द्भर॑न्ती मे॒ अप्या॒ काम्या॑नि ।
जनि॑ष्टो अ॒पो नर्यः॒ सुजा॑तः॒ प्रोर्वशी॑ तिरत दी॒र्घमायुः॑ ॥10॥
ज॒ज्ञि॒ष इ॒त्था गो॒पीथ्या॑य॒ हि द॒धाथ॒ तत्पु॑रूरवो म॒ ओजः॑ ।
अशा॑सं त्वा वि॒दुषी॒ सस्मि॒न्नह॒न्न म॒ आशृणोः॒ किम॒भुग्व॑दासि ॥11॥
क॒दा सू॒नुः पि॒तरं॑ जा॒त इ॑च्छाच्च॒क्रन्नाश्रु॑ वर्तयद्विजा॒नन् ।
को दम्प॑ती॒ सम॑नसा॒ वि यू॑यो॒दध॒ यद॒ग्निः श्वशु॑रेषु॒ दीद॑यत् ॥12॥
प्रति॑ ब्रवाणि व॒र्तय॑ते॒ अश्रु॑ च॒क्रन्न क्रन्द॑दा॒ध्ये॑ शि॒वायै॑ ।
प्र तत्ते॑ हिनवा॒ यत्ते॑ अ॒स्मे परे॒ह्यस्तं॑ न॒हि मू॑र॒ मापः॑ ॥13॥
सु॒दे॒वो अ॒द्य प्र॒पते॒दना॑वृत्परा॒वतं॑ पर॒मां गन्त॒वा उ॑ ।
अधा॒ शयी॑त॒ निर्ऋ॑तेरु॒पस्थेऽधै॑नं॒ वृका॑ रभ॒सासो॑ अ॒द्युः ॥14॥
पुरू॑रवो॒ मा मृ॑था॒ मा प्र प॑प्तो॒ मा त्वा॒ वृका॑सो॒ अशि॑वास उ क्षन् ।
न वै स्त्रैणा॑नि स॒ख्यानि॑ सन्ति सालावृ॒काणां॒ हृद॑यान्ये॒ता ॥15॥
यद्विरू॒पाच॑रं॒ मर्त्ये॒ष्ववसं॒ रात्रीः॑ श॒रद॒श्चत॑स्रः ।
घृ॒तस्य॑ स्तो॒कं स॒कृदह्न॑ आश्नां॒ तादे॒वेदं ता॑तृपा॒णा च॑रामि ॥16॥
अ॒न्त॒रि॒क्ष॒प्रां रज॑सो वि॒मानी॒मुप॑ शिक्षाम्यु॒र्वशीं॒ वसि॑ष्ठः ।
उप॑ त्वा रा॒तिः सु॑कृ॒तस्य॒ तिष्ठा॒न्नि व॑र्तस्व॒ हृद॑यं तप्यते मे ॥17॥
इति॑ त्वा दे॒वा इ॒म आ॑हुरैळ॒ यथे॑मे॒तद्भव॑सि मृ॒त्युब॑न्धुः ।
प्र॒जा ते॑ दे॒वान्ह॒विषा॑ यजाति स्व॒र्ग उ॒ त्वमपि॑ मादयासे ॥18॥

Dakshina (दक्षिणा), Mandal 10, Sukta 107

आ॒विर॑भू॒न्महि॒ माघो॑नमेषां॒ विश्वं॑ जी॒वं तम॑सो॒ निर॑मोचि ।
महि॒ ज्योति॑ः पि॒तृभि॑र्द॒त्तमागा॑दु॒रुः पन्था॒ दक्षि॑णाया अदर्शि ॥1॥
उ॒च्चा दि॒वि दक्षि॑णावन्तो अस्थु॒र्ये अ॑श्व॒दाः स॒ह ते सूर्ये॑ण ।
हि॒र॒ण्य॒दा अ॑मृत॒त्वं भ॑जन्ते वासो॒दाः सो॑म॒ प्र ति॑रन्त॒ आयुः॑ ॥2॥
दैवी॑ पू॒र्तिर्दक्षि॑णा देवय॒ज्या न क॑वा॒रिभ्यो॑ न॒हि ते पृ॒णन्ति॑ ।

अथा॒ नरः॒ प्रय॑तदक्षिणासोऽवद्यभि॒या ब॒हवः॑ पृणन्ति ॥3॥
श॒तधा॑रं वा॒युम॒र्कं स्व॒र्विदं॑ नृ॒चक्ष॑स॒स्ते अ॒भि च॑क्षते ह॒विः ।
ये पृ॒णन्ति॒ प्र च॒ यच्छ॑न्ति संग॒मे ते दक्षि॑णां दुहते स॒प्तमा॑तरम् ॥4॥
दक्षि॑णावान्प्रथ॒मो हू॒त ए॑ति॒ दक्षि॑णावान्ग्राम॒णीरग्र॑मेति ।
तमे॒व म॑न्ये नृ॒पतिं॒ जना॑नां॒ यः प्र॑थ॒मो दक्षि॑णामावि॒वाय॑ ॥5॥
तमे॒व ऋषिं॒ तमु॑ ब्र॒ह्माण॑माहुर्यज्ञ॒न्यं॑ सामगा॒मु॑क्थ॒शास॑म् ।
स शु॒क्रस्य॑ त॒न्वो॑ वेद ति॒स्रो यः प्र॑थ॒मो दक्षि॑णया र॒राध॑ ॥6॥
दक्षि॒णाश्वं॒ दक्षि॑णा॒ गां द॑दाति॒ दक्षि॑णा च॒न्द्रमु॒त यद्धिर॑ण्यम् ।
दक्षि॒णान्नं॑ वनुते॒ यो न॑ आ॒त्मा दक्षि॑णां॒ वर्म॑ कृणुते विजा॒नन् ॥7॥
न भो॒जा म॑म्रु॒र्न न्य॒र्थमी॑यु॒र्न रि॑ष्यन्ति॒ न व्य॑थन्ते ह भो॒जाः ।
इ॒दं यद्विश्वं॒ भुव॑नं॒ स्व॑श्चै॒तत्सर्वं॒ दक्षि॑णैभ्यो ददाति ॥8॥
भो॒जा जि॑ग्युः सुर॒भिं योनि॒मग्रे॑ भो॒जा जि॑ग्युर्व॒ध्वं१॒॑ या सु॒वासाः॑ ।
भो॒जा जि॑ग्युरन्तः॒पेयं॒ सुरा॑या भो॒जा जि॑ग्यु॒र्ये अहू॑ताः प्र॒यन्ति॑ ॥9॥
भो॒जायाश्वं॒ सं मृ॑जन्त्या॒शुं भो॒जाया॑स्ते क॒न्या॒३ शुम्भ॑माना ।
भो॒जस्ये॒दं पु॑ष्क॒रिणी॑व॒ वेश्म॒ परि॑ष्कृतं देवमा॒नेव॑ चि॒त्रम् ॥10॥
भो॒जमश्वाः॑ सुष्ठु॒वाहो॑ वहन्ति सु॒वृद्रथो॑ वर्तते॒ दक्षि॑णायाः ।
भो॒जं दे॑वासोऽवता॒ भरे॑षु भो॒जः शत्रू॑न्समनी॒केषु॒ जेता॑ ॥11॥

Sarma (सरमा), Mandal 10, Sukta 108

कि॒मि॒च्छन्ती॑ स॒रमा॒ प्रेदमा॑नड्दू॒रे ह्यध्वा॒ जगु॑रिः परा॒चैः ।
कास्मेहि॑तिः॒ का परि॑तक्म्यासीत्क॒थं र॒साया॑ अतरः॒ पयां॑सि ॥1॥
इन्द्र॑स्य दू॒तीरि॑षि॒ता च॑रामि म॒ह इ॒च्छन्ती॑ पणयो नि॒धीन्वः॑ ।
अ॒ति॒ष्कदो॑ भि॒यसा॒ तन्न॑ आव॒त्तथा॑ र॒साया॑ अतरं॒ पयां॑सि ॥2॥
की॒दृङ्ङिन्द्रः॑ सरमे॒ का दृ॑शी॒का यस्ये॒दं दू॒तीरस॑रः परा॒कात् ।
आ च॒ गच्छा॑न्मि॒त्रमे॑ना दधा॒माथा॒ गवां॒ गोप॑तिर्नो भवाति ॥3॥
नाहं तं वे॑द॒ द॒भ्यं॒ दभ॒त्स यस्ये॒दं दू॒तीरस॑रं परा॒कात् ।
न तं गू॑हन्ति स्र॒वतो॑ गभी॒रा ह॒ता इन्द्रे॑ण पणयः शयध्वे ॥4॥
इ॒मा गावः॑ सरमे॒ या ऐच्छः॒ परि॑ दि॒वो अन्ता॑न्सुभगे॒ पत॑न्ती ।
कस्त॑ एना॒ अव॑ सृजा॒दयु॑ध्व्यु॒तास्माक॒मायु॑धा सन्ति ति॒ग्मा ॥5॥
अ॒से॒न्या वः॑ पणयो॒ वचां॑स्यनिष॒व्यास्त॒न्वः॑ सन्तु पा॒पीः ।
अधृ॑ष्टो व॒ एत॒वा अ॑स्तु॒ पन्था॒ बृह॒स्पति॑र्व उभ॒या न मृ॑ळात् ॥6॥
अ॒यं नि॒धिः स॑रमे॒ अद्रि॑बुध्नो॒ गोभि॒रश्वे॑भि॒र्वसु॑भि॒र्न्यृ॑ष्टः ।
रक्ष॑न्ति॒ तं प॒णयो॒ ये सु॑गो॒पा रेकु॑ प॒दमल॑क॒मा ज॑गन्थ ॥7॥
एह ग॑मन्नृष॑यः॒ सोम॑शिता अ॒यास्यो॒ अङ्गि॑रसो॒ नव॑ग्वाः ।
त ए॒तमू॒र्वं वि भ॑जन्त॒ गोना॒मथै॒तद्वचः॑ प॒णयो॒ वम॒न्नित् ॥8॥
ए॒वा च॒ त्वं स॑रम आज॒गन्थ॒ प्रबा॑धिता॒ सह॑सा॒ दैव्ये॑न ।

स्वसा॑रं त्वा कृणवै॒ मा पुन॑र्गा॒ अप॑ ते॒ गवां॑ सुभगे भजाम ॥9॥
नाहं वे॑द भ्रातृ॒त्वं नो स्व॑सृ॒त्वमिन्द्रो॑ विदु॒रङ्गि॑रसश्च घो॒राः ।
गोका॑मा मे अच्छदय॒न्यदाय॒मपा॑त इत पणयो॒ वरी॑यः ॥10॥
दू॒रमि॑त पणयो॒ वरी॑य॒ उद्गावो॑ यन्तु मिन॒तीर्ऋ॒तेन॑ ।
बृह॒स्पति॒र्या अवि॑न्द॒न्निगू॑ळ्हाः॒ सोमो॒ ग्रावा॑ण॒ ऋष॑यश्च॒ विप्राः॑ ॥11॥

Juhu (जुहु), Mandal 10, Sukta 109

तेऽवदन्प्रथ॒मा ब्र॑ह्मकिल्बि॒षेऽकू॑पारः सलि॒लो मा॑त॒रिश्वा॑ ।
वी॒ळुह॑रा॒स्तप॑ उ॒ग्रो म॑यो॒भूरापो॑ दे॒वीः प्र॑थम॒जा ऋ॒तेन॑ ॥1॥
सोमो॒ राजा॑ प्रथ॒मो ब्र॑ह्मजा॒यां पुनः॒ प्राय॑च्छ॒दहृ॑णीयमानः ।
अ॒न्व॒र्ति॒ता वरु॑णो मि॒त्र आ॑सीद॒ग्निर्होता॑ हस्त॒गृह्या नि॑नाय ॥2॥
हस्ते॑नै॒व ग्रा॒ह्य॑ आ॒धिर॑स्या ब्रह्मजा॒येय॒मिति॒ चेदवो॑चन् ।
न दू॒ताय॑ प्र॒ह्ये॑ तस्थ ए॒षा तथा॑ रा॒ष्ट्रं गु॑पि॒तं क्ष॒त्रिय॑स्य ॥3॥
दे॒वा ए॒तस्या॑मवदन्त॒ पूर्वे॑ सप्तऋ॒षय॒स्तप॑से॒ ये नि॑षे॒दुः ।
भी॒मा जा॒या ब्रा॑ह्म॒णस्योप॑नीता दु॒र्धां द॑धाति पर॒मे व्यो॑मन् ॥4॥
ब्र॒ह्म॒चा॒री च॑रति॒ वेवि॑ष॒द्विषः॒ स दे॒वानां॑ भव॒त्येक॒मङ्ग॑म् ।
तेन॑ जा॒याम॒न्वविन्द॒द्बृह॒स्पतिः॒ सोमे॑न नी॒तां जु॒ह्वं॒ न दे॑वाः ॥5॥
पु॒न॒र्वै दे॒वा अ॑ददुः॒ पुन॑र्मनु॒ष्या॑ उ॒त ।
राजा॑नः स॒त्यं कृ॑ण्वा॒ना ब्र॑ह्मजा॒यां पुन॑र्ददुः ॥6॥
पु॒न॒र्दाय॑ ब्रह्मजा॒यां कृ॒त्वी दे॒वैर्नि॑किल्बि॒षम् ।
ऊर्जं॑ पृथि॒व्या भ॒क्त्वायो॑रुगा॒यमुपा॑सते ॥7॥

Vak (वाक्), Mandal 10, Sukta 125

अ॒हं रु॒द्रेभि॒र्वसु॑भिश्चराम्य॒हमा॑दि॒त्यैरु॒त वि॒श्वदे॑वैः ।
अ॒हं मि॒त्रावरु॑णो॒भा बि॑भर्म्य॒हमि॑न्द्रा॒ग्नी अ॒हम॒श्विनो॒भा ॥1॥
अ॒हं सोम॑माह॒नसं॑ बिभर्म्य॒हं त्वष्टा॑रमु॒त पू॒षणं॒ भग॑म् ।
अ॒हं द॑धामि॒ द्रवि॑णं ह॒विष्म॑ते सुप्रा॒व्ये॒ यज॑मानाय सुन्व॒ते ॥2॥
अ॒हं राष्ट्री॑ सं॒गम॑नी॒ वसू॑नां चिकि॒तुषी॑ प्रथ॒मा य॒ज्ञिया॑नाम् ।
तां मा॑ दे॒वा व्य॑दधुः पुरु॒त्रा भूरि॑स्थात्रां॒ भूर्या॑वे॒शय॑न्तीम् ॥3॥
मया॒ सो अन्न॑मत्ति॒ यो वि॒पश्य॑ति॒ यः प्राणि॑ति॒ य ईं॑ शृ॒णोत्यु॒क्तम् ।
अ॒म॒न्तवो॒ मां त उप॑ क्षियन्ति श्रु॒धि श्रु॑त श्रद्धि॒वं ते॑ वदामि ॥4॥
अ॒हमे॒व स्व॒यमि॒दं व॑दामि॒ जुष्टं॑ दे॒वेभि॑रु॒त मानु॑षेभिः ।
यं का॒मये॒ तंत॑मु॒ग्रं कृ॑णोमि॒ तं ब्र॒ह्माणं॒ तमृषिं॒ तं सु॑मे॒धाम् ॥5॥
अ॒हं रु॒द्राय॒ धनु॒रा त॑नोमि ब्रह्म॒द्विषे॒ शर॑वे॒ हन्त॒वा उ॑ ।
अ॒हं जना॑य स॒मदं॑ कृणोम्य॒हं द्यावा॑पृथि॒वी आ वि॑वेश ॥6॥
अ॒हं सु॑वे पि॒तर॑मस्य मू॒र्धन्मम॒ योनि॑र॒प्स्व१॒॑न्तः स॑मु॒द्रे ।

ततो॒ वि ति॑ष्ठे॒ भुव॑ना॒नु विश्वो॒तामूं द्यां व॒र्ष्मणोप॑ स्पृशामि ॥7॥
अ॒हमे॑व॒ वात॑ इव॒ प्र वा॒म्या॒र॒भमा॑णा॒ भुव॑नानि॒ विश्वा॑ ।
प॒रो दि॒वा प॒र ए॒ना पृ॑थि॒व्यैता॑वती महि॒ना सं ब॑भूव ॥8॥

Ratri (रात्रि), Mandal 10, Sukta 127

रात्री॒ व्य॑ख्य॒दाय॒ती पु॑रु॒त्रा दे॒व्य॑१॒क्षभिः॑ ।
विश्वा॒ अधि॒ श्रियो॑ऽधित ॥1॥
ओर्व॑प्रा॒ अम॑र्त्या नि॒वतो॑ दे॒व्यु१॒द्वतः॑ ।
ज्योति॑षा बाधते॒ तमः॑ ॥2॥
निरु॒ स्वसा॑रमस्कृतो॒षसं॑ दे॒व्या॑य॒ती ।
अपेदु॑ हासते॒ तमः॑ ॥3॥
सा नो॑ अ॒द्य यस्या॑ व॒यं नि ते॒ याम॒न्नवि॑क्ष्महि ।
वृ॒क्षे न व॑स॒तिं वयः॑ ॥4॥
नि ग्रामा॑सो अविक्षत॒ नि प॒द्वन्तो॒ नि प॒क्षिणः॑ ।
नि श्ये॒नास॑श्चिद॒र्थिनः॑ ॥5॥
या॒व॒या वृ॒क्यं१॒ वृकं॑ यव॒य स्ते॒नमू॑र्म्ये ।
अथा॑ नः सु॒तरा॑ भव ॥6॥
उप॑ मा॒ पेपि॑श॒त्तमः॑ कृ॒ष्णं व्य॑क्तमस्थित ।
उष॑ ऋ॒णेव॑ यातय ॥7॥
उप॑ ते॒ गा इ॒वाक॑रं वृणी॒ष्व दु॑हितर्दिवः ।
रात्रि॒ स्तोमं॒ न जि॑ग्युषे ॥8॥

Godha (गोधा), Mandal 10, Sukta 134

दी॒र्घं ह्य॑ङ्कु॒शं य॑था॒ शक्तिं॒ बिभर्षि॑ मन्तुमः ।
पू॒र्वेण॑ मघवन्प॒दाजो व॒यां यथा॑ य॒मो दे॒वी ज॒नित्र्य॑जीजन॒द्भद्रा ज॒नित्र्य॑जीजनत् ॥6॥
न॒किर्दे॒वा मि॑नीमसि॒ नकि॒रा यो॑पयामसि म॒न्त्रश्रु॑त्यं॑ चरामसि ।
प॒क्षेभि॑रपि॒कक्षे॑भिर॒त्राभि सं र॑भामहे ॥7॥

Shraddha (श्रद्धा), Mandal 10, Sukta 151

श्र॒द्धया॒ग्निः समि॑ध्यते श्र॒द्धया॑ हूयते ह॒विः ।
श्र॒द्धां भग॑स्य मू॒र्धनि॒ वच॑सा वेदयामसि ॥1॥
प्रि॒यं श्र॑द्धे॒ दद॑तः प्रि॒यं श्र॑द्धे॒ दिदा॑सतः ।
प्रि॒यं भो॒जेषु॒ यज्व॑स्वि॒दं म॒ उदि॑तं कृधि ॥2॥
यथा॑ दे॒वा असु॑रेषु श्र॒द्धामु॒ग्रेषु॑ चक्रि॒रे ।
ए॒वं भो॒जेषु॒ यज्व॑स्व॒स्माकमु॑दि॒तं कृ॑धि ॥3॥
श्र॒द्धां दे॒वा यज॑माना वा॒युगो॑पा उपासते ।

श्रद्धां हृद॑य्य१याकूत्या॒ श्रद्धया॑ विन्दते॒ वसु॑ ॥4॥
श्रद्धां॒ प्रातर्ह॑वामहे श्रद्धां म॒ध्यंदि॑नं॒ परि॑ ।
श्रद्धां॒ सूर्य॑स्य नि॒म्रुचि॑ श्रद्धे॒ श्रद्धाप॑येह नः ॥5॥

Indramata (इन्द्रमाता), Mandal 10, Sukta 153
ई॒ङ्खय॑न्तीरप॒स्यु॒व् इन्द्रं॑ जा॒तमुपा॑सते ।
भे॒जा॒नासः॑ सु॒वीर्य॑म् ॥1॥
त्वमि॑न्द्र ब॒ला॒दधि॑ स॒हसो॑ जा॒त ओज॑सः ।
त्वं वृ॒ष॒न्वृषेद॑सि ॥2॥
त्वमि॑न्द्रा॒सि वृ॒त्रहा॒ व्य१न्तरि॑क्षमतिर॒ः ।
उद्द्यामस्त॑भ्ना॒ ओज॑सा ॥3॥
त्वमि॑न्द्र स॒जोष॑सम॒र्कं बि॑भर्षि बा॒ह्वोः ।
वज्रं॒ शिशा॒न॒ ओज॑सा ॥4॥
त्वमि॑न्द्राभि॒भूर॑सि॒ विश्वा॑ जा॒तान्योज॑सा ।
स विश्वा॒ भुव॒ आभ॑वः ॥5॥

Saarprajni (सार्पराज्ञी), Mandal 10, Sukta 189
आ॒यं गौः पृश्नि॑रक्रमी॒दस॑दन्मा॒तरं॑ पु॒रः ।
पि॒तरं॑ च प्रय॒न्स्वः॑ ॥1॥
अ॒न्तश्च॑रति रोच॒नास्य॑ प्रा॒णाद॑पान॒ती ।
व्य॑ख्य॒न्महि॒षो दिव॑म् ॥2॥
त्रिं॒शद्धाम॒ वि रा॑जति॒ वाक्प॑त॒ङ्गाय॑ धीयते ।
प्रति॒ वस्तो॒रह॒ द्युभि॑ः ॥3॥

Shree (श्री) *Rigveda*, Parishisht Sukta 10
ॐ ॥ हिरण्यवर्णां॑ हरिणीं॑ सुवर्णरजत॒स्रजाम् ।
चन्द्रां हिरण्म॑यीं ल॒क्ष्मीं जातवेदो म॒ आवह ॥1॥
तां म॒ आवह जातवेदो लक्ष्मीमन॑पगामिनीम् ।
यस्यां॒ हिरण्यं॑ वि॒न्देयं॒ गामश्वं॒ पुरुषान॒हम् ॥2॥
अश्वपूर्वां॒ रथमध्यां हस्तिनादप्रबोधिनीम् ।
श्रियं॑ देवीमुप॑ह्वये श्रीर्मा॒देवीर्जुषताम् ॥3॥
कां॒ सो॑स्मितां॑ हिरण्यप्राकारा॑मा॒द्रां ज्वल॒न्तीं तृ॒प्तां त॒र्पयन्तीम् ।
पद्मे॒ स्थि॒तां प॒द्मव॒र्णां तामि॒होप॑ह्वये श्रियम् ॥4॥
चन्द्रां प्रभा॒सां य॒शसा॒ ज्वलन्तीं॑ श्रियं॑ लोके॒ देवजुष्टामुदाराम् ।
तां प॒द्मिनीमीं॑ शरणमहं प्रपद्ये॒ऽलक्ष्मीर्मे॑ नश्यतां॒ त्वां वृ॒णे ॥5॥
आ॒दित्यव॑र्णे तप॒सोऽधि॑जा॒तो वनस्पति॒स्तव॑ वृ॒क्षोऽथ॒ बिल्वः ।

तस्य फलानि तपसा नुदन्तु मायान्तरायाश्च बाह्या अलक्ष्मीः ॥6॥
उपैतु मां देवसखः कीर्तिश्च मणिना सह ।
प्रादुर्भूतोऽस्मि राष्ट्रेऽस्मिन् कीर्तिमृद्धिं ददातु मे ॥7॥
क्षुत्पिपासामलां ज्येष्ठामलक्ष्मीं नाशयाम्यहम् ।
अभूतिमसमृद्धिं च सर्वां निर्णुद मे गृहात् ॥8॥
गन्धद्वारां दुराधर्षां नित्यपुष्टां करीषिणीम् ।
ईश्वरीꣳ सर्वभूतानां तामिहोपह्वये श्रियम् ॥9॥
मनसः काममाकूतिं वाचः सत्यमशीमहि ।
पशूनां रूपमन्नस्य मयि श्रीः श्रयतां यशः ॥10॥
कर्दमेन प्रजाभूता मयि सम्भव कर्दम ।
श्रियं वासय मे कुले मातरं पद्ममालिनीम् ॥11॥
आपः सृजन्तु स्निग्धानि चिक्लीत वस मे गृहे ।
नि च देवीं मातरं श्रियं वासय मे कुले ॥12॥
आर्द्रां पुष्करिणीं पुष्टिं पिङ्गलां पद्ममालिनीम् ।
चन्द्रां हिरण्मयीं लक्ष्मीं जातवेदो म आवह ॥13॥
आर्द्रां यः करिणीं यष्टिं सुवर्णां हेममालिनीम् ।
सूर्यां हिरण्मयीं लक्ष्मीं जातवेदो म आवह ॥14॥
तां म आवह जातवेदो लक्ष्मीमनपगामिनीम् ।
यस्यां हिरण्यं प्रभूतं गावो दास्योऽश्वान्विन्देयं पुरुषानहम् ॥15॥
यः शुचिः प्रयतो भूत्वा जुहुयादाज्यमन्वहम् ।
श्रियः पञ्चदशर्चं च श्रीकामः सततं जपेत् ॥16॥
पद्मानने पद्म विपद्मपत्रे पद्मप्रिये पद्मदलायताक्षि ।
विश्वप्रिये विष्णु मनोऽनुकूले त्वत्पादपद्मं मयि सन्निधत्स्व ॥17॥
पद्मानने पद्म ऊरू पद्माक्षी पद्मसम्भवे ।
त्वं मां भजस्व पद्माक्षी येन सौख्यं लभाम्यहम् ॥18॥
अश्वदायी गोदायी धनदायी महाधने ।
धनं मे जुषतां देवि सर्वकामांश्च देहि मे ॥19॥
पुत्रपौत्र धनं धान्यं हस्त्यश्वादिगवे रथम् ।
प्रजानां भवसि माता आयुष्मन्तं करोतु माम् ॥20॥
धनमग्निर्धनं वायुर्धनं सूर्यो धनं वसुः ।
धनमिन्द्रो बृहस्पतिर्वरुणं धनमश्नुते ॥ 21॥
वैनतेय सोमं पिब सोमं पिबतु वृत्रहा ।
सोमं धनस्य सोमिनो मह्यं ददातु सोमिनः ॥22॥
न क्रोधो न च मात्सर्यं न लोभो नाशुभा मतिः ।
भवन्ति कृतपुण्यानां भक्तानां श्रीसूक्तं जपेत्सदा ॥23॥
सरसिजनिलये सरोजहस्ते धवलतरांशुक गन्धमाल्यशोभे ।

भगवति हरिवल्लभे मनोज्ञे त्रिभुवनभूतिकरिप्रसीद मह्यम् ॥24॥
विष्णुपत्नीं क्षमां देवीं माधवीं माधवप्रियाम् ।
विष्णोः प्रियसखींम् देवीं नमाम्यच्युतवल्लभाम् ॥25॥
महालक्ष्मी च विद्महे विष्णुपत्नी च धीमही ।
तन्नो लक्ष्मीः प्रचोदयात् ॥26॥
आनन्दः कर्दमः श्रीदश्चिक्लीत इति विश्रुताः ।
ऋषयः श्रियः पुत्राश्च श्रीर्देवीर्देवता मताः ॥27॥
श्रीवर्चस्यमायुष्यमारोग्यमाविधात् पवमानं महीयते ।
धनं धान्यं पशुं बहुपुत्रलाभं शतसंवत्सरं दीर्घमायुः ॥28॥
ऋणरोगादिदारिद्र्यपापक्षुदपमृत्यवः ।
भयशोकमनस्तापा नश्यन्तु मम सर्वदा ॥29॥

Medha (मेधा) ***Taittiriya Aranyaka*** **4, Prapataka 10: Anuvak 41–44**
ॐ यश्छन्दसामृषभो विश्वरूपः । छन्दोभ्योऽध्यमृतात्संबभूव ।
स मेन्द्रो मेधया स्पृणोतु । अमृतस्य देवधारणो भूयासम् ।
शरीरं मे विचर्षणम् । जिह्वा मे मधुमत्तमा ।
कर्णाभ्यां भूरिविश्रुवम् । ब्रह्मणः कोशोऽसि मेधया पिहितः ।
श्रुतं मे गोपाय । ॐ शान्तिः शान्तिः शान्तिः ॥

ॐ मेधादेवी जुषमाणा न आगाद्विश्वाची भद्रा सुमनस्यमाना ।
त्वया जुष्टा नुदमाना दुरुक्तान् बृहद्वदेम विदथे सुवीराः ।
त्वया जुष्ट ऋषिर्भवति देवि त्वया ब्रह्माऽऽगतश्रीरुत त्वया ।
त्वया जुष्टश्चित्रं विन्दते वसु सानो जुषस्व द्रविणो न मेधे ॥

मेधां म इन्द्रो ददातु मेधां देवी सरस्वती ।
मेधां मे अश्विनावुभावाधत्तां पुष्करस्रजा ।
अप्सरासु च या मेधा गन्धर्वेषु च यन्मनः ।
दैवीं मेधा सरस्वती सा मां मेधा सुरभिर्जुषता ॰ स्वाहा ॥

आमां मेधा सुरभिर्विश्वरूपा हिरण्यवर्णा जगती जगम्या ।
ऊर्जस्वती पयसा पिन्वमाना सा मां मेधा सुप्रतीका जुषन्ताम् ।
मयि मेधां मयि प्रजां मय्यग्निस्तेजो दधातु
मयि मेधां मयि प्रजां मयीन्द्र इन्द्रियं दधातु
मयि मेधां मयि प्रजां मयि सूर्यो भ्राजो दधातु ।
ॐ महादेव्यै च विद्महे ब्रह्मपत्नी च धीमहि । तन्नो वाणी प्रचोदयात् ।
ॐ हंस हंसाय विद्महे परमहंसाय धीमहि । तन्नो हंसः प्रचोदयात् ।

एकवर्णस्तदा लोको[1]

Ekavarṇastadā loko

CHAPTER 6

Non-discriminatory Social System

In Hindu Dharma and society, neither the scriptures nor our ancestors discriminated based on varna, jati, jatiya, jnati, skin colour, race, gender, language or region. Human dignity and respect were central to societal interactions. Most Hindu Gods and Goddesses are not depicted with fair skin; prominent examples include Bhagwan Rama, Krishna and Kali. Traditionally, Hindu deities were crafted from black granite, black hard stone or other materials such as sandstone.

The Mahabharata is one of the greatest sources of Hindu history, authored by the revered sage Maharishi Vedavyasa, one of the most renowned rishis. In addition to the Mahabharata, which includes the Bhagavad Gita, he also composed other significant works, such as the Brahmasutra (Shariraka Sutra or Vedanta Sutra or Uttar Mimansa) and a commentary (Bhashya) on Patanjali's Yogasutra. Maharishi Vedavyasa was the son of Satyavati, the daughter of a Nishad (boatman), and is described as having a darker skin tone. This detail is important because, in Hindu society, skin colour was never considered a detriment to one's character. Maharishi Vedavyasa was the son of Satyavati and Maharishi Parashar.

King Shantanu of Hastinapur wished to marry Satyavati, but her father, the Nishad (boatman), who was a subject of the king, set a condition: the marriage would only take place if Satyavati's son were to succeed Shantanu on the throne. What stands out here is that, despite being a king, Shantanu could not impose his will. The boatman had the courage to demand conditions for the marriage from a powerful ruler. He spoke to the king as an equal, without being intimidated by the king's social status, despite being his subject.

In the incorrect context of today's society, Shantanu might be seen as a member of the Kshatriya community, considered a so-called 'higher jati', while the boatman would be viewed as part of a 'lower jati'. However, this incident reveals that although the Nishad jati (the professional or occupational community of boatmen) existed, there was no hierarchy in which one jati is inherently superior to another. The fact that a king desired to marry a boatman's daughter highlights that societal divisions were not based on jati or status, as they might be perceived today.

King Shantanu's side accepted the boatman's demand. King Shantanu married Satyavati only after his eldest son, Bheeshma, agreed to renounce his claim to the throne and took a solemn vow of celibacy, promising never to marry or have children. This ensured that Satyavati's son would inherit the throne.

Satyavati had two sons with King Shantanu—Chitrangada and Vichitravirya. She was also the mother of Maharishi Vedavyasa, making her the mother of three sons. After Chitrangada died young, Vichitravirya ascended to the throne. He married Ambika and Ambalika, daughters of the King of Kashi, but after seven years of marriage, Vichitravirya died without any children. Bound by his vow, Bheeshma could not marry or produce heirs, leaving Hastinapur without a successor. On Bheeshma's advice, Satyavati summoned Vedavyasa to sire children with Vichitravirya's wives. Vedavyasa then sired three children—two with Vichitravirya's wives and one with Ambika's maid. These children were Dhritarashtra (born blind), Pandu and the youngest, Vidura.

धृतराष्ट्रे च पाण्डौ च विदुरे च महात्मनि।
एषु त्रिषु कुमारेषु जातेषु कुरुजाङ्गलम्।
कुरवोऽथ कुरुक्षेत्रं त्रयमेतदवर्धत।।1।।

dhṛtarāṣṭre ca pāṇḍau ca vidure ca mahātmani|
eṣu triṣu kumāreṣu jāteṣu kurujāṅgalam|
kuravo'tha kurukṣetraṃ trayametadavardhata||1||[2]

From the birth of all three princes—Dhritarashtra, Pandu and Vidura—the Kuruvansha (Kuru lineage) and the regions of Kurujangal and Kurukshetra experienced significant development.

Vidura was raised and educated alongside his two brothers under Bheeshma's guidance.

Bheeshma said to Vidura:

युष्मासु कुलतन्तुषु॥3॥

yuṣmāsu kulatantuṣu||3||[3]

The three of you brothers are the binding thread of this lineage.

Vidura became a great scholar in economics, politics and governance, fluent in multiple languages, including secret language or coded communication. Throughout his life, he served as a senior minister and chief advisor to the king of Hastinapur. What is particularly remarkable is that, despite being born to a maid, Vidura rose to such a high position, demonstrating that birth status does not determine one's capacity to lead and serve.

The entire Mahabharata, which remains central to Hindu society even today, unfolded among the grandchildren and great-grandchildren of Satyavati, the daughter of a boatman. Where, then, does the notion of higher or lower jati or varna exist?

Varna (वर्ण), Jati (जाति), Jatiya (जातीय) and Jnati (ज्ञाति)

Let's first explore and understand the concepts of varna (वर्ण), jati (जाति), jatiya (जातीय) and jnati (ज्ञाति) according to Pāṇini's grammar, the Nirukta of Yaskacharya, and the Nyāya Darśana (philosophy) of Gautama.

Varna (वर्ण)

वर्ण - वृञ् वरणे (Panini's Dhatupatha)

Yaskacharya's निर्वचन (interpretation) वर्णो वृणोतेः (varṇo vṛṇoteḥ) (Nirukta 2.3) Acharya Durga – 'आवृणोति हि स आश्रयम्' (āvṛṇoti hi sa āśrayam)
'आ समन्ताद् वृणोति विविधैर्धर्मैः कर्तव्यैर्वाऽऽच्छादयति नियोजयतीति वर्णः।' (ā samantād vṛṇoti vividhairdharmaiḥ kartavyairvā''cchādayati niyojayatīti varṇaḥ।) Varna refers to the classification of individuals or groups based on the

different forms of dharma—that is, the duties, responsibilities and roles in life that they either embrace or are inducted into.

वर्णो वृणोतेः (varṇo vṛṇoteḥ), वारयति = अधर्मेभ्योऽकर्तव्येभ्यो वा निवारयतीति वर्णः। (vārayati = adharmebhyoskartavyebhyo vā nivārayatīti varṇaḥ।) वर्णः निवारकः (varṇa: nivāraka:) (Sayanacharya Rigveda Commentary 9.71.8) In accordance with its inherent meaning and interpretation, varna denotes one who dissociates, distances themselves from or guides others away from unrighteousness (अधर्म – adharma), irresponsibility (अकर्तव्य – akartavya), or sinful actions. The crucial point is that an individual's acceptance of 'varna (वर्ण)' demonstrates that it is not determined by birth; the term 'varna (वर्ण)' itself implies that it is independent of birth.

Jati (जाति)

Jati is a broad term in Sanskrit grammar, literature and philosophy, with varied meanings and applications depending on the context.

As per Nyaya Darshan (philosophy) of Gautama:

आकृतिः जातिलिङ्गाख्या 70:

ākṛtiḥ jātiliṅgākhyā 70:[4]

Maharishi Vatsayan in his commentary on this Sutra: यथा जातिर्जातिलिङ्गानि च प्रख्यायन्ते तामाकृतिं विद्यात् । (yathā jātirjātiliṅgāni ca prakhyāyante tāmākṛtiṃ vidyāt |) The sign of jati is visible through aakriti (आकृति—form), and that form represents the jati. For example, the form of a human signifies the manuṣya (मनुष्य) (manuṣya jati—human species), while the form of a cow (गौ) signifies the gau jati (गौ जाति—cow species).

समानप्रसवात्मिका जातिः 71

samānaprasavātmikā jātiḥ 71[5]

Jati (जाति) refers to the recognition of common features among different objects. Although each object is distinct, they share a common feature that links them, and this essential common feature is known as जाति (jati). For example, while each human being and each cow is different, their jati is formed from their common features: manushya jati (human species) and gau jati (cow species).

The crucial point here is that many translate 'prasav' (प्रसव) as 'birth', which is incorrect. The correct interpretation is provided by Maharishi Vatsayan in his commentary on this Sutra: 'या समानां बुद्धिं प्रसूते।' This refers to the common features that appear in the mind from which they are recognized, and that constitutes their जाति jati. Jati does not refer to biological birth here.

Jati exists not only in animate beings but also in inanimate objects. Acharya Panini, in his Ashtadhyayi Sutra जातिरप्राणिनाम् (2.4.6), provides a provision for jati in inanimate objects. This refers to a copulative or coordinative compound (द्वन्द्व समास) that conveys singularity (एकवद्भाव) in inanimate entities. For example, aara (saw) and shastri (cutting tools) are both specialized cutting instruments, while dhana (rice) and shashkuli (cooked food) are food items. Among these pairs—aara and shastri, and dhana and shashkuli—there exists a commonality: based on their similarities, a single category is established. Therefore, the terms that denote these categories embody singularity: aarashastri (आराशस्त्रि) and dhanashashkuli (धानाशष्कुलि).

The concept of jati indeed encompasses broader characteristics that highlight essential commonalities among various objects, groups or entities. It suggests that identifying these common features is not dependent on birth; instead, it emphasizes the significance of shared attributes, professions, work and experiences that define a group. Thus, the concept of jati transcends hereditary notions.

Jatiya (जातीय)

जात्यन्ताच्छ बन्धुनि 5.4.9[6]

From the base noun or stem (प्रातिपदिक) that ends with the word 'jati', the suffix 'छ' is applied to convey a sense of brotherhood. This is how the word 'jatiya' (जातीय) is formed. For example,

सर्वे तुल्याभिजातीया यथा देवास्तथा वयम्।।29।।

sarve tulyābhijātīyā yathā devāstathā vayam ||29||[7]

This jatiya word in the brotherhood sense is applied and used in other languages, such as the Bengali language, also.

In Bengali, the terms 'jati' and 'jatiya' have broader meanings, often signifying both brotherhood and national identity. In Bengal, 'jatiya' was used to express a sense of brotherhood, meaning 'national' in this context.

The Tamralipta Jatiya Sarkar, or Tamluk National Government, was an independent parallel government established in the areas of Tamluk and Contai subdivisions, now in East Medinipur, West Bengal, Bharat, during the Bharat Chhodo Andolan (Quit India Movement) from 1942 to 1944. It was the first people's government to be established in British Bharat and had the distinction of being the only parallel government to run independently for two years during the British Raj. This national government was formed by Satish Chandra Samanta, who remained its supreme leader until his arrest in June 1943. He was supported by several colleagues and leaders, such as Sushil Kumar Dhara, Ajoy Mukherjee and Matangini Hazra, some of whom served as ministers. The parallel government set up police stations, military departments, courts and a revenue collection system, effectively overthrowing the British civil administration by dispensing justice, maintaining peace and security, and aiding the poor and distressed. In Bengal, the word 'jatiya' (nationhood) is employed to convey a sense of brotherhood, reflecting the concept of 'national' in this context.

Jatiya Sangha: Founded in 1945 in Howrah, Jatiya Sangha is a library and social club.

Bharat Jatiya Bahini: This organization was established by Gopal Chandra Mukhopadhyaya (Gopal Patha).

In both the Jatiya Sangha and Bharat Jatiya Bahini, the word 'jatiya' is used to convey a sense of brotherhood and nationhood.

In Bangladesh, there is Jatiya Sangsad, also known as the 'National Parliament'.

Jnati (ज्ञाति)

ज्ञाति - ज्ञायतेऽस्मात् ज्ञाति, संज्ञानाद् ज्ञाति, ज्ञायते विद्यतेऽस्मादिति ज्ञाति (From which one is known that is called 'jñāti') and (the source of cognition is called jnati.). That which is known and exists is called his/her jnati. कुल or वंश ('lineage' or 'family line').

ज्ञातिमुंखा अहुतादश्चरंन्ति ।।28।।

jñātimukhā ahutādaścaranti॥28॥[8]

For example,

विद्यते गोषु सम्पन्नं विद्यते ज्ञातितो भयम् ।।9।।

vidyate goṣu sampannaṃ vidyate jñātito bhayam ||9||[9]

अधनाद्धि निवर्तन्ते ज्ञातयः सुहृदो द्विजाः ।।20।।

adhanāddhi nivartante jñātayaḥ suhṛdo dvijāḥ||20||[10]

A person's identity is known by their 'jnati' (ज्ञाति), meaning 'lineage' or 'family line' (कुल or वंश), which refers to the family of their birth. This 'jnati' (ज्ञाति) signifies that no one can deny their birth identity, regardless of whether their lineage is ordinary or prominent. 'Jnati' (ज्ञाति), indicating 'lineage' or 'family line' (कुल or वंश), represents a family line that cannot be changed—neither in the past, present nor future.

For example,

ज्ञातिवंशस्य गोप्तारं पितॄणां वंशवर्धनम् ।।11।।

jñātivaṃśasya goptāraṃ pitṝṇāṃ vaṃśavardhanam||11||[11]

Protector of the 'lineage' or 'family line' (कुल or वंश), ensuring the continuation of the family legacy.

The problem of Intermixing between Jati (जाति) and Jnati (ज्ञाति)

In Gujarat, the term 'jnati' (ज्ञाति) is used interchangeably with 'jati' (जाति) in the Gujarati language. While this usage is technically incorrect based on the Sanskrit origins of jnati and jati, it is common in Gujarati.

ज्ञाति–जाति[12]

In the Telugu language, 'jati' is mixed up with 'jnati' (ज्ञाति). Currently, 'jati' in Telugu refers to कुलमु (kulamu), which is technically incorrect; it should be 'jnati' (ज्ञाति), meaning kulamu (कुलमु). Similar to Gujarati, the distinction between 'jnati' (ज्ञाति) and 'jati' (जाति) is also mixed in Telugu.

I have mentioned the technical inaccuracies in Gujarati and Telugu regarding 'jati' and 'jnati' according to Sanskrit vyakarana (grammar). Since both words have their roots in Sanskrit, their accuracy will be measured by Sanskrit grammar.

Like in Gujarati and Telugu, there is a common problem across Bharat in distinguishing between 'jnati' (ज्ञाति) and 'jati' (जाति), which leads to significant confusion about not understanding their differences.

'Jnati' (ज्ञाति): 'Jnati' refers to a person's identity, known through their 'Jnati' (ज्ञाति), which signifies the family of their birth, specifically their 'lineage' or 'family line' known in Sanskrit as 'kula' (कुल) or 'vamsha' (वंश). It emphasizes the familial or ancestral background from which an individual descends.

'Jati' (जाति): Jati refers to a professional and occupational grouping characterized by common essential features, shared attributes, shared qualities, specific occupations and specialized professions.

नमस्तक्षभ्यो रथकारेभ्यश्च वो नमो नमः कुलालेभ्यः कर्मारेभ्यश्च वो नमो नमो
निषादेभ्यः पुञ्जिष्ठेभ्यश्च वो नमो नमः श्वनिभ्यो मृगयुभ्यश्च वो नमः॥27॥

namastakṣabhyo rathakārebhyaśca vo namo namaḥ kulālebhyaḥ
karmārebhyaśca vo namo namo niṣādebhyaḥ puñjiṣṭhebhyaśca vo
namo namaḥ śvanibhyomṛgayubhyaśca vo namaḥ ||27||[13]

Taksha (तक्ष–mason), rathkar (रथकार–carpenter), kulal (कुलाल-कुंभकार–potter), karmar (कर्मार-लोहकार–blacksmith), niṣād (निषाद–boatman), Mrigyu (मृगयु–hunter)

Individuals from various jnati (ज्ञाति), or family lineages, come together to form or join a jati (जाति), which represents a community centred on a particular profession, occupation or grouping.

There is a significant issue arising from the lack of understanding of the difference between 'jnati' (ज्ञाति) and 'jati' (जाति). This often leads to the misinterpretation and conflation of jnati as jati.

'Jatiya' (जातीय): Jatiya refers to the concept where individuals from various 'jnati' (ज्ञाति), signifying different families and lineages, come together to form a jati (जाति)—a specialized professional and occupational grouping or community. The individuals within this jati (जाति) develop a sense of brotherhood that unites them as part of that community. This essence of togetherness and shared identity among individuals constitutes jatiya identity.

It appears that over a long period in history, the word 'jatiya' gradually became 'jati' and was often used in its place. In his final message to the nation before his death, Pandit Madan Mohan Malviya, while addressing Hindu society, used 'Hindu jati' instead of 'jatiya'.

Varna (वर्ण): Different jati (जाति), specialized professional and occupational groups based on shared attributes, align with larger professional groupings known as varnas. This reflects the organizational structure of Hindu society, where specialized communities (jati, जाति) integrate into broader professional categories or groupings (varnas). For example,

स्त्रीसङ्घाः क्षत्रसङ्घाश्च यानसङ्घसमास्थिताः।।13।।
तथा विट्शूद्रसङ्घानां महान्यतिकरोऽभवत्।
न कश्चिदकरोदीर्ष्यामभवन्धर्मबुद्धयः।।14।।

strīsaṅghāḥ kṣatrasaṅghāśca yānasaṅghasamāsthitāḥ||13||
tathā viṭśūdrasaṅghānāṃ mahānyatikaro'bhavat|
na kaścidakarodīrṣyāmabhavandharmabuddhayaḥ||14||[14]

The Stri Sangha, Kshatriya Sangha, Vaishya Sangha and Shudra Sangha all gathered. There was no enmity among them, and their minds were all aligned with dharma.

In contemporary and future societies, evolution and progress are also measured by the absence of discrimination based on varna, jati, jnati, skin colour, race, gender, language or region. While distinctions and divisions may have existed in the past among human societies based on various factors, Hindu ancestors envisioned a society without division or discrimination based on varna, jati, jnati, skin colour or race. Therefore, the sixth Hindu Sutra 'एकवर्णस्तदा लोको' '*Ekavarṇastadā loko*'—Non-discriminatory Social System.

The Singular Source and Origin of Human Beings

सर्वेषां तुल्यदेहानां सर्वेषां सदृशात्मनाम्।।14।।

Sarveṣāṃ tulyadehānāṃ sarveṣāṃ sadṛśātmanām।।14।।[15]

All human bodies are alike, and so too are their souls.

विशेषेण च वक्ष्यामि चातुर्वर्ण्यस्य लिङ्गतः।
पञ्चभूतशरीराणां सर्वेषां सदृशात्मनाम्।।11।।

Viśeṣeṇa ca vakṣyāmi cāturvarṇyasya liṅgataḥ.
Pañcabhūtaśarīrāṇāṃ sarveṣāṃ sadṛśātmanām।।11।।[16]

The bodies of the four varna are composed of the five great elements: earth, water, fire, air and space, while everyone's atma (soul) is the same.

At a fundamental level, all human bodies share common characteristics and are composed of the same basic elements. This aligns with the understanding in Hindu philosophical tradition and modern scientific systems that human bodies are made up of various physical components such as organs, tissues and cells, all of which follow similar biological principles. The mention of the five great elements—earth, water, fire, air and space—reflects the idea that regardless of one's social identity, all human bodies are ultimately made up of the same basic building blocks of the universe.

The ātmā (soul) is the existential aspect of a person, distinct from the physical body. Just as human bodies share fundamental similarities, so do their ātmā (souls). This implies equality regardless of external differences and asserts the fundamental equality of all ātmā (souls), irrespective of societal distinctions such as profession or occupation. At the existential level, each individual is identical and transcends external labels, highlighting the essential unity of humanity both physically and spiritually. This perspective emphasizes the commonality and equality among all individuals, seeking to transcend social divisions and recognize the intrinsic worth and dignity of every human being.

एकवर्णस्तदा लोको भविष्यति युगक्षये।।42।।

Ekavarṇastadā loko bhaviṣyati yugakṣaye।।42।।[17]

The whole world will either unify under a single varna or adhere to a single societal community.

In the future, the entire world may unite into a single varna, embodying a unified societal structure without discrimination.

The future, shaped by integration and evolving societal values, will see distinct social community converging or blending into a unified societal structure. This unity represents a move towards a more egalitarian and harmonious societal structure.

This envisioned social structure would embody a unified ethos or collective identity in which individuals are defined by shared values, opportunities and aspirations rather than by varna. It represents a vision of societal harmony and equality, where everyone enjoys equal opportunities and status.

The future trajectory of societal evolution suggests a global movement towards a unified and harmonious community.

No Discrimination on the Basis of Varna or Jati

न विशेषोऽस्ति वर्णानां सर्वं ब्राह्ममिदं जगत्।।10।।

Na viśeṣo'sti varṇānāṃ sarvaṃ brāhmamidaṃ jagat ।।10।।[18]

In all the varnas, there are no special signs or distinct markers. Everyone originates from Bhagwan Brahma; thus, everyone is considered a Brahmin.

The absence of a special sign or distinct marker for each varna suggests that varna is not inherently based on biological birth. Instead, it underscores the equality of all individuals in their essential nature, believed to originate from the same source. This highlights the fundamental equality of all people.

न जात्या ब्राह्मणश्चात्र क्षत्रियो वैश्य एव न
न शूद्रो न च वै म्लेच्छो भेदिता गुणकर्मभिः।।38।।

Na jātyā brāhmaṇaścātra kṣatriyo vaiśya eva na
Na śūdro na ca vai mleccho bheditā guṇakarmabhiḥ।।38।।[19]

In this world, no person is inherently born as Brahmin, Kshatriya, Vaishya, Shudra or Malechchha (Ignoble).

At birth, individuals are not predestined to belong to a particular varna or professional grouping, refuting the idea that varna is determined solely by biological birth.

सर्वे वर्णा यथा पूजां प्राप्नुवन्ति सुसत्कृताः।
न चावज्ञा प्रयोक्तव्या कामक्रोधवशादपि।।14।।

Sarve varṇā yathā pūjāṃ prāpnuvanti susatkṛtāḥ.
Na cāvajñā prayoktavyā kāmakrodhavaśādapi।।14।।[20]

The social structure and institutions within the state should be designed in a manner that ensures all varnas are honoured and respected. Even if someone is influenced by desire or anger, they should not mistreat anyone.

Advocating for social organization and governance principles that emphasize equality and respect entails promoting the dignified treatment of all societal communities. The governance and social framework of society encompass systems, laws, norms and organizations spanning government, the economy, education and family. These institutions should embody established behavioural patterns that meet societal needs. Each varna deserves dignity and esteem within society, ensuring equal rights and opportunities, regardless of social status. Fairness and justice in societal interactions preclude mistreatment or discrimination based on varna or any other factor, aligning with the principle of equality before the law and the protection of individual rights. Societal structures and institutions must safeguard against mistreatment or discrimination. Even if someone is driven by emotions such as desire or anger, they should not mistreat anyone. A social order that promotes fair treatment, regardless of societal community, and includes structures upholding equality and respect for all, is paramount.

ततोऽधिजग्मुः सर्वे ते धनुर्वेदं महारथाः।
धृतराष्ट्रात्मजाश्चैव पाण्डवाः सह यादवैः।।23।।

tato'dhijagmuḥ sarve te dhanurvedaṃ mahārathāḥ|
dhṛtarāṣṭrātmajāścaiva pāṇḍavāḥ saha yādavaiḥ||23||[21]

The Kauravas, the children of Dhritarashtra, along with the Pandavas and the Yadavas, all studied Dhanurveda*—the text and practice of archery—under Kripacharya.*

वृष्णयश्च नृपाश्चान्ये नानादेशसमागताः।
कृपमाचार्यमासाद्य परमास्त्रज्ञतां गतः।।24।।

vṛṣṇayaśca nṛpāścānye nānādeśasamāgatāḥ|
kṛpamācāryamāsādya paramāstrajñatāṃ gataḥ||24||[22]

The Vrishni prince and princes from other provinces came to learn from Kripacharya, a great scholar.

सूतस्य ववृधेऽङ्गेषु श्रेष्ठः पुत्रः स वीर्यवान्।।15।।

Sūtasya vavṛdhe'ṅgeṣu śreṣṭhaḥ putraḥ sa vīryavān।।15।।[23]

In the state of Anga, Adhiratha, the charioteer, saw his strong son Karna growing day by day.

सूतस्त्वधिरथः पुत्रं विवृद्धं समयेन तम्।
दृष्ट्वा प्रस्थापयामास पुरं वारणसाह्वयम्।।16।।

Sūtastvadhirathaḥ putraṃ vivṛddhaṃ samayena tam.
Dṛṣṭvā prasthāpayāmāsa puraṃ vāraṇasāhvayam।।16।।[24]

Adhiratha, the charioteer, realized that his son Karna had grown up, so he sent him to Hastinapur for education.

Adhiratha, the charioteer, realized that his son Karna had grown up and, at the appropriate time, sent him to Hastinapur for education. It is important to note that Adhiratha lived in Angadesh, a region mentioned in the Mahabharata that corresponds to present-day northeastern Bihar. This area includes Bhagalpur, Purnia and its surroundings, located approximately 1200 to 1300 kilometres from Hastinapur (near present-day Meerut). The gurukul (academy) of Kripacharya and Dronacharya was in Gurugram, near Delhi. Despite the distance, Adhiratha sent Karna to pursue his education there. If Adhiratha had any doubts about potential discrimination from Kripacharya and Dronacharya, he would not have sent his son to such a distant place for learning.

वृष्णयश्चान्धकाश्चैव नानादेश्याश्च पार्थिवाः।
सूतपुत्रश्च राधेयो गुरुं द्रोणमियात् तदा।।11।।

Vṛṣṇayaścāndhakāścaiva nānādeśyāśca pārthivāḥ.
Sūtaputraśca rādheyo guruṃ droṇamiyāt tadā।।11।।[25]

The Vrishnis, the Andhakas, Kshatriyas and princes from various countries, as well as Karna, the son of a suta (charioteer), all came to learn from Acharya Drona.

The Vrishnis, the Andhakas and Kshatriya princes from various countries, as well as Karna, the son of a suta (Adhiratha a charioteer), all came to learn from Acharya Drona.

There is a common misconception that Acharya Drona discriminated against Karna and denied him education because he came from a family of charioteers, considered to be of a so-called lower social stratum in the current societal order. However, this evidence suggests that in the gurukul (academy) where Drona was the main teacher of warfare and weapon, Kshatriya princes from different states, such as the Vrishnis, Andhakas and others, came to learn under Acharya Drona. Alongside the other princes, Karna, the son of a charioteer, also came to learn from Acharya Drona. Acharya Drona educated and trained all his pupils without discriminating against them based on their status, jati or varna.

तत्रोपसदनं चक्रे द्रोणस्येष्वस्त्रकर्मणि॥17॥

Tatropasadanaṃ cakre droṇasyeṣvasrakarmaṇi॥17॥[26]

Karna accepted discipleship under Acharya Drona to learn the use of weapons.

After completing the education of the Kaurava and Pandava princes, along with other students, including Karna, Dronacharya asked them to offer their gurudakshina (an offering of gratitude to their teacher). For gurudakshina, Dronacharya requested his students to capture King Drupada and bring him to him. Karna also participated in the campaign led by Dronacharya's students to capture King Drupada.

ततोऽभिजग्मुः पञ्चालान्निघ्नन्तस्ते नरर्षभाः।
ममृदुस्तस्य नगरं द्रुपदस्य महौजसः॥6॥

tato'bhijagmuḥ pañcālānnighnantaste nararṣabhāḥ|
mamṛdustasya nagaraṃ drupadasya mahaujasaḥ||6||[27]

दुर्योधनश्च कर्णश्च युयुत्सुश्च महाबलः।
दुःशासनो विकर्णश्च जलसन्धः सुलोचनः॥7॥

duryodhanaśca karṇaśca yuyutsuśca mahābalaḥ|
duḥśāsano vikarṇaśca jalasandhaḥ sulocanaḥ||7||[28]

एते चान्ये च बहवः कुमारा बहुविक्रमाः।
अहं पूर्वमहं पूर्वमित्येवं क्षत्रियर्षभाः।।8।।

ete cānye ca bahavaḥ kumārā bahuvikramāḥ|
ahaṃ pūrvamahaṃ pūrvamityevaṃ kṣatriyarṣabhāḥ||8||[29]

Duryodhana, Karna, Mahabali Yuyutsu, Dushasana, Vikarna, Jalasandh and Sulochana, along with several other prince-students, launched an attack on King Drupada.

द्रोणात् कृपाच्च रामाच्च सोऽस्त्रग्रामं चतुर्विधम्।
लब्ध्वालोकेऽभवत् ख्यातः परमेष्वासतां गतः।।18।।

Droṇāt kṛpācca rāmācca so'stragrāmaṃ caturvidham.
Labdhvāloke'bhavat khyātaḥ parameṣvāsatāṃ gataḥ।।18।।[30]

After learning all kinds of weapon systems from Dronacharya, Kripacharya and Parshurama, Karna became renowned in the world as a great warrior.

It is important to note that all three of Karna's main teachers—Dronacharya, Kripacharya and Parshurama—were Brahmins. Although Karna was publicly identified as the son of Adhiratha, a charioteer of a so-called lower social stratum in the current societal order, he was sent to Dronacharya's gurukul (academy) for education. If Adhiratha had any doubts about potential discrimination, he likely would not have sent his son such a distance to study. Furthermore, Karna was accepted as a disciple by Dronacharya and studied alongside the Kshatriya princes, receiving instruction from all his Brahmin teachers. These facts indicate that Karna did not face discrimination based on his social status or economic background in his education. The key points are that Karna was willingly sent by his father and accepted as a disciple by Dronacharya.

Discrimination Based on Varna or Jati Should Not Exist in the Military

नीतिशस्त्रास्त्रव्यूहादिनीतिविद्याविशारदाः।
अबाला मध्यवयसः शूरा दान्ता दृढाङ्गकाः।।135।।
स्वधर्मनिरता नित्यं स्वामिभक्ता रिपुद्विषः।
शूद्रा वा क्षत्रिया वैश्या म्लेच्छाः संकरसम्भवाः।
सेनाधिपाः सैनिकाश्च कार्या राज्ञा जयार्थिना।।136।।

Nītiśastrāstravyūhādinītividyāviśāradāḥ.
Abālā madhyavayasaḥ śūrā dāntā dṛḍhāṅgakāḥ।।135।।
Svadharmaniratā nityaṃ svāmibhaktā ripudviṣaḥ.
Śūdrā vā kṣatriyā vaiśyā mlecchāḥ saṃkarasambhavāḥ.
Senādhipāḥ sainikāśca kāryā rājñā jayārthinā।।136।।[31]

Any state seeking victory should appoint a capable individual as a military chief, proficient in strategy and weapon usage, adept in the phalanx formation and skilled in planning and defeating adversaries. They should not be adolescents but rather mature, brave, humble, resolute, committed to their duties, patriotic and nationalistic, showing hostility towards enemies. Regardless of their birth—be it Shudra, Kshatriya, Vaishya, Ignoble—or their birth status, including those born of mixed marriages, courageous individuals from any community should be considered for appointments as military commanders and soldiers without discrimination.

सेनापतिः शूर एव योज्यः सर्वासु जातिषु।।413।।

Senāpatiḥ śūra eva yojyaḥ sarvāsu jātiṣu।।413।।[32]

In any jati (community), a person displaying significant bravery should be appointed as a military commander.

In Hindu Society, Varna and Jati, along with Their Associated Professions and Occupations, Were Interchangeable

ब्राह्मणस्त्रिषु वर्णेषु शस्त्रं गृह्णन्न दुष्यति॥29॥

Brāhmaṇastriṣu varṇeṣu śastraṃ gṛhṇanna duṣyati॥29॥[33]

Even a Brahmin is not at fault if he takes up arms to protect the three other varnas.

महाजना ह्युपावृत्ता राजधर्मं समाश्रिताः॥160/17॥

Mahājanā hyupāvṛttā rājadharmaṃ samāśritāḥ॥160/17॥[34]

A great person like Acharya Drona moves away from his own dharma and takes refuge in Raj Dharma (Kshatriya Dharma).

अशक्तः क्षत्रधर्मेण वैश्यधर्मेण वर्तयेत्।
कृषिगोरक्ष्यमास्थाय व्यसने वृत्तिसंक्षये॥2॥

Aśaktaḥ kṣatradharmeṇa vaiśyadharmeṇa vartayet.
Kṛṣigorakṣyamāsthāya vyasane vṛttisaṃkṣaye॥2॥[35]

When a Brahmin loses his means of livelihood, he may find it challenging to survive even by adhering to Kshatriya Dharma during times of distress. In such circumstances, following Vaishya Dharma, he should seek refuge in agriculture and farming to sustain himself.

Many scholars argue that Brahmins are merely a jati or varna, rather than a professional or occupational grouping or community. The reference above demonstrates that when Brahmins lose their means of livelihood, they adhere to Kshatriya dharma (profession) and Vaishya dharma (profession) as well. This indicates that professions are interchangeable and supports the idea that Brahmins can be considered an occupational jati. Several specialized Brahmin occupational jatis come together to form a larger professional community, constituting the Brahmin varna.

अभ्युत्थिते दस्युबले क्षत्रार्थे वर्णसंकरे।
सम्प्रमूढेषु वर्णेषु यद्यन्योऽभिभवेद् बली।।35।।
ब्राह्मणो यदि वा वैश्यः शूद्रो वा राजसत्तम।
दस्युभ्योऽथ प्रजा रक्षेद् दण्डं धर्मेण धारयन्।।36।।
कार्ये कुर्यान्न वा कुर्यात् संवार्यो वा भवेन्न वा।
तस्माच्छस्त्रं ग्रहीतव्यमन्यत्र क्षत्रबन्धुतः।।37।।

Abhyutthite dasyubale kṣatrārthe varṇasaṃkare.
Sampramūḍheṣu varṇeṣu yadyanyo'bhibhaved balī।।35।।
Brāhmaṇo yadi vā vaiśyaḥ śūdro vā rājasattama.
Dasyubhyo'tha prajā rakṣed daṇḍaṃ dharmeṇa dhārayan।।36।।
Kārye kuryānna vā kuryāt saṃvāryo vā bhavenna vā.
Tasmācchastraṃ grahītavyamanyatra kṣatrabandhutaḥ।।37।।[36]

Yudhisthira questioned Bheeshma about governance issues that were being neglected by the Kshatriyas, suggesting a failure to fulfil their duty. With the increasing prevalence of bandits and looters leading to anarchy and chaos, it seemed that people from all varnas were unable to find effective solutions for governance. In such circumstances, if a powerful Brahmin, Vaishya or Shudra were to take the initiative to uphold law and order, establish societal order, and protect people from bandits and looters, could they assume governance responsibilities? Yudhisthira's response was that individuals other than Kshatriyas should indeed take up arms and actively participate in crafting governance solutions.

Shri Rama Shared a Strong Friendship with Guha, the Nishad Raj, Wherein Untouchability Had No Place

तत्र राजा गुहो नाम रामस्यात्मसमः सखा।
निषादजात्यो बलवान् स्थपतिश्चेति विश्रुतः।।33।।

Tatra rājā guho nāma rāmasyātmasamaḥ sakhā.
Niṣādajātyo balavān sthapatiśceti viśrutaḥ।।33।।[37]

King Guha ruled over Sringverpur, and he was a close friend of Sri Rama, holding a place dear to him akin to his own life. Guha hailed from the Nishad (boatman) community by birth, characterized by his remarkable physical and military strength. He was renowned as a prominent and esteemed ruler of the Nishad (boatman) people.

ततो निषादाधिपतिं दृष्ट्वा दूरादुपस्थितम्।
सह सौमित्रिणा रामः समागच्छद् गुहेन सः।।34।।

Tato niṣādādhipatiṃ dṛṣṭvā dūrādupasthitam.
Saha saumitriṇā rāmaḥ samāgacchad guhena saḥ।।34।।[38]

Upon seeing from a distance that the ruler of Nishad raj (king) had arrived, Shri Rama, along with Lakshman, proceeded to meet and receive him.

भुजाभ्यां साधुवृत्ताभ्यां पीडयन् वाक्यमब्रवीत्।।41।।
दिष्ट्या त्वां गुह पश्यामि ह्यरोगं सह बान्धवैः।
अपि ते कुशलं राष्ट्रे मित्रेषु च वनेषु च।।42।।

Bhujābhyāṃ sādhuvṛttābhyāṃ pīḍayan vākyamabravīt।।41।।
Diṣṭyā tvāṃ guha paśyāmi hyarogaṃ saha bāndhavaiḥ.
Api te kuśalaṃ rāṣṭre mitreṣu ca vaneṣu ca।।42।।[39]

Embracing Guha warmly with his rounded arms, Sri Rama said, 'Guha, it is fortunate that today I see you, my friend, in good health and joyous with friends and associates. Is everything well in your state, among your friends, and in the forest?'

In current societal norms, individuals who engage in the practice of untouchability and those often discussed in public discourse and academia in the context of untouchability within Hindu society need to understand that untouchability was never historically accepted in Hindu society.

The friendship between Shri Rama and Guha serves as an example, indicating that there is no room for any form of untouchability, even based on birth or social status, in Hindu society.

In Hindu Society, the Shudras Are a Respected Community, and They Also Have Their Own States

शूद्रास्तु मन्दगा नित्यं पुरुषा धर्मशीलिनः।।38।।

Śūdrāstu mandagā nityaṃ puruṣā dharmaśīlinaḥ।।38।।[40]

In the Mandaga Janapada (state), Shudras reside. They are known for their pious and virtuous nature (dharmasheela).

न तत्र राजा राजेन्द्र न दण्डो न च दण्डिकः।
स्वधर्मेणैव धर्मज्ञास्ते रक्षन्ति परस्परम्।।39।।

Na tatra rājā rājendra na daṇḍo na ca daṇḍikaḥ.
Svadharmeṇaiva dharmajñāste rakṣanti parasparam।।39।।[41]

In the Mandaga Janapada (state), neither a king nor punishment exists, nor is there anyone designated to administer them. Its inhabitants are deeply versed in dharma, and through steadfast adherence to it, they mutually safeguard one another.

In the Mandaga Janpada (state) of Shudra, where there is no centralized authority such as a king or ruler, punitive measures enforced by a governing body become unnecessary. This absence signifies a profound level of self-governance and mutual respect among individuals. The inhabitants of such a janpada (state), the Shudras, not only grasp the moral and ethical principles governing their society but also deeply internalize them. They possess an innate understanding of right and wrong according to the principle of dharma. Instead of relying on external authority to maintain order, the society operates smoothly because its members unwaveringly adhere to the principles of dharma. This steadfast adherence ensures that individuals act in alignment with moral principles, collectively upholding societal harmony. Within this community, people coexist harmoniously, guided solely by their inner moral compass and respect for each other's rights and duties.

शूद्राभीरगणाश्चैव ये चाश्रित्य सरस्वतीम्।।10।।

śūdrābhīragaṇāścaiva ye cāśritya sarasvatīm||10||[42]

The Ganasanghas (republican states) of the Shudras and Abhiras were located on the banks of the Saraswati River.

अश्विनौ तु स्मृतौ शूद्रौ तपस्युग्रे समास्थितौ।।24।।

Aśvinau tu smṛtau śūdrau tapasyugre samāsthitau।।24।।[43]

Two Ashvinikumars, who are practising severe penance, have been said to be Shudras.

The Ashvinikumaras are regarded as the physicians of the gods and the presiding deities of Ayurvedic medicine in Vedic tradition. Various medical operations and successful treatments are attributed to them. Remarkably, many of the medical procedures performed by the Ashvinikumaras, such as surgery, transplants and skin grafts, parallel recent advancements in modern medical science and technology.

Here are two important points to understand: First, the word 'Shudra' is not a derogatory or demeaning term, even though modern sociologists often associate it with the so-called lower stratum in Bharat. Second, the Ashvinikumaras, known as the physicians of the gods and the presiding deities of Ayurvedic medicine, were also referred to as Shudras, indicating that it is a respected term rather than a negative one.

The Dignity of a Human Being Is Paramount

शासनं त्वीदृशं कार्यं राज्ञा नित्यं प्रजासु च।।293।।
दासे भृत्येऽथ भार्यायां पुत्रे शिष्येऽपि वा क्वचित्।
वाग्दण्डपरुषं नैव कार्यं मद्देशसंस्थितैः।।294।।

Śāsanaṃ tvīdṛśaṃ kāryaṃ rājñā nityaṃ prajāsu ca।।293।।
Dāse bhṛtye'tha bhāryāyāṃ putre śiṣye'pi vā kvacit.

Vāgdaṇḍaparuṣaṃ naiva kāryaṃ maddeśasaṃsthitaiḥ||294||[44]

The head of state should always guide their people, ensuring that those living within the state refrain from speaking harshly to or punishing severely attendants, maids, servants, wives, offspring or disciples.

The head of state is not only a political leader but also a moral and ethical authority, expected to embody the virtues and values that define the society they govern. It is their duty to provide guidance to their people on interactions, particularly with those in subordinate roles such as attendants, maids, servants, family members (wives, offspring) and disciples. This extends to advocating for respectful and fair treatment according to state norms and laws, emphasizing the importance of avoiding harsh or punitive measures perceived as excessive or unjust. By promoting a culture of respect, empathy and fairness, the head of state fosters a harmonious and cohesive society where all individuals are treated with dignity and compassion, cultivating kindness and upholding fundamental principles of respect for others.

Care for the Weak and Poor without Any Form of Discrimination

अभृतानां च भरणं भृतानां चान्ववेक्षणम्||54||

Abhṛtānāṃ ca bharaṇaṃ bhṛtānāṃ cānvavekṣaṇam||54||[45]

The state should arrange for the subsistence of those without means and also provide support to those whose subsistence is arranged by the state.

The state has a responsibility to ensure that fundamental needs such as food, shelter and healthcare are met for individuals who cannot afford them independently. This responsibility can be fulfilled through programmes like welfare, free food, public housing and healthcare. Additionally, those receiving state assistance should be provided with extra support, potentially through supplementary services or resources aimed at enhancing their quality of life beyond mere survival.

कच्चिदन्धांश्च मूकांश्च पङ्गून्व्यङ्गानबान्धवान्।
पितेव पासि धर्मज्ञ तथा प्रव्रजितानपि।।125 ।।

kaccidandhāṃśca mūkāṃśca paṅgūnvyaṅgānabāndhavān|
piteva pāsi dharmajña tathā pravrajitānapi||125||[46]

The state should provide support and care for weak and vulnerable individuals, including the blind, deaf, lame, disabled, those with limb loss, and wandering monks.

Society Should Ensure Care for Everyone

साध्वी भार्या पितृपत्नी माता बालः पिता स्नुषा।
अभर्तृकाऽनपत्या या साध्वी कन्या स्वसापि च।।118।।
मातुलानी भ्रातृभार्या पितृमातृस्वसा तथा।
मातामहोऽनपत्यश्च गुरुश्वशुरमातुलाः।।119।।
बालोऽपिता च दौहित्रो भ्राता च भगिनीसुतः।।120।।
अविभवेऽपि विभवे पितृमातृकुलं सुहृत्।
पत्न्याः कुलं दासदासीभृत्यवर्गांश्च पोषयेत्।।121।।
विकलाङ्गान् प्रव्रजितान् दीनानाथांश्च पालयेत्।।122।।

Sādhvī bhāryā pitṛpatnī mātā bālaḥ pitā snuṣā.
Abhartṛkā'napatyā yā sādhvī kanyā svasāpi ca।।118।।
Mātulānī bhrātṛbhāryā pitṛmātṛsvasā tathā.
Mātāmaho'napatyaśca guruśvaśuramātulāḥ।।119।।
Bālo'pitā ca dauhitro bhrātā ca bhaginīsutaḥ।।120।।
Avibhave'pi vibhave pitṛmātṛkulaṃ suhṛt.
Patnyāḥ kulaṃ dāsadāsībhṛtyavargāṃśca poṣayet।।121।।
Vikalāṅgān pravrajitān dīnānāthāṃśca pālayet।।122।।[47]

One should take utmost care of a virtuous wife, stepmother, mother, child, father, son's wife, sister without husband and children, father's sister, mother's sister, childless elder, guru (teacher), father-in-law, mother's brother, fatherless boy, daughter's son, brother and nephew, even in times of financial hardship. When wealth is abundant, one should extend care to father and mother, relatives, friends' wives' families (in-laws), servants and maids. Similarly, the disabled, renunciates, the poor and orphans should also receive care.

It is a comprehensive ethic of care that spans familial relationships, social roles and broader humanitarian concerns. It emphasizes the importance of empathy, responsibility and solidarity in both times of abundance and financial hardship.

ये चान्नमिच्छन्ति ददस्व तेभ्यः परिश्रिता ये परितो मनुष्याः।।5।।

Ye cānnamicchanti dadasva tebhyaḥ Pariśritā ye parito manuṣyāḥ।।5।।[48]

Kunti said to Draupadi, 'Those around you who depend on you, feed them and take care of them.'

When Kunti tells Draupadi, 'Those around you who depend on you, feed them and take care of them', she is emphasizing several key principles. Kunti reminds Draupadi of her role as the wife of the Pandavas and the queen of their household, signifying a responsibility not only towards herself and her husbands but also towards others who rely on her. This underscores a compassionate attitude and a readiness to support and nurture others in their times of need. It serves as a timeless lesson in compassion, responsibility and resilience, highlighting the importance of caring for those who depend on us—not just materially but also emotionally and spiritually. This teaching embodies the noblest virtues, even in the face of adversity.

APPENDIX 1

Debating Caste: Western Constructs, Misconceptions and the Search for Clarity

A Summary of *Western Foundations of the Caste System*, edited by Martin Fárek, Dunkin Jalki, Sufiya Pathan and Prakash Shah

The problem of understanding the caste system persists in contemporary scholarship. The editors argue that, despite extensive research, many fundamental questions about caste remain unanswered. While there is consensus regarding the existence of caste and its negative impacts, there is no agreement on its nature, origin, propagation or characteristics. This lack of consensus hampers scholarly progress and raises crucial questions about how to study caste and what phenomena should be examined under the rubric of 'caste'. The work explores the difficulties scholars face in describing caste and determining its fundamental properties. The editors also examine various theories regarding the origin and spread of caste, highlighting the absence of a clear explanation for its dissemination across such a vast and diverse landscape. Furthermore, they discuss how Western scholarship has framed caste as a 'master key' to understanding Bharat, yet it struggles to define its properties and explain its prevalence and persistence. In line with the hypotheses of the research programme on the *Comparative Science of Cultures* initiated by Prof. S.N. Balagangadhara, the contributions collectively reinforce the claim that, despite its wide adoption among academicians and intellectuals in Bharat, the concept of 'the caste system' does not describe Bharat's culture and society but instead reflects the Western experience of Bharat.

S.N. Balagangadhara explores the intellectual currents shaping the debate on social justice, particularly the influence of Christian ideas. He argues that the Christian conception of social justice cannot be traced to the debates of Bharat's constituent assembly but rather to Catholic social doctrines and their secularization. Dunkin Jalki and Sufiya Pathan challenge the widespread and often unquestioned assumption that 'caste atrocities' are rampant in Bharat. They argue that data on caste crimes, collected by the National Crime Records Bureau (NCRB), does not support this claim. By examining the data, they reveal how it is often misinterpreted and misrepresented, particularly when scholars use it to argue that caste violence is on the rise. The authors highlight the problematic nature of 'soft data' on caste atrocities and how scholars frequently conflate general crime statistics with caste-related crimes. Moreover, they question the frequent use of the 'popular caveat' that caste atrocities go unreported due to caste prejudice, arguing that this assumption lacks empirical support and perpetuates the notion of widespread caste violence.

Prakash Shah addresses the debate surrounding the inclusion of caste as a protected characteristic in the UK's Equality Act 2010. The author analyses the parliamentary debates and reports used to justify the legislation, highlighting the dubious nature of the arguments presented and the lack of empirical evidence supporting them. Shah contends that the legislation reinforces a colonial and Western understanding of caste as an immoral social system and perpetuates the idea that the 'upper castes' are the sole perpetrators of discrimination against 'lower castes'.

Martin Farek examines the common assumption that the Shramana and Bhakti movements were inherently anti-caste. He analyses the teachings of the Buddha and the Vaishnava traditions, highlighting how they addressed the question who a true Brahmana is, and affirmed the value of varna. Farek argues that the unifying anti-caste hypothesis is based on a faulty understanding of these traditions and the history of society in Bharat, often relying on a Western Christian theological framework to explain the persistence of this hypothesis.

Jakob De Roover delves into the moral dimension of the dominant discourse on caste. He argues that the construction of caste as an immoral system arises from a specific historical context: the influence of Christian ideas about the Jewish nation, its laws and its priesthood on how Europeans understood Hindu society. De Roover traces the history of the 'caste system' as it evolved in the writings of European scholars, missionaries and colonial administrators, highlighting how the idea of a hierarchical caste system was constructed. He concludes that the current understanding of the caste system as immoral is derived from the Christian understanding of Judaism, which, in turn, was a product of the Reformation and its critique of Catholicism.

Marianna Keppens examines the historical account of the Aryan invasion of Bharat as a core element in understanding the caste system. She argues that the dominant account of the Aryan invasion or in-migration lacks empirical evidence and was largely driven by Christian theological frameworks that portrayed the 'heathens' of Bharat as a variant of the Jewish nation. Keppens analyses the evolution of this hypothesis, highlighting the role of the 'Indo-Aryan language family' in its development and the absence of clear evidence for an Aryan invasion of Bharat. She concludes by questioning how this hypothesis has persisted for over 200 years, despite its problematic and often unfounded nature.

The editors reiterate their claim that the caste system does not exist as a unified entity and that the dominant account of the caste system is a product of colonial consciousness, shaped by Christian ideas about religion and society. They conclude by emphasizing the need for a new understanding of Hindu society, one free from these colonial influences, while acknowledging the challenges and complexities involved in achieving such an understanding.

APPENDIX 2

Comprehensive History of Caste in Colonial Bharat

A Summary of Nicholas B. Dirks's *Castes of Mind: Colonialism and the Making of Modern India*

Castes of Mind: Colonialism and the Making of Modern India is a meticulously researched and deeply insightful exploration of the history of caste in colonial Bharat. Through archival research, ethnographic studies and textual analyses, Dirks uncovers the ways in which the British constructed caste as a central category of social and political knowledge, ultimately transforming it into the defining feature of Hindu society, both in its colonial and postcolonial incarnations.

The book challenges the conventional view of caste as a timeless and unchanging institution embedded in ancient Hindu tradition, arguing instead that it is a modern phenomenon shaped by the historical encounter between Bharat and Western colonialism. Dirks' approach is not only to document the evolution of caste within the colonial context but also to examine the ways in which colonial knowledge about caste was used to justify and legitimize colonial rule, ultimately shaping the terms of both anticolonial nationalism and contemporary caste politics in Bharat.

The Pre-colonial Background

Dirks begins by outlining the pre-colonial context in which social relations were not primarily organized around the categories of caste, but rather through more fluid and complex forms of social identity, such as clan affiliation, regional loyalties and occupational status. He challenges the common assumption that the pre-colonial state was a weak and fragmented entity, arguing instead that political power was often concentrated in the hands of powerful chieftains and local magnates, often drawn from the same groups that came to be designated as 'criminal castes' by the British. Dirks' careful reading of historical accounts, particularly those collected by the Scottish antiquarian Colin Mackenzie, reveals a vibrant and dynamic political landscape that was far more complex and nuanced than previously thought.

The Rise of the Ethnographic State

Dirks argues that the British conquest of Bharat was not the result of a sudden and decisive military victory but rather a gradual and insidious process of political and economic encroachment that relied heavily on strategies of indirect rule. The British sought to understand local political and social structures, not so much to challenge or suppress them, but rather to transform them in ways that would legitimize and stabilize British rule. The emergence of the 'ethnographic state' in the second half of the nineteenth century, marked by a growing emphasis on the systematic collection and analysis of ethnographic data, is seen as a critical turning point in the history of colonialism and its relationship to the construction of knowledge.

The ethnographic state became dependent upon the production of a new kind of knowledge that, in its focus on the systematic collection and classification of data about caste, transformed the colonial project from a largely political and economic enterprise into a social scientific endeavour. The British, having been embarrassed by their own ignorance about Bharat's society and the ways in which their attempts at social reform had backfired, sought to create a new kind of knowledge—an anthropology of Bharat—that would not only help them to govern effectively but also to justify their rule and to demonstrate that their commitment to the civilizing mission of the Empire was ultimately based on their scientific understanding of the underlying principles of Hindu society. The ethnographic project, spearheaded by the colonial ethnographers Herbert Hope Risley and Edgar Thurston, and culminating in the systematic collection of data and the creation of the decennial census, transformed the colonial archive and established a new relationship between knowledge and power.

The Problem of Custom

The British, having learned from their earlier attempts at Christianization and social reform that their attempts to impose 'civilized' values on Hindu society often backfired, sought to establish a new policy of 'non-interference' with Hindu dharma, society, tradition and customs. However, they were unable to determine with any certainty what constituted religion and custom, and they found that their efforts at non-interference often led to deeper interventions and the transformation of both religion and custom. The British discovered that their efforts at social reform often failed to produce the desired outcomes, and that the very act of interfering in traditional religious practices served to undermine the authority of those who had already taken steps to reform those practices.

The story of the hook swinging controversy, with its various protagonists, further illuminates the ways in which the colonial state sought to define and control social practices and to reify the category of caste. British officials were troubled by the violence of the practice but were also concerned that it reflected the barbarity and backwardness of Bharat's people. Although they were reluctant to interfere with religious custom, they increasingly sought to restrict and regulate practices that were seen as harmful or dangerous. The story of hook swinging also reveals the ways in which the colonial state used its own categories of custom and tradition to control and define the agency of colonial subjects.

A Postcolonial Critique of Caste

The book concludes with a reflection on the legacies of colonialism and the ways in which these legacies continue to shape the social and political landscape of contemporary Bharat. Dirks argues that caste remains a critical and enduring element of postcolonial Hindu society, and that the history of colonialism can neither be simply ignored nor used to dismiss contemporary concerns. The contemporary crisis over the implementation of reservations for backward castes, and the continuing caste violence, are seen as products of colonial history. But Dirks emphasizes that caste is not merely a vestige of the colonial past but rather a powerful force shaping the terms of political discourse and social action. He concludes the book with a plea for a postcolonial history that acknowledges the lasting legacy of colonialism and the ways in which this legacy has transformed the historical and social landscape of modern Bharat.

APPENDIX 3

Challenging Narratives: The Role and Growth of Scheduled Tribes and Castes in Medieval Bharat

A Summary of K.S. Lal's *Growth of Scheduled Tribes and Castes in Medieval India*

Challenging traditional narratives

Prof. K.S. Lal begins by critically assessing the existing historiography, which often marginalizes the role of Scheduled Castes and Tribes in medieval Bharat. He argues that traditional narratives, shaped by colonial perspectives, have overlooked the agency and contributions of these groups. By re-examining primary sources, including medieval Muslim chronicles, Lal uncovers instances where Scheduled Castes and Tribes actively shaped political events, resisted oppressive regimes and contributed to economic and cultural developments.

Active participation in political affairs

One of the pivotal arguments Lal presents is the active involvement of Scheduled Castes and Tribes in political affairs. He highlights several rebellions and movements led by these groups against foreign rulers. For instance, the role of tribal leaders in mobilizing resistance against the Delhi Sultanate is discussed, illustrating their strategic alliances and military prowess.

Economic contributions and land revenue systems

Prof. K.S. Lal uses historical and inscriptional evidence to highlight the roles of Scheduled Tribes and Castes in agriculture, trade, craftsmanship and cultural enrichment. He delves into their economic activities, emphasizing their contributions to sustaining local economies and integrating into broader economic frameworks. His analysis of the land revenue systems instituted by medieval Muslim rulers examines how these exploitative policies impacted these groups.

The chapter underscores the indispensable contributions of Scheduled Tribes and Castes to medieval Bharat's economy. Data reveals their significant economic impact: Scheduled Tribes and Castes likely constituted 20–25 per cent of the rural workforce in most regions. Their involvement in forest-based products accounted for 30–40 per cent of local trade in forested areas. Crafts and artisan groups among the Scheduled Castes produced 60–70 per cent of village-level tools and utensils. Tribal stonemasons, noted in regional inscriptions, showcased exceptional craftsmanship in temple construction.

Furthermore, Scheduled Tribes and Castes played a vital role in the construction industry, including temples, forts and public works, contributing as blacksmiths, potters, carpenters, weavers and leather workers.

Social mobility and cultural integration

The book explores the social mobility experienced by certain castes and tribes, facilitated by factors such as urbanization and involvement in trade. Lal also examines the cultural integration of different social groups, which fostered the emergence of harmonious cultural practices and mutual influences in areas such as religion, art and language.

Impact of Islamic rule: impact of Islamic invasions, rule and economic exploitation

A significant portion of Lal's analysis is dedicated to examining the impact of Islamic rule on the growth of Scheduled Tribes and Castes. He argues that the sociopolitical changes during this period created opportunities for these groups to assert their dominance or negotiate their positions within the new order. The adaptability and resilience of Scheduled Tribes and Castes in the face of changing political landscapes are highlighted as key factors contributing to their growth.

Prof. K.S. Lal highlights that the Scheduled Castes became landless labourers, forced to depend on landlords created by the Muslim feudal system, which kept them impoverished. The Scheduled Tribes, though traditionally tied to land and forest resources, faced displacement.

He emphasizes the arrival of Islamic rulers in medieval Bharat, where mass killings, forced conversions and the destruction of local economies had a devastating impact on the Scheduled Castes and Scheduled Tribes.

The imposition of high taxes under the Muslim feudal system and the jizya tax on non-Muslims disproportionately affected these groups, often coercing them into bonded labour and leading to their continued poverty.

Case studies

Lal employs detailed case studies to illustrate his arguments, including: 'The Role of the Gond Tribe: Examining how the Gond rulers in central Bharat maintained autonomy and influenced regional politics'; 'Dalit Uprisings: Analyzing rebellions led by Dalits against oppressive Muslim landlords and rulers'; and 'The Bhil and Their Resistance: Investigating the Bhil tribe's resistance to Mughal incursions, emphasizing their strategic alliances and military tactics'.

Interplay between caste and tribe identities

Lal explores the complex interplay between caste and tribe identities, noting that the boundaries are often porous and subject to change. He discusses instances where tribal groups assimilated into the caste system or maintained distinct identities while influencing caste dynamics.

Legacy of medieval growth on contemporary society

In the concluding chapters, Lal traces the historical growth of Scheduled Tribes and Castes to their present-day status in Bharat. He discusses the long-term implications of medieval sociopolitical developments on contemporary issues such as affirmative action, social mobility and political representation.

Conclusions

K.S. Lal concludes that the growth and evolution of Scheduled Tribes and Castes in medieval Bharat were significantly influenced by their active participation in sociopolitical and economic spheres. Contrary to the notion of passive subjugation, these groups demonstrated resilience, strategic acumen and agency in shaping their destinies. The interactions between scheduled castes, tribes and ruling powers created a dynamic and fluid social structure that allowed for both conflict and cooperation.

सर्वं शान्तिः[1]

Sarvam śāntiḥ

CHAPTER 7

Care for Nature

In Hindu thought, reverence for nature transcends mere appreciation, deeply intertwining with spiritual beliefs and practices. Hindus perceive life and divinity not only in humans and animals but also in natural elements such as trees, plants, rivers, mountains and the earth itself.

Trees are considered sacred in Hindu dharma and are often believed to be inhabited by various deities. Rivers hold immense significance, symbolizing purity and divinity. Both mountains and rivers are revered and worshipped, with Hindus performing circumambulations around trees, mountains and rivers as acts of devotion.

Pilgrimages to mountainous regions and rivers are considered spiritually rewarding, further highlighting their sacredness.

The earth (Prithvi) is respected as the nurturing mother (Bhudevi). Hindus perform pooja (rituals) to honour and seek blessings from the earth, acknowledging it as a source of sustenance and a manifestation of the divine.

Air (vayu) and water (jal) are integral to Hindu sacred rituals and prayers, further emphasizing the sanctity of natural elements.

This reverence for nature in Hindu dharma reflects a holistic worldview where humans are interconnected with the environment and all living beings. This perspective encourages sustainable practices, respect and care for nature, emphasizing harmony between humanity and the natural world.

If humans want to live on this earth peacefully and ensure the survival of future generations, they must respect nature and its environment by protecting forests, rivers, mountains, water and the earth itself. The exploitation of Earth's resources must be stopped, and these resources should be utilized judiciously for all living beings.

Additionally, pollution of the air, water, earth, rivers and mountains must be halted. To care for nature and safeguard its environment is the essence of the seventh Hindu Sutra. 'सर्वं शान्तिः'—'*Sarvam śāntiḥ*', Care for Nature.

Restrained Utilization of Resources

पृथिवी रत्नसम्पूर्णा हिरण्यं पशवः स्त्रियः।
नालमेकस्य तत् सर्वमिति मत्वा शमं व्रजेत्॥51॥

Pṛthivī ratnasampūrṇā hiraṇyaṃ paśavaḥ striyaḥ.
Nālamekasya tat sarvamiti matvā śamaṃ vrajet॥51॥[2]

Even if a man were to possess the entire earth, with fields brimming with gems, all the gold in the world, and countless animals, these would still not satisfy him. A man would crave more. Understanding this, he can find peace by calming his desires for material pleasures.

यत् पृथिव्यां व्रीहियवं हिरण्यं पशवः स्त्रियः।
एकस्यापि न पर्याप्तं तस्मात् तृष्णां परित्यजेत्॥13॥

Yat pṛthivyāṃ vrīhiyavaṃ hiraṇyaṃ paśavaḥ striyaḥ.
Ekasyāpi na paryāptaṃ tasmāt tṛṣṇāṃ parityajet॥13॥[3]

The paddy, barley, gold and animals on this earth are not sufficient for one person. Therefore, one should give up craving.

The insatiable nature of desire and the futility of seeking fulfilment through material possessions are evident in the pursuit of wealth. Even possessing vast riches—fields brimming with gems, all the world's gold and countless animals—fails to satisfy. This reflects desire's endless cycle: fulfilling one spawns new desires, perpetuating craving indefinitely.

Finding peace requires curbing material desires. Instead of incessantly chasing wealth, one should promote introspection and restraint. Recognizing that material goods yield only fleeting satisfaction encourages detachment from the pursuit of wealth. Embracing simpler joys fosters true contentment.

By relinquishing insatiable desires and valuing present possessions, individuals achieve inner peace surpassing materialism. It highlights material wealth's limits in sustaining happiness, endorsing balanced desire that embraces contentment.

Non-Killing of Animals

वधः पशुवराहाणां तथैव मृगपक्षिणाम्।
शान्तनौ पृथिवीपाले नावर्तत तथा नृप॥15॥

Vadhaḥ paśuvarāhāṇāṃ tathaiva mṛgapakṣiṇām.
Śāntanau pṛthivīpāle nāvartata tathā nṛpa॥15॥[4]

During Maharaja Shantanu's rule, he took great care of the earth, ensuring that animals and wild creatures such as boars, deer and birds were not killed.

Non-killing of animals was often rooted in ethical and environmental considerations, focusing on respect for life, the sanctity of nature and maintaining ecological balance. Hindu philosophy and tradition taught that all living creatures had a right to life and should not be harmed unnecessarily. States adhering to these teachings implemented policies to protect animals.

A broader ethical understanding existed that humans had a duty to protect and care for the natural world. The head of state, as a moral exemplar, was expected to demonstrate compassion and respect for all forms of life, encouraging his subjects to follow suit.

Ancient Hindus recognized the importance of maintaining ecological balance, understanding that the indiscriminate killing of animals could lead to environmental degradation, harm agricultural productivity and affect the state's overall well-being. By protecting animals such as boars, deer and birds, they aimed to preserve biodiversity and ensure the stability of natural ecosystems.

Laws were enforced by state guards and officials who patrolled forests and other wildlife habitats, with violators often subject to severe punishment and penalties. The state established wildlife sanctuaries where animals could live without the threat of being hunted, serving as safe havens that contributed to species conservation and habitat preservation.

The non-killing of animals during the ancient Hindu period reflected deep-seated ethical considerations and practical measures aimed at preserving the environment. By protecting animals, they sought to maintain ecological balance, ensure the sustainability of natural resources and uphold moral principles that valued all forms of life.

सूनाध्यक्षः प्रदिष्टाभयानामभयवनवासिनां च मृगपशुपक्षिमत्स्यानां बन्धवधहिंसायामुत्तमं दण्डं कारयेत्। कुटुम्बिनामभयवनपरिग्रहेषु मध्यमम्।

Sūnādhyakṣaḥ pradiṣṭābhayānāmabhayavanavāsinām̩ ca mṛgapaśupakṣimatsyānām̩ bandhavadhahim̩sāyāmuttamam̩ daṇḍam̩ kārayet. kuṭumbināmabhayavanaparigraheṣu madhyamam.[5]

अप्रवृत्तवधानां मत्स्यपक्षिणां बन्धवधहिंसायां पादोनसप्तविंशतिपणमत्ययं कुर्यात्, मृगपशूनां द्विगुणम्।

Apravṛttavadhānām̩ matsyapakṣiṇām̩ bandhavadhahim̩sāyām̩ pādonasaptavim̩śatipaṇamatyayam̩ kuryāt, mṛgapaśūnām̩ dviguṇam.[6]

वत्सो वृषो धेनुश्चैषामवध्याः। घ्नतः पञ्चाशत्को दण्डः। क्लिष्टघातं घातयतश्च।

Vatso vṛṣo dhenuścaiṣāmavadhyāḥ. ghnataḥ pañcāśatko daṇḍaḥ. kliṣṭaghātam̩ ghātayataśca.[7]

If any person kills, catches or injures deer, rhinoceroses, buffaloes, peacocks or fish in reserve forests and sanctuaries or in large educational institutions where killing or catching is prohibited, the officials there should inflict the severest punishment on them. If any member of the royal family violates this directive, they should also be punished. Individuals who catch, attack or kill non-violent creatures such as birds and fish should be fined. The penalty should be doubled. A person who kills deer, calves, bulls or cows among animals shall be fined. A person who kills even one of these will incur a fine. Additionally, a person who kills any other animal with cruelty shall be fined double.

Chanakya outlines strict penalties for harming or killing animals, especially in protected areas and institutions, emphasizing conservation and wildlife protection. The directive targets individuals who kill, catch or injure specific animals such as deer, rhinoceroses, buffaloes, peacocks or fish within reserve forests and sanctuaries. Officials in these areas are mandated to impose the severest punishments on violators, underscoring the importance of preserving biodiversity.

Even members of the royal family are subject to these penalties, promoting fairness and accountability by emphasizing that no one is above the law. The directive specifies fines for catching, attacking or killing non-violent creatures such as birds and fish, with fines doubled to serve as a strong deterrent.

Specific domestic animals such as calves, bulls and cows are also protected, with fines imposed for killing them, reflecting their value in agriculture and society. The fine is doubled for killing any animal with cruelty, addressing broader animal cruelty issues and ensuring all forms of animal life are protected from unnecessary harm and suffering.

Chanakya's directive promotes wildlife preservation and the ethical treatment of animals, highlighting severe consequences for violators regardless of their social status. It seeks to instil a culture of respect and protection for all living creatures, contributing to ecological balance and ethical stewardship of nature.

There Is No Killing of Animals in Yajna (Sacred Rituals) as It Is Prohibited

देवर्षिपितृयज्ञार्थमारभ्यन्त तदा क्रियाः।
न चाधर्मेण केषांचित् प्राणिनामभवद् वधः॥16॥

Devarṣipitṛyajñārthamārabhyanta tadā kriyāḥ.
Na cādharmeṇa keṣāṃcit prāṇināmabhavad vadhaḥ।।16।।[8]

In those days, yajnas (sacred rituals) were performed for the Devas, Rishis and ancestors, and no creatures were killed during these activities.

अपरिज्ञानमेतत् ते महान्तं धर्ममिच्छतः।
न हि यज्ञे पशुगणा विधिदृष्टाः पुरंदरः।।13।।

Aparijñānametat te mahāntaṃ dharmamicchataḥ.
Na hi yajñe paśugaṇā vidhidṛṣṭāḥ puraṃdaraḥ।।13।।[9]

धर्मोपघातकस्त्वेष समारम्भस्तव प्रभो।
नायं धर्मकृतो यज्ञो न हिंसा धर्म उच्यते।।14।।

Dharmopaghātakastveṣa samārambhastava prabho.
Nāyaṃ dharmakṛto yajño na hiṃsā dharma ucyate।।14।।[10]

यज बीजैः सहस्राक्ष त्रिवर्षपरमोषितैः।।16।।
एष धर्मो महान् शक्र महागुणफलोदयः।

Yaja bījaiḥ sahasrākṣa trivarṣaparamoṣitaiḥ।।16।।
Eṣa dharmo mahān śakra mahāguṇaphalodayaḥ.[11]

The desire for great dharma conflicts with individuals' readiness to kill animals. This contradiction arises from ignorance as scripture does not sanction the killing of animals in a yajna (sacred ritual).

A yajna (sacred ritual) that involves the killing of animals is harmful to dharma. Such yajnas are not in accordance with dharma because violence in a yajna is never considered part of dharma.

Conduct the yajna using seeds that are at least three years old, including rice, barley, wheat and other grains. This is a great dharma and bestows immensely meritorious results.

अजेन यष्टव्यमिति प्राहुर्देवा द्विजोत्तमान्।।

Ajena yaṣṭavyamiti prāhurdevā dvijottamān.[12]

In Vedic scripture, there are provisions for performing yajna (sacred rituals) using aja (seeds).

In ancient times, during yajna (sacred rituals), there was no animal sacrifice. The original Sanskrit text in the scriptures uses the term 'अजैर्यष्टव्यम्' 'Ajairyaṣṭavyam,' which means to perform yajna with 'aja'. In Panini's Sanskrit grammar, 'aja (अजा) – अजा न जायन्ते, न उत्पद्यन्ते, न प्ररोहन्ते इति अजाः।' 'Ajā na jāyante, na utpadyante, na prarohante iti ajāḥ' refers to seeds that are unable to germinate and are unsuitable for agricultural fields.

बीजैर्यज्ञेषु यष्टव्यमिति वै वैदिकी श्रुतिः।
अजसंज्ञानि बीजानि च्छागं नो हन्तुमर्हथ।।4।।

Bījairyajñeṣu yaṣṭavyamiti vai vaidikī śrutiḥ.
Ajasaṃjñāni bījāni cchāgaṃ no hantumarhatha।।4।।[13]

According to the Vedas and Vedic scriptures, perform yajna (sacred rituals) using seeds. The word 'aja' means seed; so do not sacrifice a goat in the yajna. Sacrificing animals in yajna is not permissible.

Later, unable to understand the actual meaning of 'aja', some began using the alternate meaning of 'aja', which is 'goat', and started sacrificing goats in yajna (sacred rituals).

एतेऽपि ये याज्ञिका यज्ञकर्मणि पशून् व्यापादयन्ति ते मूर्खाः परमार्थं श्रुतेर्न जानन्ति। तत्र किलैतदुक्तम् - 'अजैर्यष्टव्यम्' इति। अजा व्रीहयस्तावत्सप्तवार्षिकाः कथ्यन्ते, न पुनः पशुविशेषाः।।

Ete'pi ye yājñikā yajñakarmaṇi paśūn vyāpādayanti te mūrkhāḥ paramārthaṃ śruterna jānanti. tatra kilaitaduktam-

‘ajairyaṣṭavyam’ iti. ajā vrīhayastāvatsaptavārṣikāḥ kathyante, na punaḥ paśuviśeṣāḥ.[14]

Acharya Vishnu Sharma wrote that foolish people, who do not understand the meaning of the Veda and Vedic scriptures, began sacrificing animals. Actually, 'aja' means seven-year-old grain seeds that cannot germinate, aiming to clarify the mistakes of those who use goats.

यज्ञबीजैः सुरश्रेष्ठ येषु हिंसा न विद्यते ।।100।।

Yajñabījaiḥ suraśreṣṭha yeṣu hiṃsā na vidyate ।।100।।[15]

त्रिवर्षपरमं कालमुषितैरप्ररोहिभिः।।101।।

Trivarṣaparamaṃ kālamuṣitairaprarohibhiḥ।।101।।[16]

यज्ञबीजैः सुरश्रेष्ठ त्रिवर्षपरमोषितैः।।14।।

Yajñabījaiḥ suraśreṣṭha trivarṣaparamoṣitaiḥ।।14।।[17]

Perform yajna (sacred rituals) using three-year-old seeds because they cannot germinate and involve no violence.

तथाहि किल वेदे ‘अजैर्यष्टव्यम्’ इत्यादिवाक्येषु मिथ्यादृशोऽजशब्दं पशुवाचकं व्याचक्षते। सम्यग्दृशस्तु जन्माप्रायोग्यं त्रिवार्षिकं यवव्रीह्यदि, पञ्चवार्षिकं तिलमसूरादि, सप्तवार्षिकं कङ्कु-सर्षपादि धान्यर्प्यायितया पर्यवसायन्ति।

Tathāhi kila vede ‘ajairyaṣṭavyam’ ityādivākyeṣu mithyādṛśo’jaśabdaṃ paśuvācakaṃ vyācakṣate. samyagdṛśastu janmāprāyogyaṃ trivārṣikaṃ yavavrīhyadi, pañcavārṣikaṃ tilamasūrādi, saptavārṣikaṃ kaṅku-sarṣapādi dhānyarpyāyatayā paryavasāyanti।[18]

Misguided individuals misunderstand the true meaning of the Vedic word 'aja', incorrectly using it to refer to animals. Conversely, wise and knowledgeable individuals understand the genuine significance of 'aja', which denotes seeds incapable of germinating within specific time frames. For instance, grains like rice, barley and wheat do not germinate after three years, while seeds like sesame and red lentils fail to sprout after five years. Additionally, seeds such as mustard cease to germinate after seven years.

A stipulation by Acharya Vishnu Sharma was to use grain seeds that are at least seven years old in the yajna ceremony. However, other Acharyas discussed the availability of such seeds, and it was decided that if seven-year-old seeds are not available, seeds three years old or older should be used. This distinction ensures that seeds intended for food and agriculture are not used in the yajna.

It's also crucial to note that seeds or grains intended for food and agricultural purposes should not be placed into the yajna fire. Only seeds that have aged beyond germination and are unsuitable for consumption should be used in the yajna.

We should acknowledge the wisdom of our ancestors in valuing seeds meant for food and agriculture, emphasizing their exclusion from the yajna fire.

सुरा मत्स्या मधु मांसमासवं कृसरौदनम्।
धूर्तैः प्रवर्तितं ह्येतन्नैतद् वेदेषु कल्पितम्।।9।।

Surā matsyā madhu māṃsamāsavaṃ kṛsaraudanam.
Dhūrtaiḥ pravartitaṃ hyetannaitad vedeṣu kalpitam।।9।।[18]

The use of liquor, wine, meat, fish and khichdi (savoury porridge) in yajnas (sacred rituals) is promoted by misguided individuals. According to the Vedas, these items are not permitted in yajnas.

From this evidence, it is very clear that in the Hindu practice of yajna (sacred rituals), the use of liquor, wine, meat, fish and animal sacrifices involving violence were neither practised nor allowed.

In Hindu Dharma, yajnas (sacred rituals) are significant spiritual practices involving the offering of various items into a sacred fire, accompanied by the chanting of Vedic mantras. The aim of yajnas is to ensure cosmic order and harmony. The Vedas, foundational texts of Hindu dharma, and other authoritative Hindu scriptures provide detailed instructions on conducting yajnas.

The Vedas and other ancient Hindu scriptures generally condemn the use of intoxicants and explicitly forbid the consumption of alcohol. In the context of yajnas, purity is paramount, and substances that alter the mind or defile the body are considered inappropriate. The sacrifice of animals and acts of violence in yajnas are also forbidden.

The use of liquor, meat and other prohibited items in yajnas is often attributed to a lack of proper understanding or deliberate misinterpretation of Vedic principles. Such practices are not originally sanctioned by the Vedas and can lead to misconceptions about the true nature of yajnas.

The Vedas and other authoritative Hindu scriptures advocate for purity, non-violence and spiritual integrity in yajnas. The introduction of prohibited items like liquor, meat, fish, khichdi (savoury porridge) and animal sacrifices into these rituals is a deviation from traditional Vedic injunctions. Scriptural evidence clearly indicates that yajnas are intended to be conducted with non-violent and pure offerings, aligning with the broader Hindu values of sanctity.

Humans Should Be Kind to Animals

नरास्तु बुद्धिसम्पन्ना दयां कुर्वन्ति जन्तुषु।।88।।

Narāstu buddhisampannā dayāṃ kurvanti jantuṣu।।88।।[20]

Hanuman Ji said to Bhima, 'Human beings, being intelligent, should be kind to all animals.'

True intelligence encompasses more than just knowledge; it includes compassion and kindness. As beings with intellect and awareness, humans have the capacity to empathize with the suffering and needs of all creatures, not solely their own kind.

Hanuman's statement emphasizes that true humanity is revealed in how we treat the vulnerable and voiceless beings around us. It is the responsibility of intelligent beings to extend care universally, recognizing the interconnectedness of all life forms. This concept resonates with the idea of dharma, the moral duty towards all beings.

These statements offer a timeless moral lesson applicable to all societies and eras, prompting us to reflect on how we wield our intelligence and power. They urge us to exercise them responsibly and empathetically.

They signify a deep understanding of ethical conduct, compassion and the interdependence of all life. They underscore that true intelligence is demonstrated not only through knowledge and skill but also through empathy and kindness towards every living being. These principles embody universal values that transcend cultural boundaries and endure through time.

Shri Rama Never Ate Non-Vegetarian Food or Consumed Alcohol

न मांसं राघवो भुङ्क्ते न चैव मधु सेवते।
वन्यं सुविहितं नित्यं भक्तमश्नाति पञ्चमम्॥41॥

Na māṃsaṃ rāghavo bhuṅkte na caiva madhu sevate.
Vanyaṃ suvihitaṃ nityaṃ bhaktamaśnāti pañcamam॥41॥[21]

Hanuman Ji told Mata Sita that Shri Rama neither eats meat nor consumes alcohol. He partakes of the fruits, vegetables and boiled rice available in the forest every day.

Earth Is Revered and Respected

भूरसि भूमिरस्यदितिरसि विश्वधाया विश्वस्य भुवनस्य धर्त्री।
पृथिवीं यच्छ पृथिवीं दृꣳह पृथिवीं मा हिꣳसीः॥18॥

bhūrasi bhūmirasyaditirasi viśvadhāyā viśvasya
bhuvanasya dhartrī|
pṛthivīṃ yaccha pṛthivīṃ dṛꣳha
pṛthivīṃ mā hiꣳsīḥ||18 ||[22]

Mother Earth is a source of happiness. She nurtures all living beings like a divine mother, supporting them and providing for their needs. We should care for her and hold her in reverence. We must protect her and refrain from causing her pain through harmful and violent actions.

पृथिवीं नान्यदिच्छन्ति पावनं जननी यथा।।11।।

Pṛthivīṃ nānyadicchanti pāvanaṃ jananī yathā।।11।।[23]

प्रकृतिः सर्वभूतानां भूमिर्वैश्वानरी मता।।38।।

Prakṛtiḥ sarvabhūtānāṃ bhūmirvaiśvānarī matā।।38।।[24]

The Earth holds a revered status like that of a mother, being the primal birthplace and origin of all living beings.

Bheeshma imparts profound wisdom to Yudhishthira, highlighting the sanctity and maternal significance of the Earth. He emphasizes that the Earth should be revered like a mother due to its foundational role in the existence and sustenance of life. The Earth is the primal birthplace of all living beings; just as a mother nurtures her children within her womb, the Earth nurtures all forms of life, providing essential elements needed for survival and growth. This shared origin creates a fundamental bond between all life forms and the Earth, akin to the bond between children and their mother.

Bheeshma advises Yudhishthira to honour and respect the Earth, recognizing it as a sacred entity. Like a mother, the Earth endures and supports the weight of countless lives, providing sustenance and a place for all creatures to thrive. He implies that humans have a duty to protect and preserve the Earth, suggesting that, just as one would care for and respect their mother, humans should act as custodians of the Earth, ensuring its health and well-being for future generations.

This reverence translates into practical actions, advocating for sustainable living practices that honour the Earth's resources. Bheeshma encourages minimizing harm and making choices that ensure the Earth can continue to support life. His wisdom serves as an early call for environmental stewardship, emphasizing that humans must live in harmony with nature, respecting the balance and cycles of the natural world. Bheeshma's message to Yudhishthira is a timeless reminder of the Earth's vital role in our existence and the profound respect and care it deserves, akin to that of a loving and nurturing mother.

भूमौ च जायते सर्वं भूमौ सर्वं विनश्यति।
भूमिः प्रतिष्ठा भूतानां भूमिरेव परायणाम्।।20।।

Bhūmau ca jāyate sarvaṃ bhūmau sarvaṃ vinaśyati.
Bhūmiḥ pratiṣṭhā bhūtānāṃ bhūmireva parāyaṇām।।20।।[25]

Everything on this earth is created and eventually returns to it, making it the home to every living being and renowned as the ultimate refuge for all creatures.

Every living organism on Earth is born, grows, reproduces and eventually dies. The materials that compose living beings—minerals, water, carbon and other elements—originate from the Earth and are returned to it upon death. This cyclical process is fundamental to ecosystems and natural processes. Earth provides the necessary resources for life, including air, water and nutrients. It offers a habitat for countless species, each adapted to specific environments—from the deepest oceans to the highest mountains, and from the lush rainforests to arid deserts. Protecting ecosystems, preserving biodiversity and promoting sustainable practices are crucial for maintaining the health of our planet and ensuring it remains a refuge for future generations. The Earth's role in the life cycle of all beings emphasizes the natural processes of creation and return, the provision of resources and shelter, and the ecological imperative to cherish and protect our planet.

पिता भ्राता च पुत्राश्च खं द्यौश्च नरपुङ्गव।
भूमिर्भवति भूतानां सम्यगच्छिद्रदर्शाना।।76।।

Pitā bhrātā ca putrāśca khaṃ dyauśca narapuṅgava.
Bhūmirbhavati bhūtānāṃ samyagacchidradarśānā||76||[26]

If the true form of the Earth is fully known, she herself becomes the father, the mother, the progeny, the realm of virtue and the heaven.

When we fully understand the Earth's true form, we begin to see it as the source of all life and sustenance, embodying the roles of both father and mother. We recognize ourselves and all living beings as its progeny, dependent on its continued health and well-being. By viewing the Earth as a realm of virtue, we learn the importance of living in harmony with nature and adopting its inherent wisdom. This deep understanding can ultimately lead us to perceive the Earth as a kind of heaven—a place of beauty, wonder and profound significance. This reverent view of the Earth urges us to recognize and honour our deep connection to it. By doing so, we can live more harmoniously and sustainably, ensuring the well-being of both humanity and the planet.

The Ganga River Is Revered and Honoured as a Mother and Deity

तस्य शैलस्य शिखरात् क्षीरधारा नरेश्वर।
विश्वरूपापरिमिता भीमनिर्घातनिःस्वना।।28।।
पुण्या पुण्यतमैर्जुष्टा गङ्गा भागीरथी शुभा।
प्लवन्तीव प्रवेगेन ह्रदे चन्द्रमसः शुभे।।29।।

Tasya śailasya śikharāt kṣīradhārā nareśvara.
Viśvarūpāparimitā bhīmanirghātaniḥsvanā||28||
Puṇyā puṇyatamairjuṣṭā gaṅgā bhāgīrathī śubhā.
Plavantīva pravegena hrade candramasaḥ śubhe||29||[27]

From the top of Mount Himalaya flows a stream resembling white milk, in all its forms. It is infinitely powerful, sounding as terrifying as lightning. Rendered sacred by supremely virtuous individuals, it manifests as an auspicious form brimming with virtue. The Bhagirathi Ganga cascades with great force into a picturesque pond.

तस्य पार्श्वे महद् दिव्यं शुभ्रं काञ्चनवालुकम्।
रम्यं बिन्दुसरो नाम यत्र राजा भगीरथः।।43।।
द्रष्टुं भागीरथीं गङ्गामुवास बहुलाः समाः।

Tasya pārśve mahad divyaṃ śubhraṃ kāñcanavālukam.
Ramyaṃ bindusaro nāma yatra rājā bhagīrathaḥ।।43।।
Draṣṭuṃ bhāgīrathīṃ gaṅgāmuvāsa bahulāḥ samāḥ.[28]

Near the Hiranyashringa mountain, there is a large, divine, shining lake adorned with glittering sand called Bindu Sarovar. King Bhagiratha lived there for many years, wishing to have a view of the Ganga.

तपसा ब्रह्मचर्येण यज्ञैस्त्यागेन वा पुनः।
गतिं तां न लभेज्जन्तुर्गङ्गां संसेव्य यां लभेत्।।27।।

Tapasā brahmacaryeṇa yajñaistyāgena vā punaḥ.
Gatiṃ tāṃ na labhejjanturgaṅgāṃ saṃsevya yāṃ labhet।।27।।[29]

The supreme state attained through serving the Ganga cannot be achieved even through penance, rituals, yajna (sacred rituals) or renunciation.

यथोपजीविनां धेनुर्देवादीनां धरा स्मृता।
तथोपजीविनां गङ्गा सर्वप्राणभृतामिह।।52।।

Yathopajīvināṃ dhenurdevādīnāṃ dharā smṛtā.
Tathopajīvināṃ gaṅgā sarvaprāṇabhṛtāmiha।।52।।[30]

The Earth, personified as a cow, is revered by the deities for providing sustenance. Similarly, the Ganga is respected by all creatures for sustaining them in this world.

भूतभव्यभविष्यज्ञैर्महर्षिभिरूपस्थिताम्।
देवैः सेन्द्रैश्च को गङ्गां नोपसेवेत मानवः।।68।।

Bhūtabhavyabhaviṣyajñairmaharṣibhirūpasthitām.
Devaiḥ sendraiśca ko gaṅgāṃ nopaseveta mānavaḥ।।68।।[31]

People seek refuge in the Ganga, worshipped by Indra and great rishis.

प्रेक्षामि सरितां श्रेष्ठां सम्मान्यसलिलां शिवाम्।
देवमानवगन्धर्वमृगपन्नगपक्षिणाम्।।29।।

Prekṣāmi saritāṃ śreṣṭhāṃ sammānyasalilāṃ śivām.
Devamānavagandharvamṛgapannagapakṣiṇām।।29।।[32]

Sri Rama said, 'From here, I shall behold the form of the beneficent river Ganga, revered by gods, humans, Gandharvas, snakes, animals and birds, all bowing their heads before its waters.'

आचम्य च यथाशास्त्रं नदीं तां सह सीतया।
प्रणमत्प्रीतिसंतुष्टो लक्ष्मणश्च महारथः।।79।।

Ācamya ca yathāśāstraṃ nadīṃ tāṃ saha sītayā.
Praṇamatprītisaṃtuṣṭo lakṣmaṇaśca mahārathaḥ।।79।।[33]

Sri Rama, along with Sita and Lakshmana, sipped the water of the Ganga reverently, felt pleased and then bowed before the sacred river.

पुत्रो दशरथस्यायं महाराजस्य धीमतः।
निदेशं पालयत्वेनं गङ्गे त्वदभिरक्षितः।।83।।

Putro daśarathasyāyaṃ mahārājasya dhīmataḥ.
Nideśaṃ pālayatvenaṃ gaṅge tvadabhirakṣitaḥ।।83।।[34]

Sita prays to Goddess Maa Ganga, while Sri Rama, the son of the supremely intelligent ruler Dashrath, is going to the forest to obey his father's order. May you bestow your grace upon them so that they may remain safe together.

ततस्त्वां देवि सुभगे क्षेमेण पुनरागता।
यक्ष्ये प्रमुदिता गङ्गे सर्वकामसमृद्धिनी।।85।।

Tatastvāṃ devi subhage kṣemeṇa punarāgatā.
Yakṣye pramuditā gaṅge sarvakāmasamṛddhinī।।85।।[35]

Most fortunate Goddess Ganga! When I return from the forest, full of well-being and with all my desires fulfilled, I shall worship you with great delight.

पुनरेव महाबाहुर्मया भ्रात्रा च संगतः।
अयोध्यां वनवासात् तु प्रविशत्वनघोऽनघे।।91।।

Punareva mahābāhurmayā bhrātrā ca saṃgataḥ.
Ayodhyāṃ vanavāsāt tu praviśatvanagho'naghe।।91।।[36]

Goddess Ganga blesses us. May Sri Rama return to Ayodhya from the forest along with his brother and me.

अमृतान्युपजीवन्ति तथा गङ्गाजलं नराः।।53।।

Amṛtānyupajīvanti tathā gaṅgājalaṃ narāḥ।।53।।[37]

Humans sustain themselves with water from the Ganga in this world.

The river Maa Ganga is not merely a river but also a lifeline for millions of people residing along its banks. It provides water for drinking, agriculture and industry to a significant portion of Bharat. Moreover, the river supports a diverse ecosystem and plays a crucial role in people's livelihoods through activities such as farming. This underscores its multifaceted significance as both a physical and spiritual resource, sustaining not only human life but also cultural identity.

वाय्वीरिताभिः सुमनोहराभि र्द्रुताभिरत्यर्थसमुत्थिताभिः।
गङ्गोर्मिभिर्भानुमतीभिरिद्धाः सहस्ररश्मिप्रतिमा भवन्ति।।81।।

Vāyvīritābhiḥ sumanoharābhi rdrutābhiratyarthasamutthitābhiḥ.
Gaṅgormibhirbhānumatībhiriddhāḥ sahasraraśmipratimā bhavanti।।81।।[38]

Those who bathe in the wind-inspired, high-current and high-rising waves of the Ganga water become supremely delighted and bright. They are illumined and radiant like the sun in the highest realm.

Trees Are Respected in the Hindu Tradition

सार्थिका वणिजश्चापि तापसाश्च वनौकसः।
वसन्ति तत्र मार्गस्थाः सुरम्ये नगसत्तमे।।8।।
तस्य ता विपुलाः शाखादृष्ट्वा स्कन्धं च सर्वशः।
अभिगम्याब्रवीदेनं नारदो भरतर्षभ।।9।।
अहो नु रमणीयस्त्वमहो चासि मनोहरः।
प्रीयामहे त्वया नित्यं तरुप्रवर शाल्मले।।10।।
सदैव शकुनास्तात मृगाश्चाथ तथा गजाः।
वसन्ति तव संहृष्टा मनोहर मनोहराः।।11।।

Sārthikā vaṇijaścāpi tāpasāśca vanaukasaḥ.
Vasanti tatra mārgasthāḥ suramye nagasattame।।8।।
Tasya tā vipulāḥ śākhādṛṣṭvā skandhaṃ ca sarvaśaḥ.
Abhigamyābravīdenaṃ nārado bharatarṣabha।।9।।
Aho nu ramaṇīyastvamaho cāsi manoharaḥ.
Prīyāmahe tvayā nityaṃ tarupravara śālmale।।10।।
Sadaiva śakunāstāta mṛgāścātha tathā gajāḥ.
Vasanti tava saṃhṛṣṭā manohara manoharāḥ।।11।।[39]

Bheeshma explained to Yudhisthira about the shalmali tree (cotton tree) under which groups of travelling merchants, traders, ascetics living in the forest and other travellers used to rest. One day, Sage Narada approached a towering tree. Observing its broad branches and substantial trunk, he addressed it: 'O Shalmali, king of trees, you are truly delightful and charming, unparalleled among your kind. I always find joy in your presence. Countless birds find shelter on your branches, and many deer and elephants happily dwell beneath your shade.'

Trees Are Like Their Own Children, and There Is Virtue in Planting Them

अतीतानागते चोभे पितृवंशं च भारत।
तारयेद् वृक्षरोपी च तस्माद् वृक्षांश्च रोपयेत्।।26।।
तस्य पुत्रा भवन्त्येते पादपा नात्र संशयः।।27।।

पुष्पैः सुरगणान् वृक्षाः फलैश्चापि तथा पितॄन्।
छायया चातिथिं तात पूजयन्ति महीरुहः।।28।।
पुष्पिताः फलवन्तश्च तर्पयन्तीह मानवान्।
वृक्षदं पुत्रवद् वृक्षास्तारयन्ति परत्र तु।।30।।
तस्मात् तडागे सद्वृक्षा रोप्याः श्रेयोऽर्थिना सदा।
पुत्रवत् परिपाल्याश्च पुत्रास्ते धर्मतः स्मृताः।।31।।

Atītānāgate cobhe pitṛvaṃśaṃ ca bhārata.
Tārayed vṛkṣaropī ca tasmād vṛkṣāṃśca ropayet।।26।।
Tasya putrā bhavantyete pādapā nātra saṃśayaḥ।।27।।
Puṣpaiḥ suragaṇān vṛkṣāḥ phalaiścāpi tathā pitṝn.
Chāyayā cātithiṃ tāta pūjayanti mahīruhaḥ।।28।।
Puṣpitāḥ phalavantaśca tarpayantīha mānavān.
Vṛkṣadaṃ putravad vṛkṣāstārayanti paratra tu।।30।।
Tasmāt taḍāge sadvṛkṣā ropyāḥ śreyo'rthinā sadā.
Putravat paripālyāśca putrāste dharmataḥ smṛtāḥ।।31।।[40]

Bheeshma told Yudhisthira that a person who plants trees redeems their ancestors and secures the future of their progeny. Therefore, it is essential to plant trees. There is no doubt that these trees are like one's own children. Trees worship the deities with their flowers, honour ancestors with fruits and provide guests with shade. Trees that bear flowers and fruits satisfy people in this world. Those who plant such trees, nurturing them like children, are rewarded in the afterlife. Thus, a person who desires to achieve their own good should always plant trees by the side of reservoirs and water tanks and care for them like their own children. From the standpoint of dharma, those trees are considered as children.

Trees Are Living Organisms

घनानामपि वृक्षाणामाकाशोऽस्ति न संशयः।
तेषां पुष्पफलव्यक्तिर्नित्यं समुपपद्यते।।10।।

Ghanānāmapi vṛkṣāṇāmākāśo'sti na saṃśayaḥ.
Teṣāṃ puṣpaphalavyaktirnityaṃ samupapadyate।10।।[41]

Even though trees seem dense, they have space within them, leaving no doubt about it. This space makes the daily generation of fruits and flowers possible.

Despite their apparent density, trees possess internal spaces that are crucial for their physiological functions and overall vitality. These internal spaces, known as intercellular spaces or lacunae, facilitate essential processes such as gas exchange, nutrient transport and the storage of metabolites. Intercellular spaces play a pivotal role in the tree's metabolic activities, contributing to sustained growth and development. Intercellular spaces play a vital role in plant growth by allowing the transport of water and the diffusion of important gases, i.e., oxygen and carbon dioxide, on the concentration of which key processes of plant metabolism, such as photosynthesis and respiration, thrive.

The apoplast containing intercellular spaces is known to be involved in the perception and transduction of environmental signals, which further affects the growth and development of different parts of the plant. In conclusion, these spaces may not seem to be directly responsible for the daily production of fruits and flowers, but they are fundamental to the tree's health and reproductive success by supporting the physiological processes that enable fruiting and flowering.

ऊष्मतो म्लायते पर्णं त्वक् फलं पुष्पमेव च।
म्लायते शीर्यते चापि स्पर्शस्तेनात्र विद्यते।।11।।

Ūṣmato mlāyate parṇaṃ tvak phalaṃ puṣpameva ca.
Mlāyate śīryate cāpi sparśastenātra vidyate।।11।।[42]

Due to the thermal conditions inside the tree, its leaves, bark, fruit and flowers wilt and fall off, suggesting that they possess a sense of touch.

Plants, as sensitive organisms, exhibit acute responses to fluctuations in temperature. Elevated temperatures profoundly affect a number of enzymatic pathways and water balance, leading to a reduction in the growth and development of various plant parts.

Excessive warmth accelerates transpiration, leading to increased water loss, and increases the production of reactive oxygen species, which are known to have damaging effects on cellular machinery and subsequently cause the wilting of leaves and flowers.

Furthermore, heightened temperatures affect cell division as well as cell expansion, amplify biochemical reactions and cause protein degradation, influencing critical processes such as photosynthesis, respiration and fruit ripening. Disruptions in these processes can trigger premature senescence and the shedding of leaves, fruits or flowers.

Plants carefully regulate water uptake and loss to maintain turgor pressure and structural integrity. Elevated temperatures disrupt this balance, resulting in reduced turgidity and flaccid tissues.

Temperature fluctuations also dictate phenological events such as flowering and fruiting. While warmth can expedite these events, it may lead to premature senescence of leaves and flowers if plants cannot meet their metabolic demands under thermal stress. Finally, it leads to abscission, i.e., the shedding of dead organs such as leaves, flowers or fruits.

As a consequence, observable phenomena such as wilting, leaf abscission and fruit drop in plants reflect their adaptive responses to internal thermal stresses, significantly impacting metabolic pathways, water dynamics and developmental stages.

वाय्वग्न्यशनिनिर्घोषैः फलं पुष्पं विशीर्यते।
श्रोत्रेण गृह्यते शब्दस्तस्माच्छृण्वन्ति पादपाः॥12॥

Vāyvagnyaśaninirghoṣaiḥ phalaṃ puṣpaṃ viśīryate.
Śrotreṇa gṛhyate śabdastasmācśṛṇvant pādapāḥ॥12॥[43]

It is also observed that when wind, fire and thunder sound terribly, trees' fruits and flowers fall off. Sound is perceived through the ear, suggesting that trees can also hear.

When wind, fire or thunder produces intense vibrations in the air, these waves propagate through the surroundings, affecting areas occupied by plants. Once plants perceive mechanical stimuli, they register these vibrations through mechanoreceptors, initiating a signalling cascade that triggers various physiological responses. Among these responses is the shedding of fruits and flowers, a mechanism that can be interpreted as an adaptation, a protective measure or a stress response to specific environmental disturbances or stimuli.

The notion that plants 'hear' is rooted in the understanding that they can detect and respond to certain frequencies of sound. Although plants do not possess an organ analogous to human ears for perceiving acoustic signals, they have mechanoreceptors that perceive and transduce mechanical vibrations into biochemical signals. This perception is integral to their ability to adapt to and respond to their surroundings.

In conclusion, while plants do not have auditory systems like those of animals, they exhibit sensitivity to sound waves through mechanoreceptors. This enables them to perceive vibrations and potentially modulate their growth and development in response to environmental cues such as wind, fire and thunder. This sensory capability underscores the complexity of plant adaptation and interaction with their environment.

वल्ली वेष्टयते वृक्षं सर्वतश्चैव गच्छति।
न ह्यदृष्टेश्चमार्गोऽस्तितस्मात् पश्यन्ति पादपाः।।13।।

Vallī veṣṭayate vṛkṣaṃ sarvataścaiva gacchati.
Na hyadṛṣṭeścamārgo'stitasmāt paśyanti pādapāḥ।।13।।[44]

A climber winds around a tree and climbs up to its topmost branches. Without sight, no one can discover the path to traverse, suggesting that even trees perceive their surroundings.

In botanical terms, a phenomenon known as epiphytic growth occurs when a climber plant utilizes a host tree for support and elevation. Climbers, such as orchids and ferns, employ specialized structures like tendrils, aerial roots or twining stems to ascend vertical surfaces. These adaptations enable them to anchor onto the host tree and eventually reach its uppermost branches.

The process by which a climber navigates and ascends a tree involves several botanical mechanisms. Tendrils, for example, exhibit thigmotropism—a response to touch that allows them to coil around nearby objects such as branches or trunks. Some plants possess twining stems that spiral around structures, facilitating upward growth. Additionally, certain species develop aerial adventitious roots that adhere to and penetrate the bark of the host tree, providing extra support and stability.

From a sensory perspective, while plants lack sense as animals perceive them, they still exhibit responses to environmental stimuli. For instance, plants can detect light through photoreceptors and respond to touch and gravity via specialized cells and hormonal signalling. This responsiveness enables them to adjust growth patterns and optimize resource acquisition.

The scenario of a climber winding around a tree to reach its upper branches underscores the botanical adaptations and responses involved in such interactions. While plants do not possess sight or consciousness in the human sense, their ability to perceive and respond to their environment through specialized adaptations highlights their remarkable adaptability and ecological strategies in natural habitats.

पुण्यापुण्यैस्तथा गन्धैर्धूपैश्च विविधैरपि।
अरोगाः पुष्पिताः सन्ति तस्माज्जिघ्रन्ति पादपाः।।14।।

Puṇyāpuṇyaistathā gandhairdhūpaiśca vividhairapi.
Arogāḥ puṣpitāḥ santi tasmājjighranti pādapāḥ।।14।।[45]

By using both pure and mix smells, as well as various fragrances, trees become disease-free and begin to bloom and bear fruit. This demonstrates that trees can also perceive smells.

The phenomenon wherein trees and other plants respond to odours, both pure and mixed, as well as to various fragrances, enhancing their health, blooming and fruiting capabilities, indicates the presence of olfactory-like mechanisms in plants.

Plants release and detect a wide range of Volatile Organic Compounds (VOCs), which serve as chemical signals for inter- and intra-plant communication. These compounds can be emitted by neighbouring plants, herbivores, pathogens or even the plants themselves in response to environmental stimuli.

Similar to olfactory receptors in animals, plants possess receptor proteins in their cellular membranes that can bind to specific VOCs. These receptors initiate signal transduction pathways that alter gene expression and physiological responses. Upon detection of VOCs, plants activate complex signalling networks involving hormones like jasmonic acid, salicylic acid and ethylene. These pathways regulate defensive responses, growth and development processes.

Exposure to certain VOCs can prime plant immune responses, enhancing their ability to resist pathogens. For example, methyl jasmonate and green leaf volatiles can activate defence genes, making plants more resilient to infections. VOCs such as terpenes and phenolics can influence flowering and fruiting processes. These compounds may act as growth regulators, promoting or inhibiting specific physiological pathways to optimize reproductive success.

Fragrances emitted by flowers serve to attract pollinators, which is crucial for the reproductive success of many plant species. This olfactory interaction ensures effective pollen transfer and subsequent fruit and seed development.

The ability of trees and other plants to perceive and respond to VOCs demonstrates a sophisticated level of environmental interaction previously attributed mainly to animals. This olfactory-like capability suggests that trees can detect changes in their surroundings and modulate their physiological states accordingly, enhancing their survival and reproductive success.

By using VOCs strategically—whether through natural release or artificial application—horticultural practices can potentially improve plant health, increase resistance to diseases, and optimize blooming and fruiting. So, it may be hypothesized based on available literature that plants possess more than one way of sensing exogenous VOCs, which ultimately effectively induce metabolic and molecular changes. This understanding paves the way for innovative approaches in agriculture and forestry, aiming to enhance crop yields and sustain plant health in a changing environment.

पादैः सलिलपानाच्च व्याधीनां चापि दर्शनात्।
व्याधिप्रतिक्रियत्वाच्च विद्यते रसनं द्रुमे।।15।।

Pādaiḥ salilapānācca vyādhīnāṃ cāpi darśanāt.
Vyādhipratikriyatvācca vidyate rasanaṃ drume।।15।।[46]

Trees drink water through their roots and absorb medicine through them when treated for certain diseases. This indicates that trees have a sense of taste.

Trees indeed absorb water through their roots, facilitated by structures like root hairs and mycorrhizal associations.

Trees have specialized vascular tissues called xylem and phloem. Xylem transports water and minerals absorbed from the soil to the leaves, while phloem transports sugars and other organic compounds produced during photosynthesis to other parts of the tree. These tissues play a crucial role in the distribution of substances such as nutrients, pesticides, fertilizers or medications applied to the tree.

Transpiration, the primary driving force for water and nutrient uptake from roots, is a process in which water is evaporated into the atmosphere from the aerial parts of plants, primarily through the leaf surface. Stomata (small pores) on the leaf surface are responsible for water and gaseous exchange with the atmosphere. Stomatal pores sense external environmental stimuli such as light, temperature and relative humidity and open or close accordingly, maintaining plant structure through turgor pressure. Similarly, certain thickenings, such as suberin in the endodermal layer of roots, act as barriers to water transport and compel water to change its path before entering the xylem for further transport to different parts of the plant. These structures and thickenings allow plants to sense and adapt to different environments.

Trees can detect and respond to specific chemicals in their rhizospheric environment through biochemical signalling pathways rather than through taste buds or a nervous system. They can initiate defence mechanisms, such as producing defensive compounds or altering growth patterns, in response to chemical signals released by predators or pathogens. This adaptive ability enhances their survival and adaptation to different ecological conditions.

Although trees do not have taste buds or a central nervous system like animals, they possess biochemical mechanisms to detect and respond to chemical signals. This sophisticated response mechanism is critical for their survival and ecological success.

वक्त्रेणोत्पलनालेन यथोर्ध्वं जलमाददेत्।
तथा पवनसंयुक्तः पादैः पिबति पादपः।।16।।

Vaktreṇotpalanālena yathordhvaṃ jalamādadet.
Tathā pavanasaṃyuktaḥ pādaiḥ pibati pādapaḥ।।16।।[47]

Just as a person draws water through a lotus stalk straw placed to his lips, trees similarly pull water upwards through their roots with the help of air.

The process by which water and minerals move upward from the roots to the leaves and other aerial parts of plants is known as the ascent of sap. This process is driven by a combination of factors, including capillary action, cohesion-tension theory and the role of stomata.

Water molecules possess a property called cohesion, wherein they tend to stick together. This cohesion allows water to move upward through narrow tubes, such as the xylem vessels in plants, against gravity. This movement is akin to how a person can draw water through a narrow straw.

The cohesion-tension theory explains how water is pulled up from the roots to the leaves. As transpiration occurs and water evaporates from the stomata (small pores on the leaves), it creates negative pressure or tension in the xylem vessels. This tension pulls more water molecules up through the plant from the roots, similar to how a person might continue to draw water through a straw once the initial suction is established.

Just as a person can draw water through a lotus stalk straw using their lips, plants use transpiration to pull water upward through their roots, aided by air movement and the natural properties of water molecules. This process is vital for the survival and growth of plants, ensuring they receive the water and nutrients needed for photosynthesis, structural support and other biological functions.

सुखदुःखयोश्च ग्रहणाच्छिन्नस्य च विरोहणात्।
जीवं पश्यामि वृक्षाणामचैतन्यं न विद्यते।।17।।

Sukhaduḥkhayośca grahaṇācchinnasya ca virohaṇāt.
Jīvaṃ paśyāmi vṛkṣāṇāmacaitanyaṃ na vidyate।।17।।[48]

When trees are cut, new sprouts germinate, and they experience pleasure and pain. From this, one can infer that trees have a living persona; they are not inanimate.

The notion that trees experience 'pleasure and pain' when cut, and that they possess a living persona, is an anthropomorphic interpretation of their biological responses. Scientifically, trees are living organisms classified within the plant kingdom, characterized by their ability to undergo photosynthesis, reproduce and respond to environmental stimuli.

When trees are cut, they do not experience emotions such as pleasure or pain in the way animals or humans do, because they lack a nervous system and a brain. However, they do exhibit complex physiological and biochemical responses to injury and stress, which are part of their survival mechanisms. Trees have evolved mechanisms to respond to physical damage. When cut, they initiate processes to seal off wounds and prevent pathogens from entering—a process known as compartmentalization. This involves the production of chemicals and the involvement of meristems, resulting in the deposition of an unorganized mass of cells called callus tissue to protect the remaining tree structure.

Trees communicate and respond to their environment through biochemical signalling pathways. When injured, they release signalling compounds like ethylene and jasmonic acid, which trigger defence responses and immune signalling.

Many tree species have evolved the ability to regenerate from damage. When cut or pruned, dormant buds or adventitious shoots can sprout from the remaining trunk or branches. This is a survival strategy to recover lost foliage and maintain photosynthetic capacity.

Trees are dynamic and responsive organisms, but their responses are driven by biological mechanisms adapted for survival and growth.

तेन तज्जलमादत्तं जरयत्यग्निमारुतौ।
आहारपरिणामाच्च स्नेहो वृद्धिश्च जायते।।18।।

Tena tajjalamādattaṃ jarayatyagnimārutau.
Āhārapariṇāmācca sneho vṛddhiśca jāyate।।18।।[49]

The water drawn up by the tree through its roots is processed by the fire and air residing within. Trees become nourished and tranquil as they absorb nutrients, enabling growth.

Trees absorb water and minerals from the soil through their roots, primarily facilitated by osmotic processes and root pressure. This water uptake is critical for maintaining turgor pressure in the cells and providing a medium for nutrient transport.

Once water is absorbed by the roots, it ascends through the xylem vessels, driven by transpiration pull—a process facilitated by the evaporation of water from the leaves (stomatal transpiration) and other aerial parts of the tree. This evaporation creates a negative pressure that pulls water upwards through the xylem, against gravity.

Simultaneously, nutrients and dissolved minerals are transported through the same vascular system, primarily through the processes of active transport and diffusion. These nutrients include essential elements such as nitrogen, phosphorus, potassium and trace minerals, which are absorbed from the soil solution into the root cells and then transported upward alongside water.

The 'fire and air' referenced metaphorically can be understood as the metabolic, viz., catabolic and anabolic processes occurring within the leaves (where gas exchange with the atmosphere occurs) and the biochemical reactions (respiration, photosynthesis) that take place in various tissues of the tree. Photosynthesis, occurring primarily in the chloroplasts of leaf cells, uses carbon dioxide from the air, water from the xylem and energy from sunlight to produce glucose and oxygen. This glucose is used as an energy source and building material for growth and repair throughout the tree.

The water absorbed by the roots and transported through the xylem, along with nutrients and minerals, supports the metabolic processes and growth of trees. The interplay of water uptake, transpiration and photosynthesis ensures the tree's nourishment, facilitating its development and contributing to its overall health and vigour.

Planting of Tree Near the Village and Forest

उदम्बराश्ववत्थवटचिञ्चाचन्दनजम्भलाः।
कदम्बाशोकबकुलबिल्वामृतकपित्थकाः।।46।।
राजादनाम्रपुन्नागतूदकाष्ठाम्लचम्पकाः।
नीपकोकाम्रसरलदाडिमाक्षोटभिस्सटाः।।47।।
शिंशपाशिम्भुवदरनिम्बजम्बीरक्षीरिकाः।
खर्जूरदेवकरजफल्गुतापिच्छसिम्भलाः।।48।।
कुद्दालो लवली छात्री क्रमुको मातुलुङ्गकः।
लकुचो नारिकेलश्च रम्भाद्याः सत्फला द्रुमाः।
सुपुष्पाश्चैव ये वृक्षा ग्रामाभ्यर्णे नियोजयेत्।।49।।

Udambarāśvavatthavaṭaciñcācandanajambhalāḥ.
Kadambāśokabakulabilvāmṛtakapitthakāḥ।।46।।
Rājādanāmrapunnāgatūdakāṣṭhāmlacampakāḥ.
Nīpakokāmrasaraladāḍimākṣoṭabhissaṭāḥ।।47।।
Śiṃśapāśimbhuvadaranimbajambīrakṣīrikāḥ.
Kharjūradevakarajaphalgutāpicchasimbhalāḥ।।48।।
Kuddālo lavalī chātrī kramuko mātuluṅgakaḥ.
Lakuco nārikelaśca rambhādyāḥ satphalā drumāḥ.
Supuṣpāścaiva ye vṛkṣā grāmābhyarṇe niyojayet।।49।।[50]

Many important trees such as gular (cluster fig), pipal (sacred fig), banyan, tamarind, sandalwood, jambhal (type of a lemon tree), kadamba (bur flower-tree), ashok (Saraca asoca), bakul (medlar/Mimusops elengi), bilva

(Aegle marmelos), kaith (wood apple), chironji (almondette tree), mango, punnag (Calophyllum inophyllum), tudakashth (black plum), amla, champa (frangipani), neep (water kadamb), kokram, saral (cheed/Himalayan cedar), pomegranate, walnut, bhissat (beleric/bibhitaki), sheesham (rosewood/ Dalbergia sissoo), shimbhu (drumstick/Moringa oliefera), ber (jujube/ Ziziphus mauritiana), neem (Azadirachta indica), jambeer (blackberry/ Syzygium cumini), khirni (Manilkara hexandra), date palm, devkaranj (haritaki/Chebulic myrobalan), anjeer (fig), tamal (Cinnamomum tamala), simbhal (cotton tree), kuddal (kadam tree), lavli (harpharewadi/Butea monosperma), dhatri/amla (gooseberry/Phyllanthus emblica), kramuk (supari/betel nut palm, or areca palm), matulung (bijora lemon), lakuch (badhal/monkey jackfruit), coconut, banana and other significant trees that bear flowers and fruits should be planted near the village.

ये च कण्टकिनो वृक्षाः खदिराद्यास्तथापरे।
आरण्यकास्ते विज्ञेयास्तेषां यत्र नियोजनम्।।54।।

Ye ca kaṇṭakino vṛkṣāḥ khadirādyāstathāpare.
Āraṇyakāste vijñeyāsteṣāṃ yatra niyojanam।।54।।[51]

Thorny trees such as khadir (Acacia catechu) and others are categorized as wild trees and should be planted in forests.

खदिराश्मन्तशाकाग्निमन्थस्योनाकबब्बुलाः।
तमालशालकुटजधवार्जुनपलाशकाः।।55।।
सप्तपर्णशमीतुन्नदेवदारुविकङ्कताः।
करमर्देङ्गुदीभूर्जविषमुष्टिकरीरकः।।56।।
शल्लकी काश्मरी पाठा तिन्दुको बीजसारकः।
हरीतकी च भल्लातः शम्पाकोऽर्कश्च पुष्करः।।57।।
अरिमेदश्च पीतद्रुः शल्मलिश्च बिभीतकः।
नरबेलो महावृक्षोऽपरे ये मधुकादयः।।58।।
प्रतानवत्यः स्तम्बिन्यो गुल्मिन्यश्च तथैव च।
ग्राम्या ग्रामे वने वन्या नियोज्यास्ते प्रयत्नतः।।59।।

Khadirāśmantaśākāgnimanthasyonākababbulāḥ.
Tamālaśālakuṭajadhavārjunapalāśakāḥ।।55।।

Saptaparṇaśamītunnadevadāruvikaṅkatāḥ.
Karamardeṅgudībhūrjaviṣamuṣṭikarīrakaḥ।।56।।
Śallakī kāśmarī pāṭhā tinduko bījasārakaḥ.
Harītakī ca bhallātaḥ śampāko'rkaśca puṣkaraḥ।।57।।
Arimedaśca pītadruḥ śalmaliśca bibhītakaḥ.
Narabelo mahāvṛkṣo'pare ye madhukādayaḥ।।58।।
Pratānavatyaḥ stambinyo gulminyaśca tathaiva ca.
Grāmyā grāme vane vanyā niyojyāste prayatnataḥ।।59।।[52]

Khadir (Acacia catechu), ashmantak (Ficus rumphii), sagavan (teak wood), amaltas (Cassia fistula), syonak (Oroxylum indicum), babul (Vachellia nilotica), tamal (Cinnamomum tamala), shal (Shorea robusta), kutaj (Holarrhena antidysenterica), dhav (Anogeissus latifolia), arjun (Terminalia arjuna), plas (Butea monosperma), aaptparna (Alstonia scholaris), sami (Prosopis cineraria), tung (Vernicia fordii), devdaru (Cedrus deodara), vikangkat (Flacourtia indica), karonda (Carissa carandas), ingudi (Balanites aegyptiaca), bhojpatra (Betula utilis), vishmushti (kuchla/Nux vomica), karir (Capparis decidua), sallaki (Boswellia serrata), khambhar (khambhat), padhar (jacaranda), tendu (Diospyros melanoxylon), vijaysar (Pterocarpus marsupium), harad (Terminalia chebula), bhilava (Aegle marmelos), sampak (Magnolia champaca), aack (attack tree), pohakar (java fig), arimed (arimeda), peetdru (Ficus religiosa), semar (semal tree), baheda (Terminalia bellirica), narbael (Elaeocarpus angustifolius), mahavriksh (kalpavriksha), mahua (Madhuca longifolia), etc., as well as vines, creepers with long thin strands, clumps and roots, should be planted in the village if they can grow there. Those that survive in the jungle should be planted there through efforts.

State Responsibility to Protect Forest and Animal

एवं द्रव्यद्विपवनं सेतुबन्धमथाकरान्।
रक्षेत्पूर्वकृतान् राजा नवाश्चाभिप्रवर्तयेत्।।

Evaṃ dravyadvipavanaṃ setubandhamathākarān.
Rakṣetpūrvakṛtān rājā navāścābhipravartayet.[53]

The state should protect timber forests, elephant habitats (reserve forest), mines and bridges. Additionally, it should grow new forests, construct bridges and undertake other developments as needed.

Timber forests play a crucial role in biodiversity maintenance, ecosystem stability and sustainable timber production. To safeguard these vital ecosystems, the state must enforce strict laws against illegal logging and deforestation while intensifying monitoring and patrols. Involving local communities in forest management fosters ownership and responsibility. Sustainable forestry practices, such as selective logging and reforestation, are essential for the long-term viability of timber resources.

Elephant habitats, often designated as reserve forests, are pivotal for species conservation. Designating and strictly protecting these areas, including migration routes and breeding grounds, is imperative. Designating and creating new reserve forests is crucial.

Growing new forests is essential for biodiversity, carbon sequestration and mitigating climate change impacts. Strategies include planting trees on historically non-forested land, restoring degraded areas, integrating trees into agricultural landscapes for soil conservation, and planting in urban areas to improve air quality and biodiversity.

These efforts necessitate a comprehensive approach involving policy, enforcement, community engagement and scientific research for enduring success.

Water Is Invaluable and a Life-Giver

यत् प्राणः सर्वभूतानां वर्धन्ते येन च प्रजाः।
परित्यक्ताश्च नश्यन्ति तेनेदं सर्वमावृतम्।।3।।

Yat prāṇaḥ sarvabhūtānāṃ vardhante yena ca prajāḥ.
Parityaktāśca naśyanti tenedaṃ sarvamāvṛtam।।3।।[54]

Water is essential for all living creatures as it supports population growth; without access to it, living beings perish. Water covers the entire surface of the Earth.

Water, fundamental for all living organisms, plays crucial roles in metabolism and in maintaining body temperature. Plants utilize water for photosynthesis and nutrient transport. In ecosystems, water sustains habitats, biodiversity and aquatic species' breeding grounds, supporting food webs.

The availability of water directly impacts population growth and sustainability. In regions with scarce water, life struggles, resulting in reduced growth and even death. Water covers about 71 per cent of Earth's surface, primarily as oceans, seas, lakes, rivers and underground aquifers. Oceans alone hold 96.5 per cent of this water. Its presence stabilizes climate through heat distribution and precipitation.

The water cycle, driven by solar energy, involves processes such as evaporation, condensation, precipitation and runoff, which redistribute water globally. This cycle sustains terrestrial and aquatic ecosystems, regulating climate and weather.

Water distribution profoundly affects human societies, influencing agriculture, industry, transportation and energy production, shaping local economies and global geopolitics. Its critical role in supporting life and its omnipresence across Earth underscores its importance for all beings and ecosystems.

तडागानां च वक्ष्यामि कृतानां चापि ये गुणाः।
त्रिषु लोकेषु सर्वत्र पूजनीयस्तडागवान्।।4।।
अथवा मित्रसदनं मैत्रं मित्रविवर्धनम्।
कीर्तिसंजननं श्रेष्ठं तडागानां निवेशनम्।।5।।
धर्मस्यार्थस्य कामस्य फलमाहुर्मनीषिणः।
तडागसुकृतं देशे क्षेत्रमेकं महाश्रयम्।।6।।
चतुर्विधानां भूतानां तडागमुपलक्षयेत्।
तडागानि च सर्वाणि दिशन्ति श्रियमुत्तमाम्।।7।।

Taḍāgānāṃ ca vakṣyāmi kṛtānāṃ cāpi ye guṇāḥ.
Triṣu lokeṣu sarvatra pūjanīyastaḍāgavān।।4।।
Athavā mitrasadanaṃ maitraṃ mitravivardhanam.
kīrtisaṃjananaṃ śreṣṭhaṃ taḍāgānāṃ niveśanam।।5।।
Dharmasyārthasya kāmasya phalamāhurmanīṣiṇaḥ.
Taḍāgasukṛtaṃ deśe kṣetramekaṃ mahāśrayam।।6।।

Caturvidhānāṃ bhūtānāṃ taḍāgamupalakṣayet.
Taḍāgāni ca sarvāṇi diśanti śriyamuttamām।।7।।[55]

स कुलं तारयेत् सर्वं यस्य खाते जलाशये।
गावः पिबन्ति सलिलं साधवश्च नराः सदा।।16।।
तडागे यस्य गावस्तु पिबन्ति तृषिता जलम्।
मृगपक्षिमनुष्याश्च सोऽश्वमेधफलं लभेत्।।17।।

Sa kulaṃ tārayet sarvaṃ yasya khāte jalāśaye.
Gāvaḥ pibanti salilaṃ sādhavaśca narāḥ sadā।।16।।
Taḍāge yasya gāvastu pibanti tṛṣitā jalam.
Mṛgapakṣimanuṣyāśca so'śvamedhaphalaṃ labhet।।17।।[56]

Bheeshma imparted to Yudhishthira the profound benefits of digging ponds, emphasizing their universal admiration. Such endeavours, he explained, not only foster camaraderie akin to visiting a friend but also elevate one's stature, garnering recognition and renown.

According to wise counsel, the creation of ponds in villages or rural areas fulfils the triple aims of dharma, artha and kama. Such reservoirs transform their surroundings into sanctuaries teeming with life, serving as crucial resources for all living beings and ensuring prosperity across the spectrum of existence.

The reservoir, a vital source of water, quenches the thirst of renunciates, cattle and various animals. Its significance transcends mere existence, becoming a beacon of redemption for the entire community. Constructed by human hands, these ponds not only fulfil the essential need for water but also serve as sanctuaries for diverse life forms. Birds, deer and humans alike gather around their shores, drawn by the life-giving waters they provide. Digging a reservoir bestows profound merits akin to those earned from an Ashwamedha yajna (sacred rituals), symbolizing purity and sanctity.

Bheeshma underscored the universal admiration for undertaking such projects. Initially, he pointed out that digging ponds fosters camaraderie and goodwill among people. Just as visiting a friend strengthens bonds and creates harmony, creating water reservoirs for the community can unite people in a common purpose and promote social cohesion.

He highlighted that these endeavours elevate one's stature in society. By contributing to the welfare of others through pond construction, individuals earn recognition and renown. Their actions benefit the community by providing water for irrigation, drinking and other needs, while also enhancing their reputation as benefactors and contributors to the common good. Thus, these projects offer dual benefits: promoting unity and goodwill among people, akin to the warmth of visiting a friend, and enhancing one's social standing through acts of generosity and public service.

The creation of ponds in villages or rural areas serves a multifaceted purpose. It fulfils dharma, artha and kama by ensuring environmental stewardship and equitable access to water resources. Additionally, it contributes to economic prosperity through enhanced agricultural productivity, livelihood opportunities and potential economic activities. Moreover, it enriches the quality of life by transforming the surroundings into vibrant sanctuaries of life and natural beauty. These aspects together ensure holistic development and prosperity across rural communities, reflecting a balanced approach towards sustainable development and well-being.

The Natural Cycle of Rain, Food and Herbs

आदत्ते रश्मिभिः सूर्यो दिवि तिष्ठंस्ततस्ततः।
रसं हृतं वै वर्षासु प्रवर्षति दिवाकरः।।21।।
अथाभ्रेषु निगूढश्च रश्मिभिः परिवारितः।
सप्तद्वीपानिमान् ब्रह्मन् वर्षेणाभिप्रवर्षति।।23।।
ततोऽन्नं जायते विप्र मनुष्याणां सुखावहम्।
अन्नं प्राणा इति यथा वेदेषु परिपठ्यते।।22।।
ततस्तदौषधीनां च वीरुधां पुष्पपत्रजम्।
सर्वं वर्षाभिनिर्वृत्तमन्नं सम्भवति प्रभो।।24।।

Ādatte raśmibhiḥ sūryo divi tiṣṭhaṃstatastataḥ.
Rasaṃ hṛtaṃ vai varṣāsu pravarṣati divākaraḥ।।21।।
Athābhreṣu nigūḍhaśca raśmibhiḥ parivāritaḥ.

Saptadvīpānimān brahman varṣeṇabhipravarṣati||23||
Tato'nnaṃ jāyate vipra manuṣyāṇāṃ sukhāvaham.
Annaṃ prāṇā iti yathā vedeṣu paripaṭhyate||22||
Tatastadauṣadhīnāṃ ca vīrudhāṃ puṣpapatrajam.
Sarvaṃ varṣābhinirvṛttamannaṃ sambhavati prabho||24||[57]

Positioned in the sky, the sun draws moisture from the earth with its rays, later releasing it during the rainy season. Hidden behind clouds and encircled by rays, the sun showers Earth's seven continents with essential rain and water.

From this rain springs forth the food that sustains life, echoing the wisdom found in the Vedas: food is indeed the breath of life. Rainfall enables the growth of diverse herbs, medicinal plants, vines, creepers, leaves, flowers and grasses, fostering the production of various essential foods.

The sun plays a crucial role in the water cycle by energizing the evaporation of water from oceans, lakes and land, thereby forming clouds in the atmosphere. Despite being obscured at times by clouds, its energy continues to facilitate condensation and precipitation. Rainfall, essential for replenishing Earth's water sources, is also vital for agriculture, sustaining crop growth. Food production relies on rainwater, which is fundamental to sustaining life. Rainfall fosters diverse vegetation such as herbs, medicinal plants, vines, creepers, leaves, flowers and grasses—all essential for producing various foods. This diverse plant growth, including herbs crucial for human health, illustrates how the sun's energy drives the water cycle, supporting vital plant growth for human sustenance and health. This cyclical relationship underscores the significance of natural processes in providing life's necessities on Earth.

ॐ द्यौः शान्तिरन्तरिक्षँ शान्तिः पृथिवी
शान्तिरापः शान्तिरोषधयः शान्तिः।
वनस्पतयः शान्तिर्विश्वेदेवाः शान्तिर्ब्रह्म शान्तिः
सर्वँशान्तिः शान्तिरेव शान्तिः सा मा शान्तिरेधि॥
ॐ शान्तिः शान्तिः शान्तिः॥16॥

ॐ dyauḥ śāntirantarikṣa śāntiḥ pṛthivī śāntirāpaḥ
śāntiroṣadhayaḥ śāntiḥ.
vanaspatayaḥ śāntirviśvedevāḥ śāntirbrahma śāntiḥ sarva śāntiḥ
śāntireva śāntiḥ sā mā śāntiredhi॥
ॐ śāntiḥ śāntiḥ śāntiḥ॥16॥[58]

May peace prevail in the sky, the vast expanse, the earth and the waters. May peace be within herbs, creeping vines, trees and plants. Let peace flow through the entire universe and dwell within the Supreme Being, Brahman. May peace be ever-present, eternal and pure. Om Shanti, Shanti, Shanti to all beings and to us.

माता भूमिः[1]

Mātā bhūmiḥ

CHAPTER 8

Respect for the Land

In Hindu culture, people universally regard the land they inhabit or have traditionally lived in as their Motherland. The land of one's ancestors is called Punyabhumi, or Sacred Land, while the land where one resides is known as Karmabhumi.

Individuals express their love and devotion for their country through pride in its achievements, history, geography, culture and values, alongside a commitment to contribute to the common good. A patriotic populace supports national efforts to safeguard sovereignty and interests, fostering a unified and resilient society essential for progress.

This collective patriotism bolsters support for national initiatives and policies, enhancing governance effectiveness and the implementation of programmes for economic growth, social development and security. This leads not only to economic and political success but also to the preservation and promotion of cultural heritage. Sovereignty enables cultural protection, while patriotism instils pride and identity, strengthening national unity and social cohesion.

A united populace is better equipped to confront challenges and capitalize on opportunities. A lack of patriotism among the people can burden the nation, highlighting its critical importance for national progress, safety and security. Therefore, the eighth and final Hindu sutra is 'माता भूमिः' (*Mātā bhūmiḥ*): Respect for the Land.

Hindus Are Descendants of Dravideshwar Rajarshi Satyavrata, the King of Dravida

योऽसौ सत्यव्रतो नाम राजर्षिर्द्रविडेश्वरः।
ज्ञानं योऽतीतकल्पान्ते लेभे पुरुषसेवया।।2।।
स वै विवस्वतः पुत्रो मनुरासीदिति श्रुतम्।।3।।

Yo'sau satyavrato nāma rājarṣidraviḍeśvaraḥ.
Jñānaṃ yo'tītakalpānte lebhe puruṣasevayā||2||
Sa vai vivasvataḥ putre manurāsīditi śrutam||3||[2]

At the end of the last kalpa (eon), Rajarshi Satyavrata, the King of Dravid, attained knowledge and wisdom through penance (tapas) and became Vaivasvat Manu in this kalpa (eon).

The story of Rajarshi Satyavrata and his transformation into Vaivasvat Manu is a fascinating fact from Hindu history and tradition, illustrating the cyclical nature of time. In Hindu cosmology, time is divided into large cycles called kalpas. At the end of each kalpa, the universe undergoes dissolution, and a new cycle begins.

Rajarshi Satyavrata, a pious king of the ancient Dravidian region, was known for his deep devotion to God and adherence to dharma (righteousness). The term 'Rajarshi' (Raja + rishi) refers to a king who has attained the status of a sage (rishi) through virtuous deeds and spiritual practices. Satyavrata's commitment to dharma and selfless service to God distinguished him as an exemplary ruler. Through his penance (tapas) and devotion, he attained spiritual enlightenment, purifying his mind and soul and achieving a high state of spiritual knowledge and wisdom.

At the end of the last kalpa, Rajarshi Satyavrata's accumulated spiritual merits resulted in his being granted the role of Vaivasvat Manu at the beginning of the new kalpa. In Hindu tradition, each kalpa has a different Manu, responsible for establishing human civilization and guiding humanity according to divine principles. Vaivasvat Manu, the seventh Manu in the current series of fourteen Manus, plays a crucial role in the current cycle of creation, ensuring the maintenance of moral and spiritual order.

The position of Manu is highly revered, signifying the importance of leadership that upholds dharma and guides humanity. This role highlights the continuity and renewal of life and moral order across kalpas, emphasizing the perpetual cycle of time in Hindu cosmology.

It is important to note that this historical reference from the Bhagwat Mahapuran is thousands of years old, predating the now-discredited

Aryan and Dravidian theories, including both the Aryan invasion theory and the Aryan and Dravidian migration theories. This reference effectively challenges the so-called Aryan and Dravidian theories. (For general understanding, 'Dravid' is a geographical term.) This also proves that Hindus from all regions of Bharat—whether north, south, east or west—share a common origin. The present generation of Hindus are the descendants of Dravideshwar Rajarshi Satyavrata, who later became Vaivasvata Manu.

The Country Is Named Bharat

दुष्यन्तस्तु तदा राजा पुत्रं शाकुन्तलं तदा।
भरतं नामतः कृत्वा यौवराज्येऽभ्यषेचयत्।।126।।

Duṣyantastu tadā rājā putraṃ śākuntalaṃ tadā.
Bharataṃ nāmataḥ kṛtvā yauvarājye'bhyaṣecayat।।126।।[3]

भरताद् भारती कीर्तिर्येनेदं भारतं कुलम्।।131।।

Bharatād bhāratī kīrtiryenedaṃ bhārataṃ kulam।।131।।[4]

Bharat, the son of Shakuntala and Dushyant, was crowned as a prince by King Dushyanta. Later, Dushyant coronated Bharat as king.

The country was named Bharat after King Bharat.

Respect for Bharat

पृथोस्तु राजन् वैन्यस्य तथेक्ष्वाकोर्महात्मनः।
ययातेरम्बरीषस्य मान्धातुर्नहुषस्य च।।6।।
तथैव मचुकुन्दस्य शिबेरौशीनरस्य च।
ऋषभस्य तथैलस्य नृगस्य नृपतेस्तथा।।7।।
कुशिकस्य च दुर्धर्ष गाधेश्चैव महात्मनः।
सोमकस्य च दुर्धर्ष दिलीपस्य तथैव च।।8।।
अन्येषां च महाराज क्षत्रियाणां बलीयसाम्।
सर्वेषामेव राजेन्द्र प्रियं भारत भारतम्।।9।।

Pṛthostu rājan vainyasya tathekṣvākormahātmanaḥ.
Yayāterambarīṣasya māndhāturnahuṣasya ca||6||
Tathaiva macukundasya śiberauśīnarasya ca.
Ṛṣabhasya tathailasya nṛgasya nṛpatestathā||7||
Kuśikasya ca durdharṣa gādheścaiva mahātmanaḥ.
Somakasya ca durdharṣa dilīpasya tathaiva ca||8||
Anyeṣāṃ ca mahārāja kṣatriyāṇāṃ balīyasām.
Sarveṣāmeva rājendra priyaṃ bhārata bhāratam||9||[5]

Many powerful kings, such as King Prithu, the son of King Vain, King Ikshvaku, King Yayati, King Ambrish, King Mandhata, King Nahush, King Muchukunda, King Shibi (son of King Ushinar), King Rishabh, Ila (son of Pururava), King Nriga, King Kushik, King Gadhi, King Somak, King Dileep and many others, cherished the land of Bharat dearly.

Geography of Bharat

उदेति च यतः सूर्यो यत्र च प्रतितिष्ठति।।11।।
तत् सर्वं यौवनाश्वस्य मान्धातुः क्षेत्रमुच्यते।

Udeti ca yataḥ sūryo yatra ca pratitiṣṭhati||11||
Tat sarvaṃ yauvanāśvasya māndhātuḥ kṣetramucyate.[6]

The entire region where the sun rose and set was under the rule of King Mandhata, the son of Yuvanshva.

यवनाः किराता गान्धाराश्चीनाः शबरबर्बराः।
शकास्तुषाराः कङ्काश्च पह्लवाश्चान्ध्रमद्रकाः।।13।।
पौण्ड्राः पुलिन्दा रमठाः काम्बोजाश्चैव सर्वशः।।14।।

Yavanāḥ kirātā gāndhārāścīnāḥ śabarabarbarāḥ.
Śakāstuṣārāḥ kaṅkāśca pahlavāścāndhramadrakāḥ||13||
Pauṇḍrāḥ pulindā ramaṭhāḥ kāmbojāścaiva sarvaśaḥ||14||[7]

King Mandhata said that under his rule, the regions included the Yavanas (Greeks), Kiratas (Central Asia), Gandharas (Afghanistan),

Chinas (China), Shavaras, Berberas (Morocco, Algeria, Tunisia, Libya, Egypt, Mali, Niger and Mauritania), Shakas, Tusharas, Kankas, Pahallavas, Andhras, Madrakas, Paundras, Pulindas, Ramathas and Kambojas.

It is important to note that present-day China was once ruled by King Mandhata.

न शशाक वशे कर्तुं यं पाण्डुरपि वीर्यवान्।
सोऽर्जुनेन वशं नीतो राजासीद्यवनाधिपः।।21।।

na śaśāka vaśe kartuṃ yaṃ pāṇḍurapi vīryavān|
so'rjunena vaśaṃ nīto rājāsīdyavanādhipaḥ||21||[8]

Even the powerful King Pandu was unable to control or subdue the Yavan (Greek) king. Arjun defeated this Yavan king and brought him under the rule of the Indraprastha state of Bharat.

रामठान्हारहुणांश्च प्रतीच्याश्चैव ये नृपाः।।12।।
तान्सर्वान्स वशे चक्रे शासनादेव पाण्डवः।

rāmaṭhānhārahūṇāṃśca pratīcyāścaiva ye nṛpāḥ||12||
tānsarvānsa vaśe cakre śāsanādeva pāṇḍavaḥ|[9]

Nakula, the son of Pandu, defeated Ramatha, Hara, Huna and other Western kings and kingdoms, bringing them under the rule of the Indraprastha state of Bharat.

ततः सागरकुक्षिस्थान्म्लेच्छान्परमदारुणान्।
पह्लवान्वर्बरांश्चैव किरातान्यवनाञ्शकान्।।16।।

tataḥ sāgarakukṣisthānmlecchānparamadāruṇān|
pahlavānvarbarāṃścaiva kirātānyavanāñśakān||16||[10]

Nakula defeated the powerful Malechchha residing in island countries, as well as the Pahallavas, Berberas, Kiratas, Yavanas (Greeks) and

Shakas, bringing them under the rule of the Indraprastha state of Bharat.

King Yudhishthira Was Offered Gifts by Kings from around the World

चीनाञ्छकांस्तथाचौड्रान्बर्बरान् वनवासिनः॥23॥
वार्ष्णेयान् हारहुणांश्च कृष्णान् हैमवतांस्तथा।
नीपानूपानधिगतान् विविधान् द्वारवारितान्॥24॥

Cīnāñchakāṃstathācauḍrānbarbarān vanavāsinaḥ॥23॥
Vārṣṇeyān hārahūṇāṃśca kṛṣṇān haimavatāṃstathā.
Nīpānūpānadhigatān vividhān dvāravāritān॥24॥[11]

Kings from various lands with diverse appearances, such as China, Shaka, Aundara, Berbera, Varshneya, Hara, Huna and Krishna (Black), (from the upper Himalayan region), came to offer gifts to Yudhisthira during the Rajsuyajna.

Mountains of Bharat

महेन्द्रो मलयः सह्यः शुक्तिमानृक्षवानपि।
विन्ध्यश्च पारियात्रश्च सप्तैते कुलपर्वताः॥11॥

Mahendro malayaḥ sahyaḥ śuktimānṛkṣavānapi.
Vindhyaśca pāriyātraśca saptaite kulaparvatāḥ॥11॥[12]

In the land of Bharat Varsha, the seven main mountain ranges are Mahendra, Malaya, Sahya, Shuktiman, Rikshvan, Vindhya and Pariyatra.

तेषां सहस्रशो राजन् पर्वतास्ते समीपतः।
अविज्ञाताः सारवन्तो विपुलाश्चित्रसानवः॥12॥

Teṣāṃ sahasraśo rājan parvatāste samīpataḥ.
Avijñātāḥ sāravanto vipulāścitrasānavaḥ॥12॥[13]

Near these seven mountain ranges, there are thousands of other mountains abundant in minerals and gems. These mountains are vast and expansive.

Rivers of Bharat

नदीं पिबन्ति विपुलां गङ्गां सिन्धुं सरस्वतीम्।
गोदावरीं नर्मदां च बाहुदां च महानदीम्।।14।।
शतद्रूं चन्द्रभागां च यमुनां च महानदीम्।
दृषद्वतीं विपाशां च विपापां स्थूलवालुकाम्।।15।।
नदीं वेत्रवतीं चैव कृष्णवेणां च निम्नगाम्।
इरावतीं वितस्तां च पयोष्णीं देविकामपि।।16।।
वेदस्मृतां वेदवतीं त्रिदिवामिक्षुलां कृमिम्।
करीषिणीं चित्रवाहां चित्रसेनां च निम्नगाम्।।17।।

Nadīṃ pibanti vipulāṃ gaṅgāṃ sindhuṃ sarasvatīm.
Godāvarīṃ narmadāṃ ca bāhudāṃ ca mahānadīm।।14।।
Śatadrūṃ candrabhāgāṃ ca yamunāṃ ca mahānadīm.
Dṛṣadvatīṃ vipāśāṃ ca vipāpāṃ sthūlavālukām।।15।।
Nadīṃ vetravatīṃ caiva kṛṣṇaveṇāṃ ca nimnagām.
Irāvatīṃ vitastāṃ ca payoṣṇīṃ devikāmapi।।16।।
Vedasmṛtāṃ vedavatīṃ tridivāmikṣulāṃ kṛmim.
Karīṣiṇīṃ citravāhāṃ citrasenāṃ ca nimnagām।।17।।[14]

Ganga, Sindhu, Saraswati, Godavari, Narmada, Bahuda, Mahanadi, Shatadru, Chandrabhaga, Yamuna, Drishadvati, Vipasha, Vipapa, Sthulvaluka, Vetravati, Krishnavena, Iravati, Vitasta, Payoshani, Devika, Vedasmrita, Vedavati, Tridiva, Ikshula, Krimi, Karishini, Chitravaha and Chitrasena.

गोमतीं धूतपापां च वन्दनां च महानदीम्।
कौशिकीं त्रिदिवां कृत्यां निचितां लोहितारणीम्।।18।।
रहस्यां शतकुम्भां च सरयूं च तथैव च।
चर्मण्वतीं वेत्रवतीं हस्तिसोमां दिशं तथा।।19।।
शरावतीं पयोष्णीं च वेणां भीमरथीमपि।
कावेरीं चुलुकां चापि वाणीं शतबलामपि।।20।।

Gomatīṃ dhūtapāpāṃ ca vandanāṃ ca mahānadīm.
Kauśikīṃ tridivāṃ kṛtyāṃ nicitāṃ lohitāraṇīm||18||
Rahasyāṃ śatakumbhāṃ ca sarayūṃ ca tathaiva ca.
Carmaṇvatīṃ vetravatīṃ hastisomāṃ diśaṃ tathā||19||
Śarāvatīṃ payoṣṇīṃ ca veṇāṃ bhīmarathīmapi.
Kāverīṃ culukāṃ cāpi vāṇīṃ śatabalāmapi||20||[15]

Gomati, Dhutapapa, Mahanadi, Vandana, Kaushiki, Tridiva, Kritya, Nichita, Lohitarani, Rahasya, Shatakumbha, Sarayu, Charmanvati, Vetravati, Hastisoma, Dik, Sharavati, Payoshini, Vena, Bhimarathi, Kaveri, Chuluka, Vani, Shatabala.

नीवाराममहितां चापि सुप्रयोगां जनाधिप।
पवित्रां कुण्डलीं सिन्धुं राजनीं पुरमालिनीम्।।21।।
पूर्वाभिरामां वीरां च भीमामोघवतीं तथा
पाशाशिनीं पापहरां महेन्द्रां पाटलावतीम्।।22।।
करीषिणीमसिक्नीं च कुशचीरां महानदीम्।
मकरीं प्रवरां मेनां हेमां घृतवतीं तथा।।23।।
पुरावतीमनुष्णां च शैब्यां कापीं च भारत।
सदानीरामधृष्यां च कुशधारां महानदीम्।।24।।

Nīvārāmahitāṃ cāpi suprayogāṃ janādhipa.
Pavitrāṃ kuṇḍalīṃ sindhuṃ rājanīṃ puramālinīm||21||
Pūrvābhirāmāṃ vīrāṃ ca bhīmāmoghavatīṃ tathā
Pāśāśinīṃ pāpaharāṃ mahendrāṃ pāṭalāvatīm||22||
Karīṣiṇīmasiknīṃ ca kuśacīrāṃ mahānadīm.
Makarīṃ pravarāṃ menāṃ hemāṃ ghṛtavatīṃ tathā||23||
Purāvatīmanuṣṇāṃ ca śaibyāṃ kāpīṃ ca bhārata.
Sadānīrāmadhṛṣyāṃ ca kuśadhārāṃ mahānadīm||24||[16]

Nivara, Ahita, Suprayoga, Pavitra, Kundali, Sindhu, Rajani, Puramalini, Purvabhirama, Veera, Bhima, Oghavati, Pashashini, Paapahara, Mahendra, Patalavati, Karishini, Asikni, Kushachira Mahanadi, Makari, Pravara, Mena, Hema, Dhritavati, Puravati, Anushna, Shaivya, Kapi, Sadanira, Adhrishya and Kushadhara Mahanadi.

सदाकान्तां शिवां चैव तथा वीरमतीमपि।
वस्त्रां सुवस्त्रां गौरीं च कम्पनां सहिरण्वतीम्।।25।।
वरां वीरकरां चापि पञ्चमीं च महानदीम्।
रथचित्रां ज्योतिरथा विश्वामित्रां कपिञ्जलाम्।।26।।
उपेन्द्रां बहुलां चैव कुवीरामम्बुवाहिनीम्।
विनदीं पिञ्जलां वेणां तुङ्गवेणां महानदीम्।।27।।
विदिशां कृष्णवेणां च ताम्रां च कपिलामपि।
खलुं सुवामां वेदाश्वां हरिश्रावां महापगाम्।।28।।
शीघ्रां च पिच्छिलां चैव भारद्वाजीं च निम्नगाम्।
कौशिकीं निम्नगां शोणां बाहुदामथ चन्द्रमाम्।।29।।
दुर्गां चित्रशिलां चैव ब्रह्मवेध्यां बृहद्वतीम्।।
यवक्षामथ रोहीं च तथा जाम्बूनदीमपि।।30।।

Sadākāntāṃ śivāṃ caiva tathā vīramatīmapi.
Vastrāṃ suvastrāṃ gaurīṃ ca kampanāṃ sahiraṇvatīm।।25।।
Varāṃ vīrakarāṃ cāpi pañcamīṃ ca mahānadīm.
Rathacitrāṃ jyotirathā viśvāmitrāṃ kapiñjalām।।26।।
Upendrāṃ bahulāṃ caiva kuvīrāmambuvāhinīm.
Vinadīṃ piñjalāṃ veṇāṃ tuṅgaveṇāṃ mahānadīm।।27।।
Vidiśāṃ kṛṣṇaveṇāṃ ca tāmrāṃ ca kapilāmapi.
Khaluṃ suvāmāṃ vedāśvāṃ hariśrāvāṃ mahāpagām।।28।।
Śīghrāṃ ca picchilāṃ caiva bhāradvājīṃ ca nimnagām.
Kauśikīṃ nimnagāṃ śoṇāṃ bāhudāmatha candramām।।29।।
Durgāṃ citraśilāṃ caiva brahmavedhyāṃ bṛhadvatīm.
Yavakṣāmatha rohīṃ ca tathā jāmbūnadīmapi।।30।।[17]

Sadakanta, Shiva, Viramati, Vastra, Suvastra, Gauri, Kampana, Hiranyavati, Vara, Veerakara, Mahanadi Panchami, Rathachitra, Jyotiratha, Vishvamitra, Kapinjala, Upendra, Bahula, Kuvira, Ambuvahini, Vinadi, Pinjala, Vena, Mahanadi Tungavena, Vidisha, Krishnavena, Tamara, Kapila, Khalu, Suvama, Vedashrva, Harishrava, Mahapaga, Shighra, Pichhala, Bharadvaji, Kaushiki, Sona, Bahuda, Chandrama, Durga, Chintrashila, Brahmavaidhya, Brihadvati, Yavaksha, Rohi and Jambunadi.

सुनसां तमसां दासीं वसामन्यां वराणसीम्।
लीलां धृतवतीं चैव पर्णाशां च महानदीम्।।31।।
मानवीं वृषभां चैव ब्रह्ममेध्यां बृहद्धनिम्।
एताश्चान्याश्चा बहुधा महानद्यो जनाधिप।।32।।

Sunasāṃ tamasāṃ dāsīṃ vasāmanyāṃ varāṇasīm.
Līlāṃ dhṛtavatīṃ caiva parṇāśāṃ ca mahānadīm।।31।।
Mānavīṃ vṛṣabhāṃ caiva brahmamedhyāṃ bṛhaddhanim.
Etāścānyāścā bahudhā mahānadyo janādhipa।।32।।[18]

Sunasa, Tamasa, Dasi, Vasa, Varanasi, Nila, Dhritavati, Mahanadi, Parnasha, Manavi, Vrishabha, Brahmamedhya and Brihadhini.

सदा निरामयां कृष्णां मन्दगां मदवाहिनीम्।
ब्राह्मणीं च महागौरीं दुर्गामपि च भारत।।33।।
चित्रोपलां चित्ररथां मञ्जुलां वाहिनीं तथा।
मन्दाकिनीं वैतरणीं कोषां चापि महानदीम्।।34।।
शुक्तिमतीमनङ्गां च तथैव वृषसाह्वयाम्।।35।।
कुमारीमृषिकुल्यां च मारिषां च सरस्वतीम्।
मन्दाकीनीं सुपुण्यां च सर्वां गङ्गां च भारत।।36।।

Sadā nirāmayāṃ kṛṣṇāṃ mandagāṃ madavāhinīm.
Brāhmaṇīṃ ca mahāgaurīṃ durgāmapi ca bhārata।।33।।
Citropalāṃ citrarathāṃ mañjulāṃ vāhinīṃ tathā.
Mandākinīṃ vaitaraṇīṃ koṣāṃ cāpi mahānadīm।।34।।
Śuktimatīmanaṅgāṃ ca tathaiva vṛṣasāhvayām।।35।।
Kumārīmṛṣikulyāṃ ca māriṣāṃ ca sarasvatīm.
Mandākīnīṃ supuṇyāṃ ca sarvāṃ gaṅgāṃ ca bhārata।।36।।[19]

Sadaniramaya, Krishna, Mandaga, Mandavahini, Brahmini, Mahagauri, Durga, Chitratpla, Chitraratha, Manjula, Vahini, Mandakini, Vaitarani, Kosha Mahanadi, Shuktimati, Ananga, Vrisha, Lohitya, Karatoya, Vrishaka, Kumari, Rishikulya, Marisha, Sarasvati, Mandakini, Supunya, Sarva and Ganga.

Janapada of Bharat

तत्रेमे कुरुपाञ्चालाः शाल्वा माद्रेयजाङ्गलाः।
शूरसेनाः पुलिन्दाश्च बोधा मालास्तथैव च॥39॥
मत्स्याःकुशल्याःसौशल्याःकुन्तयःकान्तिकोसलाः।
चेतिमत्स्यकरूषाश्च भोजाः सिन्धुपुलिन्दकाः॥40॥
उत्तरमाश्वदशार्णाश्च मेकलाश्चोत्कलैः सह।
पञ्चालाः कोसलाश्चैव नैकपृष्ठा धुरंधराः॥41॥
गोधामद्रकलिङ्गाश्च काशयोऽपरकाशयः।
जठराः कुक्कुराश्चैव सदशार्णाश्च भारत॥42॥
कुन्तयोऽवन्तयश्चैव तथैवापरकुन्तयः।
गोमन्ता मण्डकाः सण्डा विदर्भा रूपवाहिकाः॥43॥
अश्मकाः पाण्डुराष्ट्राश्च गोपराष्ट्राः करीतयः।
अधिराज्यकुशाद्यश्च मल्लराष्ट्रं च केवलम्॥44॥

Tatreme kurupāñcālāḥ śālvā mādreyajāṅgalāḥ.
Śūrasenāḥ pulindāśca bodhā mālāstathaiva ca॥39॥
Matsyāḥkuśalyāḥsauśalyāḥkuntayaḥkāntikosalāḥ.
Cetimatsyakarūṣāśca bhojāḥ sindhupulindakāḥ॥40॥
Uttaramāśvadaśārṇāśca mekalāścotkalaiḥsaha.
Pañcālāḥ kosalāścaiva naikapṛṣṭhā dhuraṃdharāḥ॥41॥
Godhāmadrakaliṅgāśca kāśayo'parakāśayaḥ.
Jaṭharāḥ kukkurāścaiva sadaśārṇāśca bhārata॥42॥
Kuntayo'vantayaścaiva tathaivāparakuntayaḥ.
Gomantā maṇḍakāḥ saṇḍā vidarbhā rūpavāhikāḥ॥43॥
Aśmakāḥ pāṇḍurāṣṭrāśca goparāṣṭrāḥ karītayaḥ.
Adhirājyakuśādyaśca mallarāṣṭraṃ ca kevalam॥44॥[20]

The Kuru-Panchala, the Shalva, the Madreya, the Jangala, the Shurasena, the Pulinda, the Bodha, the Mala, the Matsya, the Kushalya, the Saushalya, the Kunti, the Kanti, the Koshala, the Chedi, the Matsya, the Karusha, the Bhoja, the Sindhu-Pulinda, the Uttamashrava, the Dasharana, the Mekal, the Utkal, the Panchal, the Koshala, the Naikaprishtha, the Dhurandhara, the Godhas, the Madrakalinga, the Kashi, the Aparkashi, the Jathara, the Kukura, the Sadadasharana, the Kunti, the Avanti, the apar Kunti, the Gomanta, the Mandaka, the

Sanda, the Vidarabha, the Rupavahik, the Ashmaka, the Pandurashtra, the Goparashtra, the Kareeti, the Adhirajya, the Kushadhya and the Mallarashtra.

वारवास्यायवाहाश्च चक्राश्चक्रातयः शकाः।
विदेहा मगधाः स्वक्षा मलजा विजयास्तथा।।45।।
अङ्गा वङ्गाः कलिङ्गाश्च यकृल्लोमान एव च।
मल्लाः सुदेष्णाः प्रह्लादा माहिकाः शशिकास्तथा।।46।।
बाह्लिका वाटधानाश्च आभीराः कालतोयकाः।
अपरान्ताः परान्ताश्च पञ्चालाश्चर्ममण्डलाः।।47।।
अटवीशिखराचैव मेरुभूताश्च मारिष।
उपावृत्तानुपावृत्ताः स्वराष्ट्राः केकयास्तथा।।48।।
कुन्दापरान्ता माहेयाः कक्षाः सामुद्रनिष्कुटाः।
अन्ध्राश्च बहवो राजन्नन्तर्गिर्यास्तथैव च।।49।।
बहिर्गिर्याङ्गमलजा मगधा मानवर्जकाः।
समन्तराः प्रावृषेया भार्गवाश्च जनाधिप।।50।।

Vāravāsyāyavāhāśca cakrāścakrātayaḥ śakāḥ.
Videhā magadhāḥ svakṣā malajā vijayāstathā।।45।।
Aṅgā vaṅgāḥ kaliṅgāśca yakṛllomāna eva ca.
Mallāḥ sudeṣṇāḥ prahlādā māhikāḥ śaśikāstathā।।46।।
Bāhlikā vāṭadhānāśca ābhīrāḥ kālatoyakāḥ.
Aparāntāḥ parāntāśca pañcālāścarmamaṇḍalāḥ।।47।।
Aṭavīśikharācaiva merubhūtāśca māriṣa.
Upāvṛttānupāvṛttāḥ svarāṣṭrāḥ kekayāstathā।।48।।
Kundāparāntā māheyāḥ kakṣāḥ sāmudraniṣkuṭāḥ.
Andhrāśca bahavo rājannantargiryāstathaiva ca।।49।।
Bahirgiryāṅgamalajā magadhā mānavarjakāḥ.
Samantarāḥ prāvṛṣeyā bhārgavāśca janādhipa।।50।।[21]

The Varavasya, the Aayavaha, the Chakara, the Chakarati, the Shaka, the Videha, the Magadha, the Savksha, the Malaja, the Vijaya, the Anga, the Vanga (Bengal), the Kalinaga, the Yakrilloma, the Malla, the Sudeshna, the Prahlada, the Mahika, the Shashika, the Balhika, the Vatadhana, the Abhira, the Kalatoyaka, the Aparanta, the Paranta, the Panchala, the Charamamandala, the Atavishikhara, the Merubhuta, the Upavritta, the Anupavritta, the Svarashtra, the Kaikeya, the Kundaparanta, the Maheya, the Kaksha, the Samudranishkuta, the Bahusankhyak Andhra, the Antargiri, the Bahirgiri, the Angamalaja, the Magadh, the Manavarjaka, the Samantra, the Pravrisheya and the Bharagava.

अथापरे जनपदा दक्षिणा भरतर्षभ।
द्रविडाः केरलाः प्राच्या भूषिका वनवासिकाः।।58।।
कर्णाटका महिषका विकल्पा मूषकास्तथा।
झिल्लिकाः कुन्तलाश्चैव सोहृदा नभकाननाः।।59।।
कौकुट्टकास्तथा चोलाः कोङ्कणा मालवा नराः।
समङ्गाः करकाश्चैव कुकुराङ्गारमारिषाः।।60।।
ध्वजिन्युत्सवसंकेतास्त्रिगर्ताः शाल्वसेनयः।
व्यूकाः कोकबकाः प्रोष्ठाः समवेगवशास्तथा।61।।
तथैव विन्ध्यचुलिकाः पुलिन्दा वल्कलैः सह।
मालवा बल्लवाश्चैव तथैवापरबल्लवाः।।62।।
कुलिन्दाः कालदाश्चैव कुण्डलाः करटास्तथा।
मूषकाः स्तनबालाश्च सनीपा घटसृंजयाः।।63।।
अठिदाः पाशिवाटाश्च तनयाः सुनयास्तथा।
ऋषिका विदभाः काकास्तङ्गणाः परतङ्गणाः।।64।।

Athāpare janapadā dakṣiṇā bharatarṣabha.
Draviḍāḥ keralāḥ prācyā bhūṣikā vanavāsikāḥ।।58।।
Karṇāṭakā mahiṣakā vikalpā mūṣakāstathā.
Jhillikāḥ kuntalāścaiva sohṛdā nabhakānanāḥ।।59।।
Kaukuṭṭakāstathā colāḥ koṅkaṇā mālavā narāḥ.
Samaṅgāḥ karakāścaiva kukurāṅgāramāriṣāḥ।।60।।
Dhvajinyutsavasaṃketāstrigartāḥ śālvasenayaḥ.
Vyūkāḥ kokabakāḥ proṣṭhāḥ samavegavaśāstathā।।61।।
Tathaiva vindhyaculikāḥ pulindā valkalaiḥ saha.
Mālavā ballavāścaiva tathaivāparaballavāḥ।।62।।
Kulindāḥ kāladāścaiva kuṇḍalāḥ karaṭāstathā.
Mūṣakāḥ stanabālāśca sanīpā ghaṭasṛṃjayāḥ।।63।।
Aṭhidāḥ pāśivāṭāśca tanayāḥ sunayāstathā.
Ṛṣikā vidabhāḥ kākāstaṅgaṇāḥ parataṅgaṇāḥ।।64।।[22]

The southern janapadas of Bharat include the Dravida, Kerala, Prachya, Bhushika, Vanavasika, Karantaka, Mahishaka, Vikalpa, Mushaka, Jhillika, Kuntal, Sauhrida, Nabhakanana, Kaukuttaka, Chola, Konkan, Malava, Nara, Samanga, Karaka, Kukkura, Angara, Marisha, Dhvajini, Utsava-Sanketa, Trigarta, Shalvaseni, Vyuka, Kokabaka, Proshta, Samavegavasha, Vindhyachulik, Pulinda, Valkala, Malava, Ballava, Apar Ballava, Kulinda, Kalada, Kundala, Karata, Mushaka, Stanabala, Saneep, Ghata, Srinjya, Adida, Pashivata, Tanay, Sunay, Rishika, Vidabha, Kaka, Tangana and Partangana.

उत्तराश्चापरम्लेच्छाः क्रूरा भरतसत्तम।
यवनाश्चीनकाम्बोजा दारुणा म्लेच्छजातयः।।65।।
सकृद्ग्रहाः कुलत्थाश्च हुणाः पारसिकैः सह।
तथैव रमणाश्चीनास्तथैव दशमालिकाः।।66।।
क्षत्रियोपनिवेशाश्च वैश्यशूद्रकुलानि च।
शूद्राभीराश्च दरदाः काश्मीराः पशुभिः सह।।37।।
खाशीराश्चान्तचाराश्च पह्लवा गिरिगह्वराः।
आत्रेयाः सभरद्वाजास्तथैव स्तनपोषिकाः।।68।।
प्रोषकाश्च कलिङ्गाश्च किराताना च जातयः।
तोमरा हन्यमानाश्च तथैव करभञ्जकाः।।69।।

Uttarāścāparamlecchāḥ krūrā bharatasattama.
Yavanāścīnakāmbojā dāruṇā mlecchajātayaḥ।।65।।
Sakṛdgrahāḥ kulatthāśca hūṇāḥ pārasikaiḥ saha.
Tathaiva ramaṇāścīnāstathaiva daśamālikāḥ।।66।।
Kṣatriyopaniveśāśca vaiśyaśūdrakulāni ca.
Śūdrābhīrāśca daradāḥ kāśmīrāḥ paśubhiḥ saha।।37।।
Khāśīrāścāntacārāśca pahlavā girigahvarāḥ.
Ātreyāḥ sabharadvājāstathaiva stanapoṣikāḥ।।68।।
Proṣakāśca kaliṅgāśca kirātānāṃ ca jātayaḥ.
Tomarā hanyamānāśca tathaiva karabhañjakāḥ।।69।।[23]

The janapadas of the West and North include the Yavana, China, Kamboja, Malechchha, Sakridgraha, Kulatha, Huna, Parasika, Ramana-China, Dashamalika, Shudra, Abhira, Darda, Khashmira, Pashu, Khasir, Antachar, Pahllava, Girigahavar, Atreya, Bharadvaja,

Stanoposhika, Proshaka, Kalinag and many other Kirata janapadas, as well as the Tomaras, Hanyaman and Karabhanjaka.

Identifying Anti-National Elements and Their Activities: Ensuring Accountability and Punishment

ये च राष्ट्रोपरोधेन वृद्धिं कुर्वन्ति केचन।
तानेवानुम्रियेरंस्ते कुणपं कृमयो यथा।।21।।

ye ca rāṣṭroparodhena vṛddhiṃ kurvanti kecana|
tānevānumriyeraṃste kuṇapaṃ kṛmayo yathā||21||[24]

Those who seek to increase their fortune through unscrupulous means, harming and betraying their country, are like vermin feeding on a corpse.

Anti-national individuals are parasitic to society. Just as vermin thrive on decay, these unscrupulous people exploit the suffering and decline of their country. Their actions perpetuate a cycle of destruction, where values such as loyalty, duty and societal well-being are disregarded in favour of self-serving pursuits.

Anti-national behaviour and activities must be condemned, as they signify a betrayal of the shared values and collective responsibilities that unite individuals with their nation. Such individuals should face severe punishment to deter others from engaging in similar actions.

Selected Vedic Mantras from *Atharvaveda*, Kanda 12, Sukta 1, for the Reverence of the Motherland

सत्यं बृहदृतमुग्रं दीक्षा तपो ब्रह्म यज्ञः पृथिवीं धारयन्ति ।
सा नो भूतस्य भव्यस्य पत्न्युरुं लोकं पृथिवी नः कृणोतु ॥1॥

Satyaṃ bṛhadṛtamugraṃ dīkṣā tapo brahma
yajñaḥ pṛthivīṃ dhārayanti.
Sā no bhūtasya bhavyasya patnyuruṃ
lokaṃ pṛthivī naḥ kṛṇotu॥1॥

O beloved Motherland, endowed with the qualities of truth, enterprise, professional knowledge, patience, courage and sacrifice, and with the aspiration to accomplish good work, we pledge to defend and protect you at all times. You, who have provided for our nourishment in the past, present and future, may you enhance our repute.

असंबाधं बध्यतो मानवानां यस्या उद्वतः प्रवतः समं बहु ।
नानावीर्या ओषधीर्या बिभर्ति पृथिवी नः प्रथतां राध्यतां नः ॥2॥

Asaṃbādhaṃ badhyato mānavānāṃ yasyā udvataḥ pravataḥ samaṃ bahu.
Nānāvīryā oṣadhīryā bibharti pṛthivī naḥ prathatāṃ rādhyatāṃ naḥ॥2॥

O beloved Motherland, our people should not harbour enmity among themselves. Instead, they should unite, especially our leaders, who must work together for the country's betterment. Your land nurtures a variety of vegetation and herbs that cure diseases and provide nourishment. O beloved Motherland, elevate our reputation across the world.

यस्यां समुद्र उत सिन्धुरापो यस्यामन्नं कृष्टयः संबभूवुः ।
यस्यामिदं जिन्वति प्राणदेजत्सा नो भूमिं पूर्वपेये दधातु ॥3॥

Yasyāṃ samudra uta sindhurāpo yasyāmannaṃ kṛṣṭayaḥ saṃbabhūvuḥ.
Yasyāmidaṃ jinvati prāṇadejatsā no bhūmiḥ pūrvapeye dadhātu॥3॥

O beloved Motherland, your land is enriched with oceans, large rivers, ponds, lakes and canals that irrigate the fields. Because of this, a variety of grains, fruits and vegetables grow in abundance, providing enough nourishment for everyone and ensuring happiness for all. The artisans, technicians and farmers are skilled and enterprising. O Motherland, you bless us with prosperity, peace and happiness.

गिरयस्ते पर्वता हिमवन्तोऽरण्यं ते पृथिवि स्योनमस्तु ।
बभ्रुं कृष्णां रोहिणीं विश्वरूपां ध्रुवां भूमिं पृथिवीमिन्द्रगुप्ताम् ।
अजीतोऽहतो अक्षतोऽध्यष्ठां पृथिवीमहम् ॥11॥

Girayaste parvatā himavanto'raṇyaṃ te pṛthivi syonamastu.
Babhruṃ kṛṣṇāṃ rohiṇīṃ viśvarūpāṃ dhruvāṃ bhūmiṃ pṛthivīmindraguptām.
Ajīto'hato akṣato'dhyaṣṭhāṃ pṛthivīmaham॥11॥

O beloved Motherland, your snow-clad mountains and forests bring happiness. May your mountains and forests always be free from enemies. Your fertile lands, abundant with plants and vegetation, provide nourishment to everyone. Beloved Motherland, we must protect you from harm and ensure you remain undefeated by enemies, so that we may live with great dignity.

यत्ते मध्यं पृथिवि यच्च नभ्यं यास्त ऊर्जस्तन्वः संबभूवुः ।
तासु नो धेह्यभि नः पवस्व माता भूमिः पुत्रो अहं पृथिव्याः पर्जन्यः पिता स उ नः पिपर्तु ॥12॥

Yatte madhyaṃ pṛthivi yacca nabhyaṃ yāsta ūrjastanvaḥ saṃbabhūvuḥ.
Tāsu no dhehyabhi naḥ pavasva mātā bhūmiḥ putro ahaṃ pṛthivyāḥ parjanyaḥ pitā sa u naḥ pipartu॥12॥

O beloved Motherland, we protect the resources both beneath and above you from enemies. Scholars, warriors and the wealthy unite in their efforts to safeguard you, and I will join their ranks to protect you. You are our beloved Motherland, and we are your children. The clouds regularly shower rain; they are like our father, nurturing us with their downpour.

यो नो द्वेषत्पृथिवि यः पृतन्याद्योऽभिदासान् मनसा यो वधेन ।
तं नो भूमे रन्धय पूर्वकृत्वरि ॥14॥

Yo no dveṣatpṛthivi yaḥ pṛtanyādyo'bhidāsān manasā yo vadhena.
Taṃ no bhūme randhaya pūrvakṛtvari॥14॥

O beloved Motherland, may those who hate and attack us with their armies, seeking to conquer and destroy us, and wishing to enslave us, be vanquished by your blessings.

म॒ह॒त्स॒धस्थं॑ मह॒ती ब॒भूवि॑थ म॒हान् वेग॑ ए॒जथु॑र्वे॒पथु॑ष्टे ।
म॒हांस्त्वेन्द्रो॑ रक्ष॒त्यप्र॑मादम् ।
सा नो॑ भूमे॒ प्र रो॑चय॒ हिर॑ण्यस्येव सं॒दृशि॒ मा नो॑ द्विक्षत॒ कश्च॒न ॥18॥

Mahatsadhasthaṃ mahatī babhūvitha mahān vega ejathurvepathuṣṭe.
Mahāṃstvendro rakṣatyapramādam.
Sā no bhūme pra rocaya hiraṇyasyeva
saṃdṛśi mā no dvikṣata kaścana॥18॥

O beloved Motherland, the earth provides space for all of us to live together, and her vast expanse is sufficient for everyone. The earth moves swiftly across the sky. Wise and valiant warriors, endowed with courage and alertness, protect you and are capable of destroying any enemy. You shine like gold; may you bless us so that we all may shine as well, and may there be no enmity among us.

शि॒ला भू॒मिरश्मा॑ पां॒सुः सा भू॒मिः संधृ॑ता धृ॒ता ।
त॒स्यै हिर॑ण्यवक्षसे पृ॒थि॒व्या अ॑क॒रं नम॑ः ॥26॥

Śilā bhūmiraśmā pāṃsuḥ sā bhūmiḥ saṃdhṛtā dhṛtā.
Tasyai hiraṇyavakṣase pṛthivyā akaraṃ namaḥ॥26॥

O beloved Motherland, your soil is abundant with stones, mountains and mines rich in gold and other precious resources. May our Motherland bestow upon us knowledge, strength and valour, ensuring the protection of your sacred land.

मा न॑ः प॒श्चान् मा पु॒रस्ता॑न्नुदिष्ठा॒ मोत्त॒राद॑ध॒रादु॒त ।
स्व॒स्ति भू॑मे नो भव॒ मा वि॑दन् परिप॒न्थिनो॒ वरी॑यो यावया व॒धम् ॥32॥

Mā naḥ paścān mā purastānnudiṣṭhā mottarādadharāduta.
Svasti bhūme no bhava mā vidan paripanthino varīyo yāvayā vadham॥32॥

O beloved Motherland, no one from the north, south, east or west can defeat us. We shall always emerge victorious, with our enemies remaining unaware of our strategies. May our Motherland bless us, and may our best warriors always vanquish our foes.

सा नो भूमिरा दिशतु यद्धनं कामयामहे ।
भगो अनुप्रयुङ्क्तामिन्द्र एतु पुरोगवः ॥40॥

Sā no bhūmirā diśatu yaddhanaṃ kāmayāmahe.
Bhago anuprayuṅktāmindra etu purogavaḥ॥40॥

O beloved Motherland, you provide us with all the wealth and prosperity we seek. Prosperous people support the warrior with their wealth. May our Motherland bless us, and may our warriors stand at the forefront to defeat the enemy.

यस्यां गायन्ति नृत्यन्ति भूम्यां मर्त्या व्यैलबाः ।
युध्यन्ते यस्यामाक्रन्दो यस्यां वदति दुन्दुभिः ।
सा नो भूमिः प्र णुदतां सपत्नान् असपत्नं मा पृथिवी कृणोतु ॥41॥

Yasyāṃ gāyanti nṛtyanti bhūmyāṃ martyā vyailabāḥ.
Yudhyante yasyāmākrando yasyāṃ vadati dundubhiḥ.
Sā no bhūmiḥ pra ṇudatāṃ sapatnān asapatnaṃ mā pṛthivī kṛṇotu॥41॥

O beloved Motherland, in your embrace, people sing, dance and inspired warriors fight to protect the nation; where the thundering hooves and the beating of war drums sound loudly, we must defeat our enemies and drive them away. May the Motherland bless us and grant us freedom from our foes.

जनं बिभ्रती बहुधा विवाचसं नानाधर्माणं पृथिवी यथौकसम् ।
सहस्रं धारा द्रविणस्य मे दुहां ध्रुवेव धेनुरनपस्फुरन्ती ॥45॥

Janaṃ bibhratī bahudhā vivācasaṃ nānādharmāṇaṃ pṛthivī yathaukasam.
Sahasraṃ dhārā draviṇasya me duhāṃ dhruveva dhenuranapasphurantī॥45॥

O beloved Motherland, upon your soil, people speak different languages and follow diverse philosophical schools, yet they live together under your embrace. O indestructible Motherland, like a cow, you provide us with myriad forms of prosperity and abundance.

अहमस्मि सहमान उत्तरो नाम भूम्याम् ।
अभीषाडस्मि विश्वाषाडाशामाशां विषासहिः ॥54॥

Ahamasmi sahamāna uttaro nāma bhūmyām.
Abhīṣāḍasmi viśvāṣāḍāśāmāśāṃ viṣāsahiḥ॥54॥

O beloved Motherland, we stand ready to endure all hardships and joys, to protect and defend you. We are prepared to face any suffering and pain. May our Motherland bless us as we strive to utterly defeat our enemies.

अश्वं इव रजो दुधुवे वि तान् जनान् य आक्षियन् पृथिवीं यादजायत ।
मन्द्राग्रेत्वरी भुवनस्य गोपा वनस्पतीनां गृभिरोषधीनाम् ॥57॥

Aśva iva rajo dudhuve vi tān janān ya ākṣiyan pṛthivīṃ yādajāyata.
Mandrāgretvarī bhuvanasya gopā vanaspatīnāṃ gṛbhiroṣadhīnām॥57॥

O beloved Motherland, anyone who comes and unjustly settles on your land should be removed like dust from a horse's hooves. You should nurture herbs, plants and vegetation to protect the world. May our Motherland bless all patriots so that we can defend and care for you.

यद्वदा॑मि मधु॑मत्तद्व॑दामि यदीक्षे तद्व॑नन्ति मा ।
त्विषीमान् अस्मि जूतिमान् अवान्यान् हन्मि दोधतः ॥58॥

Yadvadāmi madhumattadvadāmi yadīkṣe tadvananti mā.
Tviṣīmān asmi jūtimān avānyān hanmi dodhataḥ॥58॥

O beloved Motherland, let us always speak sweetly and in ways that benefit our nation. Let everything we envision be for the good of our country. May all our actions be dedicated to you, Motherland. Bless us with wisdom, courage and strength. If our enemies threaten you, let us stand ready to defend and protect you.

उपस्थास्ते अनमीवा अयक्ष्मा अस्मभ्यं सन्तु पृथिवि प्रसूताः ।
दीर्घं न आयुः प्रतिबुध्यमाना वयं तुभ्यं बलिहृतः स्याम ॥62॥

Upasthāste anamīvā ayakṣmā asmabhyaṃ santu pṛthivi prasūtāḥ.
Dīrghaṃ na āyuḥ pratibudhyamānā vayaṃ tubhyaṃ balihṛtaḥ syāma॥62॥

O beloved Motherland, we are born of your soil. May we be healthy, strong, long-lived, learned and wise. For the sake of our Motherland, let us awaken and be ready to sacrifice our interests. May our Motherland bless us so that we are always prepared to sacrifice for you.

APPENDIX 1

Bhumi Sukta: Vedic Prayer for the Reverence of the Motherland

Athervaveda, Kanda 12, Sukta 1

सत्यं बृहदृतमुग्रं दीक्षा तपो ब्रह्म यज्ञः पृथिवीं धारयन्ति ।
सा नो भूतस्य भव्यस्य पत्न्युरुं लोकं पृथिवी नः कृणोतु ॥1॥

Satyaṃ bṛhadṛtamugraṃ dīkṣā tapo
brahma yajñaḥ pṛthivīṃ dhārayanti.
Sā no bhūtasya bhavyasya patnyuruṃ lokaṃ pṛthivī naḥ kṛṇotu॥1॥

O beloved Motherland, endowed with the qualities of truth, enterprise, professional knowledge, patience, courage and sacrifice, and with the aspiration to accomplish good work, we pledge to defend and protect you at all times. You, who have provided for our nourishment in the past, present and future, may you enhance our repute.

असंबाधं बध्यतो मानवानां यस्या उद्वतः प्रवतः समं बहु ।
नानावीर्या ओषधीर्या बिभर्ति पृथिवी नः प्रथतां राध्यतां नः ॥2॥

Asaṃbādhaṃ badhyato mānavānāṃ yasyā udvataḥ pravataḥ
samaṃ bahu.
Nānāvīryā oṣadhīryā bibharti pṛthivī naḥ
prathatāṃ rādhyatāṃ naḥ॥2॥

O beloved Motherland, our people should not harbour enmity among themselves. Instead, they should unite, especially our leaders, who must work together for the country's betterment. Your land nurtures a variety of vegetation and herbs that cure diseases and provide nourishment. O beloved Motherland, elevate our reputation across the world.

यस्यां समुद्र उत सिन्धुरापो यस्यामन्नं कृष्टयः संबभूवुः ।
यस्यामिदं जिन्वति प्राणदेजत्सा नो भूमिं पूर्वपेये दधातु ॥3॥

Yasyāṃ samudra uta sindhurāpo
yasyāmannaṃ kṛṣṭayaḥ saṃbabhūvuḥ.
Yasyāmidaṃ jinvati prāṇadejatsā no bhūmiḥ
pūrvapeye dadhātu॥3॥

O beloved Motherland, your land is enriched with oceans, large rivers, ponds, lakes and canals that irrigate the fields. Because of this, a variety of grains, fruits and vegetables grow in abundance, providing enough nourishment for everyone and ensuring happiness for all. The artisans, technicians and farmers are skilled and enterprising. O Motherland, you bless us with prosperity, peace and happiness.

यस्याश्चतस्रः प्रदिशः पृथिव्या यस्यामन्नं कृष्टयः संबभूवुः ।
या बिभर्ति बहुधा प्राणदेजत्सा नो भूमिर्गोष्वप्यन्ने दधातु ॥4॥

Yasyāścatastraḥ pradiśaḥ pṛthivyā yasyāmannaṃ
kṛṣṭayaḥ saṃbabhūvuḥ.
Yā bibharti bahudhā prāṇadejatsā no
bhūmirgoṣvapyanne dadhātu॥4॥

O beloved Motherland, your farmers are highly skilled and enterprising in agriculture. As a result, food grain production and prosperity abound. Consequently, all animals, birds, plants and other living beings enjoy nourishment and protection. May our Motherland bless us with an abundance of cows, horses, wealth and prosperity.

यस्यां पूर्वे पूर्वजना विचक्रिरे यस्यां देवा असुरान् अभ्यवर्तयन् ।
गवामश्वानां वयसश्च विष्ठा भगं वर्चः पृथिवी नो दधातु ॥5॥

Yasyāṃ pūrve pūrvajanā vicakrire yasyāṃ devā asurān abhyavartayan.
Gavāmaśvānāṃ vayasaśca viṣṭhā bhagaṃ varcaḥ pṛthivī no dadhātu॥5॥

O beloved Motherland, where our ancestors—learned and wise individuals drawing upon their knowledge, warriors displaying valour, businessmen excelling in trade and enterprise and artisans mastering their craft—have collectively achieved greatness, overcoming violent, oppressive and coarse forces. Our beautiful land provides shelter to all. May our Motherland bless us and enhance our knowledge, valour and strength.

विश्वंभरा वसुधानी प्रतिष्ठा हिरण्यवक्षा जगतो निवेशनी ।
वैश्वानरं बिभ्रती भूमिरग्निमिन्द्रऋषभा द्रविणे नो दधातु ॥6॥

Viśvaṃbharā vasudhānī pratiṣṭhā hiraṇyavakṣā jagato niveśanī.
Vaiśvānaraṃ bibhratī bhūmiragnimindrarṣabhā draviṇe no dadhātu॥6॥

O beloved Motherland, you sustain and nourish everyone, holding all treasures and providing shelter to all. Beneath your surface lie mines of gold, gems and resources, offering space for both animate and inanimate beings. You embrace people of all kinds who contribute to the development of our nation. May our Motherland bring prosperity and renown to our leaders, learned individuals and courageous warriors.

यां रक्षन्त्यस्वप्ना विश्वदानीं देवा भूमिं पृथिवीमप्रमादम् ।
सा नो मधु प्रियं दुहामथो उक्षतु वर्चसा ॥7॥

Yāṃ rakṣantyasvapnā viśvadānīṃ devā bhūmiṃ pṛthivīmapramādam.
Sā no madhu priyaṃ duhāmatho ukṣatu varcasā॥7॥

O beloved Motherland, free from slumber, idleness and ignorance, may our smart and intelligent businessmen, traders, scholars and warriors protect and defend this land that provides everything for us. May our Motherland, which furnishes resources and nurtures our knowledge, courage and prosperity, also shield and safeguard us.

यार्णवेऽधि'सलिलमग्र आसीत्यां मायाभिरन्वचरन् मनीषिणः ।
यस्या हृदयं परमे व्योमन्त्सत्येनावृतममृतं पृथिव्याः ।
सा नो भूमिस्त्विषिं बलं राष्ट्रे दधातूत्तमे ॥8॥

Yārṇave'dhi salilamagra āsītyāṃ māyābhiranvacaran manīṣiṇaḥ.
Yasyā hṛdayaṃ parame vyomantsatyenāvṛtamamṛtaṃ pṛthivyāḥ.
Sā no bhūmistviṣiṃ balaṃ rāṣṭre dadhātūttame॥8॥
Yarnave'dhi salilamagra dsidydm mdydbhiranvacaranmamsinah.
Yasyd hrdayam parame vyomantsatyendvrtama-mrtam prthivydh.
Sd no bhumistvisirh balam rdstre dadhdtuttame.

O beloved Motherland, once submerged beneath the sea, is now revered. Omnipotent and wise, individuals devoted to this land serve with perfection. May our Motherland bless us with growth in our nation, knowledge, courage and strength.

यस्यामापः परिचराः समानीरहोरात्रे अप्रमादं क्षरन्ति ।
सा नो भूमिर्भूरिधारा पयो दुहामथो उक्षतु वर्चसा ॥9॥

Yasyāmāpaḥ paricarāḥ samānīrahorātre apramādaṃ kṣaranti.
Sā no bhūmirbhūridhārā payo duhāmatho ukṣatu varcasā॥9॥

O beloved Motherland, just as water flows continuously, so too do wandering monks travel everywhere, practising and imparting knowledge and wisdom to all. May our Motherland, which provides us with grain, food, fruit and vegetables, bless us with the growth of knowledge, courage and strength.

यामश्विनावमिमातां विष्णुर्यस्यां विचक्रमे ।
इन्द्रो यां चक्र आत्मनेऽनमित्रां शचीपतिः ।
सा नो भूमिर्वि सृजतां माता पुत्राय मे पयः ॥10॥

Yāmaśvināvamimātāṃ viṣṇuryasyāṃ vicakrame.
Indro yāṃ cakra ātmane'namitrāṃ śacīpatiḥ.
Sā no bhūmirvi sṛjatāṃ mātā putrāya me payaḥ॥10॥

O beloved Motherland, beloved by those who tirelessly nurture all, conquer adversaries and accomplish great deeds, cherished by the wise and the brave. Just as a mother gives milk to her child, may our Motherland provide food-grains, fruits and vegetables to all of us.

गिरयस्ते पर्वता हिमवन्तोऽरण्यं ते पृथिवि स्योनमस्तु ।
बभ्रुं कृष्णां रोहिणीं विश्वरूपां ध्रुवां भूमिं पृथिवीमिन्द्रगुप्ताम् ।
अजीतोऽहतो अक्षतोऽध्यष्ठां पृथिवीमहम् ॥11॥

Girayaste parvatā himavanto'raṇyaṃ te pṛthivi syonamastu.
Babhruṃ kṛṣṇāṃ rohiṇīṃ viśvarūpāṃ dhruvāṃ bhūmiṃ pṛthivīmindraguptām.
Ajīto'hato akṣato'dhyaṣṭhāṃ pṛthivīmaham॥11॥

O beloved Motherland, your snow-clad mountains and forests bring happiness. May your mountains and forests always be free from enemies. Your fertile lands, abundant with plants and vegetation, provide nourishment to everyone. Beloved Motherland, we must protect you from harm and ensure you remain undefeated by enemies, so that we may live with great dignity.

यत्ते मध्यं पृथिवि यच्च नभ्यं यास्त ऊर्जस्तन्वः संबभूवुः ।
तासु नो धेह्यभि नः पवस्व माता भूमिः पुत्रो अहं पृथिव्याः पर्जन्यः पिता स उ नः पिपर्तु ॥12॥

Yatte madhyaṃ pṛthivi yacca nabhyaṃ yāsta ūrjastanvaḥ saṃbabhūvuḥ.
Tāsu no dhehyabhi naḥ pavasva mātā bhūmiḥ putro ahaṃ pṛthivyāḥ parjanyaḥ pitā sa u naḥ pipartu॥12॥

O beloved Motherland, we protect the resources both beneath and above you from enemies. Scholars, warriors and the wealthy unite in their efforts to safeguard you, and I will join their ranks to protect you. You are our beloved Motherland, and we are your children. The clouds regularly shower rain; they are like our father, nurturing us with their downpour.

यस्यां वेदिं परिगृह्णन्ति भूम्यां यस्यां'यज्ञं तन्वते विश्वकर्माणः ।
यस्यां'मीयन्ते स्वरवः पृथिव्यामूर्ध्वाः शुक्रा आहुत्याः पुरस्तात्।
सा नो भूमिर्वर्धयद्वर्धमाना ॥13॥

Yasyāṃ vediṃ parigṛhṇanti bhūmyāṃ yasyāṃ yajñaṃ tanvate viśvakarmāṇaḥ.
Yasyāṃ mīyante svaravaḥ pṛthivyāmūrdhvāḥ śukrā āhutyāḥ purastāt.
Sā no bhūmirvardhayadvardhamānā॥13॥

O beloved Motherland, continuous efforts for growth and development are underway across your lands, with courageous and inspiring discourses everywhere. May our Motherland serve as a catalyst for the progress and development of all its inhabitants.

यो नो द्वेषत्पृथिवि यः पृतन्याद्योऽभिदासान् मनसा यो वधेन ।
तं नो भूमे रन्धय पूर्वकृत्वरि ॥14॥

Yo no dveṣatpṛthivi yaḥ pṛtanyādyo'bhidāsān manasā yo vadhena.
Taṃ no bhūme randhaya pūrvakṛtvari॥14॥

O beloved Motherland, may those who hate and attack us with their armies, seeking to conquer and destroy us, and wishing to enslave us, be vanquished by your blessings.

त्वज्जातास्त्वयि चरन्ति मर्त्यास्त्वं बिभर्षि द्विपदस्त्वं चतुष्पदः ।
तवेमे पृथिवि पञ्च मानवा येभ्यो ज्योतिरमृतं मर्त्येभ्य उद्यन्त्सूर्यो'रश्मिभिरातनोति ॥15॥

Tvajjātāstvayi caranti martyāstvaṃ bibharṣi dvipadastvaṃ catuṣpadaḥ.
Taveme pṛthivi pañca mānavā yebhyo jyotiramṛtaṃ martyebhya udyantsūryo raśmibhirātanoti॥15॥

O beloved Motherland, we are born on you and are dependent upon you. You provide sustenance and nourishment for all animals, birds, human beings and every other living creature. Just as the sun spreads its rays everywhere, we too, as learned people, warriors, entrepreneurs, farmers and artisans, are always ready to serve.

ता नः प्रजाः सं दुह्रतां समग्रा वाचो मधु पृथिवि धेहि मह्यम् ॥16॥

Tā naḥ prajāḥ saṃ duhratāṃ samagrā vāco madhu pṛthivi dhehi mahyam॥16॥

O beloved Motherland, as your children, we should communicate with each other amiably. May our Motherland bless us and give us the strength to interact with love and affection towards one another.

विश्वस्वं मातरमोषधीनां ध्रुवां भूमिं पृथिवीं धर्मणा धृताम् ।
शिवां स्योनामनु चरेम विश्वहा ॥17॥

Viśvasvaṃ mātaramoṣadhīnāṃ dhruvāṃ bhūmiṃ pṛthivīṃ dharmaṇā dhṛtām.
Śivāṃ syonāmanu carema viśvahā॥17॥

O beloved Motherland, just as herbs, creepers, vegetation, trees and plants grow tall, wide, strong and stable, the people nurture and protect them with truth, knowledge, valour and compassion. The Motherland provides us with all resources and happiness. May the Motherland bless us so that we may all serve her.

महत्सधस्थं महती बभूविथ महान् वेग एजथुर्वेपथुष्टे ।
महांस्त्वेन्द्रो रक्षत्यप्रमादम् ।
सा नो भूमे प्र रोचय हिरण्यस्येव संदृशि मा नो द्विक्षत कश्चन ॥18॥

Mahatsadhasthaṃ mahatī babhūvitha mahān vega ejathurvepathuṣṭe.
Mahāṃstvendro rakṣatyapramādam.
Sā no bhūme pra rocaya hiraṇyasyeva saṃdṛśi mā no dvikṣata kaścana॥18॥

O beloved Motherland, the earth provides space for all of us to live together, and her vast expanse is sufficient for everyone. The earth moves swiftly across the sky. Wise and valiant warriors, endowed with courage and alertness, protect you and are capable of destroying any enemy. You shine like gold; may you bless us so that we all may shine as well, and may there be no enmity among us.

अग्निर्भूम्यामोषधीष्वग्निमापो बिभ्रत्यग्निरश्मसु ।
अग्निरन्तः पुरुषेषु गोष्वश्वेष्वग्नयः ॥19॥

Agnirbhūmyāmoṣadhīṣvagnimāpo bibhratyagniraśmasu.
Agnirantaḥ puruṣeṣu goṣvaśveṣvagnayaḥ॥19॥

O beloved Motherland, there is fire in the earth, fire in the herbs and trees, fire in the waters, fire in the stones, fire in humans, fire in cows and fire in horses. Various beings shine with this fire. May our Motherland bless us all so that we may be strong and shine with this fire.

अग्निर्दिव आ तपत्यग्नेर्देवस्योर्वन्तरिक्षम् ।
अग्निं मर्तास इन्धते हव्यवाहं घृतप्रियम् ॥20॥

Agnirdiva ā tapatyagnerdevasyorvantarikṣam.
Agniṃ martāsa indhate havyavāhaṃ ghṛtapriyam॥20॥
Agnirdiva a tapatyagnerdevasyorvantariksam. Agnim martdsa indhate havyavdham ghrtapriyam.

O beloved Motherland, a great fiery sun in the sky spreads light everywhere. The same fire exists in different forms, like the ghee offered in the yajna that is consumed by the flames. May our Motherland bless us so that we too may perform the yajna in the sacred fire.

अग्निवासाः पृथिव्यसितज्ञूस्त्विषीमन्तं संशितं मा कृणोतु ॥21॥

Agnivāsāḥ pṛthivyasitajñūstviṣīmantaṃ saṃśitaṃ mā kṛṇotu॥21॥

O beloved Motherland, the earth is filled with fire and shrouded in darkness. May you bless us, cultivate our knowledge and enhance our reputation and renown.

भूम्यां देवेभ्यो ददति यज्ञं हव्यमरंकृतम् ।
भूम्यां मनुष्या जीवन्ति स्वधयान्नेन मर्त्याः ।
सा नो भूमिः प्राणमायुर्दधातु जरदष्टिं मा पृथिवी कृणोतु ॥22॥

Bhūmyāṃ devebhyo dadati yajñaṃ havyamaraṃkṛtam.
Bhūmyāṃ manuṣyā jīvanti svadhayānnena martyāḥ.
Sā no bhūmiḥ prāṇamāyurdadhātu jaradaṣṭiṃ mā pṛthivī kṛṇotu॥22॥

O beloved Motherland, people offer the finest quality offerings in yajna (sacred rituals), resulting in the earth producing abundant, high-quality food grains. People thrive and find joy in consuming these grains. May the Motherland bless us with strength and longevity.

यस्ते गन्धः पृथिवि संबभूव यं बिभ्रत्योषधयो यमापः ।
यं गन्धर्वा अप्सरसश्च भेजिरे तेन मा सुरभिं कृणु मा नो द्विक्षत कश्चन ॥23॥

Yaste gandhaḥ pṛthivi saṃbabhūva yaṃ
bibhratyoṣadhayo yamāpaḥ.
Yaṃ gandharvā apsarasaśca bhejire tena mā
surabhiṃ kṛṇu mā no dvikṣata kaścana॥23॥

O beloved Motherland, from your earth's sweet odour, herbs and vegetation flourish. Water absorbs and retains this fragrance, while sunrays enhance it. May our Motherland bless us so that we, too, may be imbued with this fragrance, and may we refrain from harbouring enmity among ourselves, choosing instead to live in friendship.

यस्ते गन्धः पुष्करमाविवेश यं संजभ्रुः सूर्याया विवाहे ।
अमर्त्याः पृथिवि गन्धमग्रे तेन मा सुरभिं कृणु मा नो द्विक्षत कश्चन ॥24॥॥

Yaste gandhaḥ puṣkaramāviveśa yaṃ saṃjabhruḥ sūryāyā vivāhe.
Amartyāḥ pṛthivi gandhamagre tena mā surabhiṃ kṛṇu mā no
dvikṣata kaścana॥24॥

O beloved Motherland, the lotus absorbs your essence. In the morning, the air absorbs that fragrance. May our Motherland bless us with that fragrance, and may we not harbour enmity among ourselves but instead live in friendship.

यस्ते गन्धः पुरुषेषु स्त्रीषु पुंसु भगो रुचिः ।
यो अश्वेषु वीरेषु यो मृगेषूत हस्तिषु ।
कन्यायां वर्चो यद्भूमे तेनास्माँ अपि सं सृज मा नो द्विक्षत कश्चन ॥25॥

Yaste gandhaḥ puruṣeṣu strīṣu puṃsu bhago ruciḥ.
Yo aśveṣu vīreṣu yo mṛgeṣūta hastiṣu.
Kanyāyāṃ varco yadbhūme tenāsmāṃ api saṃ sṛja
|mā no dvikṣata kaścana॥25॥

O beloved Motherland, the essence of your soil nourishes courageous warriors, ordinary people, women, Brahmacharis, Brahmacharinis, horses, animals, elephants and all others, infused with strength, radiance and fragrance. May our Motherland bless us and unite us with this essence. May we live in harmony and avoid harbouring enmity towards one another.

शिला भूमिरश्मा पांसुः सा भूमिः संधृता धृता ।
तस्यै हिरण्यवक्षसे पृथिव्या अकरं नमः ॥26॥

Śilā bhūmiraśmā pāṃsuḥ sā bhūmiḥ saṃdhṛtā dhṛtā.
Tasyai hiraṇyavakṣase pṛthivyā akaraṃ namaḥ॥26॥

O beloved Motherland, your soil is abundant with stones, mountains and mines rich in gold and other precious resources. May our Motherland bestow upon us knowledge, strength and valour, ensuring the protection of your sacred land.

यस्यां वृक्षा वानस्पत्या ध्रुवास्तिष्ठन्ति विश्वहा ।
पृथिवीं विश्वधायसं धृतामच्छावदामसि ॥27॥

Yasyāṃ vṛkṣā vānaspatyā dhruvāstiṣṭhanti viśvahā.
Pṛthivīṃ viśvadhāyasaṃ dhṛtāmacchāvadāmasi॥27॥

O beloved Motherland, may the trees, plants and vegetation always grow and flourish upon your earth, upholding all the noble qualities you possess. May our Motherland bless us as we sing your glory.

उदीराणा उतासीनास्तिष्ठन्तः प्रक्रामन्तः ।
पद्भ्यां दक्षिणसव्याभ्यां मा व्यथिष्महि भूम्याम् ॥28॥

Udīrāṇā utāsīnāstiṣṭhantaḥ prakrāmantaḥ.
Padbhyāṃ dakṣiṇasavyābhyāṃ mā vyathiṣmahi bhūmyām॥28॥

O beloved Motherland, whether sitting or standing, moving around or walking in every direction, may our Motherland bless us so that we do no harm to anyone on this earth.

विमृग्वरीं पृथिवीमा वदामि क्षमां भूमिं ब्रह्मणा वावृधानाम् ।
ऊर्जं पुष्टं बिभ्रतीमन्नभागं घृतं त्वाभि नि षीदेम भूमे ॥29॥

Vimṛgvarīṃ pṛthivīmā vadāmi kṣamāṃ bhūmiṃ brahmaṇā vāvṛdhānām.
Ūrjaṃ puṣṭaṃ bibhratīmannabhāgaṃ ghṛtaṃ tvābhi ni ṣīdema bhūme॥29॥

O beloved Motherland, your sacred earth is upheld by the Almighty. Your land produces all the materials necessary for nourishment and strength, such as food grains and ghee. Your soil is habitable for all living beings. May our Motherland bless us, and may we find refuge in you.

शुद्धा न आपस्तन्वे क्षरन्तु यो नः सेदुरप्रिये तं नि दध्मः ।
पवित्रेण पृथिवि मोत्पुनामि ॥30॥

Śuddhā na āpastanve kṣarantu yo naḥ sedurapriye taṃ ni dadhmaḥ.
Pavitreṇa pṛthivi motpunāmi॥30॥

O beloved Motherland, upon your soil, pure waters flow for our purification. May you separate us from those who seek to harm us, so that we may treat them accordingly. May our Motherland bless us that we may flourish in all our endeavours.

यास्ते प्राचीः प्रदिशो या उदीचीर्यास्ते भूमे अधराद्याश्च पश्चात्।
स्योनास्ता मह्यं चरते भवन्तु मा नि पप्तं भुवने शिश्रियाणः ॥31॥

Yāste prācīḥ pradiśo yā udīcīryāste bhūme adharādyāśca paścāt.
Syonāstā mahyaṃ carate bhavantu mā ni paptaṃ bhuvane śiśriyāṇaḥ॥31॥

O beloved Motherland, in all corners of your vast expanse—east, west, north, south and their every nuanced direction—reside people who are devoted to your welfare. May our Motherland bless us, ensuring that we never falter from our standing. Wherever we dwell, let us strive for your prosperity and goodwill.

मा नः पश्चान् मा पुरस्तान्नुदिष्ठा मोत्तरादधरादुत ।
स्वस्ति भूमे नो भव मा विदन् परिपन्थिनो वरीयो यावया वधम् ॥32॥

Mā naḥ paścān mā purastānnudiṣṭhā mottarādadharāduta.
Svasti bhūme no bhava mā vidan paripanthino varīyo yāvayā vadham॥32॥

O beloved Motherland, no one from the north, south, east or west can defeat us. We shall always emerge victorious, with our enemies remaining unaware of our strategies. May our Motherland bless us, and may our best warriors always vanquish our foes.

यावत्तेऽभि विपश्यामि भूमे सूर्येण मेदिना ।
तावन् मे चक्षुर्मा मेष्टोत्तरामुत्तरां समाम् ॥33॥

Yāvatte'bhi vipaśyāmi bhūme sūryeṇa medinā.
Tāvan me cakṣurmā meṣṭottarāmuttarāṃ samām॥33॥

O beloved Motherland, with the guidance of wisdom and light, we shall regard and care for you diligently. May Motherland bless us, and may we continue to serve and protect you with our wisdom and senses for as long as they endure.

यच्छयानः पर्यावर्ते दक्षिणं सव्यमभि भूमे पार्श्वम् । उत्तानास्त्वा प्रतीचीं यत्पृष्टीभिरधिशेमहे ।
मा हिंसीस्तत्र नो भूमे सर्वस्य प्रतिशीवरि ॥34॥

yacchayānaḥ paryāvarte dakṣiṇaṃ savyamabhi bhūme pārśvam.
uttānāstvā pratīcīṃ yatpṛṣṭībhiradhiśemahe.
Mā hiṃsīstatra no bhūme sarvasya pratiśīvari॥34॥

O beloved Motherland, we are all devoted to you, and wherever we go to rest—left, right, up or down—please give us refuge. May our Motherland bless us, and may no one ever destroy us.

यत्ते भूमे विखनामि क्षिप्रं तदपि रोहतु ।
मा ते मर्म विमृग्वरि मा ते हृदयमर्पितम्॥35॥

Yatte bhūme vikhanāmi kṣipraṃ tadapi rohatu.
Mā te marma vimṛgvari mā te hṛdayamarpitam॥35॥

O beloved Motherland, when we till your soil and plant seeds, may they grow quickly. We should be careful not to harm you or cause you pain while tilling. May you, our Motherland, bless us, your devoted children, so that we may always be happy and free from sorrow.

ग्रीष्मस्ते भूमे वर्षाणि शरद्धेमन्तः शिशिरो वसन्तः ।
ऋतवस्ते विहिता हायनीरहोरात्रे पृथिवि नो दुहाताम् ॥36॥

Grīṣmaste bhūme varṣāṇi śaraddhemantaḥ śiśiro vasantaḥ.
Ṛtavaste vihitā hāyanīrahorātre pṛthivi no duhātām॥36॥

O beloved Motherland, within you exist six seasons: summer, monsoon, autumn, pre-winter winter and spring. May our Motherland abundantly bless us with grains, food, fruits and vegetables throughout all these seasons, and may their days and nights bring us joy and comfort.

यापं सर्पं विजमाना विमृग्वरी यस्यामासन्न अग्नयो ये अप्स्वन्तः ।
परा दस्यून् ददती देवपीयून् इन्द्रं वृणाना पृथिवी न वृत्रं शक्राय दध्रे वृषभाय वृष्णे ॥37॥

Yāpa sarpaṃ vijamānā vimṛgvarī yasyāmāsanna
agnayo ye apsvantaḥ.
Parā dasyūn dadatī devapīyūn indraṃ vṛṇānā pṛthivī na vṛtraṃ
śakrāya dadhre vṛṣabhāya vṛṣṇe॥37॥

O beloved Motherland, your soil is abundant with treasures; the more we search, the more valuable things we discover. In your skies and clouds, there is a fire that can destroy evil. Bless us, O Motherland, and accept wise warriors who can defeat our enemies.

यस्यां सदोहविर्धाने यूपो यस्यां निमीयते ।
ब्रह्माणो यस्यामर्चन्त्यृग्भिः साम्ना यजुर्विदः। युज्यन्ते यस्यामृत्विजः सोममिन्द्राय
पातवे ॥38॥

Yasyāṃ sadohavirdhāne yūpo yasyāṃ nimīyate.
Brahmāṇo yasyāmarcantyṛgbhiḥ sāmnā yajurvidaḥ. yujyante
yasyāmṛtvijaḥ somamindrāya pātave॥38॥

O beloved Motherland, where learned and wise priests continuously perform yajna with Vedic mantras, our Motherland is blessed and sacred.

यस्यां पूर्वे भूतकृत ऋषयो गा उदानृचुः ।
सप्त सत्रेण वेधसो यज्ञेन तपसा सह ॥39॥

Yasyāṃ pūrve bhūtakṛta ṛṣayo gā udānṛcuḥ.
Sapta satreṇa vedhaso yajñena tapasā saha॥39॥

O beloved Motherland, in your soil, extraordinary individuals have been born who protect the good people of society and perform great deeds. May the Motherland bless us so that we all may sing her praises.

सा नो भूमिरा दिशतु यद्धनं कामयामहे ।
भगो अनुप्रयुङ्क्तामिन्द्र एतु पुरोगवः ॥40॥

Sā no bhūmirā diśatu yaddhanaṃ kāmayāmahe.
Bhago anuprayuṅktāmindra etu purogavaḥ॥40॥

O beloved Motherland, you provide us with all the wealth and prosperity we seek. Prosperous people support the warrior with their wealth. May our Motherland bless us, and may our warriors stand at the forefront to defeat the enemy.

यस्यां गायन्ति नृत्यन्ति भूम्यां मर्त्या व्यैलबाः ।
युध्यन्ते यस्यामाक्रन्दो यस्यां वदति दुन्दुभिः ।
सा नो भूमिः प्र णुदतां सपत्नान् असपत्नं मा पृथिवी कृणोतु ॥41॥

Yasyāṃ gāyanti nṛtyanti bhūmyāṃ martyā vyailabāḥ.
Yudhyante yasyāmākrando yasyāṃ vadati dundubhiḥ.
Sā no bhūmiḥ pra ṇudatāṃ sapatnān asapatnaṃ
mā pṛthivī kṛṇotu॥41॥

O beloved Motherland, in your embrace, people sing, dance and inspired warriors fight to protect the nation; where the thundering hooves and the beating of war drums sound loudly, we must defeat our enemies and drive them away. May the Motherland bless us and grant us freedom from our foes.

यस्यामन्नं व्रीहियवौ यस्या इमाः पञ्च कृष्टयः ।
भूम्यै पर्जन्यपत्न्यै नमोऽस्तु वर्षमेदसे ॥42॥

Yasyāmannaṃ vrīhiyavau yasyā imāḥ pañca kṛṣṭayaḥ.
Bhūmyai parjanyapatnyai namo’stu varṣamedase॥42॥

O beloved Motherland, you produce rice, wheat, barley and other grains abundantly on your soil during the monsoon season, nourishing everyone. Wise and learned scholars, warriors, entrepreneurs, farmers and artisans live together in harmony. We ought to pay homage to our Motherland.

यस्याः पुरो देवकृताः क्षेत्रे यस्या विकुर्वते ।
प्रजापतिः पृथिवीं विश्वगर्भामाशामाशां रण्यां नः कृणोतु ॥43॥

Yasyāḥ puro devakṛtāḥ kṣetre yasyā vikurvate.
Prajāpatiḥ pṛthivīṃ viśvagarbhāmāśāmāśāṃ
raṇyāṃ naḥ kṛṇotu॥43॥

O beloved Motherland, in your provinces, many cities have been established, populated and settled. People are engaged in various types of industry, trade and commerce on your soil. Everything is produced within your borders. May our Motherland bless us, and may your land be blessed and prosperous from every side.

निधिं बिभ्रती बहुधा गुहा वसु मणिं हिरण्यं पृथिवी ददातु मे ।
वसूनि नो वसुदा रासमाना देवी दधातु सुमनस्यमाना ॥44॥

Nidhiṃ bibhratī bahudhā guhā vasu maṇiṃ
hiraṇyaṃ pṛthivī dadātu me.
Vasūni no vasudā rāsamānā devī dadhātu sumanasyamānā॥44॥

O beloved Motherland, your soil has yielded abundant riches, from precious stones to metals. May our Motherland bless us and grant us prosperity abundantly.

जनं बिभ्रती बहुधा विवाचसं नानाधर्माणं पृथिवी यथौकसम् ।
सहस्रं धारा द्रविणस्य मे दुहां ध्रुवेव धेनुरनपस्फुरन्ती ॥45॥

Janaṃ bibhratī bahudhā vivācasaṃ nānādharmāṇaṃ
pṛthivī yathaukasam.
Sahasraṃ dhārā draviṇasya me duhāṃ dhruveva
dhenuranapasphurantī॥45॥

O beloved Motherland, upon your soil, people speak different languages and follow diverse philosophical schools, yet they live together under your embrace. O indestructible Motherland, like a cow, you provide us with myriad forms of prosperity and abundance.

यस्ते सर्पो वृश्चिकस्तृष्टदंश्मा हेमन्तजब्धो भृमलो गुहा शये ।
क्रिमिर्जिन्वत्पृथिवि यद्यदेजति प्रावृषि तन्नः सर्पन् मोप सृपद् यच्छिवं तेन नो मृड ॥46॥

Yaste sarpo vṛścikastṛṣṭadaṃśmā hemantajabdho
bhṛmalo guhā śaye.
Krimirjinvatpṛthivi yadyadejati prāvṛṣi tannaḥ sarpan mopa sṛpad
yacchivaṃ tena no mṛḍa॥46॥

O beloved Motherland, on your soil during the wet season, snakes, scorpions and various types of poisonous insects and reptiles are born and emerge, whose bites are harmful and venomous. May our Motherland bless us so that these creatures do not harm us, and may you bring us joy and comfort.

ये ते पन्थानो बहवो जनायना रथस्य वर्त्मानसश्च यातवे ।
यैः संचरन्त्युभये भद्रपापास्तं पन्थानं जयेमानमित्रमतस्करं यच्छिवं तेन नो मृड ॥47॥

Ye te panthāno bahavo janāyanā rathasya vartmānasaśca yātave.
Yaiḥ saṃcarantyubhaye bhadrapāpāstaṃ panthānaṃ
jayemānamitramataskaraṃ yacchivaṃ tena no mṛḍa॥47॥

O beloved Motherland, upon your soil and along your diverse pathways, both good and bad individuals traverse, while vehicles move, and food grains are transported. It is imperative that these pathways remain safe and secure from enemies, robbers, looters, smugglers and thieves. May our Motherland bestow upon us its blessings, ensuring our safety, victory, joy, and comfort.

मल्वं बिभ्रती गुरुभृद्भद्रपापस्य निधनं तितिक्षुः ।
वराहेण पृथिवी संविदाना सूकराय वि जिहीते मृगाय ॥48॥

Malvaṃ bibhratī gurubhṛdbhadrapāpasya nidhanaṃ titikṣuḥ.
Varāheṇa pṛthivī saṃvidānā sūkarāya vi jihīte mṛgāya॥48॥

O beloved Motherland, you attract heavy materials towards you, bearing both good and bad people. Despite this, you provide abundant rain and pure water. You orbit the sun, whose rays purify the impure.

ये त आ<u>र</u>ण्याः <u>प</u>शवो <u>मृ</u>गा वने <u>हि</u>ताः <u>सिं</u>हा <u>व्या</u>घ्राः पु<u>रु</u>षा<u>द</u>श्चरन्ति ।
<u>उ</u>लं वृकं पृथिवि दुच्छुनामि<u>त</u> <u>ऋ</u>क्षीकां रक्षो अप बाध<u>या</u>स्मत्॥49॥

Ye ta āraṇyāḥ paśavo mṛgā vane hitāḥ siṃhā vyāghrāḥ puruṣādaścaranti.
Ulaṃ vṛkaṃ pṛthivi ducchunāmita ṛkṣīkāṃ rakṣo apa bādhayāsmat॥49॥

O beloved Motherland, in your forests roam lions, tigers, wolves, wild dogs, bears and other carnivorous quadrupeds. May our Motherland protect us from these wild animals.

ये गन्<u>ध</u>र्वा अ<u>प्स</u>र<u>सो</u> ये <u>चा</u>रायाः कि<u>मी</u>दिनः ।
<u>पिशा</u>चान्त्स<u>र्वा</u> रक्षां<u>सि</u> ता<u>न्</u> अस्मद्भूमे यावय ॥50॥

Ye gandharvā apsaraso ye cārāyāḥ kimīdinaḥ.
Piśācāntsarvā rakṣāṃsi tān asmadbhūme yāvaya॥50॥

O beloved Motherland, please protect us from the violent and the lazy, and those who unjustly seize wealth from others. Shield us from the evil in our midst and keep them far from our shores. May our Motherland safeguard us from these threats and preserve our peace and prosperity.

यां <u>द्वि</u>पादः <u>प</u>क्षिणः <u>सं</u>पतन्ति <u>हं</u>साः सु<u>प</u>र्णाः श<u>कु</u>ना वयांसि ।
य<u>स्यां</u> वातो मा<u>त</u>रिश्वेय<u>ते</u> रजांसि <u>कृ</u>ण्वं<u>श्च्या</u>वर्यश्च <u>वृ</u>क्षान् ।
वातस्य <u>प्र</u>वा<u>मु</u>पवामनु वा<u>त्य</u>र्चिः ॥51॥

yāṃ dvipādaḥ pakṣiṇaḥ saṃpatanti haṃsāḥ suparṇāḥ śakunā vayāṃsi.
yasyāṃ vāto mātariśveyate rajāṃsi kṛṇvaṃścyāvayaṃśca vṛkṣān.
vātasya pravāmupavāmanu vātyarciḥ॥51॥

O beloved Motherland, where swans and eagle-like birds roam joyfully in your skies, and powerful winds blow, carrying dust and uprooting plants in our sacred land.

यस्यां कृष्णम<u>रु</u>णं <u>च</u> संहिते अहो<u>रा</u>त्रे विहि<u>ते</u> भू<u>म्या</u>मधि ।
<u>वर्षे</u>ण भूमिः पृ<u>थि</u>वी <u>वृ</u>तावृ<u>ता</u> सा नो दधातु <u>भ</u>द्रया <u>प्रि</u>ये धामनिधामनि ॥52॥

Yasyāṃ kṛṣṇamaruṇaṃ ca saṃhite ahorātre vihite bhūmyāmadhi.
Varṣeṇa bhūmiḥ pṛthivī vṛtāvṛtā sā no dadhātu bhadrayā priye dhāmanidhāmani॥52॥

O beloved Motherland, may you shine both day and night upon your land. May your vast expanse be covered with the blessings of rain, ensuring prosperity and happiness for all of us.

द्यौश्च म इदं पृथिवी चान्तरिक्षं च मे व्यचः ।
अग्निः सूर्य आपो मेधां विश्वे देवाश्च सं ददुः ॥53॥

Dyauśca ma idaṃ pṛthivī cāntarikṣaṃ ca me vyacaḥ.
Agniḥ sūrya āpo medhāṃ viśve devāśca saṃ daduḥ॥53॥

O beloved Motherland, between your earth and the vast sky above, the radiant sun illuminates everything. May our Motherland bless us with learned and wise people who are victorious, granting us the gifts of memory, strength, wisdom and radiance.

अहमस्मि सहमान उत्तरो नाम भूम्याम् ।
अभीषाडस्मि विश्वाषाडाशामाशां विषासहिः ॥54॥

Ahamasmi sahamāna uttaro nāma bhūmyām.
Abhīṣāḍasmi viśvāṣāḍāśāmāśāṃ viṣāsahiḥ॥54॥

O beloved Motherland, we stand ready to endure all hardships and joys, to protect and defend you. We are prepared to face any suffering and pain. May our Motherland bless us as we strive to utterly defeat our enemies.

अदो यद्देवि प्रथमाना पुरस्ताद्देवैरुक्ता व्यसर्पो महित्वम् ।
आ त्वा सुभूतमविशत्तदानीमकल्पयथाः प्रदिशश्चतस्रः॥55॥

Ado yaddevi prathamānā purastāddevairuktā vyasarpo mahitvam.
Ā tvā subhūtamaviśattadānīmakalpayathāḥ pradiśaścatastraḥ॥55॥

O beloved Motherland, in the past, learned, wise and victorious people have sung praises for you. May your name and fame continue to spread in all directions, blessing us as they have in times gone by.

ये ग्रामा यदरण्यं याः सभा अधि भूम्याम् ।
ये संग्रामाः समितयस्तेषु चारु वदेम ते ॥56॥

Ye grāmā yadaraṇyaṃ yāḥ sabhā adhi bhūmyām.
Ye saṃgrāmāḥ samitayasteṣu cāru vadema te॥56॥

O beloved Motherland, in your villages, forests, cities, councils and assemblies of war, we should discuss ways to improve rather than harm you, and we should all sing your praises.

अश्वं इव रजो दुधुवे वि तान् जनान् य आक्षियन् पृथिवीं यादजायत ।
मन्द्राग्रेत्वरी भुवनस्य गोपा वनस्पतीनां गृभिरोषधीनाम् ॥57॥

Aśva iva rajo dudhuve vi tān janān ya ākṣiyan pṛthivīṃ yādajāyata.
Mandrāgretvarī bhuvanasya gopā vanaspatīnāṃ
gṛbhiroṣadhīnām॥57॥

O beloved Motherland, anyone who comes and unjustly settles on your land should be removed like dust from a horse's hooves. You should nurture herbs, plants and vegetation to protect the world. May our Motherland bless all patriots so that we can defend and care for you.

यद्वदामि मधुमत्तद्वदामि यदीक्षे तद्वनन्ति मा ।
त्विषीमान् अस्मि जूतिमान् अवान्यान् हन्मि दोधतः ॥58॥॥

Yadvadāmi madhumattadvadāmi yadīkṣe tadvananti mā.
Tviṣīmān asmi jūtimān avānyān hanmi dodhataḥ॥58॥

O beloved Motherland, let us always speak sweetly and in ways that benefit our nation. Let everything we envision be for the good of our country. May all our actions be dedicated to you, Motherland. Bless us with wisdom, courage and strength. If our enemies threaten you, let us stand ready to defend and protect you.

शन्तिवा सुरभिः स्योना कीलालोध्नी पयस्वती ।
भूमिरधि ब्रवीतु मे पृथिवी पयसा सह ॥59॥

Śantivā surabhiḥ syonā kīlālodhnī payasvatī.
Bhūmiradhi bravītu me pṛthivī payasā saha॥59॥

O beloved Motherland, you provide us with peace, happiness, food, water and all the resources for enjoyment and prosperity. May our Motherland bless and protect us.

यामन्वैच्छद्धविषा विश्वकर्मान्तरर्णवे रजसि प्रविष्टाम् ।
भुजिष्यं पात्रं निहितं गुहा यदाविर्भोगे'अभवन् मातृमद्भ्यः ॥60॥

Yāmanvaicchaddhaviṣā viśvakarmāntararṇave rajasi praviṣṭām.
Bhujiṣyaṃ pātraṃ nihitaṃ guhā yadāvirbhoge abhavan mātṛmadbhyaḥ॥60॥

O beloved Motherland, your land was divinely created, where virtuous and dedicated people have tirelessly served. Through their hard work, they have ensured survival and prosperity, producing everything needed for a thriving life.

त्वमस्यावपनी जनानामदितिः कामदुघा पप्रथाना ।
यत्त ऊनं तत्त आ पूरयाति प्रजापतिः प्रथमजा ऋतस्य ॥61॥

Tvamasyāvapanī janānāmaditiḥ kāmadughā paprathānā.
Yatta ūnaṃ tatta ā pūrayāti prajāpatiḥ prathamajā ṛtasya॥61॥

O beloved Motherland, you do not bring sorrow; instead, you provide all the necessary things that your land can produce. We pray to the Almighty that anything lacking in your land may be fulfilled by Him.

उपस्थास्ते अनमीवा अयक्ष्मा अस्मभ्यं सन्तु पृथिवि प्रसूताः ।
दीर्घं न आयुः प्रतिबुध्यमाना वयं तुभ्यं बलिहृतः स्याम ॥62॥

Upasthāste anamīvā ayakṣmā asmabhyaṃ santu pṛthivi prasūtāḥ.
Dīrghaṃ na āyuḥ pratibudhyamānā vayaṃ tubhyaṃ
balihṛtaḥ syāma॥62॥

O beloved Motherland, we are born of your soil. May we be healthy, strong, long-lived, learned and wise. For the sake of our Motherland, let us awaken and be ready to sacrifice our interests. May our Motherland bless us so that we are always prepared to sacrifice for you.

भूमे मातर्नि धेहि मा भद्रया सुप्रतिष्ठितम् ।
संविदाना दिवा कवे श्रियां मा धेहि भूत्याम् ॥63॥

Bhūme mātarni dhehi mā bhadrayā supratiṣṭhitam.
Saṃvidānā divā kave śriyāṃ mā dhehi bhūtyām॥63॥

O beloved Motherland, bless us and grant us wisdom so that we may always think diligently for you. May our Motherland bless us and bestow prosperity upon us from its abundant earth.

Notes

Introduction

1 Published by Gita Press Gorakhpur (37th Reprint).
2 Published by Gita Press Gorakhpur (14th Reprint).
3 Published by Chawkhamba Vidya Bhawan (5th Edition).
4 Published by Rishidevi Rooplal Kapoor Dharmarth Trust.
5 MBAPAnAP, Ch. 62.
6 MBShPRaDP, Ch.109.
7 MBAPAnAP, Ch. 62.

Chapter 1: Prosperity for All

1 KS 2.
2 MBShPApDP, Ch. 167.
3 MBVPArAP, Ch. 33.
4 KA Adh. 1, Prak. 3, Ch. 6.
5 MBShPRaDP, Ch. 109.
6 MBUPBhYP, Ch. 90.
7 MBUPBhYP, Ch. 137.
8 KS.
9 MS, Ch. 6.
10 KA, Adh. 1, Prak. 3, Ch. 6.
11 Hitopadesha, Prakaran 1.
12 MBShPRaDP, Ch. 90.
13 MBShPRaDP, Ch. 130.
14 MBVPArAP, Ch. 33.
15 MBShPRaDP, Ch. 8.
16 MBShPApDP, Ch. 167.
17 MBUPBhYP, Ch. 72.
18 MBShPRaDP, Ch. 15.
19 MBVPArAP, Ch. 33.
20 MBVPArAP, Ch. 33.
21 MBShPApDP, Ch. 167.
22 MBShPRaDP, Ch. 8.
23 MBShPRaDP, Ch. 8.

24 MBShPRaDP, Ch. 8.
25 MBShPRaDP, Ch. 8.
26 MBShPRaDP, Ch. 8.
27 MBShPApDP, Ch. 167.
28 MBShPApDP, Ch. 167.
29 AV, Kanda 3, Sukta 24.
30 MBShPMoDP, Ch. 228.
31 MBShPMoDP, Ch. 228.
32 MBVPArAP, Ch. 33.
33 MBShPRaDP, Ch. 120.
34 MBAnPDaDP, Ch. 6.
35 MBAnPDaDP, Ch. 11.
36 MBAnPDaDP, Ch. 11.
37 MBVPMaSP, Ch. 193.
38 MBUPBhYP, Ch. 172.
39 MBUPBhYP, Ch. 172.
40 KS.
41 MBShPRaDP, Ch. 8.
42 MBAPLoSP, Ch. 5.
43 KA, Adh. 2, Prak. 40, Ch. 24.
44 MBAPLoSP, Ch. 5.
45 MBAPLoSP, Ch. 5.
46 KA, Adh. 2, Prak. 17, Ch. 1.
47 MBSPLoSP, Ch. 5.
48 MBAnPDaDP, Ch 2.
49 MBAnPDaDP, Ch 2.
50 MBShPRaDP, Ch. 24.
51 YV, Ch. 16.
52 SS, Ch. 5.
53 MBVPRaOP, Ch. 283
54 MBShPRaDP, Ch. 130.
55 MBShPApDP, Ch. 133.
56 SS, Ch. 4. Prak.2
57 MBShPRaDP, Ch. 15.
58 MBShPRaDP, Ch. 8.
59 MBShPRaDP, Ch. 120.
60 MBShPRaDP, Ch. 87.
61 MBShPRaDP, Ch. 87.
62 MBSPLoSP, Ch. 5.

63 MBSPLoSP, Ch. 5.
64 MBSPLoSP, Ch. 5.
65 MBShPRaDP, Ch. 89.
66 KA, Adh. 2, Prak. 32, Ch. 16,
67 KA, Adh. 2, Prak. 37, Ch. 21,
68 MBShPRaDP, Ch. 89.
69 MBShPRaDP, Ch. 71.
70 MBShPRaDP, Ch. 69.
71 VRArK, C. 6.
72 KA, Adh. 2, Prak. 32, Ch. 16.
73 MBShPApDP, Ch. 135.
74 MBUPBhYP, Ch. 172.
75 MBUPBhYP, Ch. 172.
76 MBUPBhYP, Ch. 172.
77 VRBK, C. 5.
78 VRBK, C. 5.
79 VRBK, C. 5.
80 VRBK, C. 5.
81 VRBK, C.5.
82 VRBK, C.5.
83 VRBK, C.6.
84 The World Economy: A Millennial Perspective, Development Centre Studies, OECD Publishing Organization for Economic Cooperation and Development, Appendix B, p. 263.
85 Ibid.
86 R.C. Dutt, *The Economic History of India*, Publication Division, Ministry of Information and Broadcasting, Volume 1, p. 263. Fifth Reprint 2006.
87 Will Durant, *Case for India*, Simon and Schuster, New York, 1930, pp. 8–13.
88 Will Durant, *Case for India*, Simon and Schuster, New York, 1930, pp. 14–17.
89 Will Durant, *Case for India*, Simon and Schuster, New York, 1930, pp. 31–43.
90 R.C. Dutt, 'Preface to the First Edition', *The Economic History of India*, Publication Division, Ministry of Information and Broadcasting, Vol. 1, pp. XXIII-XXVI.
91 Will Durant, *Case for India*, Simon and Schuster, New York, 1930, p. 43.
92 R.C. Dutt, 'Preface to the First Edition', *The Economic History of India*, Publication Division, Ministry of Information and Broadcasting, Vol. 1, p. XX1.

93 R.C. Dutt, 'Preface to the First Edition', *The Economic History of India*, Publication Division, Ministry of Information and Broadcasting, Vol. 1, p. 285.

94 Indian Industrial Commission, set up by the British Government in 1916, member's note by Pandit Madan Mohan Malaviya. First published by the Superintendent of Government Printing, Calcutta, in 1918 (pp. 292-355). Republished by the Mahamana Malviya Mission, Banaras Hindu University Unit, Varanasi.

95 Ibid.

96 Ibid.

Chapter 2: Defeating Enemy, Defending Citizens

1 MBShPRaDP, Ch. 89/9.

2 MBAPSaP, Ch. 135.

3 SS, Ch. 4, Prak. 7.

4 MBShPRaDP, Ch. 130.

5 MBShPRaDP, Ch. 130.

6 SS, Ch. 4. Prak. 2.

7 MBShPApDP, Ch. 133.

8 MBShPRaDP, Ch. 99.

9 MBShPRaDP, Ch. 99.

10 MBShPRaDP, Ch. 78.

11 MBShPRaDP, Ch. 100.

12 MBSPLoSP, Ch. 5.

13 MBAPSaP, Ch. 139.

14 MBAPSaP, Ch. 139.

15 MBAPSaP, Ch. 139.

16 MBVPNaP, Ch. 52.

17 Kiratarjuniyam, C. 1.

18 MBVPArAP, Ch. 33.

19 VRAK, C. 5.

20 MBAPLoSP, Ch. 5.

21 MBAPLoSP, Ch. 5.

22 VRAK, C. 5.

23 MBShPRaDP, Ch. 85.

24 SS, Ch. 2

25 MBShPRaDP, Ch. 101.

26 MBShPRaDP, Ch. 101.

27 MBShPRaDP. Ch. 101.

28 MBShPRaDP. Ch. 101.
29 MBShPRaDP. Ch. 101.
30 MBShPRaDP. Ch. 101.
31 MBShPRaDP. Ch. 101.
32 MBShPRaDP. Ch. 101.
33 VRAK, C. 100.
34 MBAPLoSP, Ch. 5.
35 MBShPRaDP, Ch. 107.
36 MBSPLoSP, Ch. 5.
37 MBVPAaP, Ch. 175.
38 MBVPAaP, Ch. 175.
39 MBShPRaDP, Ch. 69.
40 MBShPRaDP, Ch. 100.
41 MBAPPaSP, Ch. 2.
42 MBAPPaSP, Ch. 2.
43 MBAPPaSP, Ch. 2.
44 MBAPPaSP, Ch. 2.
45 MBAPPaSP, Ch. 2.
46 MBAPPaSP, Ch. 2.
47 MBAPPaSP, Ch. 2.
48 MBAPPaSP, Ch. 2.
49 MBUPSeP, Ch. 19.
50 MBUPSeP, Ch. 19.
51 MBUPSeP, Ch. 19.
52 MBUPSeP, Ch. 19.
53 MBUPSeP, Ch. 19.
54 MBUPSeP, Ch. 19.
55 MBUPSeP, Ch. 19.
56 MBUPSeP, Ch. 19.
57 MBUPSeP, Ch. 19.
58 MBUPSeP, Ch. 19.
59 MBUPSeP, Ch. 19.
60 MBUPSeP, Ch. 19.
61 MBUPSeP, Ch. 19.
62 MBUPSeP, Ch. 19.
63 MBUPSeP, Ch. 19.
64 MBUPSeP, Ch. 19.
65 MBUPSeP, Ch. 19.
66 SS, Ch. 4, Prak. 7.

67 SS, Ch. 4, Prak. 7.
68 Ram Gopal Mishra, *Indian Resistance to Early Muslim Invaders Up to 1206 AD.*
69 Ibid.
70 Ibid.
71 Ibid.
72 Ibid.

Chapter 3: Quality Education for All

1 MBShPMoDP, Ch. 277/35.
2 MBShPMoDP, Ch. 277.
3 MBAnPDaDP, Ch. 145, GPGKP, P. 4948.
4 SS, Ch. 3.
5 MBUPPrP, Ch. 33.
6 Bhartruhari Nitishatkam.
7 MBAnPDaDP, Ch 145, GPGKP, P. 5955
8 MBAnPDaDP, Ch. 145. ,GPGKP, P. 5955
9 KA, Prak. 8, Ch. 3.
10 SS, Ch. 3.
11 MBShPRaDP, Ch. 120.
12 SS, Ch. 3.
13 SS, Ch. 3.
14 SS, Ch. 4, Prak. 3.
15 SS, Ch. 1.
16 MBUPPrP, Ch. 33.
17 MBAnPDaDP, GPGKP, P. 5956.
18 SS, Ch. 1.
19 SS, Ch. 1.
20 MBAPLoSP, Ch. 5.
21 Dharampal, *The Beautiful Tree: Indigenous Indian Education in the Eighteenth Century*, Biblia Impex, New Delhi, 1983. Also published in J.K. Bajaj and M.D. Srinivas (eds), *Dharampal Classics Series* Vol. 4, Centre for Policy Studies and Rashtrotthana Parishad, Bengaluru, 2021.
22 J.K. Bajaj and M.D. Srinivas (eds), *Dharampal Classics Series*, Vol. 4, Centre for Policy Studies and Rashtrotthana Parishad, Bengaluru, 2021, pp. 267–268.
23 Ibid., pp. 349–350.
24 Ibid., pp. 245–246.
25 Ibid., p. 350.

26 Ibid., p. 24.
27 J.K. Bajaj and M.D. Srinivas (eds), *Dharampal Classics Series*, Vol. 4, Centre for Policy Studies and Rashtrotthana Parishad, Bengaluru, 2021, pp. 182–184.
28 Ibid., pp. 183–184.
29 Ibid., p. 279.
30 J.K. Bajaj and M.D. Srinivas (eds), *Dharampal Classics Series*, Vol. 4, Centre for Policy Studies and Rashtrotthana Parishad, Bengaluru, 2021, p. 349.
31 Ibid., p. 357.

Chapter 4: Responsible Democracy

1 Abhigyan Shakuntalam, Act 5.
2 MBShPRaDP, Ch. 56.
3 MBShPRaDP, Ch. 56.
4 MBShPRaDP, Ch. 64.
5 MBShPRaDP, Ch. 64.
6 MBShPRaDP, Ch. 64.
7 MBShPRaDP, Ch. 64.
8 MBShPRaDP, Ch. 63.
9 MBShPRaDP, Ch. 63.
10 MBShPRaDP, Ch. 63.
11 MBShPRaDP, Ch. 63.
12 MBShPRaDP, Ch. 66.
13 MBShPRaDP, Ch. 58.
14 MBShPRaDP, Ch. 65.
15 MBShPRaDP, Ch. 66.
16 AV, Kanda 6, Sukta 64.
17 RV, Mandal 10, Sukta 191.
18 AV, Kanda 5, Sukta 19.
19 AV, Kanda 12, Sukta 1.
20 MBShPRaDP, Ch. 68.
21 MBShPRaDP, Ch. 77.
22 MBShPRaDP, Ch. 77.
23 MBAnPDaDP, Ch. 2.
24 MBShPRaDP, Ch. 68.
25 VRBK, C. 6.
26 VRBK, C. 6.
27 VRBK, C. 6.
28 VRBK, C. 6.

29 VRBK, C. 6.
30 VRBK, C. 6.
31 VRBK, C. 7.
32 MBDPAbVP, Ch. 59.
33 VRBK, C. 1.
34 VRBK, C. 1.
35 VRBK, C. 1.
36 VRBK, C. 1.
37 VRYK, C. 128.
38 VRYK, C. 128.
39 VRYK, C. 128.
40 VRYK, C. 128.
41 VRYK, C. 128.
42 VRBK, C. 100.
43 MBSPLoSP, Ch. 5.
44 MBAsPAshP, GKP.
45 MBAsPAshP, GKP.
46 MBAPSaP, Ch. 108.
47 MBAPSaP, Ch. 108.
48 MBAPSaP, Ch. 108.
49 MBAPSaP, Ch. 108.
50 MBAPSaP, Ch. 108.
51 MBAPSaP, Ch. 108.
52 MBAPSaP, Ch. 108.
53 MBAPSaP, Ch. 108.
54 MBAPSaP, Ch. 108.
55 MBAPSaP, Ch. 108.
56 MBAPSaP, Ch. 108.
57 MBAPSaP, Ch. 108.
58 MBAsPAshP, Ch. 14, GPGKP, P. 6129.
59 MBAsPAshP, Ch. 14, GPGKP, P. 6129.
60 MBShPRaDP, Ch. 59.
61 MBBPBhuP, Ch. 11.
62 MBBPBhuP, Ch. 11.
63 KA, Adh. 11, Praks. 160–161, Ch. 1.
64 MBShPRaDP, Ch. 107.
65 MBShPRaDP, Ch. 107.
66 MBShPRaDP, Ch. 107.
67 MBShPRaDP, Ch. 107.

68 MBShPRaDP, Ch. 107.
69 MBShPRaDP, Ch. 107.
70 MBShPRaDP, Ch. 107.
71 MBShPRaDP, Ch. 107.
72 MBShPRaDP, Ch. 107.
73 MBShPRaDP, Ch. 130.
74 SS, Ch. 2.
75 SS, Ch. 2.
76 SS, Ch. 4, Prak. 5.
77 MBAPAsP, Ch. 49.
78 MBAPAsP, Ch. 49.
79 KA, Adh. 1, Prak. 2, Ch. 2.
80 MBShPRaDP, Ch. 25.
81 MBShPRaDP, Ch. 24.
82 MBShPRaDP, Ch. 56.
83 MBShPRaDP, Ch. 56.
84 MBShPRaDP, Ch. 57.
85 MBUPBhYP, Ch. 129.
86 MBShPRaDP, Ch. 69.
87 MBShPRaDP, Ch. 69.
88 MBShPRaDP, Ch. 70.
89 MBShPRaDP, Ch. 70.
90 MBShPRaDP, Ch. 70.
91 MBShPRaDP, Ch. 70.
92 MBShPRaDP, Ch. 70.
93 MBShPRaDP, Ch. 70.
94 MBShPRaDP, Ch. 70.
95 MBShPRaDP, Ch. 70.
96 MBShPRaDP, Ch. 70.
97 MBShPRaDP, Ch. 70.
98 MBAnPDaDP, Ch. 145, GPGKP, P. 5949.
99 MBAnPDaDP, Ch. 145, GPGKP, P. 5954.
100 MBShPRaDP, Ch. 69.
101 MBShPRaDP, Ch. 69.
102 SS, Ch. 1.
103 MBAnPDaDP, Ch. 145, GPGKP, P. 5948.
104 SS, Ch. 1.
105 SS, Ch. 1.
106 MBShPRaDP, Ch. 83.

107 MBShPRaDP, Ch. 83.
108 MBShPRaDP, Ch. 83.
109 MBShPRaDP, Ch. 85.
110 MBShPRaDP, Ch. 118.
111 VRBK, C. 7.
112 VRBK, C. 7.
113 VRBK, C. 7.
114 VRBK, C. 7.
115 VRBK, C. 7.
116 VRBK, C. 7.
117 VRBK, C. 7.
118 VRBK, C. 100.
119 VRBK, C. 100.
120 MBShPRaDP, Ch. 83.
121 VRYK, C. 63.
122 VRYK, C. 63.
123 MBShPRaDP, Ch. 15.
124 MBShPRaDP, Ch. 121.
125 MBShPRaDP, Ch. 15.
126 MBShPRaDP, Ch. 15.
127 MBShPRaDP, Ch. 15.
128 MBShPRaDP, Ch. 59.
129 MBShPRaDP, Ch. 15.
130 MBShPRaDP, Ch. 15.
131 MBShPRaDP, Ch. 69.
132 MBShPRaDP, Ch. 69.
133 MBShPRaDP, Ch. 15.
134 MBShPApDP, Ch. 135.
135 VRAK, C. 100.
136 SS, Ch. 1.
137 KA, Adh. 2, Ch. 1.
138 KA, Adh. 2, Ch. 1.
139 MBAPAsP, Ch. 49.
140 MBShPRaDP, Ch. 59.
141 MBAnPDaDP, Ch. 61.
142 MBAnPDaDP, Ch. 61.
143 MBAPLoSP, Ch. 5.
144 VRAK, C. 100.
145 MBShPRaDP, Ch. 71.

146 MBShPRaDP, Ch. 122.
147 MBAPLoSP, Ch. 5.
148 MBAPLoSP, Ch. 5.
149 VRBK, C. 52.
150 SS, Ch. 2.
151 SS, Ch. 2.
152 SS, Ch. 2.
153 VRAK, C. 100.
154 MBShPRaDP, Ch. 58.
155 MBShPRaDP, Ch. 58.
156 MBAnPDaDP, Ch. 154.
157 SS, Ch. 1.
158 SS, Ch. 1.
159 MBShPRaDP, Ch. 130.
160 MBShPRaDP, Ch. 57.
161 MBShPRaDP, Ch. 69.
162 MBAnPDaDP, Ch. 61.
163 MBAnPDaDP, Ch. 154.
164 SS, Ch. 1.
165 SS, Ch. 2.
166 MBAnPDaDP, Ch. 61.
167 K.P. Jayaswal, *Hindu Polity*, Chaukambha Sanskrit Pratisthanam, Delhi 2005, pp. 12–13.
168 K.P. Jayaswal, *Hindu Polity*, Chaukambha Sanskrit Pratisthanam, Delhi, pp. 186–187.

Chapter 5: Highest Respect for Women

1 RV, 7/80/2.
2 Brihat Devta, Ch. 2, Shlokas 82–84.
3 MBAnPDaDP, Ch. 45.
4 MBAPArVP, Ch. 214.
5 MBSPDiVP, Ch. 31.
6 MBAPSaP, Ch. 74.
7 MBAPSaP, Ch. 74.
8 MBAPSaP, Ch. 74.
9 MBAPSaP, Ch. 74.
10 MBAPSaP, Ch. 74.
11 MBAPSaP, Ch. 74.
12 MBAPSaP, Ch. 74.

13 MBAPBaP, Ch. 156.
14 MBViPPaPP, Ch. 3.
15 MBVPArAP, Ch. 27.
16 MBSPAaDP, Ch. 165.
17 KS.
18 MBShPMoDP, Ch. 190.
19 MBVPKuP, Ch. 307.
20 MBAnPDaDP, Ch. 20.
21 MBAnPDaDP, Ch. 20.
22 MBAnPDaDP, Ch. 20.
23 MBShPRaDP, Ch. 68.
24 VRAK, C. 61.
25 MBAPSaP, Ch. 110.
26 MBVPArAP, Ch. 12.
27 MBVPArAP, Ch. 12.
28 MBVPNaP, Ch. 69.
29 KA, Adh. 2, Prak. 17, Ch. 1.
30 MBAPBaP, Ch. 157.
31 MBShPAaDP, Ch. 135.
32 MBSPAaDP, Ch. 135.
33 MBAPArVP, Ch. 216.
34 MBAnPDaDP, Ch. 154, GPGKP, P. 5954
35 MBVPMaSP, Ch. 206.
36 VRAK, C. 78.
37 MBAnPDaDP, Ch. 45.
38 VRAK, C. 26.
39 VRKK, C. 16.
40 VRKK, C. 17.
41 VRKK, C. 21.
42 VRKK, C. 22.
43 Malti Madhav, Act 1.
44 MBVPDrSSP, Ch. 232.
45 MBSPAnP, Ch. 78.
46 MBSPDyP, Ch. 52.
47 MBSPDyP, Ch. 72.
48 MBSPDyP, Ch. 72.
49 MBVPNaP, Ch. 61.
50 MBVPArnP, Ch. 313.

51 MBVPArnP, Ch. 313.
52 MBShPAaDP, Ch. 144.
53 MBShPAaDP, Ch. 135.
54 MBUPBhYP, Ch. 113.
55 MBUPBhYP, Ch. 90.
56 MBUPBhYP, Ch. 137.
57 VRKK, C. 18.
58 MBShPMoDP, Ch. 166.
59 MBShPMoDP, Ch. 166.
60 MBAsPVaDP, Ch. 92, GPGKP, P. 6362.
61 MBAnPDaDP, Ch. 62.
62 YV, Ch. 10.
63 MBShPRaDP, Ch. 32
64 VRAK, C. 37.
65 MBShPMoDP, Ch. 166.
66 MBShPMoDP, Ch. 166.
67 MBShPMoDP, Ch. 166.
68 KA, Adh. 3, Ch. 2.
69 MBAnPDaDP, Ch. 44.
70 MBAnPDaDP, Ch. 44.
71 MBAnPDaDP, Ch. 44.
72 YV, Ch. 5.
73 VRAK, C. 9.
74 VRAK, C. 9.
75 KA, Adh. 3, Prak. 58, Ch. 2.
76 KA, Adh. 4, Prak. 87, Ch. 12.

Chapter 6: Non-discriminatory Social System

1 MBVPMaSP, Ch. 190/42.
2 MBAPSaP, Ch. 108.
3 MBAPSaP, Ch. 109.
4 GND, Ch. 2, Anhik 2.
5 GND, Ch. 2, Anhik 2.
6 Panini Ashthadhyayi.
7 MBShPApDP, Ch. 166.
8 AV, Kanda 18, Sukta 2.
9 VRYK, C. 16.
10 MBUPBhYP, Ch. 72.

11 MBAPSaP, Ch. 105.
12 https://hi.wiktionary.org/wiki/विक्षनरी:गुजराती–हिंदी_शब्दकोश
13 YV, Ch. 16
14 MBAPSaP, Ch. 125.
15 MBAnPDaDP, Ch. 164.
16 MBAnPDaDP, Ch. 164.
17 MBVPMaSP, Ch. 190.
18 MBShPMoDP, Ch. 188.
19 SS, Ch. 1.
20 VRBK, C. 13.
21 MBAPSaP, Ch. 129.
22 MBAPSaP, Ch. 129.
23 MBVPKuP, Ch. 309.
24 MBVPKuP, Ch. 309.
25 MBAPSaP, Ch. 131.
26 MBVPKuP, Ch. 309.
27 MBAPSaP, Ch. 137.
28 MBAPSaP, Ch. 137.
29 MBAPSaP, Ch. 137.
30 MBVPKuP, Ch. 309.
31 SS, Ch. 2.
32 SS, Ch. 2.
33 MBShPRaDP, Ch. 78.
34 MBShPMoDP, Ch. 160.
35 MBShPRaDP, Ch. 78.
36 MBShPRaDP, Ch. 78.
37 VRAK, C. 50.
38 VRAK, C. 50.
39 VRAK, C. 50.
40 MBBPBhuP, Ch. 11.
41 MBBPBhuP, Ch. 11.
42 MBSPDiVP, Ch. 32.
43 MBShPMoDP, Ch. 208.
44 SS, Ch. 1.
45 MBShPRaDP, Ch. 59.
46 MBSPLoSP, Ch. 5.
47 SS, Ch. 3.
48 MBAPSwP, Ch. 191.

Chapter 7: Care for Nature

1 YV, 36/17.
2 MBAPSaP, Ch. 75.
3 MBAPSaP, Ch. 85.
4 MBAPSaP, Ch. 100.
5 KA, Adh. 2, Prak. 42, Ch. 26.
6 KA, Adh. 2, Prak. 42, Ch. 26.
7 KA, Adh. 2, Prak. 42, Ch. 26.
8 MBAPSaP, Ch. 100.
9 MBAsPAnGP, Ch. 91.
10 MBAsPAnGP, Ch. 91.
11 MBAsPAnGP, Ch. 91.
12 MBShPMoDP, Ch. 337.
13 MBShPMoDP, Ch. 337.
14 Panchtantra , 105/106, Tantra 3.
15 Vayu Puran, Purvardham, Ch. 57
16 Vayu Puran Purvardham, Ch. 57
17 Matasya Puran Ch. 143
18 Syadvaad Manjiri, Shloka 23 explanation.
19 MBShPMoDP, Ch. 265.
20 MBVPTiP, Ch. 147.
21 VRSK, C. 37.
22 YV, Ch. 13.
23 MBAnPDaDP, Ch. 62.
24 MBAnPDaDP, Ch. 62.
25 MBBPJaVP, Ch. 4.
26 MBBPBhuP, Ch. 9.
27 MBBPJaVP, Ch. 6.
28 MBBPJaVP, Ch. 6.
29 MBAnPDaDP, Ch. 26.
30 MBAnPDaDP, Ch. 26.
31 MBAnPDaDP, Ch. 26.
32 VRAK, C. 50.
33 VRAK, C. 52.
34 VRAK, C. 52.
35 VRAK, C. 52.
36 VRAK, C. 52.
37 MBAnPDaDP, Ch. 26.
38 MBAnPDaDP, Ch. 26.

39 MBShPApDP, Ch. 154.
40 MBAnPDaDP, Ch. 58.
41 MBShPMoDP, Ch. 184.
42 MBShPMoDP, Ch. 184.
43 MBShPMoDP, Ch. 184.
44 MBShPMoDP, Ch. 184.
45 MBShPMoDP, Ch. 184.
46 MBShPMoDP, Ch. 184.
47 MBShPMoDP, Ch. 184.
48 MBShPMoDP, Ch. 184.
49 MBShPMoDP, Ch. 184.
50 SS, Ch. 4, Prak. 4.
51 SS, Ch. 4, Prak. 4.
52 SS, Ch. 4, Prak. 4.
53 KA, Adh. 2, Prak. 17, Ch. 1.
54 MBShPMoDP, Ch. 183.
55 MBAnPDaDP, Ch. 58.
56 MBAnPDaDP, Ch. 58.
57 MBAnPDaDP, Ch. 95.
58 YV, Ch. 36.

Chapter 8: Respect for the Land

1 AV 12/12.
2 Srimad Bhagwat Mahapuran, Skandh 9, Ch. 01.
3 MBAPSaP, Ch. 74.
4 MBAPSaP, Ch. 74.
5 MBBPJaVP, Ch. 9.
6 MBDPAbVP, Ch. 74.
7 MBShPRaDP, Ch. 65.
8 MBAPSaP, Ch. 138.
9 MBSPDiVP, Ch. 32.
10 MBSPDiVP, Ch. 32.
11 MBSPDyP, Ch. 51.
12 MBBPJaVP, Ch. 9.
13 MBBPJaVP, Ch. 9.
14 MBBPJaVP, Ch. 9.
15 MBBPJaVP, Ch. 9.
16 MBBPJaVP, Ch. 9.
17 MBBPJaVP, Ch. 9.

18 MBBPJaVP, Ch. 9.
19 MBBPJaVP, Ch. 9.
20 MBBPJaVP, Ch. 9.
21 MBBPJaVP, Ch. 9.
22 MBBPJaVP, Ch. 9.
23 MBBPJaVP, Ch. 9.
24 MBShPApDP, Ch. 135.

References

Bajaj, J.K., and M.D. Srinivas, (eds). *Dharampal Classics Series Volume 4.* Bengalure: Centre for Policy Studies and Rashtrotthana Parishad, 2021.

Dharampal. *The Beautiful Tree: Indigenous Indian Education in the Eighteenth Century.* New Delhi: Biblia Impex, 1983.

Dirks, Nicholas B. *Castes of Mind: Colonialism and the Making of Modern India.*

Durant, Will. *Case for India.* New York: Simon and Schuster, 1930.

Dutt, R.C. *The Economic History of India Volume 1* (Fifth Reprint). New Delhi: Publication Division, Ministry of Information and Broadcasting, 2006.

Dutt, R.C. *The Economic History of India Volume 1* (First Edition). New Delhi: Publication Division, Ministry of Information and Broadcasting,

Fárek, Martin, Dunkin Jalki, Sufiya Pathan, and Prakash Shah. *Western Foundations of the Caste System.*

Jayaswal, K.P. *Hindu Polity.* Delhi: Chaukambha Sanskrit Pratisthanam.

Lal, K.S. *Growth of Scheduled Tribes and Castes in Medieval India.*

Malaviya, Madan Mohan. Member's Note, Indian Industrial Commission, set up by the British Government in 1916. Calcutta: Superintendent of Government Printing, 1918. Republished by the Mahamana Malviya Mission, Banaras Hindu University Unit, Varanasi.

Mishra, Ram Gopal, *Indian Resistance to Early Muslim Invaders up to 1206 AD.*

The World Economy: A Millennial Perspective, Development Centre Studies, Organisation for Economic Cooperation and Development.

Sacred Books Consulted

The Mahabharata
Valmiki Ramayana
Kautilya Arthashastra
Kautilya Sutra
Shukranitisar
The Rigveda
The Atharvaveda
The Yajurveda
Manu Smriti
Gautam's Nyaya Darshan

About the Author

Swami Vigyananand is a sannyasi (monk), scholar and key organizer of the Hindu renaissance. He holds a BTech degree from the Bharatiya Praudyogiki Sansthan (IIT) and later pursued advanced studies in Sanskrit Vyakaran (grammar) and Hindu Darshan (philosophy) at a traditional gurukul, earning the titles of Acharya and Vidyāvaridhi in Pāṇini Vyakaran and Darshan.

He currently serves as the Joint General Secretary of the Vishva Hindu Parishad (VHP), where he leads International Coordination—a role in which he spearheads Hindu resurgence and organizational initiatives worldwide.

Swami Vigyananand is the visionary behind the World Hindu Congress (WHC)—a global platform designed to connect, inspire and mobilize Hindus to accelerate the Hindu renaissance—and the World Hindu Economic Forum (WHEF), which works to promote economic prosperity in society. Under his leadership, the WHC has been successfully organized in Delhi (2014), Chicago (2018) and Bangkok (2023). He has also convened nine WHEF conferences across the globe: Hong Kong (2012), Bangkok (2013), Delhi (2014), London (2015), Los Angeles (2016), Chicago (2018), Mumbai (2019), Bangkok (2023) and again in Mumbai (2024).

Renowned for his profound understanding of Hindu dharma, Swami Vigyananand has also championed the institutionalization of Hindu studies as a formal academic discipline in leading universities across Bharat. He advocates for strategic and structured organization among Hindus to reclaim the Hindu nation and establish Bharat and the global Hindu community as a formidable presence on the world stage.

www.ingramcontent.com/pod-product-compliance
Lightning Source LLC
LaVergne TN
LVHW091613070526
838199LV00044B/782